JANUA LINGUARUM

STUDIA MEMORIAE
NICOLAI VAN WIJK DEDICATA

edenda curat
C. H. VAN SCHOONEVELD
Indiana University

Series Minor, 207

THE THREAD
OF
DISCOURSE

by

JOSEPH E. GRIMES

Cornell University
and
Summer Institute of Linguistics

1975

MOUTON

THE HAGUE · PARIS

LIBRARY OF CONGRESS CATALOG CARD NUMBER: 74–78506

ISBN 90 279 3164 X

Printed in The Netherlands

PREFACE

New ideas in linguistics take time to formulate well. Their merit cannot be guessed at on the basis of one article or even a book. They need to be put to work on a wide scale to see how well they clarify things. Otherwise it is easy to confuse a technique that succeeds for explaining what happens in one language with a fundamental principle of the speech of humans regardless of what language they speak.

In the past three years I have had the privilege of organizing field workshops in seven countries for the purpose of explaining to practicing linguists in the field how I think we can use linguistic tools to understand the way complete discourses go together, then helping those linguists put the ideas into practice. The National Science Foundation made this possible with a grant to Cornell University for the Cross Language Study of Discourse Structures. The Summer Institute of Linguistics, Inc., which is affiliated with the University of Oklahoma and conducts linguistic research around the world, organized the workshops, though not all the participants were with the Institute.

The workshops were held in Brazil, Papua New Guinea, the Philippines, the United States of America, Nigeria, Ivory Coast, and Ghana in that order, with an eighth workshop still to go in Nepal. Material from the first three was used in a seminar held at Cornell University in the spring of 1972. The bibliography (page 369) includes 69 articles on various aspects of discourse that have either appeared in print as a result of the project or are at the moment in the process of publication.

This book grew out of a report by the same title submitted a year ago to the Anthropology Program of the National Science Foundation as Technical Report No. 1 on NSF Grant GS-3180. Every chapter in it has been revised in the light of later field experience, and some chapters (15, 17, 20, 22, 23, 24) which had only been projected at the time the report was written have been filled in. I am delighted with the alacrity with which colleagues to whom copies of that report were sent came back with comments on better ways to look at things, especially Dwight Bolinger, Bruce and Barbara Ericson Hollenbach, George Huttar, Anthony J. Naden, Gloria Risser Poedjosoedarmo, and Ladislav Zgusta.

What has the project established about the linguistic nature of discourse? First, it has shown that theoretical models of language worked out at the level of the sentence and below can be successfully expanded to account for larger structures without becoming unrecognizable. Second, it has shown that discourse provides a context within which even prosaic phenomena like morphological categories begin to make sense instead of just being there to be listed. Third, it has shown that linguists who are beginning their field work can carry out meaningful studies on discourse structure as well as they can on any other part of language; discourse is neither a territory accessible only to superlinguists nor a far-off goal to which one can only aspire while plowing through phonology, morphology, syntax, and lexicon as he works off his apprenticeship before moving on to higher things. Fourth, it has shown that there is both consistency and variety in the worldwide range of ways in which we express ourselves to one another.

The least expected result of this research was the discovery of the overlay structure described in Chapter 19. Related to it are Thomas Bearth's distinction between primary and secondary centers of information in Toura of Ivory Coast and Roberta Huisman's primary and secondary event inflections in Angaataha of Papua New Guinea: an organization of information into given, new, and highlighted categories instead of the simpler given-new categories we are accustomed to in other languages.

The place of thematic patterns in discourse came to the fore in a number of languages. In Bacairí of Brazil, Wheatley finds pronouns that distinguish two thematic levels. Marked topicalizations are used to introduce paragraphs in several languages of the Philippines. In West Africa, a thematic distinction among primary, secondary, and tertiary characters is common, with different patterns of introduction and subsequent identification for each giving a rather detailed stage management effect. Ennulat even finds a special participant category in Fali of Cameroun: regardless of what characters have taken part in a story, and regardless of what the story is about, it ends with a collection of dogs of various colors going out and hunting antelopes, by way of telling the hearers that the story is ended.

Distinct genres in oral discourse came to be recognized in several studies, notably one by Ilse Bearth on Toura that distinguishes parables and riddles from ordinary narratives on the basis of remarkably tight constraints on the first two.

Not only were linkage patterns involving repetition of a preceding sentence found to be widespread (Chapter 21); they were found to fall quite regularly into four types: exact repetition, less specific repetition with verbs like 'do', linkage via a logical consequence of the last event, and (in a few languages) conditional linkage. As for their use, some of the languages examined use linkage to indicate boundaries between units like paragraphs, while others break a sequence of sentence-to-sentence linkages at similar boundaries.

Litteral's development of a topological index for time (Chapter 3) made possible a simpler view of rhetorical relations (Chapter 14). The display of text elements devised by Robert C. Thurman (Chapter 6) provided a means of getting started on discourses that was used by nearly everybody who came after.

In relating morphological categories to discourse, most of the work centered around pronominal systems on the one hand and tense-aspect systems on the other. Pronominal systems split into sequential systems like that of English, in which the characteristic way of finding what a pronoun refers to involves scanning back through the text for the nearest likely referent, and thematic systems like those of Bacairí of Brazil and Longuda of Nigeria, in which the topic of a paragraph is assigned pronouns from a special set regardless of what other things have just been mentioned.

The initial insight into the relationship between tense-aspect systems and discourse came from Ruth McLeod's work on Xavante of Brazil. She found that what appeared morphologically to be a single aspect system broke apart into two upon observing where verbs bearing each of the aspects occurred in discourse. John and Bonnie Newman investigated aspect sequences in Longuda, and Lynell Marchese found tense to be a high level discourse feature with recursive organization in Godié of Ivory Coast. Peter Kruesi pinpointed specialized uses of certain aspects in the introduction of narratives.

Several colleagues who did not participate directly in the workshops nevertheless made contributions to them and to my own studies: Ivan Lowe in Brazil, Paul Freyberg in Papua New Guinea, Nellie Hidalgo in the Philippines, Anthony J. Naden and Alan Duthie in Ghana. Robert Litteral acted as my assistant in the Philippines, David J. Cranmer at Cornell, Mona Perrin and Norris P. McKinney in Nigeria, and Thomas Bearth, Lynell Marchese, Eva Flik, and Keith Dawson in Ivory Coast.

Anything as complex as a three-month field workshop requires more than scholarly steam to keep its momentum up. We could not have accomplished nearly as much without the administrative and logistic help of the workshop coordinators: James and Dorothy Wheatley in Brazil, John Abernethy in Papua New Guinea, Carl DuBois and Charles Walton in the Philippines, Karl Grebe and James Hoskison in Nigeria, Donald and Thelma Webster in Ivory Coast, and Martin and Sharon Huyett in Ghana. Peggy Pittman, Barbara Grimes, and Ursula Poltéra assisted me considerably by typing the manuscript and several others that lie behind it.

Here are some of the things we worked out together.

Tamale, Ghana

June 1973

CONTENTS

1

WHY DISCOURSE STUDY?

Linguistics started small, concentrating on sounds and words before phrases and sentences. There is always excitement in new ideas about those areas, and the subject matter has always shown itself tough enough to be challenging. A linguist could fill a lifetime without needing to ask whether the framework he worked in might also extend to take in larger segments of verbal behavior.

Now that some of us are trying to expand our horizons beyond the sentence to paragraphs and even entire discourses, we seem to draw two kinds of reactions. One is encouraging and a little wistful. Colleagues see that linguistics can go in that direction and wish they had time to join us in finding out how. The other reaction is mildly surprising for a field in which one or another set of young Turks has nearly always held the center of the stage: it is suggested either that we can't work on discourse, because it has been convincingly demonstrated that such work is impossible, or that we shouldn't, because everything beyond the sentence is the fiefdom of the rhetoricians, or the critics, or the logicians.

Since I take it as a principle that the way to sell soap is not to waste time arguing that Brand X won't get the dirt out, but rather to show the way your own product does its job, I propose no lengthy critique that will demolish one by one the negative arguments about discourse. In Section One of this chapter I will touch lightly on the criticisms I am aware of, then go on in Section Two to the reasons why I think it is not only possible but also downright enlightening to study discourse. The third section of the chapter will sketch some possible consequences of discourse study.

1. WHY LINGUISTS SHOULD NOT STUDY DISCOURSE

The first thing that has kept many linguists away from the serious study of discourse is probably the magnitude of the subject matter.[1] Like the Dutch boy with his finger in the dike, they look at how much they have to cope with and get the understandable feeling that the whole wild sea is out there. Beyond the ordered paradigms and mildly controversial counterexamples of sentence grammar they see business letters, conversations, restaurant menus, novels, laws, nonverbal behavior, movie scripts, editorials, without end. They are right. Yet there are ways of bringing a good deal of this under control, as I hope this book will show.

Totally apart from the question of magnitude there are limitations built into linguistic theory that have made it difficult to work on discourse from inside the discipline. The most obvious of these is the theoretical restriction of linguistics to relationships within the sentence. Bloomfield, for example, in defining the sentence as "an independent form, not included in any larger (complex) linguistic form",[2] clamped a lid on linguistics that few have tried to lift. Dik[3] rightly criticizes the effect of this limitation on our understanding of the kinds of relations between sentences that have to be assumed in order to account for things like conjunctions.

Chomsky not only perpetuated Bloomfield's restriction uncritically, but made it even stronger by having the sentence, or something very much like it, be the distinguished symbol of the kind of grammar that can be constructed as a formal system.[4] His statements about the aim of grammar being to account for all the sentences of a language and only the sentences of a language had a similar effect.

---

[1]   Langendoen, *Essentials of English Grammar* (1970), p. 4.
[2]   Bloomfield, *Language* (1933), p. 170. See also Benveniste, *Problèmes de linguistique générale* (1966), p. 128: "Une phrase ne peut donc pas servir d'intégrant à un autre type d'unité." p. 129: "Les phrases n'ont ni distribution ni emploi." Martinet, *La linguistique synchronique* (1965), p. 223: "Rien ne se trouve dans le discours qui ne soit déjà dans la phrase."
[3]   Dik, *Coordination* (1968).
[4]   Chomsky, *Syntactic Structures* (1957), *Aspects* (1965).

Chomsky's theoretically motivated view said that as far as linguistics is concerned no relationships beyond the sentence exist. Yet ignoring them has had odd consequences. In Katz and Fodor's important 1963 article on semantics, for example, they were forced to adopt the fiction that in order to make a semantic interpretation of a text, all the sentences of the text have to be conjoined into a single supersentence, which is then amenable to interpretation by projection rules. Postal also has to exclude some of the information carried by pronouns from his linguistic analysis, although he points out correctly that a good deal of the information necessary for what he has to say about pronouns is contained within the sentence in which they occur.[5]

One cannot criticize Bloomfield, Chomsky, or anyone else who has operated like them for making a clear distinction between what they choose to talk about and what they lay aside. Restriction of a field is essential for any kind of scientific thinking. If someone wishes to focus on what happens within certain bounds, anyone else who accepts the rules of the game has to agree to those bounds. Trouble comes only when we are given to understand that those are the only reasonable or possible or interesting bounds, and he who would disturb them is disrupting the peace of the kingdom. In our discipline we do this by invoking the name of Linguistic Theory, presented more as an eternal verity than as the way some eminent and generally sensible person happens to look at things at the moment.

Frankly, at the time Bloomfield wrote, sticking to the sentence was probably the wisest thing he could have done. It gave him and those who came after him breathing space to get a grasp on a broad range of phenomena like word structure and the lower reaches of phonology. Later on the limitation to sentences permitted a thorough classification of patterns within phrases and sentences. In the same way, Chomsky really needed a restricted field within which to work out the consequences of his ideas about the formalization of grammar. But now that we have a grasp both of the

---

[5] Postal, "Underlying and Superficial Linguistic Structures" (1964).

classifying side of grammar and of its expression in the form of generalizations within a formal system, it is high time to make room for less narrow limitations.

A different reason for urging linguists to hold back from discourse is that the kinds of relationships that are involved once we go beyond the sentence are different from those that operate within sentences.[6] For example, it is often asserted that stylistic relationships have little in common with the relationships of ordinary grammar, that perhaps they are a statistical property of speech that linguists cannot deal with directly. In the opinion of others style has an intangible nature that cannot be approached with the combinatorial tools of linguistics. What is overlooked should become plain later in this book: First, there are perfectly straightforward combinatorial relationships that operate in discourse, and second, no matter what is meant by style, the problem is just as prominent inside sentences as it is anywhere else in language.

To maintain that linguists should not work with complete discourses because that is the province of rhetoric and literary criticism is a little like saying that physicists should not work with chemistry or that information scientists should have nothing to do with law. As a matter of fact, chemists and lawyers have both profited because those outside their discipline applied the concepts of a different field to it; there is no reason why both rhetoric and literary criticism should not be better off as a result of linguists having tried their tools in those areas.

2. WHY LINGUISTS SHOULD STUDY DISCOURSE

As I suggested in the last section, linguists can and should work with discourse. None of the reasons given why linguists should leave discourse alone is more than a tactical barrier. Those reasons impede linguistic study mainly because we do not yet have much experience in finding our way around them.

[6]   Kelkar, "Some Notes on Language and Literature" (1970).

For example, the magnitude of the subject matter, while vast, is not impossible to cope with. Progress in scientific thinking always. implies distinguishing between generalizations that can be broadened on the one hand and kinds of complexity that can be left out of consideration on the other. Certainly in fields like mathematical biology, genetics, and astronomy, numberless observed phenomena have been successfully brought into the scope of a relatively small number of generalizations. Kemeny discusses optimistically the application of mathematical models in the social sciences even where problems "are much too large to get explicit solutions for them and yet the number of parts is not large enough, nor are they homogeneous enough, to be able to pass to the limit".[7] In discussing optimal sequences of decisions that involve a large number of factors, Bellman starts from the working assumption that at any point in such a sequence the number of parameters that have to be taken into consideration is very small.[8] The answer to complexity is not to give up the whole thing, but to find generalizations and simplifying assumptions that put their finger on the essential factors behind the complexity.

Suppose we were to look at what has already been accomplished in linguistics by taking the point of view of a hypothetical elf who is a good phonetician but who knows nothing of the kinds of generalizations linguists have made since the times of the Hindu grammarians. We could imagine how he might quail at the hopelessness of ever doing anything about the mass of phonetic data that a linguist collects in an ordinary working day. He knows, after all, that he is dealing with sequences of motions in a many-dimensioned continuous space, and that the exact correspondence even between two successive utterances of what is supposed to be the same word are rare. Yet, because we non-elvish linguists have evolved a conceptual framework that takes in all this complexity, it no longer bothers us. We are even tempted (wrongly) to regard the study of phonological systems as the most cut and dried part

---

[7] Kemeny, "Facing Up to Large Systems" (1969).
[8] Bellman, "The Theory of Dynamic Programming" (1956).

of linguistics. Where discourse is concerned, however, we still feel in the position of the elf; we have not yet come up with generalizations that can cope with the magnitude of the subject matter. I suggest that such generalizations are possible, and that we are already on the track of some of them, for example in Winograd's inclusion of a model of what the speaker knows about the world as part of his theory of language.[9]

As mentioned, some of the relationships that we find between sentences are the same as those we find between elements of a single sentence.[10] The first consequence of this is a redefinition of the notion of grammar that does away with its traditional limitation to sentences. I personally prefer to symbolize this change of scope by choosing a psychologically neutral starting symbol such as F for "form" to represent the distinguished symbol in a formal grammar.[11]

Relationships that I have characterized as belonging to outline-like structures are well recognized in sentences, where statements of constituency based on the partitionings of strings are the backbone of the grammatical tradition.[12] Pike anticipated discourse studies in showing how the notion of constituency applies from within the word clear up to the "behavioreme", a major unit with a culturally recognizable beginning and ending on the one hand and internal structure on the other.[13] His characterization of a discourse as a verbal behavioreme is still as good for getting things started as anything we can think of, since it emphasizes that discourse, like

[9]   Winograd, *Procedures* (1971).
[10]   John Austing, "Semantic Relationships in Omie" (ms).
[11]   Substituting one symbol for another in a formal grammar does not change the grammar, of course. A formal grammar beginning with S is perfectly capable of being developed into a discourse grammar rather than restricted to a sentence grammar. But it is linguists' secondary and even tertiary responses to the idea of grammatical systems that seem to keep the lid on their thinking. Reshaping of perspectives, in linguistics as in politics, is aided by switching symbols.
[12]   Grimes, "Outlines and Overlays" (1972).
[13]   Pike, *Language*, Part 1 (1954), pp. 33, 57.

the sentence in the older grammars, is a primitive notion that is not definable from within the system.

Although the field of rhetoric is independent of linguistics, many of the relationships rhetoricians talk about can be formalized quite well as constituency grammars. The first example of this that came to my attention was Daniel P. Fuller's *Inductive Method of Bible Study*, which applies rhetorical concepts to exegesis in such a way as to parse texts in a tree representation, sometimes going down as far as relationships among elements of a sentence, but also uniting major segments of texts in terms of the same relationships.

This rhetorical approach, incidentally, gives an analysis of a text that is much more like that of a modern propositional grammar[14] than it is like a pure constituency grammar like Longacre's.[15] The rhetorical structure consists of underlying relationships — generalization and example, say — for which there is explicit but indirect evidence in the output form itself.

At the same time, the organization of a text above the level of the sentence has more to it than can merely be extrapolated from relationships within sentences. It is for this reason that I have distinguished between lexical and rhetorical predicates for a propositional model of discourse. Rodgers, writing for a College Conference of Composition symposium on the sentence and the paragraph,[16] criticized the work of Christensen and Becker on paragraph structure as being nothing more than "extrapolations from the sentence"; but he was only half right. Some relationships on which paragraphs are built can apply at any level of constituency including between words within a sentence; only a few like those expressed by *therefore* do not seem to have a place in sentence structure. The important point for discourse studies is what John Austing documents for Omie: each relationship has several different forms of expression, depending on what things are being related,

---

[14] Langendoen, *The Study of Syntax* (1969); Frantz, *Toward a Generative Grammar of Blackfoot* (1970).
[15] Longacre, *Discourse ... in Philippine Languages* (1968).
[16] Rodgers, "Contribution" (1966).

and relationships that have distinct expressions in some contexts may have identical, ambiguous expressions in others.

Gerald A. Sanders has gone a step beyond simply saying that the familiar relationships of sentence grammar apply on up the line.[17] His claim, with which I agree, is that a sentence grammar will not work unless it is part of a discourse grammar, because certain factors are needed for the understanding of elements in sentences that are not available within those sentences themselves but only elsewhere in the discourse.

A number of concepts have been developed specifically for the study of discourse. Although from one point of view it could be argued that these are relationships that are different in kind from the ones linguists work with in sentence grammars, it is important to notice that they all relate to familiar concepts in grammar rather than being totally from without. Among these are the notions of kinds of information, participant orientation, information structure, thematization, clause permutation, and variable frequency rules, all of which are discussed later in this book.

3. THE USE OF DISCOURSE STUDIES

Curiosity is, of course, adequate justification for studying nearly anything, even discourse. Going beyond that motivation, discourse study does seem to have some implications in other areas. The most obvious is the likelihood that discourse studies will require a reshaping of linguistic theory, certainly by extending its scope if nothing else. H. A. Gleason, Jr., reported to me in conversation that when he worked out both a sentence grammar and a discourse grammar of Kâte of Papua New Guinea, the discourse grammar, which included everything in the sentence grammar as well, contained fewer irregularities and was in some sense simpler. It is possible that the closure of grammar on discourse, as Sanders maintains, will round off our view of language in a much more

---

[17]   Sanders, "On the Natural Domain of Grammar" (1970).

integrated way than can be achieved by truncating grammar at the sentence.

The implications of discourse study for language teaching, while . probably not a primary concern for first year language textbook writers (though Willis and Agard[18] take it into account in their discussion of Spanish tenses), are nevertheless there. One can no more string sentences together at random in another language than he can in his own. Certainly in intermediate and advanced level language courses, and in the study of literature, the results of discourse study should come to be a part of the picture.[19]

Young, Becker, and Pike have already attempted to put the results of their research on discourse into the teaching of composi-·tion.[20] In the area of Bible translation, which in some ways is very close to composition, Hollenbach, Beekman, Frantz, and Kathleen Callow have made suggestions based on discourse oriented models.[21]

One can only speculate about the effect linguistic studies of ·discourse might have in the field of criticism, granted the traditional lack of interaction between them. I think that as linguists we can at least double check the critic in matters of structure. It also seems possible from within linguistics to pin down certain aspects of the coherence of a text, and even to show why some passages are incoherent. This is not the same as being able to say whether a particular passage is clear or not, though again linguistics may be able to raise a warning flag and tell the critic (or the writer when he is criticizing his own draft) that there are obstacles to clarity in the road ahead. Some aspects of style seem to be approachable from within a linguistic view of discourse.[22] By no means can everything stylistic be broken to our bridle, but neither are all the horses wild.

Illustrations have already been given of inputs from the field of

---

[18] Willis and Agard, *Spanish from Thought to Word* (1941).
[19] Gleason, "Contrastive Analysis in Discourse Structure" (1968).
[20] Young, Becker, and Pike, *Rhetoric* (1970).
[21] Hollenbach, "A Method for Displaying Sentence Structure" (1969); Beekman, "Propositions and Their Relations within a Discourse" (1970); Frantz, *Blackfoot* (1970); Kathleen Callow, "More on Propositions and Their Relations within a Discourse" (1970).
[22] Grimes and Glock, "A Saramaccan Narrative Pattern" (1970).

exegesis to linguistics. This looks like a two-way street. The rules of evidence in exegesis embody what can equally well be thought of as linguistic relationships, while the treatment of those relationships as part of a linguistic system should in turn help remove some of the fuzziness from exegesis.

One area of exegesis in which I am not aware that there has been interaction with linguistics, but where there could be, is in the interpretation of law. Reading the law is essentially an exegetical process, deciding what it says and what it excludes. Writing laws involves using language that seems designed to keep things from being said too clearly, but using it in such a way that the necessary lines of demarcation are unambiguously drawn. How parallel legal exegesis is to, say, Biblical exegesis or historical exegesis bears looking into.[23]

Now that information retrieval is taking on greater importance because of the proliferation of circulated information, linguistics may have something to contribute to it through discourse studies.[24] In the first place, studies of discourse seem to show that the essential information in some discourses is localized, which implies that for retrieval it might be possible to specify parts of the discourse that do not have to be taken into account. There is definitely a pattern of organization of information in any discourse that can be recognized and should therefore be explored for its usefulness in retrieval; for example, Halliday's notion of the distribution of given and new information.[25]

Grammar contains clues to semantic structure. Sometimes,

---

[23] Boeckh, *On interpretation and criticism*, John Paul Pritchard, transl. (1886, translated 1968).

[24] Information scientists, it should be said, are not standing by waiting for linguists to show them how to do their job. Gerard Salton, for example, in *Automatic Information Organization and Retrieval* (1968), pp. 196-99, found that by using the Kuno-Oettinger syntactic analyzer he got retrieval results that were essentially no better than the ones he got by bypassing all considerations of linguistic structure completely. I would like to see research done on this Salton Effect in the expectation that we would learn something about linguistics through it.

[25] Halliday, "Notes on Transitivity and Theme, Part 2" (1967).

unfortunately, they are no easier to read than are phonological clues to grammatical structure. Taken together with other discourse signals, however, the work of Winograd shows how it might prove possible to disambiguate mappings from semantics to grammatical structure sufficiently well that a semantic analysis can build on a grammatical analysis.[26]

There are also clues to semantic structure that do not fit into the notion of grammatical structure directly but which are still recognizable. Word collocations are one such clue; patterns of pronominal reference may also fit here.

Linguistics should be able to come up with a theory of abstracting. This theory should account for varying degrees of compactness in abstracts. For any degree of compactness it should give a basis for saying whether or not an abstract is COMPLETE in that it includes everything that should be in an abstract of that degree of compactness, and whether it is CONCISE, in that it includes nothing that is superfluous. It should also be able to distinguish a non-abstract that sounds like an abstract from a real one.

Connected with abstracting is the problem of retrieval indexing. This is a matter of providing a representation of the meaning of a discourse that is easy to find and work through, and that somehow interlocks with the text itself in such a way as to facilitate retrieval. Specification of key terms is one approach that is commonly used; it involves not only the identification of those terms in a text that are truly its key words, but also the formation of thesauri to identify semantic neighborhoods of terms.

[26] Winograd, *Procedures* (1971).

2

DISCOURSE SO FAR

This chapter is a quick review of ideas in linguistics and related fields that have fed into the formation of the views I present later in the book. I have not gone to any lengths to trace these topics out, because that is material for several books in itself.

1. RHETORIC

In Western culture the tradition is a long one that insists that there is a right way and a wrong way to put arguments and other kinds of discourses together, and that the right way can be taught. This attitude has given rhetoric a prescriptive tone for two and a half millenia: say this; don't put those things together; form the rhythmic pattern thus. Rhetorical works tend to be schoolbook treatises, not descriptive statements associated with science and research. Yet this is the area where discourse phenomena have traditionally been brought up and discussed, to the extent that a very good start on the study of discourse patterns in any of the major European languages could probably be made simply by bringing together systematically all the things that rhetoricians have said that speakers of that language either should or should not do.[1]

[1] Linguists today would point out that the gap between what rhetoricians and grammarians in the prescriptive tradition say should be done and what accomplished speakers and writers do is always noticeable. My point, however, is that the rhetoricians raise questions that need to be discussed in the analysis of discourse patterns, not that they dispose of those questions in a uniformly satisfactory way.

Linguistics can, I think, go beyond the insights of rhetoric in its traditional form by providing a language independent framework within which the rhetorical patterns of each language fit as special cases. Insofar as linguistics explains language as well as describing it, it also has something to say about what various rhetorical phenomena contribute to the process of communication, about the reasons why they are there.

Classical rhetoric is epitomized by the work of Aristotle, whose *Rhetoric* contains acute observations about the structure of discourses aimed at changing other people's behavior, and later by that of Quintilian and Cicero. The ancient sophists, some of whom were Aristotle's contemporaries, have usually been cast on the side opposite that of the angels because Socrates caught them out on the philosophical worth of their arguments. While we side with Socrates on the larger question, it is perhaps good to remember that men like Prodicus of Ceos and Gorgias of Leotini did at least pay attention to the forms and techniques of discourse construction. In the so-called Second Sophistic Period of the second to fourth centuries A. D. Aristotle's structural categories of speech were set aside. [2]

The medieval trivium combined rhetoric with philosophy and grammar as the standard course of instruction. Here the object was not to teach effective communication in the pupil's native tongue, but rather in Latin as the international vehicle. The models were found in the writings of medieval writers rather than in the literary but non-Christian Latin of the classical period, so that notions of innovation and exploitation of the full resources of the language were marginal.

Rhetoric now has split into composition, or the construction of written discourses, and speech, or the construction and delivery of oral discourses. In both there is the attempt to force certain aspects of discourse structure to the pupil's attention, to make him accustomed to working with time-tested models rather than stringing what he has to say together in a jumble. Rhetoric at its

---

[2]   Chase , *The Classical Conception of Epideictic* (1961).

best tries to teach the pupil to exploit the possibilities the language gives him. Nowadays this is carried out more fully in creative writing and advanced composition than it is in speech. Academic work is focused on writing, while creative speaking is heard of more often in Dale Carnegie courses and Toastmaster's Clubs.

The do's and dont's of the prescriptive tradition are still the watchword of rhetoric; but it is becoming more accepted that the models to be followed are not the deductively fabricated dicta of the rhetoricians, based on logic or principles of usage, but rather the accepted writers themselves, regardless of the reasons the rhetoricians or the authors themselves might give for why a particular thing is said in a particular way.

My impression is that most of the points taught in modern rhetoric of writing or speaking are still taught mainly by osmosis. It is possible that by developing a general scheme that accounts for different patterns of expression we might eventually be able to present a rhetoric based on what is known about the nature of language. Young, Becker, and Pike have attempted this,[3] and the outlook is promising. Vast numbers of students are exposed to writing courses in high school and university; yet an extremely small proportion of those who go into business and the scholarly fields can write an intelligible paragraph.

It would therefore be no waste of effort to explore further what a linguistic understanding of discourse could do as a basis for a new prescriptive approach. I do, however, find insights that contribute to discourse linguistics coming from people who are primarily skillful practitioners of the art of teaching writing, yet whose knowledge of linguistics itself precludes their making the kind of systematizations a linguist would make. They are doing something right, and linguists need to find out why it works.

2. CRITICISM

Literary criticism has never been noticeably close to linguistics,

---

[3]   Young, Becker, and Pike, *Rhetoric* (1970).

yet the critic and the linguist who works on discourse react to some ʳ of the same patterns in language. For example, the notion of literary structure seems to be handled in similar ways by critic and linguist. The critic asks what the structure of a literary work contributes to the total effect, more or less taking it for granted that he knows what the structure is. The linguist, on the other hand, is interested in the range of structures that are available, the signals that identify them, and the scope of what a given structure can be used to express. He is also interested in the structure of discourses that the critic might not even deign to look at: a conversation at a party, for example, or a description in the Sears, Roebuck catalogue.

With the publication of Propp's *Morphology of the Folktale* in English in 1958 another aspect of structure came into view. Propp, followed by Alan Dundes,[4] analyzed the plots of folk tales in a way that George Lakoff, in a paper read at a Summer Meeting of the Linguistic Society of America, pointed out could be generated by a very simple grammar. There have been questions raised about whether this structure, which seems to characterize not only the Russian fairy tales Propp worked with but also such disparate things as Westerns and scientific papers, is linguistic at all, or merely represents a kind of psychological template imposed on nearly anything to make it sound interesting.[5] June Austing, however, finds that for Omie some uses of the transitional particle *iae* are accounted for best on the assumption that the speaker is aware of a transition from one segment of a plot structure to the next.[6]

Some other points that seem to be relevant in criticism have their counterparts in discourse theory: characterization, viewpoint, pre- ʳ suppositions, diction, and lexical organization, to name some that seem most easily accessible. Characterization involves providing information about a character, either by talking about him descriptively or by reporting selected actions he performs. This

---

[4] Dundes, "Structural Typology in North American Indian Folktales" (1963), *The Morphology of North American Indian Folktales* (1964).

[5] Grimes and Glock, "Saramaccan" (1970).

[6] June Austing, "Omie Discourse" (ms).

information must be given in such a way that when the character comes to do something that has particular significance in the plot, it will then be plausible for him to do it because it is consistent with what else is known about him. Linguistically this is a constraint on the presentation of identificational information and background in relation to action information. Characterization also has the sense of establishing empathy between the hearer or reader and a character, and in that sense depends heavily on the richness and accuracy of the speaker's assessment of who the hearer is and what his background is. Technically it is possible for the speaker's perception of the hearer to be embodied in the notion of the performative, as discussed in Chapter 3.

The spatial and social viewpoint from which an action is told is well known as a trouble spot in criticism. "The author fails to show us the world through Marcy's eyes", "it is hard to tell whose side he is really on", "the payoff seems to hinge on the hero's knowing about Burlington's tendency toward alcoholism, but there is no conceivable way presented by the author by which he could have found this out". Discourse studies have already uncovered patterns of spatial viewpoint that permit considerable complexity, yet a complexity that is totally different from that of, say, the handling of viewpoint in Conrad's *Lord Jim*.[7]

The problem of the speaker's assumptions comes up both in literary studies and in discourse theory. "Writing down" and "writing up" are cases in which the writer misjudges the reader in making his assumptions about what the reader already knows. In the first instance he tells the reader things that he already takes for granted; in the second he leaves the reader behind by skipping

---

[7] The term 'viewpoint' has two uses: (1) How the author or speaker looks at life, in the sense of his philosophy, and (2) how the author or speaker looks at a particular scene, in the sense that he views it either as a whole — the so-called omniscient viewpoint — or in terms of the way one of the participants sees it, or in terms of the way a nonparticipating observer sees it. In the study of discourse the second use comes up constantly. The first use may be in an area in which a linguist cannot operate as a linguist, but where the critic comes into his own. For a complex handling of spatial viewpoint see Helen Lawrence, "Viewpoint and Location in Oksapmin" (1972).

essential points. The study of how these assumptions affect linguistic form not only involves what the speaker expects the hearer to know in general, but also the development of presuppositional complexes within a text, where the way the speaker expresses himself reflects what he thinks the hearer has gotten clear from what he already said.[8]

Diction, the choice of the right word in the right place, also reflects whatever knowledge the speaker imputes to the hearer at the moment. Part of it appears as a gradient going from specific expressions to more general expressions for the same reference throughout a segment of text. The tendency away from specific expression is balanced by a tendency to overload the hearer's memory when general terms for several different things become easy to confuse, and also by the need in some kinds of texts to maintain a certain level of novelty and spice. Another factor tends to be more pervasive: the effect of the situation of speaking on the choice between nearly equivalent forms of expression.

The whole problem of how a speaker's internal lexicon is organized and how that organization agrees with that of the hearer is of interest to the student of discourse. It is also of interest to the critic, most notably when a discrepancy in organization introduces a bar between the writer and the reader. Some writers are said to have a private vocabulary, others to be highly experimental in their use of words, others to use a symbolism that we cannot penetrate; it all seems to come back to the comparability of different people's lexical systems. In another direction, psychologists have used crude measures of lexical structuring like word association and the semantic differential to get at abnormal mental states in a way that does not seem too different from a critic's feeling that, say, "Zabrowski's incessant reference to milk bottles in his metaphors for nearly anything unpleasant makes us wonder if he is reporting the way an average Eastern European sees things or if he is projecting his unhappy years on a dairy farm on the rest of the world".

Source criticism and its derivatives have been practiced, in my

[8] Weizenbaum, "Contextual Understanding by Computers" (1967).

opinion, with relatively little reference to finding out what points of structure actually are invariant in a particular person's pattern of usage, yet serve to discriminate his works from those of others. The points from which proof is derived tend to be things that are easy to count, without any normalization to take care of observable effects of style, genre, or subject matter. Having done this kind of thing myself within extremely tentative statistical limits,[9] I feel it is legitimate to engage in this sort of counting in order to get a rough approximation to the notion of similarity; but I would insist that no theory of source criticism that is realistic from the point of view of discourse has yet been propounded. The idea of parametric predicates may have implications for source criticism.[10]

Ideally the factors on which a critic bases his judgment ought to be built into a writer before he starts writing. To the extent that they can be specified linguistically, I see no reason why they cannot be taught. There is a sense in which parts of this book depend on observations made not only in teaching writing to freshmen, but also in specialized teaching on the short story, the novel, and expository and argumentative prose. Here, however, the emphasis is on putting things that teachers of composition know into a systematic framework; any of their expertise that I cannot fit in readily has been left to one side for the present.

3. EXEGESIS

In this section I discuss primarily those aspects of discourse that have come to light in the area of Biblical studies, with which I am considerably more familiar than with legal or historical exegesis. The standard exegetical question concerns the way factors external to a text influence the content and diction of the text. The idea seems to be, put simply, that once those factors are written off, the remainder represents the sense of the text in a more abstract,

---

[9] Grimes, "Measuring Naturalness" (1963).
[10] Grimes and Glock, "Saramaccan" (1970). See also Chapter 23.

general, and therefore more applicable form. The factors themselves relate to the communicative situation, the lexical and
rhetorical resources of the language itself, and the reasons why
the particular text is put together the way it is.

The area of exegesis generally labeled "introduction" comes
close to being a specification of the performative elements of a text.
Here it is customary to discuss authorship, the audience to whom
the text was directed, and the historical setting, both in terms of the
culture of the period (for example, Edersheim or Conybeare and
Howson)[11] and the specific local situations that called forth the
text.

Studies of authorship involve not only who might have written
a work, but also, assuming it was a particular person, what his
personal experiences up to that point were and where he must have
been. Statements like "it is less plausible to assume that the author
of *Hebrews* had been involved in the actual temple ritual in Jeru-
salem than it is to assume that his familiarity with those rites was
from a distance and so was couched in the terms of the Pentateuch"
illustrate the kind of working back from the text itself to deductions
about the person who formed the text that is characteristic of
exegetical method. Similarly structured arguments concerning the
audience rather than the author appear in commentaries on the
Epistle to the Galatians,[12] where it is uncertain just who the
Galatians were to whom the epistle was directed, and knowing who
they were seems to influence how some statements in the epistle
are to be taken. In terms of discourse theory, these studies are
parallel to my deduction that a certain Saramaccan text had to
have been uttered in Paramaribo, based on an analysis of the
pattern of distribution of "come" and "go" verbs.[13]

In Biblical lexicography the problem of semantic structure in
general has been raised in ways that have linguistic implications

---

[11]   Edersheim, *The Life and Times of Jesus the Messiah* (1883); Conybeare and
Howson, *The Life and Epistles of St. Paul* (1860).
[12]   Lightfoot, *Galatians* (1892), Burton, *Galatians* (1920).
[13]   Grimes and Glock, "Saramaccan" (1970).

even though they are not usually phrased in linguistic terms. Studies of the use of a particular word in different contexts by a particular individual, or by a group of individuals, are parallel to the tracing of lexical idiosyncrasies referred to in the section on criticism. Barr, in his *Semantics of Biblical Language*,[14] makes a distinction between text- and usage-based lexicography and etymologically-based lexicography that has implications for any semantic study. The influence of grammatical position and form, and to a certain extent the influence of position in a text, on the meaning of a lexical item, are traced carefully in, for example, the Arndt and Gingrich entry for *pistéuo*.[15]

Daniel P. Fuller's characterization of the recursive relations that link both clauses and the textual units formed from linked clauses has been a major stimulus to this study.[16] It has shown that the grammatical trees that characterize sentences can be extended upward to groups of sentences, without essential discontinuity, as is exemplified in John Austing's paper on Omie. Although I feel that grammars based purely on constituency relations, even beginning with semantics, have certain inherent limitations, Fuller's work shows that if one is willing to set aside those limitations, a tree representation of text structure can be enlightening.

Ethel Wallis's study of the structure of the four gospels illustrates the kind of contribution to exegetical studies that can be made by a person who thinks linguistically.[17] Although her analysis does not fit any of the models of discourse that we have yet, and so cannot quite be put forth as an example of high level linguistics, it appears nevertheless to be linguistically motivated on the one hand and exegetically useful on the other.

---

[14] See my review (1963).

[15] Arndt and Gingrich, *Greek-English Lexicon* (1965).

[16] Fuller, *The Inductive Method of Bible Study* (1959). Note also Ballard et al., "The Deep and Surface Grammar of Interclausal Relations" (1971), "More on the Deep and Surface Grammar of Interclausal Relations" (1972); Grimes, "Outlines and Overlays" (1972).

[17] Wallis, "Contrastive Plot Structures of the Four Gospels" (1971).

4. LINGUISTICS

So far the greatest attention to discourse within the field of modern American linguistics has been paid by scholars of the so-called tagmemic school, which developed in the middle 1950's under the stimulus of Kenneth L. Pike.[18] Elson and Pickett's textbook and the work of Robert E. Longacre furthered the work of the school, which is summarized by Pike.[19]

In my opinion Pike's most fundamental contribution to discourse studies was his insistence that certain chunks of human behavior can be taken as culturally given. They are recognizable to those who participate in them, and often to bystanders who understand the cultural systems involved, as having a definite beginning and end. Behavior that is characterized thus by CLOSURE is Pike's starting point for the analysis of both verbal and nonverbal behavior. The behavioreme, as he calls such a segmentable chunk of behavior, has an internal structure, so that successive segmentations of the behavioreme lead to the units of a grammar, again either verbal or nonverbal (as exemplified by Bock's analysis of cultural conceptions of space and time).[20]

Since "discourse" is a primitive term in the notional system I build up in this book, it is obviously not possible to give a strict definition of it. Nevertheless, Pike's notion of discourse as a verbal behavioreme is a better starting point than any other I know of for communicating what a discourse is. Like any other behavioreme, it is recognized by the culture as an entity with a beginning and an ending, and has an internal structure. Even when it is not immediately obvious to an analyst what the beginning and ending signals are or how the internal structure fits together, it is possible to find particular discourses for which corroboration of discreteness can be gotten from speakers, and use that evidence to build general

---

[18]   Pike, *Language*, Part 1 (1954).
[19]   Elson and Pickett, *Morphology and Syntax* (1969); Longacre, *Grammar Discovery Procedures* (1964); Pike, "A Guide to Publications Related to Tagmemic Theory" (1966).
[20]   Bock, *The Social Structure of a Canadian Indian Reserve* (1962).

models of discourse in such a way that apparently dubious cases are seen to be special instances of some model, just as linguists do for everything else in language.

From the very beginning Pike pointed out the implications of the behavioreme concept for studies of discourse. James Loriot seems to have been the first to attempt to work this out on a large scale in a 1958 manuscript which unfortunately was not published until much later.[21] Pike's ideas were worked out in the area of rhetoric by Alton Becker,[22] and in application to various languages by Loos[23] and doctoral dissertations by Bridgeman, Wise, and Powlison.[24] Pike gave a programmatic statement of his view of the way discourse grammars might be written in a 1964 article.

Although a formal theory of reference has been no more prominent in tagmemics than in any other American brand of linguistics, Pike and Ivan Lowe did work out systematic relationships between pronouns and their referents for the case of embedded quotations, with an elegant, exhaustive, and probably universal solution that is quite atypical of attempts to apply mathematical models to language.[25] Lowe then worked with Mary Ruth Wise on applying a similar model to sequential pronominal reference in a text, with results that will be given in Chapter 9.[26]

Although most of the early work of the Pike school was directed toward the analysis and cataloguing of output forms of language without much greater attention to the semantics that lay behind those forms than that which could be conveniently embodied

[21]   Loriot and Hollenbach, "Shipibo Paragraph Structure" (1970).
[22]   Becker, "A Tagmemic Approach to Paragraph Analysis" (1965); with Young and Pike, *Rhetoric* (1970).
[23]   Loos, "Capanahua Narration Structure" (1963).
[24]   Bridgeman, *Oral Paragraphs in Kaiwa* (1966); Wise, *Identification of Participants in Discourse* (1968); Powlison, *Yagua Mythology and its Epic Tendencies* (1969).
[25]   Pike and Lowe, "Pronominal Reference in English Conversation and Discourse" (1969); Lowe, "An Algebraic Theory of English Pronominal Reference" (1969).
[26]   Wise and Lowe, "Permutation Groups in Discourse" (1972).

in the labels of tagmemes,[27] Pike did foreshadow the development
of case grammar, so important in current work on discourse. An
article by Janette Forster,[28] written under Pike's guidance, shows
the emergence of a notion of "situational role", the part someone
plays in an action regardless of how it is reported, as opposed to
"grammatical role", the place that participant fills in the most
immediately apparent grammatical structure. Donna Hettick's
study of verb stem classes in northern Kankanay carries this idea
a good deal farther, putting emphasis on how the tightly constrained
grammatical structure serves to express a highly flexible system of
semantic distinctions.[29]

Robert E. Longacre has contributed heavily to the literature on
discourse. In keeping with the tagmemic tradition of surface
grammars based on partitionings of classes of strings, his earlier
work was devoted largely to classifying the discourse patterns he
found; but more recently he has also moved in the direction of
including semantics. His major contributions are based on studies
of languages of the Philippines and a similar volume on languages
of Papua New Guinea.[30] His semantic emphasis appears in two
articles by Ballard, Conrad, and Longacre.[31] The Philippines
volumes is also significant because in it he begins the development
of a typology of discourse features.

The stratificational school of linguistics, originated by Sydney
Lamb, is free from inherent limitations to the sentence.[32] I have
drawn heavily on the work of H. A. Gleason, Jr. and his students
Taber, Cromack, and Stennes, in regard to the notion of different
kinds of information that appear at various places in discourse

---

[27] Postal, *Constituent Structure* (1964).
[28] Forster, "Dual Structure of Dibabawon Verbal Clauses" (1964).
[29] Hettick, "Verb Stem Classes in Northern Kankanay" (ms).
[30] Longacre, *Discourse, Paragraph, and Sentence Structure in Selected Philippine Languages* (1968), *Hierarchy and Universality of Discourse Constituents in New Guinea Languages* (1972).
[31] "The Deep and Surface Grammar of Interclausal Relations" (1971), "More on ... Interclausal Relations" (1972).
[32] Lamb, *Outline of Stratificational Grammar* (1966).

and how they are related to the forms that appear in text.[33]
Furthermore, Gleason has made a major contribution in suggesting
how the text of discourse might be represented as an aid both to
discovering and to displaying interesting linguistic relationships.
While discovery of relationships is not particularly germane to
the way those relationships are presented in a grammar that is fully
worked out, as Chomsky has made clear in *Syntactic Structures*,
at the stage where we do not yet know exactly what it is we expect
to find, anything that helps us see patterns as a whole is an advance;
and the work of Gleason and his associates seems to me to be such
a contribution.

In Europe, where some scholars appear not to have felt so
strongly as some in America that the sentence is the last frontier of
linguistics, linguists associated with the Linguistic Circle of Prague
investigated what I am calling information structure and thematization in a productive way. Chafe gives a resume of their work in
Meaning and the Structure of Language, but I sense that it is colored
by his simplifying assumption that thematization and information
structure are both concerned with the introduction of new information. A valuable summary of studies made on the Continent is
embodied in Halliday's three articles on transitivity and theme in
English,[34] on which I have drawn heavily in Chapters 19 and 21.
I have found Halliday's work extremely productive in the field,
though I observe that many readers find it hard to follow. Since I
think what he says ought to be more widely available, I attempt
to restate it in a form that is easier to comprehend in Chapters 19
and 21. Winograd has applied Halliday's grammatical notions in
a model of language that handles complete discourses.[35]

Generative transformational grammar of the Chomsky school
has been reluctant to peer out over the boundaries of the sentence.

---

[33] Gleason, "Contrastive Analysis in Discourse Structure" (1968); Taber,
The Structure of Sango Narrative (1966); Cromack, *Language Systems and
Discourse Structure in Cashinawa* (1968); Stennes, *Participant Identification in
Adamawa Fulani* (1969).
[34] Parts 1 and 2 (1967), Part 3 (1968).
[35] Winograd, *Procedures* (1971).

Nevertheless, in the area of reference it has operated under the assumption that some information has to be available from outside the actual productions of the grammar. This assumption is not necessarily incompatible with any theory of the generative transformational variety; but it does imply a form of grammar that looks a little different from today's standard brands.

The theory of reference that a generative transformational theory ought to cope with makes its lack felt in the matter of pronominalization. In the Chomsky tradition (which by no means represents the total family of theories that are both generative and transformational) there have been two approaches to pronominalization: deletion and insertion.

Pronominalization by deletion holds that whenever two noun phrases that are not distinct in reference stand in a particular relation to one another, one of the noun phrases is deleted and a pronoun is left in its place. The extreme form of deletion would be one in which not only must the noun phrases not be distinct in reference; they must also be identical in form. George Lakoff has also followed the line that pronominalization arises transformationally by deletion.[36]

Emmon Bach proposed a different theory of pronominalization, followed with modifications by McCawley and Langendoen.[37] He pointed out the complicated nature of underlying representations that required identity of noun phrases in deletion; for example, in *The tall teenager who came in here for a couple of hours yesterday while it was raining must have forgotten his guitar*, identity implies that the word *his* derives from *the tall teenager who came in here for a couple of hours yesterday while it was raining's*. It would be less cumbersome, he points out, if we could say that the sentence represents on the one hand a proposition like *x must have forgotten y* coupled with *x is the tall teenager who came in here for a couple of hours yesterday while it was raining* (without going further into

[36]   Lakoff, "Pronouns and Reference" (ms).
[37]   Bach, "Nouns and Noun Phrases" (1968); McCawley, "Where Do Noun Phrases Come From?" (1970); Langendoen, *Essentials of English Grammar* (1970).

the internal structure of that identification), *y is a particular guitar*, and *y belongs to x*, together with a principle that inserts the noun phrase identifying *x* when *x* is first mentioned and supplies the corresponding pronoun elsewhere.[38]

Not only does pronominalization by insertion give a clear account of pronominalization phenomena;[39] it also fits neatly with the idea proposed here that different kinds of information in discourse are characteristically encoded in different ways and at different points in the discourse (Chapter 3). This makes it possible to think of the information in a discourse as partitioned into identifications, actions, evaluations, and the like, linked together grammatically by thoroughly regular patterns.

I have cautiously bypassed some things that have been said about discourse because I do not yet see how they lead anywhere. The one I have most obviously skipped is Zellig Harris's discourse analysis.[40] Harris has found that within a text it is possible to form equivalence classes of substrings of sentences. A substring *a* occurs along with a substring *b* in one sentence and with *c* in another, say; *b* also occurs with *d* in some other sentence and *c* with *e* in still another, giving sentences of the form *ab, ac, db, ec* somewhere in the text. *b* and *c* then constitute one equivalence class, and *a, d,* and *e* constitute another. It is possible to analyze an entire text into equivalence classes, especially if the sentences are normalized in form.

What I think we have is an effect for which we cannot yet account: call it the Harris effect. It may be similar to the Edison effect in electronics. Thomas Edison mentioned in 1875 that if a metal plate

---

[38]   This is an oversimplification of English pronominalization. Limitations on this basic pattern are discussed extensively in the literature.

[39]   Pronominalization by insertion seems to be capable of accounting for Bach-Peters sentences without becoming trapped in infinite regress: in *the man who discovered it never realized the value of the process he stumbled on*, the referent of *it* is *the process he stumbled on*, which involves *he* in its definition, while the referent of *he* is *the man who discovered it*, which involves *it* in its definition.

[40]   Harris, "Discourse Analysis" (1952), "Discourse Analysis: A Sample Text" (1952), *Discourse Analysis Reprints* (1963).

were placed on the outside of one of his newly invented electric lights, a current could be made to flow between it and the filament when the filament was lit. He made a note of the "etheric effect" (and in 1883, patented it under the name of the Edison effect), then went on to other things. Thirty years later, in 1905, Lee De-Forest capitalized on the Edison effect and gave us the vacuum tube. I suspect that we may be in the same position as Edison was regarding the Harris effect. It is worth noting, but for the time being we do not know what to do with it.

It is also of interest that the normalizing of sentences to make it possible to get an analysis of a text into fewer equivalence classes seems to have been directly related to the development of the idea of transformations.[41] Harris's term "discourse analysis", though defined very tightly by him, is too useful to allow it to remain attached exclusively to equivalence chain analysis. I prefer to speak of different kinds of discourse analysis, one of which is Harris's.

Another effect to be noted and shelved for the time being is the Salton effect. In his work on information retrieval noted earlier, Gerard Salton attempted to evaluate the quality of retrieval he was able to get by computer. He found that if he analyzed texts syntactically before processing them against retrieval requests, the quality of retrieval was not significantly greater than what he got by taking into account only the frequency of occurrence of particular lexical items in the text as a whole, independently of their syntactic position. To the extent of establishing what a text is talking about, then, the Salton effect points to semantics without syntax. This kind of information retrieval does not tell what the text says about the things it is talking about, however; to say that a text has to do with disarmament does not tell whether the author is for it or against it.

Another line of thinking I have not followed up because it may be a theoretical blind alley is Katz and Fodor's treatment of a

[41] Harris, "Co-occurrence and Transformation in Linguistic Structure" (1957).

text as a supersentence formed by conjoining all the sentences of the text.[42] This manipulation did allow them to apply their projection rules and develop their notions of semantic structure, and from that point it is justified. But it appears more than anything else to be an artifact of the limitations under which they were working, a ghost if you like of the assumption that the task of linguistics is to explicate the sentences of a language.

5. EMPIRICAL STUDIES

Studies of discourse phenomena have been made already for more than seventy languages. These have served as a testing ground for theories about discourse, and have consistently resulted in an enrichment of our understanding of discourse phenomena. There is no language for which the discourse structure has been described thoroughly; yet the composite picture from a number of languages certainly points toward an increasingly consistent conceptual framework for discourse studies. If we applied what we know now to a single language, we might be able to cover its discourse phenomena fairly thoroughly, though there would be points where we probably could not yet relate one part of the picture to the other parts coherently.

Studies by Pike and his students have, as already mentioned, touched on English and Nomatsiguenga of Peru, and have influenced studies in Kaiwa, a Guaraní language of Brazil, Capanahua of Peru, and Shipibo of Peru, among others. Longacre's work on discourse in the Philippines involved Ata Manobo, Dibabawon Manobo, Ilianen Manobo, Sarangani Bilaan, Tagabili, Atta Negrito, Botolan Sambal, Bontoc, Mansaka, Itneg, and Maranao. He also worked with Reid, Bishop, and Button on Totonaco of Mexico,[43] and on a number of languages in New Guinea.

---

[42] Katz and Fodor, "The Structure of a Semantic Theory" (1963).
[43] Reid, Bishop, Button, and Longacre, *Totonac: From Clause to Discourse* (1968).

Gleason's group has studied Sango of the Central African Republic, Cashinawa of Peru, and Fulani of Nigeria. Gleason himself has worked on Kâte of New Guinea.

In the series of workshops that formed the background for the writing of this book I was able, with the assistance of a grant from the National Science Foundation, to guide discourse studies in Bacairí, Borôro, Xavante, Nambiquara, Kayapó, and Paressí of Brazil, Halia, Omie, Wantoat, Angaataha, Oksapmin, Sanio-Hiowe, Anggor, and Chuave of New Guinea, and Sarangani Manobo, Ilianen Manobo, Kalinga, Keley-i Kallahan, Ivatan, and Mamanwa of the Philippines. Prior to that series of workshops I had had a hand in discourse studies in Mundurukú of Brazil, Ayoré of Bolivia, Jibu of Nigeria, and Otomí of Mexico, plus doing some work of my own on Huichol of Mexico. More recently I have assisted on studies on Goajiro of Columbia, Arabela of Peru, Sanuma of Brazil, Fali of Cameroun, Mumuye, Kaje, Longuda, and Mambila of Nigeria, Godié, Wobé, Tépo Krou, Gagou, Toura, and Loron of the Ivory Coast, and several languages of Ghana.

The point of all these field studies, of course, is not simply to collect data for data's sake. Instead, the attempt to work out each kind of discourse pattern as it comes up puts pressure on the theory of language that has guided the analysis, bending it one way or another. For my own part, the studies have been carried out in an atmosphere of interest and excitement, with the feeling that although in general we think we know how and why language is put together the way it is, there are areas that can be developed best under the stimulus of unforeseen phenomena.

Another result of the field studies is the beginnings of a typology of discourse. Longacre has extracted the parameters of sequence and accomplishment, for example, as the basis for his two-by-two division of discourse types.[44] Thurman has surveyed broad classes

---

[44] Longacre, *Discourse ... in Philippine Languages* (1968). Aristotle (*Rhetoric* 1:3) distinguishes deliberative, forensic, and epideictic or ceremonial rhetoric as respectively future (giving advice), past (accusation and defense), and present (praise and blame).

of cohesive phenomena and categorized them under the headings of linking and chaining.[45] I have looked at patterns of presentation of information in texts and have come up with the typological notion of the outline as over against the overlay pattern.[46] These regularities across languages and language families help us to narrow down the field of what to expect, and provide some control for other kinds of cross language studies.

6. THE APPROACH OF THIS BOOK

Since I have deliberately taken discourse as undefined, characterized only in terms of Pike's notion of a verbal behavioreme,[47] there is very little in human speech behavior that does not somehow fall within the scope of this book. To me this is an advantage at this stage of our understanding: look at anything that might conceivably fit, and if it does, then make sure the conceptual system provides a place for it. I suspect that this approach is a pendulum's swing in the other direction from starting out with an arbitrary limitation like Chomsky's and seeing how far it will go, so that the next person to try his hand at a theory of discourse may well go back to a more restricted starting point.

The generalizations I try to make in the book relate to the family of theories currently known as generative semantics. That is, I assume that we can say the most about language by factoring out two different things: the decisions a speaker can make regarding what and what not to say, and the mechanisms and patterns that are available to him for implementing the results of those decisions in a way that communicates with another person. The decisions that the speaker makes, and the relations among them, are referred

---

[45] Thurman, "Chuave Medial Verbs" (ms).
[46] Grimes, "Outlines and Overlays" (1972).
[47] Even though Pike's behavioreme is the starting point, the reader should be aware that my treatment of it is not that of the tagmemic school. For tagmemic studies of discourse and my reasons for wanting a more revealing theory, see Chapter 4.

to as the underlying formational structure (underlying in the sense that it is verifiable only indirectly from the forms he utters and the behavior that is associated with the uttering) or the semantic structure. The relation between this underlying structure and the speech forms that are uttered is called the transformation, or better yet the Transformation with a capital T, which is usually talked about by decomposing it into a number of less complex transformations with small t's.

An increasingly strong impression that has built up throughout the period of study that resulted in this book is that one of the things that current linguistic theory lacks is a viable theory of reference. As already mentioned, an implicit but formally unrecognized theory of reference has been in use for years, expressed principally in discussions of referential indices and coreferentiality. I see no way to avoid bringing this into linguistic theory; but in doing so, I suspect that something more than the minimum needed to recognize coreferentiality will have to be defined. Winograd has taken the bull by the horns by making reference to the external world part of his explicit model of language. Chapter 20 discusses how his model works.

Each of the linguistic traditions being talked about today is good for certain things and spotty for others. Even though when wearing the theoretician's hat I try to be consistent with one particular way of looking at things, I find that useful insights have been developed by people with other points of view. It is all to the good when I can put them into my perspective and find that they fit; when they don't, the problem is then to revise my perspective to make room for the insight, not to throw out the insight.

A good example of this is tagmemics. I find, possibly because much of my early training in linguistics was in tagmemics, that it is an extremely useful tool for getting the facts of language sorted out and organized. I also recognize that when it came on the scene around 1954 it was like a breath of fresh air in that it made it possible to incorporate a certain amount of semantic information into grammar via the notion of function.

Since moving off in a different direction in the early 1960's, however, I find that tagmemics leaves something to be desired as a view of what language is like, especially at the point where the idea of function seems in practice to turn into an arbitrary and almost mystical process for assigning tagmeme labels. Nevertheless, I feel quite free here to use tagmemic ideas. I recognize first of all that they do enable people to manage linguistic data without getting lost regardless of how the labels are assigned. I also realize that whatever the defects of their results may be as seen through the theoretical lenses I am currently wearing, I am likely to agree with at least ninety-five per cent of the analysis that is made when all is said and done, and there is no point in throwing out all that just because I find that there are more consistent ways of understanding another few per cent.

In work that is as exploratory as this it is not surprising that a large amount of methodology for organizing data is mixed with theorizing. It is not really worth the trouble to state relationships among data elements or classes of data elements unless someone else can find the same data elements and verify the relationships. At this stage I am not even sure that it is possible to squeeze a pure theory of language out of the practice of discourse study. Where I have seen abstractions that can be made I have tried to call attention to them, but many of the components of a real theory of discourse are probably hidden within recipes for lining up information of a particular kind. I warn the reader about this, but do not apologize for it.

Along with the intermixing of theory and practice goes an inevitably large number of loose ends. We are not yet ready for a compendium or a formal summing up of what we know, because in some senses what we know is like a few galaxies and what we do not know but hope to is like the interstellar space that surrounds the galaxies: not very crowded. Yet I do not feel that having large numbers of unresolved questions about discourse is a bad thing as long as we see progress in pulling together a core of theory that allows us to work out toward the less explored areas.

3

EVENTS AND PARTICIPANTS IN DISCOURSE

To analyze discourse from a linguistic point of view requires a starting point. The work of Gleason and his group has provided such an entering wedge. The basic idea behind their work is that different parts of a discourse communicate different kinds of information. The kinds of things that are communicated in each part seem to be recognizable in any language, at least well enough that a meaningful preliminary breakdown of texts can be made.[1]

Empirically this distinction among various kinds of information has proved useful, not only in the studies on Sango, Cashinawa, Fulani, and Kâte that have already been mentioned in connection with Gleason, but also in papers on Xavante by McLeod, Munduruku by Sheffler, Maxakalí by Popovich, Halia by Jan Allen (all referred to in the bibliography), and others.

The distinction among different kinds of information is most obvious in narrative discourse as opposed to the procedures, explanations, and exhortations of Longacre's typology. Procedures, which like narratives are based on the notion of temporal sequence, are the next most productive.

Parenthetically, the texts that yield the most consistent analysis are edited texts. Certain people in any society have a reputation for consistently producing the kind of discourses that other people want to listen to. Part of the reason people like these discourses

---

[1] Part of this chapter and the next three was presented in a paper, "Kinds of Information in Discourse", read before the Linguistic Circle of Papua and New Guinea on February 24, 1971, and subsequently published in *Kivung* (1971).

appears to lie in their well formedness; that is, they are constructed according to plans that make it maximally easy for hearers or readers to comprehend them. Furthermore, even people who produce highly valued discourses recognize that certain parts of what they say can be improved by being reshaped or edited. The principles that guide their editing behavior are likely (unless they are imposed artificially from without, as for example under pressure of a more prestigious language) to represent a replacement of expressions that are less consistent with the discourse as a whole by other expressions that fit the structure and the context better. Speakers of unwritten languages display editorial reactions just as regularly as editors who work with paper and pencil.[2] The analysis of discourse that has been edited is likely to be easier, and at the same time more truly representative of those patterns of expression that speakers of the language react to as appropriate. Practiced discourses like folk tales are less likely to be told poorly than, say, personal narratives brought out on the spur of the moment with no opportunity to shape the expression first.

Even edited narratives cover quite a range. To begin analysis it is best to concentrate on simple narratives. These are characterized by having well separated participants: little or no merging of individual participants into groups or combining of one group with another. A simple narrative may, however, contain a large number of distinct participants. Two-participant narratives, though common, are not the best kind to start with, because the mechanisms needed to keep reference straight in them are usually rudimentary. Three-participant narratives are more likely to be revealing.

The other characteristic that identifies simple narratives is that in them telling matches time. That is, the sequence in which events are told matches the sequence in which the events actually happened. Many languages have this as a strict requirement for all narration; others have techniques whereby the temporal scene can be shifted

---

[2] I am indebted to Larry Jordan for calling to my attention the value of beginning with texts edited by proficient speakers, based on his experience with Mixteco of Apoala in Mexico.

at will without losing the hearer. Texts with flashbacks, or that begin in the middle of things, should be left to one side at the start.

To begin analysis with simple narratives does not, of course, imply that we stop with the study of simple narratives. Like any exploration of the complex, discourse study should begin in shallow water and only later progress into the depths. What is learned in the study of simple narratives becomes the starting point that allows progress into other areas.

The notion that different parts of a discourse communicate different kinds of things agrees with other conclusions about language that have been suggested for reasons totally unconnected with the study of discourse. McCawley's suggestion that noun phrases constitute a separate kind of grammatical production from the verb-centered part of sentences, and that the two are laced together loosely and late in the derivational process, is motivated as far as I can tell by a need to account adequately for pronominalization patterns within sentences.[3] It fits, however, with the distinction I make here between event information and identificational and other kinds of information. It also illustrates the notion that different kinds of information tend to be communicated by grammatically distinctive forms in surface structure.

1. EVENTS

The first distinction made in the analysis of discourse is between events and non-events. In *Garner, the halfback, made six yards around end* we are told two kinds of things: a particular person did something (that is, an event took place), and furthermore, the particular person is named Garner and is a halfback (neither of which is an event). Sometimes entire paragraphs are devoted to non-events, as in the description of a scene or a person. At other times, especially in languages like Anggor, long stretches of speech

[3]   McCawley, "Where Do Noun Phrases Come From?" (1970).

may be devoted to nothing but event information, the rules of the reference system being such that the hearer always knows by deduction who is doing what.[4]

Gleason, who pioneered in exploiting the difference between events and non-events, pointed out that different languages approach the time sequences between neighboring events in different ways. In Kâte, for example, events that are contiguous in time are distinguished from those that are separated by a lapse during which nothing of significance for the story happens.[5] The lapse may be long or short; but if it is noticeable in terms of the stream of action of the narrative, it must be mentioned. Ronald Huisman finds a similar situation in Angaataha with regard to both time sequence and logical sequence.[6] Cromack, on the other hand, finds that Cashinawa requires a distinction between completing one event before the next begins and continuing the earlier event on into the next.[7] In terms of Kâte, a Cashinawa completion might be either with or without lapse; but Cashinawa speakers are not required to report contiguity or lapse unless they want to call attention to it. Cashinawa continuation, on the other hand, would undoubtedly be equated with Kâte contiguity.

We can envision numerous logical possibilities for temporal relations between two events that are reported as a sequence. If we take A as the earlier of the two events and B as the later, we can distinguish several cases: A finishes significantly long before B begins, A finishes by the time B begins, A finishes just as B begins, and A does not finish by the time B begins. In the last case we might have to specify further whether A ends during B, A ends when B ends, or A contains all of B and continues on after B is finished.

Robert Litteral has applied the mathematical notion of TOPOLOGY to the linguistic treatment of time.[8] He notes first that when time

4   Shirley Litteral, "Orientation Shifts in Anggor" (ms).
5   Gleason, "Contrastive Analysis in Discourse Structure" (1970).
6   Ronald Huisman, "Angaataha Verb Morphology" (1973).
7   Cromack, *Cashinawa* (1968).
8   Robert Litteral, "Rhetorical Predicates and Time Topology in Anggor" (1972).

is handled by language, it is measured only rarely. For example, in *I went down town and bought a shirt* the first event, going down town, may have taken half an hour, while the second may have taken four minutes, or vice versa, depending on transportation facilities and shopping habits. Most languages would not give even a relative indication of the duration of the events, although they have the capacity to add this information if there is some reason to, as in *It took me half an hour to go down town; then I bought a shirt in four minutes.* The normal thing is for the two events, regardless of their relation to time by the clock, by the stars, by the seasons, physiological time, or even psychologically perceived time, to be reported simply as Event A and Event B. For this reason it is useful to model the linguistic handling of time in a non-metric fashion, which suggests a topology.

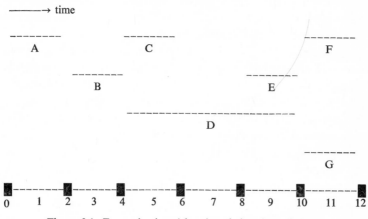

Figure 3.1. Events in time (above) and time base (below).

Suppose the relationship of events in a narrative fits Figure 3.1. Here Event A is followed by B, which is followed in turn by both C and D. D continues after C finishes, and also keeps going through the end of E. F and G follow, simultaneous with each other. A sample narrative with these relationships might be **(A)** *They got up before dawn and* **(B)** *ate breakfast together.* **(C)** *Curly rode into town, but* **(D)** *Slim headed off to the canyon to look for* *lost cattle.* (E) *Another cowpuncher he met at the mouth of a draw told him he had seen a yearling farther up.* (F) *Slim went after it* (G) *while the puncher watered his horse.*

It is also characteristic of the linguistic handling of time that the boundaries between events are rarely clear cut. For example, unless we are saying it in Kâte, we give no idea whether or not time elapsed between getting up (A) and eating breakfast (B) in the example above. The only thing that is certain is that there was a time (A) when they were getting up and not eating breakfast, and that later there was a time (B) when they were eating breakfast and not getting up. This lack of interest in the transition period is represented appropriately by a line that represents time, and open sets of points along that line that represent events; open sets do not include their own boundaries.[9] The time line thus appears to be a special case of what is known as a Hausdorff space, a kind of topological space in which for any pair of distinct points, there are neighborhoods of each that have no points in common.

Litteral takes the events as a SUBBASE for the topology of the time line. This means that each event that is in the narrative is represented by an open set of points along the time line in such a way that the finite intersections of those open sets are a BASE for the topology that expresses the linguistic organization of time. The base itself consists of open sets such that each event set is a union of sets in the base. (The intersection of two sets is the elements that are common to both; the union of two sets is the elements that are found in either.) By arranging the members of the base and the boundaries between them along the time line, an OPEN CHAIN that COVERS the time line results. It consists of open sets representing linguistically significant stretches of time, alternating with the boundaries between the open sets. From this Litteral is able to

---

[9] The elementary notions of topology are presented in Lipschutz, *Outline of Theory and Problems of General Topology* (1965), Arnold, *Intuitive Concepts in Elementary Topology* (1962), or Mendelson, *Introduction to Topology* (1963). The presentation of them here is informal, but is capable of being formalized. Technical terms used here include *open set, boundary, Hausdorff space, neighborhood, subbase,* and *base.*

construct the index illustrated in Figure 3.1 at the bottom. There the open set of points associated with an event is represented by a horizontal line and the boundary between two events by a vertical bar. The alternating boundary and event segments are matched to the set of nonnegative integers (whole numbers) in such a way that even numbers match boundaries and odd numbers match events. There is also an even number α that denotes an undefined beginning boundary instead of 0, and a corresponding even number ω that denotes an undefined terminating boundary. The index of an event is an ordered pair *(a,b)* with $a \leq b;$ *a* tells when on the time index line the event begins and *b* tells when it ends. For events that span more than one segment of the time base, *(a,b)* refers to the simple chain that begins with segment *a* and ends with segment *b*, including all the intervening event spans and boundaries. Thus in Figure 3.1 the index of event A is (1,1), since A begins and ends with the same time segment. Similarly the other single span indexes are B(3,3), C(5,5), E(9,9), F(11,11), and G(11,11). The index of D, however, is (5,9); D spans the times of C and E and the boundary times between them as well.

This representation of time makes it possible to distinguish simultaneous actions like F and G from partially simultaneous actions like C and D or D and E. It is precise, but with a precision that is something other than the precision of a stopwatch. Neither is it the precision of a frame counter on a motion picture projector, as was used in analyzing films of the assassination of John F. Kennedy. It is rather the kind of precision that is appropriate to the linguistic system itself. Furthermore, the distinction Litteral makes between events as open sets of points on the time line and the boundaries of those sets is valuable for making explicit certain kinds of aspectual distinctions like inchoative ("starting to ...") and completive ("finishing ..."). By providing a framework for time that is related directly to the referential system of language itself, Litteral has also made it simpler to talk about apparent referential incongruities such as *My wife*$_{n,\omega}$ *was born*$_{n-k,n-k}$ *in San Diego*$_{\alpha,\omega}$ in which obviously the person being talked about at time *n* was not the speaker's wife at the time she was born, *n-k*, but became his wife later.

Another kind of sequencing between events is what Ronald Huisman has characterized as tight vs. loose.[10] In Angaataha, a language of the Eastern Highlands of Papua New Guinea, Huisman reports two kinds of sequencing, temporal and logical, each of which may be tight or loose. Tight temporal sequencing corresponds rather well to the Kâte notion of contiguity in time, while loose temporal sequencing corresponds to Kâte lapse. In logical sequencing, however, tight sequence implies that one event has another as its direct consequence, while loose sequence implies that one event has a continuing effect that persists indefinitely, or at least to the point of influencing a second event even when that second event cannot be considered its direct consequence. The notion of a persisting effect is also present in the perfect tenses of ancient Greek.

The time sequence of a narrative is rarely expressed as though events simply followed one another like beads on a string. Instead, there is usually a grouping of events into smaller sequences; then each of these smaller sequences as a unit is put together with other subsequences of the same kind. Time structuring can be carried on through several levels of partitioning, so that the grouping of subsequences of events can be diagrammed as a tree. Over the whole narrative, however, a single index in Litteral's sense can be constructed. The moving finger of time moves on from event to event; yet from another point of view the events themselves are clustered together.

In asserting this independence of temporal sequences from the hierarchical grouping of linguistic elements, Litteral has, I think, rightly, eliminated my earlier notion[11] of TEMPORAL SEQUENCE as one of several rhetorical relations (see Chapter 6). Instead he has moved temporal sequence into the area of reference. The clumping together of a series of events which are also in temporal sequence

---

[10] Ronald Huisman, "Angaataha Verb Morphology" (1973).
[11] Grimes, "Outlines and Overlays" (1972).

with one another turns out to be based on organizing factors which probably are part of the rhetorical structure. For example, all the events that take place at a particular setting tend to be treated as a unit, as Glock and I found to be the case in Saramaccan.[12] When rhetorical organization and temporal sequence match, the order of elements can be considered normal or unmarked.

Another grouping principle that partitions events in a single temporal sequence could be called the principle of COMMON ORIENTATION. A sequence of events is distinguished from a later part of the same time sequence in that all the actions in each part involve uniform relations among their participants. Alton Becker speaks of this as one of the bases of paragraphing in English.[13] Sheffler finds something similar but more explicitly communicated in her manuscript on Munduruku. There the patient or goal of an action is singled out at the beginning of each paragraph. It defines the characteristic orientation of the participants for that paragraph, in that the rest of the actions in the paragraph are implicitly taken to be directed toward that patient or goal. Uniformity of participant orientation will be discussed in detail in Chapter 9, and is related to thematization, discussed in Chapter 11.

Besides common setting and common orientation, some event sequences appear to be grouped together by the way they relate to PLOT structures. In our study of Saramaccan, Glock and I had questioned whether plot structure was actually part of linguistics at all. I suggested it might rather be a perceptual template whereby a discourse could be rendered interesting by casting the more prominent referents in it in standard roles like hero and villain. June Austing finds in Omie, however, that the particle *iae*, which marks the beginning of temporal subsequences that are grouped together for other reasons, also begins temporal subsequences that do not appear to be grouped together in any of those ways, but do correspond to boundaries between Propp's basic plot elements.[14]

[12]   Grimes and Glock, "Saramaccan" (1970).
[13]   Becker, "A Tagmemic Approach to Paragraph Analysis" (1965).
[14]   June Austing, "Omie Discourse" (ms). Propp, *Morphology of the Folktale* (1958).

This would suggest that plot structure is a factor in the linguistic behavior of Omie speakers and must therefore be considered as interacting with the time sequencing system of the language. The high predictability of the Labov-Waletzky suspension point, at which English speakers (but not Saramaccan speakers, I notice) inject evaluative comments or questions into a narrative between the complication and the resolution, also argues in favor of plot as a semantic complex rather than as a principle of referential selection alone.[15]

Not all events, of course, are in sequence. Language is capable of communicating FORKED action[16] as in *you take the high road and I'll take the low road*, which is not a description of a sequence of events. Forked actions may be related only by their simultaneity, or they may be different sides of a single complex action as in *the dog chased the fleeing cat* or *they got the car started by him pulling and her pushing*.

In other cases a language may mark certain stretches within which sequence is irrelevant. Janet Briggs cites part of an Ayoré text in which many things happen during a raid on a jungle encampment.[17] Although all the events, which involve several individuals fighting and others getting killed or being captured, took place in some real sequence, they are explicitly marked in Ayoré by the particle *jéque* as part of a single hurly-burly in which attention to sequence, normally a prominent part of Ayoré discourse structure, is suspended.

Ayoré is also typical of many languages in that the sequence of telling normally has to parallel the sequence of happening. Even when the sequence is suspended, the suspension covers an interval of time whose relative position in relation to other events is kept

---

[15] Labov and Waletzky, "Narrative Analysis" (1967). See also Section 5 of this chapter.

[16] The term FORKED is taken from the terminology used to describe simultaneous computational processes in the design of multiprocessing systems. It is matched by JOINED, which refers to the point in the total sequence where all the simultaneous processes are known to have been completed so that another step that depends upon their joint results can then proceed.

[17] Briggs, "Ayoré Narrative Analysis" (ms).

in the right order. Other languages, however, make use of a set of signals that allows events to be told out of order. The Odyssey, for example, consists of a series of flashbacks from a rather short main sequence of events; but it is constructed in such a way that there is no doubt about where each episode fits into the whole. True flashbacks are part of the main sequence of events that are told out of order. They are distinct from narrative subsequences that are told in an explanatory fashion without being in the main stream of events (Section 4).

2. PARTICIPANTS

The information that identifies the participants in an event not only links participants to events, but also links one mention of a participant with other mentions of the same participant. It obeys rules of its own in addition to combining with event information.

There may be a distinction in language between PARTICIPANTS and PROPS. Certainly in the folk tale of Little Red Riding Hood, in which the little girl's mother sends her off to take a basket of goodies to her grandmother, what her mother put in her basket has a different relation to the rest of the tale than Little Red Riding Hood herself does. On the other hand, it is not a simple matter to distinguish participants from props. One could suggest that the animate objects that are involved in actions are the participants and the inanimate ones the props; but this does not square with Propp's observation that the helper in a plot, who assists the hero to attain his goal, is inanimate as often as animate.[18] Furthermore, many other texts have the form of a folk tale without necessarily intending to be one. In a considerable amount of scientific writing the hero, the author, slays a dragon, ignorance or the bumbling of former investigators, by means of a helper, a second order differential equation, and thus rescues the victim, his branch of

---

[18] Propp, *Morphology of the Folktale* (1958).

science. In folk tales of this kind many or all of the participants
may be abstractions.

The role ranking developed in Chapter 5 gives a scale of relative
involvement in an action, from deliberate involvement expressed
by the agent, to being acted upon in the patient and instrument,
and from there on down to zero involvement. This ranking might
make it possible to divide the things mentioned in a text into those
that never appear in the more active semantic roles, the props, and
those that do, the participants. This kind of classification, for
example, seems implicit in Wise and Lowe's partitioning of objects
into participants and props in their analysis of a Nomatsiguenga
text.[19]

The distinction between participants and props does seem to be
related to plot, possibly in the sense just mentioned. That is, even
if activity is not relative to the role system as such, yet it may be
relative to the plot within which it takes place. Little Red Riding
Hood's lunch basket contents seem not to matter in the plot of the
tale because they never do anything; Digory's rings in C. S. Lewis's
The Magician's Nephew do matter because they transport him to
another world. On the other hand, Rosencrantz and Guildenstern
in *Hamlet* have always impressed me more as props than as
participants; what they do only implements what somebody else
has decided. Barnard and Longacre confront this problem in a
Dibabawon text, and Perrin finds different identification patterns
for props and participants in Mambila of Nigeria.[20]

A fourth possibility for distinguishing between participants and
props is suggested by the study of orientation systems (Chapter 9).
If we assume that changes in the orientation of participants toward
actions are systematic, then any elements that would break the
regularity of orientation patterns if considered as participants are
probably props. This notion combines two things: the relative
involvement in a particular action that is implied by a ranking of

[19]   Wise and Lowe, "Permutation Groups in Discourse" (1972).
[20]   Barnard and Longacre, "Dibabawon Procedural Narrative" (1968).
Perrin, "Who's Who in Mambila" (ms).

underlying role categories, and relative involvement in the more comprehensive categories of plot. Even so, it remains to be seen whether the distinction between participants and props can ultimately be generalized to plotless and nonsequential texts.

Reference to who and what is involved in an event is partially independent of the means used to identify each referent. For example, here are six sentences that could conceivably refer to exactly the same situation, and therefore to the same set of referents, but that use different means of identifying them.

(a) The butler it was that killed him.
(b) Someone in a tuxedo killed him.
(c) That one killed him.
(d) He killed him.
(e) He killed the prime minister.
(f) Killed him.

Throughout this book REFERENCE and IDENTIFICATION are kept distinct. Reference has to do with who or what is being talked about. It goes back to the speaker's assumption that the hearer knows who or what is involved. Identification, on the other hand, has to do with the linguistic means that the speaker uses to communicate to the hearer who or what is involved. In (f) the doer of the deed is not identified, but he is still the doer of the deed; there is reference with no identification. The way in which identification is accomplished depends upon the circumstances, linguistic and nonlinguistic, under which reference is made.

Participants are referred to as individuals or in groups. Reference to individuals presents relatively few problems. Group reference, on the other hand, takes a number of forms. It may be individual centered, as in *the President and his staff* or *me and my gal*. It may be collective, referring to members of the group en masse: *the Presidential staff, today's consumer*. The group reference may imply that a further partitioning of the group is possible: *representatives of the major labor unions* invites a matching up of representatives with labor unions. It may be undefinable, as in *they say it's going to rain*, for which it is considered impertinent to

ask who *they* are. Some languages have a conventional *they* as
well: *they were camping near the rapids* in the absence of any more
explicit identification means 'those members of our tribe who were
alive at the time' by default.

Sometimes reference shifts during the course of a text. There
are three kinds of shift: introduction and deletion, recombination,
and scope change. Introduction and deletion involve expanding
and contracting reference by adding or subtracting individuals
from a group. For example, in *We met George at the airport. We
all took the same plane.* a group (we_1) is introduced, then expanded,
then the expanded group (we_2) remains as the referent. The Jibu
text cited by Bradley involves extensive expansion and contraction
of groups.[21]

Recombination is slightly different from expansion and contraction. In expansion and contraction individuals are introduced
only to the extent necessary to enable them to be incorporated
into a group; once in it, they have no further identity, like George
in the preceding example. When a group contracts, as in the Jibu
example, individuals who leave it are not referred to again, but
are lost to view. In the merging and splitting of groups, however,
the constituent subgroups of which the original group was composed remain as referential entities. For example, in *We had dinner.
Then we went to work on the nominations while the children went
to a basketball game*, the first *we* includes the children while the
second *we* does not; the children remain as a newly defined group
split off from the original group. Thus although the original group
is split, all its members remain in view, but the groups they are
assigned to are not the same as in the earlier identification.

The third kind of referential shift, scope change, is like the effect
of a zoom lens on a camera. It changes the area that is under
attention. It may combine individuals who were formerly seen as
individuals and treat them as a group, not because they start to
act as a group as in the case of expansion and merger, but because
they and everything else being talked about are seen in a different

---

[21]   Bradley, "Jibu Narrative Discourse Structure" (1971).

perspective. Bradley's Jibu text, already mentioned, includes an example of zooming in from an overall perspective to a closeup, with a corresponding shift in reference. She has a group of individuals, namely a bridegroom, priest, and bride, interacting as a single group with the guests at a wedding. At one point in the text, however, the guests are left out of the picture and the narrator tells what the members of the bridegroom's group say to each other. They are treated as distinct individuals for the duration of that scene only. Later the scope zooms back out to the entire wedding proceedings, and the reference picks up the bridegroom's group again as a single entity as it was before.

Where there is a shift in the spatial viewpoint from which events are reported there may also be a shift in reference. When a narrator has been speaking as though he were omniscient and knows everything that goes on both inside and outside the heads of the participants, he may shift, for example, to presenting events as a certain one of the participants sees them, or vice versa. When he shifts, what at first he had treated as reference to individuals may change to reference to groups, or one pattern of grouping may be replaced by another through merging and splitting.

Identification, or the linguistic indication of reference, will be discussed in detail in Chapter 20. The next paragraphs here are a preliminary sketch of it. The basic problems in identification are first, establishing reference sufficiently well that the hearer is clear about who or what is being talked about, and second, confirming or maintaining it sufficiently well to keep the hearer from becoming confused.

Unique reference is established, and to a certain extent maintained, by naming in some cases.[22] In others, as is often the case where naming in itself would not be enough to fix reference adequately for the hearer, some kind of description is used to narrow down the range of possible referents to where the speaker thinks the hearer can proceed on his own. Bach, McCawley, Langendoen, and Postal have discussed the relation between grammatical forms of de-

[22] Jakobson, *Shifters, Verbal Categories, and the Russian Verb* (1957).

scription and the referential problem of keeping the entity that is being described distinct from other entities.[23] Postal adds that even single nouns used to characterize a referent descriptively may have a time dependent element. In *she married the poor bachelor and made a happy husband out of him* the same individual is referred to twice, but with two different descriptions appropriate to two different time segments with Litteral indices $(\alpha,1)$ and $(3,\omega)$ corresponding to before marriage and from the time of marriage onward.

From the point of view of discourse studies the striking thing about the identificational information that goes with participants in events is the different grammatical forms that are used to communicate the different kinds of information. Whereas events tend to be communicated by independent verbs in most languages, transformed from underlying predicates whose role sets include nearly anything,[24] identifications tend to involve the embedding of sentences. They also include nouns, which may be the limiting case of embedded equative sentences. Surface constructions of the equative and stative varieties are also characteristic of identifications.[25]

Identification is also maintained through the use of anaphoric elements. The most general of these, as pointed out by Lakoff and Langendoen,[26] are not pronouns, but nouns used as umbrella

---

[23]   Bach, "Nouns and Noun Phrases" (1968), p. 105. McCawley, "Where Do Noun Phrases Come From?" (1970), p. 136. Langendoen, *Essentials of English Grammar* (1970), p. 47. Postal, "Problems in Linguistic Representation of Reference" (1971), p. 13.

[24]   Frantz, *Blackfoot* (1970).

[25]   This is true even in languages like those of the Philippines where it is traditional in translation into English to render verbs nominally: *as for Bill, the hitting of him was by John*, or something of the kind. The nonverbal glossing of sentences in languages of this kind helps convince the reader that he is not dealing with English, but it rather obscures the fact that these languages also use true equative constructions to indicate the topicalization of units larger than the clause (in a manner parallel to English *what Bill did was to hit John*). This is discussed further in Chapter 11.

[26]   Lakoff, "Pronouns and Reference" (ms); Langendoen, *Essentials of English Grammar* (1970).

terms to cover a wide area of more specific nouns. They include nouns that are easily recognized as generic, like *thing, one, person,* and *idea.* They also include nouns that are generic relative to the particular referents, like *dish* in *All they had was chili and apple pie. He ate them, but the first dish gave him nightmares.*

Pronouns are the common means of maintaining identification. How efficient they are depends partly on the richness of the categories of appropriateness of reference that are available within the pronominal system. As long as two referents in English, for example, can be referred to by *he* and *she,* pronouns alone are enough to maintain their distinctiveness indefinitely; but if two referents both fall within the scope of *he,* other measures have to be taken to keep them from becoming confused. What a pronoun can refer to may be indicated explicitly when the pronoun agrees with nouns that are used to initiate identification of the referent. Spanish *la,* for example, is used to identify many referents that are introduced with nouns that end in *a* like *cola* 'tail' and *mesa* 'table', as well as with a few nouns that lack the *a* ending but are conventionally treated in the same way like *mano* 'hand'. The applicability of a pronoun may simply be known by convention, as when English *she* is used to identify something that was introduced with *ship.* In other cases neither explicit form nor convention suffices, as in the case of Spanish *sobrecargo* 'airplane cabin attendant', where *la* is used if the specific attendant in question is female and *lo* if male.

Inflectional reference is closely enough related to pronouns that the two are sometimes discussed together. From the point of view of identification, however, it is important to notice that the categories of appropriateness of reference for inflectional systems are, as far as I know, never more finely divided than those of the pronouns with which they may stand in cross reference. The inflectional categories may be identical with the pronominal categories, or the pronominal system may be richer in distinctions than the inflectional system, but the inflectional system probably never has more categories than the corresponding pronouns.

Even though this section is about participants, so far in discussing means of identification I have phrased things almost exclusively in terms of the identification of physical objects. The notion of identification is, of course, much broader. It is just as appropriate to speak of identification of time spans ("then") or actions ("did so") or directions ("there") or anything else. All these kinds of things are identified both descriptively and anaphorically; and even inflectional systems may index any of them.

Before leaving identification it is useful to point out that the notion of zero or implicit identification helps to bridge the gap between identification and reference. There are many cases where the hearer is expected to know who the participants are by deducing it from the context; he is not told by any overt linguistic signal. The rules for this kind of deduction are most important for the way they shed light on the entire process of identification. Like any zero element in linguistics, zero identification must be approached with caution; there must be a way to recover the reference from the context by rule, and there must be no possibility that the zero identification could contrast with its own absence.[27]

A possible way to make a theory of reference an integral part of linguistic theory is sketched in Chapter 20.

---

[27]   Haas, "Zero in Linguistic Description" (1957).

4

NON-EVENTS IN DISCOURSE

1. SETTING

Where, when, and under what circumstances actions take place constitute a separate kind of information called SETTING. Setting is important in the study of discourse not only because it characteristically involves distinctive grammatical constructions like locatives, but also because it is a common basis for segmentation of sequential texts into their constituent parts.

There is a difference, not always easy to perceive, between the setting of part of a text and the underlying relation of an action to its surroundings that I speak of later (5.1) as the range role. Range is part of the definition of certain actions, not part of the definition of every action. For example, with the English word *climb*, the surface on which the climbing is done is an essential semantic element of the action; if reference to it is omitted, it is because the range is readily deducible from the context, never because it is irrelevant to the action. Other actions like *think* and *say*, on the other hand, do not have a range element as part of their semantics. For example, if a person uses *climb* without making clear the surface on which the climbing was done, and a hearer asks him about it, he will get either a definite answer like *on the roof* or *under the porch*, or he will elicit the equally determinate *I don't know*, implying that it was legitimate for the hearer to have asked. But if asked where a particular event of thinking took place, the speaker is more likely to come back with a bewildered *huh?* and the kind of look in his eyes that shows he has no idea what the hearer is talking about, because range is not part of the normal semantics of those actions. On the other hand, a true setting is capable of extending over a sequence of actions and is independent of the meaning of any one of them. Setting can apply to predicates that do not have range as part of their meaning: *While I was in Phoenix I had a great idea.*

It is tricky to distinguish setting from the range role. Either may, for example, take the form of a locative like a prepositional phrase. One test that seems to work in a number of languages is the test of SEPARABILITY. Setting information can be paraphrased naturally in the form of a complete *when*, *where*, or *while* clause. It may even take the form of a separate sentence or block of sentences: *Finally we arrived in London. It was ten in the morning.* Range information, on the other hand, cannot be separated. *When he was at the street corner, he climbed* does not give the range for *climb*; it is necessary to make range part of the same clause, as in *he climbed the flagpole* or *he climbed the path that led from there.*

Settings in space are frequently distinguished from settings in time. All languages probably have the capability for defining a spatial setting by description, as in Gilbert and Sullivan's *On a tree by a river a little tom-tit* ... Maxakalí of Brazil characteristically goes heavy on describing spatial reference.[1] Up to half of each paragraph may be taken up with describing exactly where the action of that paragraph took place. Other languages give descriptions of spatial setting more sparingly. Especially in societies in which the physical environment is well known and most reported actions take place within it, a few cryptic and conventional reference points seem to be all the definition of setting that is normally needed. In Cora of Mexico, for example, each dwelling area has the physical features surrounding it catalogued through conventional combinations of verbal affixes, so that more explicit description of the setting is necessary only in talking about actions that take place outside that part of the tribal area.[2] In Anggor the

---

[1] Popovich, "Large Grammatical Units and the Space-Time Setting in Maxakali" (1967).
[2] Ambrose McMahon, personal communication.

factors of location of high ground, direction of river flow, and the sun's path combine in the selection of locatives in a way that gives almost a precut definition of the setting, changed only if those properties are radically different in the settings of some actions.[3]

Spatial settings may be redefined during the course of a text either by describing where each new setting is located, as seems normal for English, or by a relative redefinition that takes the most recent setting as its point of departure. Maxakalí does this frequently. When a setting is established in one paragraph, certain other points are related to that setting, yet stand outside it. The paragraph may end with one of the participants going to one of those peripheral points. A new paragraph that begins with a signal that the setting is to be changed may then pick up the peripheral point at which the action of the last paragraph ended and make that into the setting for the next paragraph. Oksapmin of Papua New Guinea does something similar, except that the shifting of setting does not seem to be related so closely to the division of the text into paragraphs as in Maxakalí.[4] A setting is established; then verbs of motion like "go" and "come back" are used for excursions out from that setting and back. If a "go" is not matched by a corresponding "come back", however, then a following "arrive" or similar verb establishes a new setting. On the other hand, a "come back" or "return" that is not preceded by a corresponding "go" switches the setting back to whatever setting was defined at the beginning of the text.

Huichol of Mexico defines spatial setting either by motion from one place to another, like Oksapmin but on a much less extensive scale, or by a more static characterization of one area in its relation to the area where earlier actions occurred. For example, "up on top" is used to characterize an area on top of a mountain range as it is seen from the perspective of previous actions that took place in a valley below. From then on all reference to the setting is from the

---

[3] Shirley Litteral, "Orientation Shifts in Anggor" (ms).
[4] Helen Lawrence, "Viewpoint and Location in Oksapmin" (1972).

new perspective of the top of the mountains until that in turn is changed.

The scope of a spatial setting may be broad or narrow. Oksapmin, for example, takes as the first setting of a narrative the place where the person stood from whose spatial viewpoint the story is told. The setting also includes his immediate surroundings. The extent of those surroundings, however, may take in as little as part of a room, or it may include part of a country. There is no explicit indication of where the boundaries of an Oksapmin setting lie; it must be deduced by the hearer from the speaker's pattern of use of prefixes like *ma-* 'here', or more exactly 'within the setting area', as opposed to *a-* 'there, outside the setting area'.

Settings in time are equally important. Temporal setting, like spatial setting, must be distinguished from the temporal properties inherent in a particular action. Whether an action followed its predecessor immediately or after a lapse, whether it is viewed as having an extension in time or taking place as a single unit, whether its effects are said to persist, all are independent of the general time framework of the narrative, just as the place where an action or series of actions happens is independent of those elements of location (range) that are an integral part of the definition of the action.

Descriptive definition of time is usually with reference to some kind of calendric system. The term is used broadly to include not only explicit calendric references like Longfellow's *'Twas the eighteenth of April in seventy-five ...* but also references to uncodified but culturally recognized temporal events like *at the first new moon after the solstice* or *when the corn developed its second joint* or even the Old Testament's *at the time when kings go forth to battle.*

Another kind of time definition makes use of reference to memorable events. This can shade off into a calendric system of its own in the case of dynasties or definitions of years by outstanding events as in the Kiowa calendar.[5] St. Luke, for example, places the birth of Christ "in the days of Herod" (1:5) as a general time, then

[5]   Mariott, *The Ten Grandmothers* (1945).

more specifically "in those days ... the first enrollment, when Quirinius was governor of Syria" (2:1-2). One episode of a Bororo story begins with "John fished", not as an event in the story, which is about jaguars killing cattle, but as a means of placing the episode both in time and in space with reference to John's fishing trip.[6] The notion of a mythological "dream time" or "in the time of the ancestors", common in Australia and Papua New Guinea, is a still different kind of establishment of setting, not too different in some ways from the English *once upon a time*.

As with spatial settings, temporal settings within a narrative can be established relative to earlier temporal settings. This is usually done by mentioning the amount of time that intervened between the earlier group of actions and the later group: "after three years", "the next day", "when the next chief came to power". The time may also be established with reference to the time of telling: "last year ... within the last three weeks, however". Aging of the participants serves as a mechanism for establishing settings in other cases: "Now he was three years older", "by the time she got married", "later, after he had stepped down from his heavier responsibilities".

McLeod suggests that the psychological atmosphere of a series of events may be treated linguistically in a fashion parallel to spatial and temporal setting.[7] Mumuye of Nigeria has behavior like "the horns were blowing for the ceremony" or "the ancestors were making beer" handled grammatically as setting rather than as events.[8]

2. BACKGROUND

Some of the information in narratives is not part of the narratives themselves, but stands outside them and clarifies them. Events, participants, and settings are normally the primary components of

---

[6] Crowell, "Cohesion in Bororo Discourse" (ms).

[7] McLeod, "Paragraph, Aspect, and Participant in Xavante" (ms).

[8] Kruesi, "Mumuye Discourse Structure" (ms).

narrative, while explanations and comments about what happens have a secondary role that may be reflected in the use of distinctive grammatical patterns, as it is in Munduruku.[9]

On the other hand, in nonsequential texts, explanatory information itself forms the backbone of the text, and narrative sequences may be used to illustrate it. Thus it appears that the narrative oriented model used to begin the analysis of discourses points toward a generalized model that can be used for more than just narratives. In the generalized model of kinds of information in discourse there is no need to single out one kind, events, as the one we expect to be the central thread of all discourses. Other kinds of information may be made the central thread instead.

Much of the secondary information that is used to clarify a narrative (called BACKGROUND for convenience, even though the term may be misleading for nonsequential texts when explanatory information could be thought of as being in the foreground) has a logical sounding structure, frequently tied together with words like *because* and *therefore*. It is an attempt to explain. It has this explanatory form even when the logic in it is invalid or when it falls short of really explaining what it purports to explain. As far as natural language is concerned, it seems enough that the sound of logic be there, though the substance and structure of logic be nowhere in sight. The logic may be shaky and the premises flawed, but to the dismay of real logicians it is usually accepted anyway as long as it is cast in the right linguistic mold.

Explanations, either as secondary part of narratives or as the central theme of texts, often involve premises that the speaker feels are generally accepted and therefore can be left unsaid. Sometimes what is unstated brings consternation to a linguist from another culture who is not yet in a position to supply the missing pieces of the argument. Even Aristotle, however, recognized the legitimate use of ENTHYMEMES, or partially filled in arguments, rather than complete arguments, and pointed out that the debater might have to contend with sham enthymemes.[10]

[9] Sheffler, "Munduruku Discourse" (ms).
[10] Aristotle, *Rhetoric* 2:22,24.

The handling of the structure of explanations actually sheds light on the depth and sensitivity of the speaker's estimate of who the hearer is; because even in cultures where nearly all parts of an explanation or argument are assumed, if the hearer makes it sufficiently clear that he does not follow, most speakers will restate themselves in an attempt to make up for his lack of understanding. This is less likely to hold in relatively homogeneous and isolated cultures, where many of life's activities depend upon the assumption that everyone shares the same fund of information. In these cultures only the more imaginative may entertain the thought that an outsider might not automatically share all the assumptions that the members of the society hold. The pervasiveness of this belief about the pervasiveness of belief could in fact serve as a measure of ethnocentrism.

A speaker may leave out elements of an explanation, whether it is given as background to a narrative or whether it is the main thread of a text, in several ways. He may, for example, state premises in his argument that fill the place of premises in the structure but that are far removed from the real premises, either because they are superficial derivatives of them or because the real premises on which the argument is based would not be palatable to the hearer.

One recalls, for example, a statement by a President of the United States in which he justified an economic action on the grounds that it had been called forth by the activities of international monetary speculators. This, if carried deeper, would point back to a premise that the internal economy of a large nation can be controlled by a small number of individuals on another continent; but few of the people who saw the statement delivered on television would have accepted that premise. On the other hand, it would have been politically disastrous to admit that his country's economy had been allowed to work itself into a state that was noncompetitive on the international market, which one suspects is much closer to the real reason for the action. So a premise of sorts was dropped into the necessary slot in the argument.

Another type of gap in explanations is found in the connection made between premises and conclusions. In the European tradition there is a long history of trying to make connections of this kind clear. The tradition of *topoi*, or familiar skeleton arguments, goes back at least to Aristotle.[11] In other traditions there are modes of connection which, though not necessarily acceptable in the European tradition, are taken as valid. An example is the so-called "rabbinical logic" in which the presence of a word in the Biblical text is taken as proof for an argument in which that word is involved. St. Matthew, for example (2:15), cites *Hosea* 11:1, "I called my son out of Egypt", as a prophecy referring to Christ's time spent as a child in Egypt, even though in Hosea's own context it is related to God's attempts to bring about a reconciliation with the nation of Israel.

In general explanations tend to contain as little information and have as uncomplex a structure as the speaker thinks he can get away with. The belief system that is being invoked may be rich and intricate, and the number of steps when fully traced out may be great; but unless a speaker foresees some misunderstanding on the part of the hearer he can be counted on to hit only enough of the high spots to suggest the general nature of his argument. He appears to count on the hearer to have most of the elements and relations of the argument already present in his own head, so that touching a few points is sufficient to activate the whole logical structure.

Certain events are told as background, not as part of the event sequence. In Saramaccan of Surinam, for example, a story that deals with a canoe trip that ended when the canoe capsized in the rapids goes back at the very point of the disaster to a series of events that took place before the trip started. The man of the family that made the trip had brought in cassava, his wife had grated it and cooked it into bread, and they had made bundles of it to take with them. As far as I can tell the reason this sequence of events is put into the story is not because those events should have been told before as part of the main sequence and were overlooked or played down, but rather because the speaker wanted the hearer to under-

[11]   Aristotle, *Rhetoric* 2:23.

stand the magnitude of the loss when the canoe overturned. So he gives details on the labor that went into producing the load.[12] Aristotle likens these exemplary events to steps of an induction in logic; they make a case by proceeding from instances, not principles.[13]

Sequences of events that are told as background are in a sense embedded narratives, though the ones I have noticed so far are much less rich in structure than the main narratives on which they are supposed to shed light. Their structure is, however, their own; it is independent of the structure of the main narrative. Furthermore, there is no requirement that the participants in the embedded narrative be connected with the participants in the main narrative. In the Saramaccan case they are the same. In parables, which are a special kind of narrative used to shed light on something else, there is usually no connection of participants with those of the main story except by analogy. In between lies, for example, St. Matthew's account of the death of John the Baptist. It is brought in to explain the apprehensions of King Herod about Jesus, who Herod thought must be John come back to life. Then the supporting narrative goes back to the death of John and brings in Herod's brother Philip and his former wife Herodias, whom Herod had married, together with Herodias's daughter (14:1-12). None of the events involved in this peripheral story touch the main narrative directly. They rather serve to explain an attitude reported in the main narrative. Only two of the participants, Herod and John, appear in both narratives.

Antecedent events occur in a time framework that is removed from that of the main narrative. In terms of Litteral's time index they are removed from the main time of the narrative by a constant factor k, so that an antecedent event sequence that relates to time segment n in the main narrative has indices of the form $n - k + i$, where $i = 1, 3, 5, \ldots$, for the events within it.[14] This time DIS-

---

[12] Grimes and Glock, "Saramaccan" (1970).
[13] Aristotle, *Rhetoric* 1:2.
[14] Robert Litteral, "Rhetorical Predicates and Time Topology in Anggor" (1972); Hajičová, Panevová, and Sgall, "Recursive Properties of Tense in Czech and English" (1970).

PLACEMENT is signalled overtly in some languages. English, for example, uses the past perfect tense to point out a displacement: in the preceding paragraph I find I wrote *whom Herod had married* for just this reason.

Another kind of background involves an event sequence used to explain things, but displaced forward in time rather than backward. Such FORESHADOWING has a displaced index of the form $n + k + i$. Again, the internal structure and cast of participants of such a displaced event sequence are essentially independent of the structure and cast of the main sequence.

Foreshadowing has two uses in narrative. First, it explains the main events by stating a sequence of events that might result later from the main action. Second, it may fill in the semantic content of part of the main event sequence well before the events are actually asserted to have taken place. This is seen in narrative sequences like *He married Cindy so that he could drain her fortune off to a numbered account in a Swiss bank. When he attempted to do so, however, Dapper Dan got wind of it and advised Cindy to switch to municipal bonds over which her husband had no control.* Here *drain her fortune off* is not asserted as having happened; the actual assertion of an event is *attempted to do so*, with the semantic content of *do so* already specified. In the same way *switch to municipal bonds* is a foreshadowing in terms of the time base of the event *advise*. As we leave this drama we are not told whether Cindy ever got to her stock broker in time. It is of such interplay between foreshadowing and assertion that soap operas are woven; but the pattern also has its serious uses.

Foreshadowing shades off into collateral information, discussed in Section 4 of this chapter. There is a slight difference in emphasis between the two, but which of them is intended may not always be clear. Foreshadowing, like other background information, intends to explain something, whereas collateral information intends to lay out a range of possible actions so as to set off the main action by contrast with the other alternatives to it.

3. EVALUATIONS

Not only do speakers report the state of the world; they tell how they feel about it. The addition of internal feelings to other kinds of information (which is not the same as a simple reporting of what one's internal feelings are) involves specific modes of linguistic expression, as we shall see.

The reactions that are expressed come from several sources. The most obvious is the speaker's own evaluation: *Here comes that blackguard Jones* not only identifies Jones and sets the action in the speaker's immediate environment, but also lets the hearer know what the speaker thinks of Jones. Aristotle points out the difference between "Orestes the matricide" and "Orestes the avenger of his sire", depending on what the speaker thinks of Orestes.[15] Winograd shows how a word like "nice" tells us nothing about the object it is applied to, but only about the attitude of the person who uses the word expressively.[16]

Often evaluations are imputed to the hearer or to other people referred to in the discourse. Any participant in a discourse can be assumed to have his own opinions of things, and the speaker may feel that he knows what those opinions are sufficiently well to include them. There is, however, a restriction that is pointed out in manuals of short story writing.[17] The speaker, or the person from whose spatial viewpoint a story is being told, must have established himself as being in a position to know what a particular character thinks before he can say what that character thinks, or else a viewpoint constraint is violated. Only under the assumption of an omniscient viewpoint can the speaker dart in and out of people's minds with impunity; otherwise the speaker must connect any

---

[15]   Aristotle, *Rhetoric* 3:2.
[16]   Winograd, *Procedures* (1971).
[17]   Meredith and Fitzgerald, *The Professional Storywriter and his Art* (1963). As a linguist I do not yet see how to incorporate this kind of viewpoint constraint into linguistic theory directly. It is either an involved kind of referential constraint, or else stands clear outside linguistics.

evaluation that he gives with the possibility that he can give it legitimately.

Another kind of evaluation is that of the culture within which the speaker is speaking, the conventions of the society he represents. The ancient Greek chorus brought society's expectations of what was proper into the play, and weighed the actions of the participants less against the personal factors that influenced their choices than against the factors that all agreed should have been decisive. In some ways the omniscient viewer of modern story telling represents this function.

Not everything in a discourse has to be evaluated. For this reason it is useful to recognize the SCOPE of an evaluative statement. It may be global, embracing an entire discourse; if so, it is likely to be found either at the beginning as an introductory statement that tells why the rest of the discourse is being told, or at the end as a moral to the story or the tag line to a fable. Frequently the evaluation is local, as when one participant tells another that as far as he was concerned what they just did was the wrong thing to have done. Labov and Waletzky discuss the use of evaluative statements of this kind.[18] They occur in English between the complication part of a narrative and the resolution. An evaluation, which may evaluate the immediately preceding event or the entire situation of the story or even the situation of the telling of the story, suspends the flow of events at a structurally significant break.

Bolinger discusses the influence of evaluations on choice of words.[19] Not only is one man's meat another man's poison, but what is prudence for one is cowardice for another, what is beautiful for one is garishness for another, and what one calls love another sees as sentimentality. It all depends on how one looks at it, literally. Thus there are words that always represent Good Things, such as *loyal*, *true*, *Mother*, and the whole list that includes "Remember the Maine, Plymouth Rock, and the Golden Rule" in the song "Trouble" from Meredith Willson's *The Music Man*. On the other

---

[18]   Labov and Waletzky, "Narrative Analysis" (1967).
[19]   Bolinger, *Aspects of Language* (1968).

hand, there are words that always represent Bad Things: *ghastly*, *traitor*, *decay*. Other words float in between, depending partly on the temper of the times (the chorus function) and partly on the immediate context. Charles Osgood shows how the evaluative component of words can be represented, and how it shifts in terms of varying psychological states.[20]

Labov and Waletzky point out that evaluative information is the most mobile part of a narrative in that it can occur nearly anywhere without changing the meaning of the narrative as a whole. They apply a permutation or MOBILITY test that consists of inter-changing pairs of clauses, then finding which interchanges destroy the meaning of a narrative and which merely produce what subjects react to as another version of the "same" narrative. Evaluative clauses characteristically can be moved anywhere within the text. Event clauses, however, cannot be taken out of their text order without making a different story, unless the reordering is heavily marked. Other types of clauses can move over a limited range. This capability of evaluative clauses to occur anywhere makes the consistency with which they appear at the Labov-Waletzky sus-pension point (between the complication and the resolution) all the more interesting.

Evaluations bring the hearer more closely into the narration; they communicate information about feelings to him that goes beyond the bare cognitive structure of what happened or what deduction is to be made. In conversations, and even in monologues, the hearer may be pressed to give his own evaluation: *What do you think? How do you suppose they took that?*

Evaluations may also be an aim of the discourse. By communi-cating how the speaker feels, there is often an implication that the hearer ought to adopt the same attitude. Stories with a moral are characteristically of this kind. Where the evaluation itself is the punch line, the discourse is hortatory in form, and may take the form "Because these things happened, you should feel as I do", or "Because this principle holds for the reasons I give, here is the

[20]   Osgood, Suci, and Tannenbaum, *The Measurement of Meaning* (1957).

attitude you must take".[21] A story with a moral is thus likely to be an exhortation within which there is embedded a narrative.

Evaluative information shades off into background information or even into setting in cases where it serves to build up the psychological tone of a series of events. Here the general form would be "Because people felt this way, or because I think things were exceptionally good, this is what happened as a consequence". Evaluations also mark the development and release of tension in a plot, giving cues as to how the action affects the participants' view of things and vice versa.

4. COLLATERAL

Some information in a narrative, instead of telling what did happen, tells what did not happen. It ranges over possible events, and in so doing sets off what actually does happen against what might have happened.

For example, in the Saramaccan text referred to in Section 2, the narrator breaks the sequence of events after the capsizing of the canoe: "The canoe overturned. The father did not die. The mother did not die. The children did not die. Instead, they all escaped to land." By telling what did not happen to the participants, he throws their escape into relief. Aristotle lists "describing a thing in terms of what it is not" as a device for impressiveness of style; he attributes its recognition to Antimachus.[22]

The idea of collateral information was brought to my attention by William Labov in a lecture which as far as I know remains unpublished. He also pointed out that collateral information (his term for it was "comparators") is not restricted to things that might have taken place but did not. Collateral information also fits into projected time. Questions, for example, raise alternatives that might or might not turn out to be so; future tense forms predict

[21]   Longacre, *Discourse ... in Philippine Languages* (1968).
[22]   Aristotle, *Rhetoric* 3:6.

actions that might or might not take place; imperatives direct
people to do things that might or might not be accomplished.
All of these have the effect of setting up alternatives. Later in the
text it is usually made clear which of the alternatives happens. At
that point the fact that alternate possibilities were mentioned earlier
makes what actually does happen stand out in sharper relief than
if it were told without collateral.

Collateral information, simply stated, relates non-events to
events. By providing a range of non-events that might take place,
it heightens the significance of the real events.

Collateral information also has the effect of anticipating content
when, with reference to projected time, a number of alternative
possibilities are spelled out in advance. If one of these alternatives
is the real one, much of what has to be said about it has already
been said ahead of time. In this respect collateral information is
not very different from foreshadowing.

I have already mentioned some of the grammatical forms that
are characteristic of collateral information. These are closely
related to mood (Chapter 15.3). The rest of this section gives
details concerning collateral forms.

Negation, first of all, is almost always collateral, whether its
temporal reference is in accomplished time or in projected time.
Events that do not take place have significance only in relation to
what actually does happen. Events that are not supposed to happen
still may take place; if they do not, then we are concerned with
what else might happen in their place; while if they do happen
contrary to the prediction, the fact that a negative prediction was
made about them contributes to the highlighting effect.

Adversatives are a form of negation. Some imply parallel but
disjoint action: *They brought pickles but we brought mustard*
conveys implicitly *they did not bring mustard and we did not bring
pickles*. Other adversatives imply that the speaker assumes the
hearer to have inferred an event that is plausible but that did not
in fact happen: *We arrived late but were received immediately*
implies *I, the speaker, think that you, the hearer, must expect that
if we were to arrive late the logical thing would be for our reception*

to be postponed. Contrary to your expectation, we were received immediately.

Other negatives are not really collateral, but are hidden forms of positive statements. St. Paul's "we do not want you to be ignorant" in *1 Thessalonians* 4:13 is of this type; the meaning is 'we want you to realize' followed by the content of what the readers ought to know. Here the negative has apparently been raised into the main clause "we want X" from the embedded "you should not fail to realize", in which the Greek negative *ouk* is cancelled by the privative *a-* of *agnoeîn* to give the whole meaning equivalent to 'you should realize', incorporated in the stylistic device known as LITOTES. The same privative enters into the composition of lexical items that denote certain events. These events are named by negation from some other word that also denotes an event, but of a different (not necessarily antithetical) kind: for example, Greek *athetéō* 'disregard' from *títhēmi* 'establish'. Negatives of this kind are not necessarily collateral.

Questions are another grammatical form used for indicating collateral information. They have been discussed frequently in the linguistic literature with regard to the information they presuppose or assume as over against what they inquire about.[23] *When did John get here?* presupposes that John did get here, so that the area of uncertainty is restricted to the time of his arrival. *When did you stop beating your wife?* is more complex; it assumes that you have a wife, that there was a time when you beat her, and that there was a time after which you no longer beat her. The question is directed toward ascertaining that time. The presuppositions in a question are almost like conditions laid down by the speaker for the hearer to give an acceptable answer. If the hearer accepts the presuppositions, then he can give the missing information that is requested; if not, he is in a bind.

The questions that are most characteristically collateral are polar or yes-no questions, since they invariably impose alternatives. *Will Reginald escape?* presupposes an exclusive disjunction, a

---

[23]   Fillmore and Langendoen, *Studies in Linguistic Semantics* (1971).

pair of alternatives only one of which is acceptable: *Either Reginald will escape or Reginald will not escape; please tell me which is the case.* In English, a positive answer like *yes* or *he will* asserts the positive alternative even if the question is stated by using the negative member of the pair. *Won't Reginald escape?* expresses the same disjunction, differing from the positive question principally in communicating in the latter case that the speaker already has his own opinion, but that he is interested in getting the hearer's reaction.[24]

In any case, polar questions express at least a pair of alternatives. The alternatives remain open regardless of the answer given to them; just because at one point in a discourse one participant expresses an opinion that Reginald will escape does not guarantee that he will. Polar questions are therefore a useful device for introducing more than one alternative at once. Even nonpolar questions with *who, what, when, where, how, why,* and the like may carry the implication, for a particular discourse, that the person asking the question thinks that there may be more than one possible answer. *Which* regularly presupposes a set of alternatives from which a choice is to be made. And the expression of several alternatives in order to highlight the particular one of them that actually takes place is central to the idea of collateral information.

---

[24] Some languages, including New Guinea Pidgin and Huichol, have a different rationale for phrasing answers to polar questions. The answer in English depends upon selecting the positive or negative member of the implied disjunction, which explains why disjunctions that are not formed around truth values as such have to be answered in other ways (*yes*, for example, is not an acceptable answer for *will you have coffee or tea?*). The languages named, however, answer with agreement or disagreement with whichever member of the disjunction is given in the question. *Bai Rejinal i ranewe, o nogat?* is equivalent in Pidgin to the English example, and states the positive member of the pair, so that *yes* 'agreed' is equivalent to English *yes* and *nogat* 'I disagree' as an answer is equivalent to English *no*. But if the question is negative, *bai Rejinal i no ranewe, o nogat?*, then *yes* 'agreed' means that the person giving the answer does not expect him to escape, and *nogat* 'I disagree with the member of the disjunction that was expressed in the question' means that he does expect him to escape. See Robert Litteral, *A Programmed Course in New Guinea Pidgin* (1969). Moravcsik, "Yes-No Questions and Their Answers" (1971), traces this pattern in detail.

Rhetorical questions form a special case in the study of discourse. These are questions for which the answer is implied by regular rules, so that none is actually given in the text, or else for which the same person who asks the question immediately supplies the answer. A well known example of the first is at the climax of Patrick Henry's speech of March 1775 to the Virginia Convention: "Is life so dear, or peace so sweet, as to be purchased at the price of chains and slavery?" The second is found in St. Paul's *Epistle to the Romans* 6:1–2: "Shall we keep on doing wrong, so that we may be treated all the more graciously? Of course not!"

Some languages, including Huichol, make use of rhetorical questions combined with answers, but never of unanswered rhetorical questions. There may be certain points in discourse at which rhetorical questions are permitted, whereas they do not fit elsewhere; this is the case in Mundurukú.[25]

Insofar as rhetorical questions introduce information that is different from what actually turns out to be the case, they can be considered devices for introducing collateral information. This is the case with both the examples given above. Patrick Henry is not really inquiring into the prospects of a life in chains and slavery; he is setting up a foil against which his use of *liberty* in the next sentence rings out more clearly than it would if he had simply stood up and said *I want liberty*. St. Paul brings up the possibility of keeping on doing wrong only for the purpose of making his negation of that plan of action stronger.

In Sarangani Manobo, however, what sounds like a rhetorical question is used in a way that is distinctly not collateral, but identificational.[26] The rhetorical question is followed immediately by its answer; but it is used regularly to keep track of participants when a group is split. One of DuBois's examples illustrates this: "Then Ken's wife disembarked and the two of them including Lauretta stayed there at the airstrip. Where were we? We rode the airplane first, the three of us. Then the airplane flew going to

[25] Sheffler, "Munduruku Discourse" (ms).
[26] DuBois, "Connectives in Sarangani Manobo Discourse" (1973).

Davao. Where were they, Lauretta and Ken's wife? They waited for the airplane to return."

Given the world the way it is, predicting an event is no guarantee that that event will take place. Instead, a prediction states one of several things that might happen and expresses the opinion of the predictor that that is what will happen, not something else. Other possible happenings may also be predicted or brought into the discourse by means of other collateral expressions.

The information about what actually does happen, then, may take several forms. If none of the collateral expressions give what really happened as one of the alternatives, it must be stated as a distinct event. If it was mentioned ahead of time, however, then it is not necessary to repeat the content that was mentioned as part of the collateral, but only to affirm which of the possibilities took place. *They were going to Florida for vacation, but ended up camping in the Adirondacks* illustrates an event that is not foreshadowed; *They were either going to go to Florida for vacation or camp in the Adirondacks. They did the latter* illustrates the introduction in collateral of the event, followed by an anaphoric reference that gives it the status of a true event.

Predictions come in several degrees of relative firmness: total expectation, probable, possible, and on the negative side, unlikely and impossible predictions. From the point of view of using predictions as collateral information that points out alternatives in discourse, it seems irrelevant which modality is used unless there is a dual sense of collaterality: perhaps the alternative and the information about whether it actually happened or not make up one component, and the expectation of the person making the prediction and his feeling in relation to it when the event happens are a second component.

Quotations often give collateral information. An act of speaking mentioned in a discourse is, of course, an event in itself; but what is said is usually not. If it has the form of a denial, a question, or a prediction, the three regular forms of collateral I have just discussed, then it is clearly collateral. *She said, "He isn't in the house." But when we unlocked the door, there he was* uses a negative quotation to add significance by contrast to *there he was. She said, "Are you looking for Gorham?" When we unlocked the door, there was Simmons* uses a question to suggest a possible find that turns out to be different from the actual find. *She said, "You will find him in the second room on the right." When we unlocked the door, there he was* sets up a prediction in the quotation.

Not all quotations give collateral information. Quotations may also express background information and evaluations: *The doctor said she should watch her weight. So she went on a diet* explains going on a diet by quoting (indirectly in this case) what the doctor said. *As the rocket curved toward orbit, a reporter whispered, "Beautiful!"* conveys an evaluation.

As Longacre points out, in certain kinds of discourse there is a standing assumption that what is quoted is what happened.[27] This DIALOGUE form of discourse can be considered a specialized version of narrative; it is sequentially oriented in accomplished time. It could be considered the default or unmarked case of collateral quotation, in which only one possibility for each event is introduced via quotation, and since there are no alternatives, what is mentioned is tacitly taken to be what happened: *The canoe glided between the islands. "Closer in to the shore." "Far enough?" No answer from the forest. "Try again." "Hello the island!" "Marlowe!" "Take her ashore."* Radio drama without narration developed this kind of discourse into an art form; even stage and television plays depend heavily on it, and it is a popular form of oral narration in many languages.

---

[27] Longacre, *Discourse ... in Philippine Languages* (1968).

5

THE SPEAKER AND HEARER IN DISCOURSE

Both the form and the content of any discourse are influenced by who is speaking and who is listening. The speaker-hearer-situation factors can be represented in linguistic theory via the notion of PERFORMATIVE information.

The idea is this: in any language there are certain words called PERFORMATIVES which under the right conditions denote actions that are performed in the uttering of the words themselves.[1] When the minister says *I pronounce you man and wife* a couple are thereby made man and wife; if I say *I bet you ten dollars the Cubs will win* you can hold me to it if they lose.

There are, however, restrictions on performative utterances. They must be in the first person and the present tense; the minister cannot say to someone else *you pronounce them man and wife* and thereby perform a marriage, and if he says *I pronounced you man and wife* he is reminiscing, not exercising his office.[2] There are also extralinguistic conditions that are required to make those performatives stick; in American society, for example, a bartender or a ship captain on shore or a seminary student or an elementary school pupil can utter *I pronounce you man and wife*, but only

---

[1] Austin, *How to Do Things with Words* (1962); Searle, *Speech Acts* (1969); Ross, "On Declarative Sentences" (1970).

[2] George Huttar has called to my attention uses of *ask* that permit the future and the plural in a performative sense: *I will now ask Brother Jones to lead in prayer*, and *We are enclosing some letters, and will ask if you will please get them distributed*. He suggests that the future is raised into the main clause from the complement clause.

a minister of religion, a justice of the peace, or a ship captain on the high seas can say it in a way that performs the action. In the same way, the people it is addressed to must be of different sexes, above a certain age, and not married to anyone else.

Certain performatives are quite common and are free of special limitations on their use. *I hereby order you to turn left* and numerous equivalent forms are one kind that is so common that there is a grammatical shorthand for it: *turn left*, an imperative. Another large family of performatives can be paraphrased into a form like that of *Somebody stole the garlic. I hereby request you to identify that person.* The grammatical shorthand for this is the question form *Who stole the garlic?* By far the largest family of performatives fit the pattern *I hereby inform you that your back porch just fell off*, for which the conventional shorthand is the declarative *Your back porch just fell off.* Behind even simple utterances, then, it is possible to say that there stands a performative element that recognizes the identity of the speaker, the hearer, and the situation within which they are communicating. [3]

The recognition of implicit performatives behind commands, questions, and statements, as well as explicit performatives, paves the way for a linguistic handling of situational factors in discourse. Specifically, it gives a place in linguistic analysis for what are conventionally known as DEICTIC (pointing) elements like "this" and "that" or "here" and "there", and for person categories like "me" and "you". Assuming a performative behind every discourse, and even behind parts of discourses in addition to the global performative, makes it possible to talk about persons, time, and place in a way that would be very hard to explain otherwise within the bounds of a theory of language.

In the case of persons (and for that matter, objects) the recogni-

---

[3]   There is a weakness in the structure of the performative argument. If we say *I hereby order you to turn left*, there is nothing in the argument that restricts us from saying that this is equivalent to *I hereby inform you that I hereby order you to turn left*, and so on forever. The idea of performatives, however, is so useful that I prefer to stick with it with caution about its potentially infinite regress, trusting that the philosophers will eventually find a way to make it respectable.

tion of the speaker-hearer axis in communication is the basis for assignment of person categories. This seems trivial or obvious for a discourse that has a single performative like "I, the speaker, hereby inform you, the hearer, that ..." that dominates it; there the person speaking is always *I* and the person spoken to is always *you*. Pike and Lowe, however, have probed one class of discourses in which this simple assignment is not possible.[4]

Their case involves a situation in which three individuals, call them Al, Bill, and Charlie, or A, B, and C, are talking. Suppose that A is speaking to B; then A is *I* and B is *you* and C is *he*. But now suppose A says to B, "You said to him, 'I see you.'" The last instance of *I* does not refer to A but to B, and the last instance of *you* does not refer to B but to C, even though the whole thing is spoken by A to B. The key to understanding the person assignment is that every instance of direct discourse introduces a new, limited, and local performative in which the person who utters the direct quotation is *I* and his hearer is *you*, regardless of what other performative dominates the whole. Lowe presents a theorem based on the theory of finite permutation groups, which as far as I can tell predicts all cases and works for all languages, for any depth of embedding of performatives via direct quotations.

Performatives are pertinent in the identification of participants in other cases besides direct discourse, but in a different way. In direct discourse person assignments are derived by Lowe's Theorem from the immediately dominating verb of saying or thinking. The assignment of participants in that performative utterance is taken from the one that dominates it, and so on up the ladder until the performative for the discourse itself is reached.

In indirect discourse, person assignments are taken from some performative more remote than the one that dominates the statement immediately; that is, the one that constitutes the nearest verb of saying that dominates direct discourse higher up the tree of

---

[4] Pike and Lowe, "Pronominal Reference in English Conversation and Discourse — A Group Theoretical Treatment" (1969). See also Lowe, "An Algebraic Theory of English Pronominal Reference" (1969).

quotations. This shows up if we paraphrase the example just given in such a way as to show the performative elements:

(a) I, the author, hereby inform you, the reader:
(b)   A said to B, quote (direct)
(c)   "I, A, hereby inform you, B, that (indirect)
(d)   you, B, said to him, C, quote (direct)
(e)   'I, B, hereby inform you, C, that (indirect)
(f)   I, B, see you, C.'"

Any paraphrase of this that uses only indirect discourse goes into the third person and is highly ambiguous in English even with full intonation, because neither A nor B nor C is the author or the reader: *A said to B that he said to him that he saw him.* With explicit identification of C there is less ambiguity, but still enough to inhibit communication: A said to B that he said to C that he saw him. Mona Perrin reports a complex situation involving indirect and three different kinds of direct speech in Mambila of Nigeria.[5]

In addition to the identifications that relate to performatives, there are other less easily recognizable factors whose effects can be seen in the outer form of language and that find their place in the conceptual scheme of linguistics by virtue of their relation to performatives. Here, first of all, is where the speaker's entire image of himself as a person is accessible to the linguistic system.[6] Here also is the place in linguistic structure for registering the speaker's assessment of who the hearer is, what he knows, how he feels, and what he might do as a result of what the speaker says. Both images may change during the course of speech as a result of feedback signals from the hearer to the speaker; but it is in terms of what the speaker holds about both himself and the hearer at the moment that he phrases what he says next.

---

[5] Perrin, "Direct and Indirect Speech in Mambila" (ms).
[6] As Aristotle says, "the speaker ... must give the right impression of himself" (*Rhet.* 2:1). He also points out constraints between who the speaker is and what he says: "In a young man, uttering maxims is — like telling stories — unbecoming, and to use them in a realm where one lacks experience is stupid and boorish" (*Rhet.* 2:21).

For example, I, the author, estimate you, the reader, to be generally informed about the field of linguistics, and as a consequence
I write *noun phrase* without bothering to give you an explanation.
I expect that you are mildly interested in the subject of discourse
and highly interested in one or two points. Because I do not know
which of the points I am making those are, I try to say enough on
each that you can grasp what I think about it. At the same time I
try to give enough signals about the relationships between one
point and another that you can skim anything of which all you
want is the drift.

On the other hand, if I, the author, thought that you, the reader,
were a high school student, required perhaps by a state board of
education to take a course in the discourse patterns of English
in order to graduate, but were really more interested in what is
going to happen at football practice, the whole presentation would
be different. I might tell better jokes. I would certainly leave out
most of the explanations and alternative hypotheses, and would
present English discourse structure on a take-it-or-leave-it-but-it-
makes-sense-to-take-it basis. Rather than giving only enough
examples that a motivated person could pick up one and then
supply as many others as he wants on his own, I would give a
range of examples for each point and reinforce them with exercises
in which you would either have to find your own examples or show
how some new examples (called "problems") relate to ones already
given. I would not talk about Mundurukú or Manobo unless I
thought that doing so might make something in English easier to
understand. Furthermore, my estimate of you would not change,
because the only feedback I could get would be after I had finished
writing the book and had tried it out in the classroom.

Aristotle notes that "whatever the quality an audience esteems,
the speaker must attribute that quality to the object of his praise,
whether the audience be Scythians, or Spartans, or scholars".[7]

The performative element not only serves to relate persons to
the discourse, but also sets the zero point for time reference. In

---

[7]   Aristotle, *Rhetoric* 1:9.

terms of Litteral's time index, discussed in 3.1, the time axis of a discourse can be represented by the real number line. Zero matches the time the actual activity of uttering the discourse begins, the negative part of the line matches things that happen before then, and the positive part matches both the uttering of the discourse itself and future events that are talked about. Each event, including the uttering of the discourse itself, is then represented by an open set of points on the time line, indexed as described earlier.

English words like *now*, *ago*, and *yet* have explicit reference to the relation between the time of speaking and a time referred to. Other words are independent of this relation; Pidgin *nau*, for example, even though it comes from English *now*, refers in narrative to the next thing in the sequence being narrated, not to the time of narration.

Tense systems are defined at least partly in terms of this correspondence between the time relations that are inherent in what happens and the relation of the happening to the telling. Some tense systems, like that of Halia, divide this area rather fine:[8] the Halia past tense includes events up to and including the day before the day on which speech takes place. The nonpast is further divided into completive, progressive, and intentive aspects, which in terms of the time framework correspond to events that took place earlier on the day of speaking, events in progress at the time of speaking, and contemplated events.

Relationships between the time of happening and the time of speaking may be indicated overtly as in Halia, or they may be established by a single time reference and then not mentioned again. This is somewhat like the English historical present: *First he goes and finds the girl, then he shows her the ring* can be either a blow-by-blow description of something that is happening at the time of speaking (visualize a detective hidden in the arras whispering into a tape recorder) or a narration of something that happened, say, three thousand years ago, told so as to create an air of im-

---

[8]   Jerry Allen, "Tense-Aspect in Halia Narratives" (ms). See also Marchese, "Tense-Aspect in Godié" (ms).

mediacy. Intermediate between the use of tense to index every event for time and the total absence of time indexing is the indexing by paragraphs reported by Dye for Bahinemo of Papua New Guinea.[9] A dependent clause at the beginning of each Bahinemo narrative paragraph gives the relation of the paragraph as a whole to the time of narration; from there on the narration of the events that take place is tenseless.

Tense displacement was mentioned in connection with the use of antecedent events and foreshadowings for explanation in 4.2. In English the past perfect forms regularly indicate displacement out of the main time line of a discourse into a subsidiary time line (or into a segregated section of a single time line, more properly): *The car arrived at ten. They had been delayed by a flash flood outside of town. We got in and left anyway, hoping to make up the time on the open highway.* Dependent temporal clauses with nonpast verbs, introduced with words like *after, before,* and *while,* or independent clauses with future verbs, denote time displacements projected into the future from the time of speaking. Collateral forms (4.4) involving questions and predictions regularly signal displacement into the future.

The place where an act of speech occurs is also part of the performative information for that act of speech. The position of speaker and hearer relative to each other, their surroundings, and the relationships between all this and the things they are talking about influence to a certain extent the linguistic forms they choose.

For example, when talking about things in the immediate speech situation, English speakers distinguish *this,* something near the speaker, from *that,* something not near the speaker, though possibly near the hearer. When talking about abstractions or about things outside the speech situation, however, the use of *this* and *that* loses its spatial component and takes on a reference to what the speaker has or has not said already: *The point is this: you have to forget all that* has *this* pointing ahead to what the speaker is

9 Longacre, *Discourse ... in New Guinea Languages* (1972).

about to say and *that* pointing back to what has already been said.[10] Portuguese makes a three-way spatial distinction: *este* for something near the speaker, *esse* for something near the hearer, and *aquele* for something relatively remote from both. Ilocano has four degrees: near the speaker, near the hearer, near both, and remote from both.[11] In Huichol there is a complex system of reference either to the surface of the earth as seen by the speaker or to position on the body of a human or animal.[12]

Bacairí makes a four-way distinction in pronouns that depends partly upon how they are related to the situation of speaking.[13] *Mira* 'this one' refers only to someone relatively close to the speaker; in the case of an embedded performative, it can be used with reference to the speaker who uttered the embedded performative. *Maca* when defined in relation to the performative refers to someone far away but in sight of the speaker, while *auaca* refers to someone closer. Overlapping the performative oriented pronouns, however, is a discourse oriented system that makes no reference to the situation of speaking, but only to what is being said. At the end of this scale is *inara* 'he', which can refer only to someone who has already been identified verbally. *Maca* and *auaca* also play a part in this system; but when they are used in relation to the verbal context rather than the context of the act of speaking *maca* refers to a participant who has been placed in focus,[14] in the center of the stage as it were, and *auaca* refers to any other nonfocal participant. (There are also inanimate and athematic counterparts for the four mentioned here, which are animate and thematic.) Some discourses have a point of confusion that comes about like this: First *maca* 'he, far' and *auaca* 'he, near' are used to introduce participants that are present in the situation of speaking. Then the

---

[10] Halliday, "Notes on Transitivity and Theme in English, Part 2" (1967).
[11] Thomas, "Three Analyses of the Ilocano Pronoun System" (1955).
[12] Grimes, *Huichol Syntax* (1964).
[13] Wheatley, "Pronouns and Nominal Elements in Bacairí Discourse" (ms).
[14] In terms of Chapters 19 and 21, David Cranmer suggests that Wheatley's focus is a kind of high level theme, and Wheatley tentatively agrees (personal communications).

nearer participant is taken as focal with reference to the discourse, and the system shifts so that the speaker is using *maca* 'he, focal' for the nearer character and *auaca* 'he, nonfocal' for the more distant one. This shift from situational to textual reference gives the effect of a flip in pronoun reference in the middle of a text.

In Oksapmin events are told relative to a setting.[15] This setting may be defined by where the speaker is located as he is speaking, or it may be defined by where somebody who reported the scene to the speaker was located when he observed it. In either case the setting has an imaginary boundary: the walls of a room, the rim of a valley, the bounds of a village, the shores of the island of New Guinea. This boundary is never made explicit. The use of words like *matai* 'here' and *atai* 'there', *moh* 'this one' and *oh* 'that one', *masoh* 'along here' and *asoh* 'along there', however, is always split with reference to that boundary, so that the proximal words (the ones that begin with *m-*) refer to locations inside the boundary and their distal counterparts refer to locations outside the boundary. The hearer is left to deduce where the boundary is. English *near/far* seem to be distinguished in a similar way. Bierwisch has discussed a number of relative factors of this kind in reference.[16]

In addition to position relative to the speaker and hearer, some languages distinguish motion relative to the speaker and hearer. These motions may involve a reference surface in addition to the position of the speaker and hearer themselves, as in the Anggor distinction between motion upstream from the speaker, downstream from the speaker, down a declivity from the speaker, or across a stream from the speaker.[17]

The properties of English *go* and *come* when used in relation to speaker and hearer have been discussed by Fillmore.[18] It seems to be a quirk of English that *come* not only implies motion in the direction of the speaker, as in *come here*, but also motion in the

[15] Helen Lawrence, "Viewpoint and Location in Oksapmin" (1972).
[16] Bierwisch, "Some Semantic Universals of German Adjectivals" (1967).
[17] Shirley Litteral, "Orientation Shifts in Anggor" (ms).
[18] Fillmore, "Deictic Categories in the Semantics of 'Come'" (1966).

direction of the hearer, as in *I'm coming to your side of the room*. Furthermore, in the case of projected time, the motion is not necessarily in terms of where the speaker and the hearer are at the time of speaking, but may be in terms of where either the speaker or the hearer expects to be at the time of the projected action: *I'll come over to your house on Tuesday* implying that the speaker expects to find the hearer home, or *Come to the park for supper*, implying that the speaker expects to already be in the park. Longuda of Nigeria has a directional suffix -*wa* that refers to an action terminating where the theme character is located; but if it is the theme character who is performing the action, then -*wa* refers to the place where he expects to be when he finishes.[19]

In Saramaccan Naomi Glock and I found that the distribution of verbs meaning 'come' and 'go' permitted me to identify where Glock had recorded one text.[20] *kam* 'come' always implies motion in the direction of the speaker, while *go* 'go' is used for motion in any other direction. Every *kam* in the text but one pointed toward the city of Paramaribo, which is outside the Saramaccan area but is where the recording was in fact made. The exception involved a local performative in which one participant sent a message requesting his brother to *kam* to where he was when he sent the message, so that that instance fitted the pattern defined by the performative as well.

Pull and *push*, *bring* and *take*, and *get* and *put* seem to parallel *come* and *go* not only in English but in other languages. In a number of languages of the Philippines the stems for 'bring' and 'take' are the same, as are the stems for 'get' and 'put'; but the possibilities for taking grammatical focus markers differ.[21] In terms of semantic roles (Chapter 8) verbs of the 'bring' variety uniformly fit a pattern of acquisition verbs, in which the agent moves an object toward himself as goal; while their 'take' counterparts involve the same stems potentially inflected to show that the

[19]   Bonnie Newman, "The Longuda Verb" (ms).
[20]   Grimes and Glock, "Saramaccan" (1970).
[21]   For example, see Hettick, "Verb Stem Classes in Northern Kankanay" (ms).

agent moves an object away from himself as source; the agent may move with the object, as in the case of verbs for 'carry', or the object may move away without the agent, as in 'throw'. The 'get' and 'put' set, in addition, take on perfective or resultative meanings that link them respectively with 'have' and 'be'.

Some languages link expressions of time to expressions of motion in terms of the performative. Paul Freyberg in a personal communication has called to my attention the repetition in New Guinea Pidgin of *i kam i kam i kam* 'on and on he comes' or *i go i go i go* 'on and on he goes' in a temporal sense. The repeated forms follow the main verb in a verb phrase. They come in an aspect position that can also be filled by *stap* 'continue' and *pinis* 'complete'. *I kam i kam* in the aspect slot refers to the time of an earlier event that is extended toward the time of speaking, while *i go i go* refers to the same extension from the point of view of a participant in the action and the time of happening (repetition is part of the expression, but the particular number of repetitions is more like an iconic representation of extent, with more repetitions for more time).

Both Huichol and ancient Greek seem to conceptualize time linguistically in terms of a hillside on which the speaker stands. In Greek the past is uphill *(ana)* and the future downhill *(kata)*. In Huichol, on the other hand, future time is uphill from the speaker and past time downhill. Some Huichol time words, furthermore, have the form of verbal words with directional prefixes appropriate to a hillside perspective. For time ahead, for example, the usual words are *Puza+Páa* 'tomorrow', *waaríe* 'day after tomorrow', *Paayei+mána* 'the day after the day after tomorrow, three days hence', the verb-like *ranuti+Páayéi+mána* 'up over the top of the day after the day after tomorrow, four days hence', and *zei máná+yaari +cíe* 'on one time unit ahead, five days hence'. The analogous series in the past is *tákái* 'yesterday', *Paatu* 'day before yesterday', the verb-like *ranuka+Páatu* 'down behind the day before yesterday, three days ago', and *zei Páatú+yaari+ cíe* 'on one time unit behind, four days ago'.

6

KINDS OF INFORMATION IN DISCOURSE

1. A WORK SHEET

The idea of different kinds of information in a text is more easily put to use if there can be a display of text that lays out each kind of information in a way that can be seen at a glance. Figure 6.1 is the skeleton of such a display. It is a development of the diagrams used by Gleason and Cromack. Mickey Stout developed a horizontal version of it which she fastened at eye level around the walls of a room to display an entire Kayapó text. The current form was worked out by Robert C. Thurman, who used it in his study of Chuave.[1]

The vertical columns on the chart correspond to the various kinds of information distinguished in texts: events, identification, setting, background (which to save space includes both explanations and evaluations), collateral, and performative. To keep the chart from being crowded, I use the convention that information of a particular kind begins under the corresponding heading, but may be carried as far to the right as needed; this is more convenient than trying to squeeze everything into narrow vertical columns.

The parallel vertical lines are for the participants, one line per participant. For each event a line is drawn from the lexical elements that represent the event to the vertical lines that represent the participants in the event. Where identifications are given for the

---

[1] Thurman, "Chuave Medial Verbs" (ms).

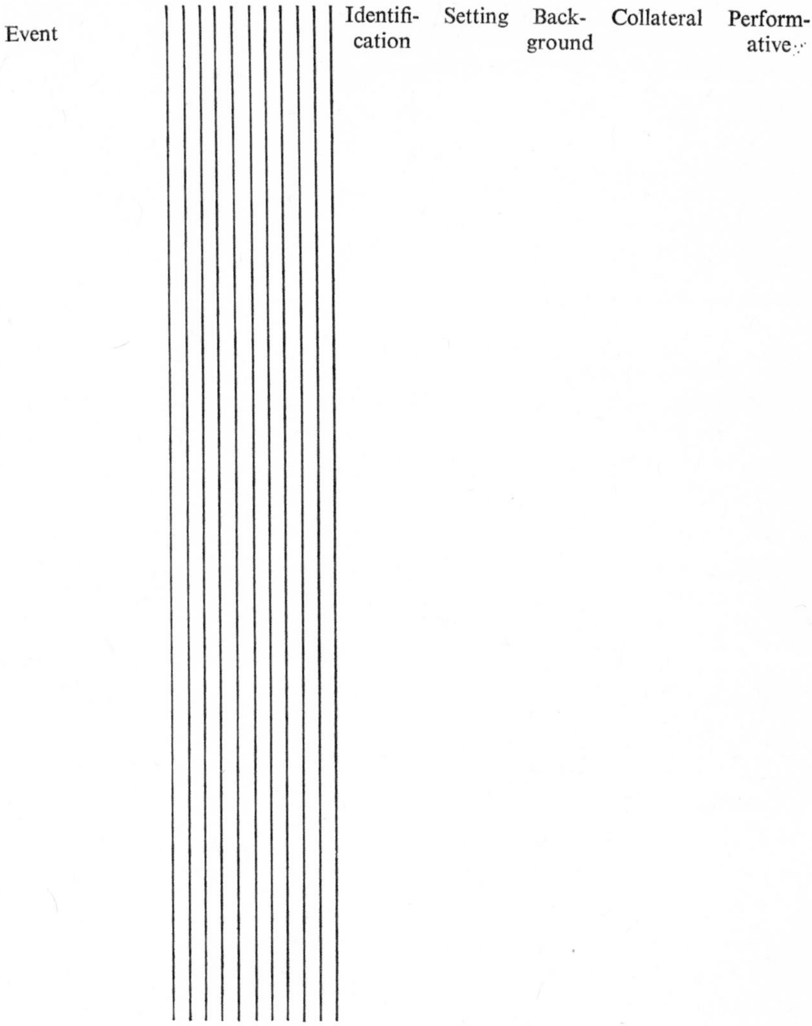

Event		Identifi-cation	Setting	Back-ground	Collateral	Perform-ative

Figure 6.1 A blank Thurman chart.

participants, lines are also drawn from the other side to show which identification belongs with which participant.

The most comfortable working format is to match a Thurman chart with a page of text. The text is written out, double spaced,

1. The last drops of the thundershower had hardly ceased falling
2. when the Pedestrian stuffed his map into his pocket,
3. settled his pack more comfortably on his tired shoulders,
4. and stepped out from the shelter of a large chestnut-tree into the middle of the road.
5. A violent yellow sunset was pouring through a rift in the clouds to westward,
6. but straight ahead over the hills the sky was the colour of dark slate.
7. Every tree and blade of grass was dripping,
8. and the road shone like a river.
9. The Pedestrian wasted no time on the landscape
10. but set out at once with the determined stride of a good walker
11. who has lately realized that he will have to walk farther than he intended.
12. That, indeed, was his situation.
13. If he had chosen to look back,
14. which he did not,
15. he could have seen the spire of Much Nadderby,
16. and, seeing it ...

Figure 6.2a Text written out by clauses. C. S. Lewis, *Out of the silent planet*, p. 1.

at about one clause per line. Some clauses require more than one line, and it may not be clear exactly what a clause is until after the analysis is finished; but in general the clause is convenient chunk to work with. The text page is fastened to the Thurman chart with the text on the left and the chart on the right, as in Figure 6.2. Then the information from each clause is copied into the appropriate place on the chart. If there seems to be no place on the chart that is appropriate for some piece of the clause, as sometimes happens, that information is put in one of the margins of the chart as a residue.

I have taken for illustration a narrative in English, the opening sentences of C. S. Lewis's *Out of the Silent Planet*. Its first clauses appear on the left in Figure 6.2. On the Thurman chart on the right of Figure 6.2 the events in this section of the narrative are copied opposite the clauses they come from, and each event is connected to a single participant line to indicate that the person who *stuffed his map into his pocket* (2) is the same one who *settled his pack on his shoulders* (3), *stepped out* (4), and *set out at once* (10). If other participants were involved in the events, each of them would be connected to a separate participant line.

Figure 6.3 takes the chart one step farther. Here the identifica-

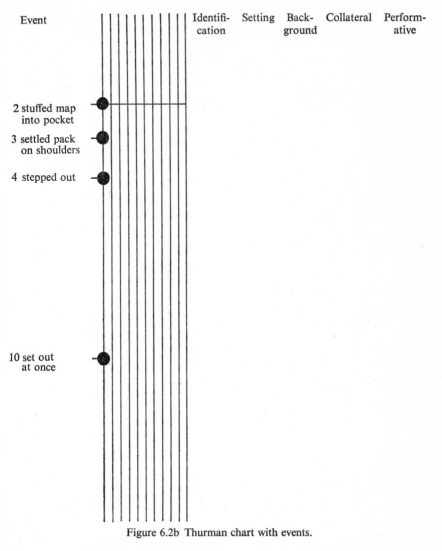

Figure 6.2b Thurman chart with events.

tional material connected with each event is added and connected up to show reference. (Since there is but one participant on stage here, the connections are obvious; but where there are two or more participants this is not always so.) The participant is first

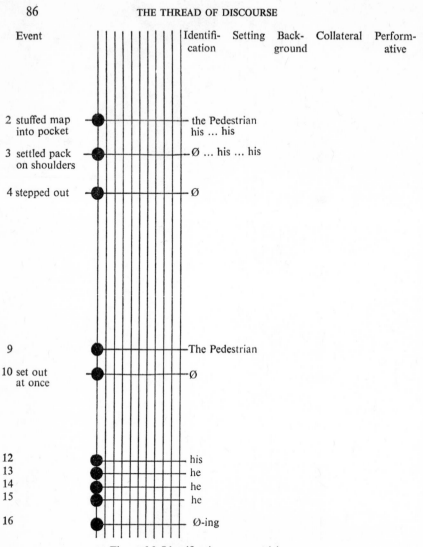

Figure 6.3 Identification, one participant.

brought on the scene as *the Pedestrian* (2). In the next two clauses, which represent a tightly knit sequence of actions that could be taken as aspects of a single action, he is not identified at all as the doer of the actions, but is only mentioned indirectly by *his* (3).

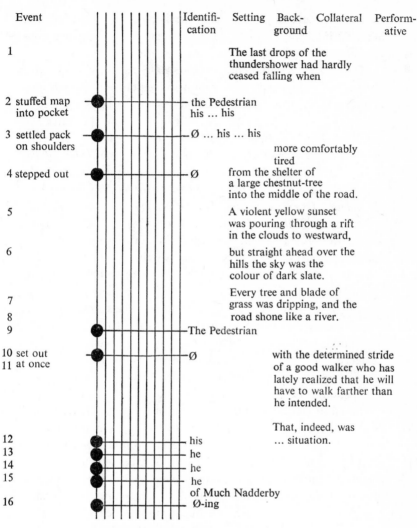

Figure 6.4 Setting and background.

The Pedestrian is repeated in 9, after a scenic interlude, in an identification that spans the event in 10 as well as 9 by means of the conjunction *but* in 10. In non-events 12 through 15 the participant is identified by *he* and *his*, but in 16, even though he is the one who would have done the seeing, he is not identified explicitly, but only implicitly through the agreement of the participial construction.

Figure 6.4 adds setting information. Many narratives begin with nothing but setting and identification and get down to the business of events only after a few hundred words of the other. Here, however, events are interspersed with setting from the start: *The last drops of the thundershower had hardly ceased falling when* ⋯ (1), ⋯ *from the shelter of a large chestnut-tree into the middle of the road* (4), *A violent yellow sunset was pouring through a rift in the clouds to westward* (5), *but straight ahead over the hills the sky was the colour of dark slate* (6), *Every tree and blade of grass was dripping* (7) *and the road shone like a river* (8). The village name *Much Nadderby* (15), though found in a collateral section, is secondarily part of the setting system as well.

Figure 6.4 also includes background information. A bit of minor background in 3 tells how the Pedestrian felt as the scene opened: *more comfortably* suggests that his pack was less than maximally comfortable, and *tired* explains the basis for his subsequent thoughts about the hospitality of Much Nadderby. Sentence 12 refers to the same feeling anaphorically in *That, indeed, was his situation*, which uses the hypothetical description in 10–11 to expand on the simple physical weariness of 3.

The ninth clause is a classical piece of collateral. It highlights what the Pedestrian did by telling first what he did not do: *wasted no time on the landscape but* ⋯ The last four clauses also tell what he did not do, and what the consequences would have been if he had done it; in the process information about the setting, and later on about background, also comes in almost incidentally. Figure 6.5 shows the collateral information added to the chart.

The performative information, in which the relation of speaker to hearer (author to reader in this case) and the speech situation (here, reading what is known to be a work of fiction) are taken into account, does not show up as coherent stretches, as in *I am going to tell you what happened to a friend of mine on a walking tour* or *Bet you thought he would stop to admire the landscape,*

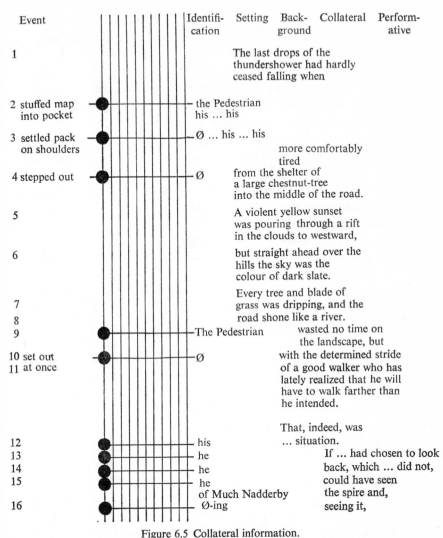

Figure 6.5 Collateral information.

didn't you?, which a less skilled raconteur might use. Instead, the author cuts corners by forcing the reader into making many small assumptions that project him more precipitously into the scene; the narrator does not have to lay his groundwork in the way a trial lawyer does. The definite article of *the thundershower* in 1 says, "I know and you know what thundershower we are talking about; so I won't delay things by telling you that one took place." *The Pedestrian* (2), *the road* (4), *the clouds to westward* (5), and *the hills* (6) manipulate the definite article in the same way, treating them as already introduced and therefore needing no further preliminaries. (*Pedestrian* actually sneaks in a good amount of information at the same time that *the* is cozying up to the reader by suggesting experiences previously shared by him and the author. If Lewis had actually been talking to a friend about a situation they both knew, however, he would not have had to make sure, as he does here, that before too many paragraphs went by the Pedestrian had been identified as a Cambridge don named Ransom out on a holiday and had given his height, age, and dress. The friend would have known.)

Other performative information appears under other guises. *His map* (2) and *his pack* (3) are also definite, and in the same way suggest "I know you remember what he looked like; just let me remind you of a couple of details of it". *Grass* (7) is a mass noun used in the same definite sense: "You know the place. There was a chestnut-tree beside the road that went through a grassy place, then on into the hills; and he was not headed west." Even the introduction of the village is by name, direct, as though it were a common scene for the author and the reader alike.

A few of the definite forms do not reflect the assumed relationship between author and reader in this way. Instead they reflect what the author assumes the reader knows in terms of broadly shared experiences of life. *The last drops* (1) are a natural part of any thundershower, a *pocket* (2) is standard equipment of any pedestrian in temperate climates (though the use of clothing plus the distinctively English form of village name could be construed as indirect information, "I expect you to realize that all this took place in the English countryside"), and once we admit a pedestrian we would be highly surprised unless he had *shoulders* (3). Even the *spire* (15) is a standard landmark of the kind of small English towns that get described in literature, and is therefore highly predictable.

The descriptive phrase of 10 and 11 relates to the speaker's shared background with the hearer that is implicit in the performative in the following sense: "You know how a good walker goes into a determined stride if he has lately realized that he will have to walk farther than he intended? Let me evoke that image to help give you a feel for what happened." On the other hand, since anything at all in the vocabulary evokes some sort of image in the same sense, it might be better not to lay stress here on the immediate speaker-hearer relation, especially since the author is not suggesting that the reader should be thinking of a particular good walker who has revised his navigation. If it were that particular, it would put the descriptive into the category of an embellishment of the event itself.

Displaying a text on a Thurman chart is the first step toward looking for systematic relations among parts of the text. It gets things out where we can see them.

2. SPAN ANALYSIS

From the Thurman chart it is possible to go on to another level of abstraction further removed from the text itself, namely the plotting of SPANS. Spans represent stretches of text within which there is some kind of uniformity. Certain kinds of uniformity have already turned out to be useful for characterizing discourse structure in several languages, and so are mentioned here. It would be surprising if there were not other kinds of spans that are relevant.

If we take a page and write clause numbers down the left hand margin corresponding to the clause numbers on the Thurman chart, though more closely spaced, we have a framework for a plot of the spans in a text as in Figure 6.6. Each span is represented by a vertical line, sometimes broken by a horizontal line or interspersed by symbols. This representation makes it possible to put many spans on a single page so that they can be compared with one another.

Setting spans are the most obvious ones to look for in narratives.

One vertical line indicates all the actions that take place in a single spatial location, and another vertical line indicates all the actions that take place in a single time sequence. A horizontal line that shows where a span is broken is useful for matching spans across the page. If a time index backs up to repeat a sequence, or if there is a resetting of the time of an action in terms of another hour or day, this starts a new time span.

It is possible to plot spans for each of the seven distinct kinds of information in discourse that I have discussed: events, identifications, settings, explanations, evaluations, collateral, and performatives. A series of clauses that gives a sequence of events, for example, appears as a vertical line, while another series dedicated to background information is represented by another line. If seven lines are dedicated to different kinds of information, this part of the span chart is equivalent to a compressed Thurman chart. It presents the same information in a less detailed way that makes it comparable with still other spans.

For plotting identification within this framework, however, it is useful to go into more detail than simply to show which clauses are identificational. In Figure 6.3, for example, there is a regularity about the ways in which the identity of the sole participant is expressed. First he is *the Pedestrian;* then there are four references that involve him: *his map, his pocket, his pack,* and *his tired shoulders.* In the next clause he is referred to but is identified only implicitly. Then four clauses go by without any reference to him. The next time he appears he is given an identification that is as complete as the identification by which he was brought on stage: again he is *the Pedestrian.* The reference to him that follows in 10, like the one in 4, lacks explicit identification. Then 12 through 15 use *his* and *he,* followed by no identification in 16.

The pattern here is common enough in different languages that I would label it a series of IDENTIFICATION SPANS. An identification span consists of a series of identifications of the same participant, not necessarily in contiguous clauses, in which no identification is stronger than the one before it. STRENGTH of identification is a ranking that goes from proper names like *George Washington*

Carver to explicit descriptives like *the mechanic who fixed our generator in Arkansas* to common nouns like *the teacher* to nouns used generically like *the fellow* to pronouns like *him*, and from there to reference without identification. The text in the example contains three identification spans for the lone participant. First comes *the Pedestrian* in 2, used somewhat like a common noun and somewhat like a proper noun. The rest of that span takes in the pronouns in 2 and 3 and ends with the zero identification of 4. The second span begins with the explicit *the Pedestrian* in 9 and ends with the zero identification of 10. The third begins with the pronouns of 12 through 15 and ends with the zero identification of 16. Where identification spans are plotted, it is wise to plot spans for each participant on different vertical lines.

Since tense and aspect sequences seem to be closely tied to the structure of discourse, and since they rarely have simple explanations, spans within which all the verbs have the same tense or the same aspect should be plotted. When this was done for Xavánte, comparing the points where the aspect changed with the spans for each kind of information showed that confusion in understanding the aspect system had arisen from the fact that events operated under one aspect system and nonevents under another.[2] Some of the aspectual indicators were used in both systems, but with different values.

Another column of the span chart should be dedicated to a problem that is so widespread in linguistic analysis that I think of it as the PLP column, for Pesky Little Particle. Most languages have particles whose use seems to be related to gluing the parts of discourses together but which are never easy to pin down. In English they are words like *now, either, moreover*, when used to relate more than one sentence. In Huichol they include both words like *mérí+kʌʌte* 'well, then' and postfixes (suffix-like forms that follow enclitics) like *-ríi* 'definitely'. Writing them out in the PLP column makes it possible to compare their pattern of occurrence with the beginnings and endings of other spans and often leads

---

[2] McLeod, "Paragraph, Aspect, and Participant in Xavante" (ms).

to a useful understanding of what they are for, as for example in June Austing's study of Omie.[3]

There are three other types of phenomena that lend themselves to representation on a span chart, but that cannot be described compactly enough here to mention further in this chapter. They are participant orientation sequences (Chapter 18), placement of new information (Chapter 19), and theme sequences at various levels (Chapter 21). By the time they are discussed it should be obvious to the reader how to fit them in.

Figure 6.6 is a span chart for the same text fragment that was used as an example in the earlier part of this section. The lines representing kinds of information are a condensation of Figure 6.5; the plots of identification spans, tenses, and particles are likely to

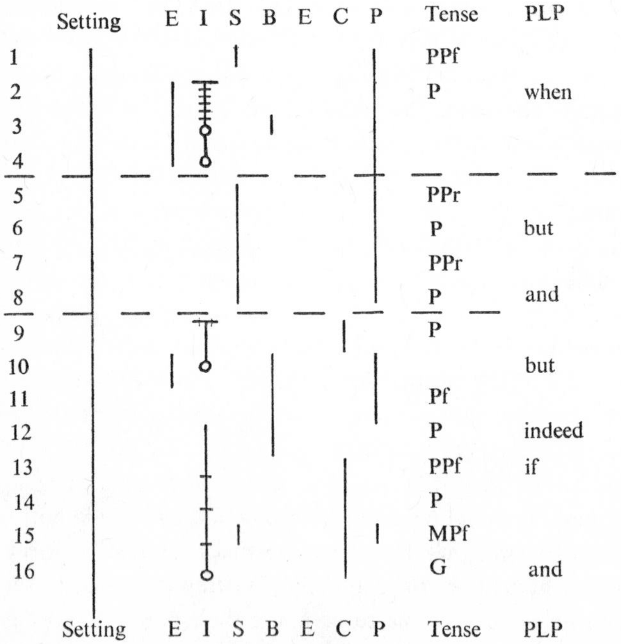

Figure 6.6 Span analysis.

³ June Austing, "Omie Discourse" (ms).

be relevant for a discourse grammar of English. As can be seen, there are correspondences between spans. For example, the new identification span begun in 9 follows the extensive setting span that begins in the latter part of 4 and continues through 8. The use of the past perfect tense in 13 and 15 goes with the collateral relationship of that string of clauses to the rest. Other regularities are not so noticeable from this chart alone, but would appear on examination of a number of texts: for example, the zero identification of the subject or agent in 3 and 4 is possible if the actions are closely related as phases of a single action that begins in 2, and if no other kinds of information such as background or collateral clauses break the sequence. The zero identification in 10, however, is an instance of a different pattern. Rather than representing a tight sequence of actions, it is one side of a collateral pair; but a condition similar to that of the event sequence holds in that the pair cannot be interrupted at that point by, say, background if zero identification is used in the second member.

Other relationships are not so readily represented on a chart of spans because they involve inflections and function words within clauses. They can, however, be marked on the Thurman chart itself with colored arrows. This is the place where anaphoric and cataphoric relationships can be plotted out, for example. In ANAPHORA a pronoun or pronoun-like element has the reference of something before it in the text. In the sample *his* in 2 has been defined earlier by *the Pedestrian* in the same clause, while *That, indeed, was his situation* of 12 has had its semantic content fully specified by 10 and 11; both are anaphoric. CATAPHORA, on the other hand, presents a reference together with a promise to identify it later. *Here's what we'll do* is cataphoric; *here* has no previous reference in the text (if there were a previous reference, *there* or *that* would be the normal form to show anaphora) and *do* has no content.

Thurman has singled out two special kinds of text relationship that deserve notice.[4] LINKAGE is his name for a particular kind of

---

4   Thurman, "Chuave Medial Verbs" (ms).

anaphoric relation, and CHAINING for a particular kind of cataphoric relation. In a number of languages events must be linked to preceding events by a repetition of those events: *They went down to the river. Having gone to the river, they entered the canoe. Having entered the canoe, they began to paddle. Having begun to paddle ...* In a system that makes extensive use of linkages it is the absence of a linking clause that catches the hearer's attention; this ASYNDETON or break in the sequence may be used to signal a change of scene or a shift of participants or a transition to background information or even a point of special emphasis.[5] The most striking linkage pattern I have come across is in Kayapó, where each paragraph of a narrative is preceded by a linking paragraph that is an almost exact repetition of the preceding narrative paragraph.[6]

Chaining is cataphoric. It is the prediction of some of the information that a following clause will contain. It is common throughout the New Guinea highlands, though unreported elsewhere. Joy McCarthy's 1965 article "Clause Chaining in Kanite" describes verb inflections that predict whether the subject of the second of two clauses will be the same as the subject of the first. If the second clause is to have a different subject, the chaining systems of some languages predict what person and number the new subject is to have, while others simply predict that there is going to be a change. Chaining systems may go with linkage systems, so that an event in a sequence of events may be chained forward to the next event and at the same time may be linked backward to the preceding event. As with linkage, breaking a chained sequence may have special significance.[7]

---

[5] Longacre, *Discourse ... in Philippine Languages* (1967), uses the terms *figure* and *ground* for linkage relationships; the central element or figure in one sentence becomes the ground for the introduction of a new figure in the next. I find this terminology, which is taken from Gestalt psychology, less than satisfactory because of the necessity of divesting it of the Gestalt principle that without the ground we can't perceive the figure. That is not the point; we are dealing only with a mechanism for linear cohesion between adjacent event tellings.

[6] Stout and Thomson, "Kayapó Narrative" (1971).

[7] Marshall Lawrence, "Oksapmin Sentence Structure" (ms).

3. USE OF SURFACE CONSTRUCTIONS

It is useful to note down on a Thurman chart just where and for what kind of information particular grammatical constructions are used. Our grasp of grammar has changed sufficiently in the past decade that instead of simply saying that a language has, for example, thirty-two clause types, we can now ask legitimately what the various clause types are for, and by tracing their pattern of use within a discourse we can get an answer.

Most of the languages I have looked at so far regularly use some kind of active clause type to report events; that is, the instigator of the action is regularly the grammatical subject. Passive constructions may be used to report events, but they assert a special kind of relationship to them, discussed in Chapter 21.

There are two kinds of phenomena frequently called passive that should be kept distinct. The first is the kind found in English, in which the agent who instigates an action is expressed in a prepositional phrase and some other element of the action is the grammatical subject, as in *the ball was hit by the batter*. As Halliday points out,[8] this construction gives two options. One treats the agent as new information by placing it at the end of the clause as the nucleus of an intonation contour without using a marked form of either the information center (Chapter 19) or the thematic organization (Chapter 21). The other option omits the agent: *the ball was hit*, which permits *hit* to be the new information in the information center and makes *ball* the theme; the agent either is irrelevant or is recoverable from the context. The second kind of passive, which I distinguish as the NONAGENTIVE, sounds like the second of the two English patterns but has no parallel in the first. In other words, it is incapable of stating who the agent of the action is, and is often used to sidestep the question of who instigated something. Nonagentives are common in languages of the Americas, and not unknown in the Old World. Of the Indo-European languages, Spanish illustrates nonagentive semantics

---

8   Halliday, "Notes on Transitivity and Theme in English, Part 2" (1967).

in one use of the impersonal *se:* for example, *se me pasó una desgracia en el camino* 'an unfortunate thing happened to me on the road' in circumstances where English would say *I had an accident on the road.* Passives of both kinds may be used in explanations.

Confusion between the use of passives for reporting events and their use in explanations seems to be involved in the justly parodied bent of some writers in the physical sciences to try to sound objective by using the passive voice in all their writings, with the result that they really sound as though they were trying to evade the responsibility for their work: *The apparatus was mounted and the observation begun. The dials were read every hour. The process was interrupted briefly because an important connection was broken. After the results were tabulated, it was concluded that the Heatherington-Smedley hypothesis was capable of being modified as had been suggested by this investigator. The tabulation is given in Appendix B for verification by the reader.*

Identificational information tends to make heavy use of equatives as well as of nouns, which there is reason to believe may represent a surface form of embedded equative.[9] Equative constructions are also the basis for thematically partitioned (cleft) forms of sentences (Chapter 11) like *what this country needs is a good five cent cigar* and its extraposed counterpart *it is a good five cent cigar that this country needs.*

Locative constructions appear frequently in connection with setting information: *It is chilly in the mountains in November. There is a valley there, however, where the frost always comes late.*

Grammatical embedding of sentences within sentences is commonly used for relatively short stretches of background information or for identification: *The tickets for which Sam had paid his week's salary were for the wrong night* contains an embedded *for which Sam had paid his week's salary* that is on the borderline between background and identification. The embedded clause may inform the hearer about the events that led up to Sam's having the tickets;

---

[9]   Bach, "Nouns and Noun Phrases" (1968); Frantz, *Blackfoot* (1970).

on the other hand it may distinguish those tickets from some others. The distinction in this instance is paralleled by the well known grammatical distinction between nonrestrictive and restrictive relative clauses, though I am not sure the correspondence fits all cases.[10]

Quotative constructions in connection with collateral information have already been mentioned. Some languages also use quotations regularly as a means of presenting background information, using a verb of thinking to introduce the quotation rather than a verb of saying: "he took the money, thinking 'she owes it to me'" is equivalent to *he took the money because she owed it to him* in English.

Specific grammatical elements in a language are seen to stand in a special relationship to discourse structure. McLeod demonstrates the difference in aspect systems in Xavánte of Brazil when the aspect refers to an event and when it refers to a nonevent.[11] In Angaataha of Papua New Guinea Roberta Huisman reports a difference between primary and secondary verbal inflections in event-oriented texts.[12] The speaker uses primary verbs to single out events that are important to his story in contrast to those he puts in for detail or color using secondary inflection. Bacairí of Brazil makes use of a distinction between focal and nonfocal pronouns in a kind of stage management system, telling the hearer who is prominent in the discourse at the moment and who is upstage.[13] The focus and topic system of some Philippine languages (the term "voice" used by some authors obscures what the system is for; see Austin 1962) is similar in that sequences of related grammatical constructions are used to tell what a discourse or paragraph is about and to introduce characters.[14] This system has

10 Thompson, "The Deep Structure of Relative Clauses" (1971).
11 McLeod, "Paragraph, Aspect, and Participant in Xavánte" (ms).
12 Roberta Huisman, "Angaataha Narrative Discourse" (1973).
13 Wheatley, "Pronouns and Nominal Elements in Bacairí Discourse" (ms).
14 Helen Miller, "Thematization in Mamanwa" (1973). For a critique of the analysis of Philippine focus as voice see Austin, *Attention, Emphasis, and Focus in Ata Manobo* (1966).

parallels in Nambiquara of Brazil, though the specific grammatical expressions used are not comparable on the surface; see the paper by Menno Kroeker that is Appendix A of this volume.

7

CONSTITUENCY IN DISCOURSE

Sentences and parts of sentences can be broken into their constituent parts. So can entire discourses. Larger units of language are made up of smaller units in a particular arrangement; or looked at from a different angle, larger units can be partitioned into smaller ones according to a particular principle.

One kind of linguistic analysis of discourse is therefore a division of large units into their constituent parts, labeling the parts so as to reflect how they are related. This type of study has been carried farthest in the area of discourse by Longacre and his associates.[1] It is a valuable phase of discourse study, even though it is subject to the criticisms Postal brought up against constituency grammars in general.[2] One could say that constituent analysis makes use of a universal property of surface grammars, partitionability, which could be thought of equally well as a property of the transformational systems that produce surface structures from deep structures. It proceeds by successive partitioning to catalog the kinds of elements and kinds of relationships among elements that a language makes use of in its discourse system. What these elements express, and what the relationships are good for, is an aspect of discourse study that I would suggest can be investigated best when the cataloguing is done. Constituent analysis is not the end of linguistics, but rather a systematic way of doing the spade work.

---

[1] Longacre, *Discourse ... in Philippine Languages* (1967), *Discourse ... in New Guinea Languages* (1972).
[2] Postal, *Constituent Structure* (1964).

1. PARTITIONING PRINCIPLES

Texts can be divided into sections in a number of ways, and the sections themselves can be further divided. The principles of partitioning discourses involve more distinct relationships than the principles of partitioning sentences. There is also no inherent ordering of the partitioning principles; for example, one text may be divided into two settings in which a single cast operates, while another may have a single setting within which a series of casts of characters play their parts. Link finds different principles of partitioning in different discourse types in Wobe of Ivory Coast.[3]

The first kind of partition to look for in a narrative text is one based on SETTING. Change of scene is usually marked explicitly, and almost always comes near the beginning of the stretch of text that is characterized by unity of setting. Even in the case of procedures and explanations, the place where the action is to be carried out or the region where the principle holds good may give a partitioning of the text.

TEMPORAL setting, as has been mentioned, is different from spatial setting in that it is always changing. The trees and buildings of a spatial setting remain constant throughout the scene for all practical purposes; but each tick of the clock changes the temporal setting. Nevertheless, it makes sense to speak of a single temporal setting whenever actions take place without mention being made of discontinuities in the temporal line. If we talk, for example, of *the major battles of World War I*, we refer to a sequence of events in a temporal setting but fail to take any note of the times that passed between battles. If we were taking a closer look at that time interval, we might use the boundary periods between major battles as segmentation points for stretches of speech which indicate no discontinuity within themselves, but do use linguistic means to talk about discontinuity with the preceding and following stretches: *not long after the final action of that battle ...*

SPATIAL setting is very much like stage scenery; it remains stable

---

[3]   Link, "Units in Wobe Discourse" (ms).

from the time the curtain goes up until the curtain is brought down again, except when there are overt actions of the participants that rearrange it. When a text is divided into parts on the basis of spatial settings, each part is like a different scene of a play. A special kind of spatial setting is what Naomi Glock and I have labelled a TRAJECTORY, or a moving sequence of spatial settings through which a participant travels.[4] A trajectory is like a temporal setting in that even though no two actions take place at the same location, the setting is considered a unit unless a discontinuity in it, a boundary between it and another setting, is mentioned. All the actions along a trajectory belong to the same segment of text.

THEME is a partitioning principle for some languages. It will be gone over in more detail in Chapter 11; but in this context it is enough to say that as long as the speaker continues talking about the same thing, he remains within a single segment of the text at some level of partitioning. When he changes the subject he passes from one element of the organization of the text to the next element.

Mundurukú paragraphing is tied tightly to thematic organization. I would interpret Sheffler's analysis as thematic:[5] First comes a particle which says, 'I am going to talk about something else'. Then the new theme is introduced as either the grammatical object or the goal of the clause. From there on the theme can be referred to without explicit identification, even though other elements in the text have to be identified. Both Nambiquara of Brazil and Longuda of Nigeria have a hierarchy of thematic organization that includes at least a global theme for the entire discourse and local themes which cover sections of the discourse and thus define segments of the discourse.[6]

Christensen's discussion of the place of topic sentences in English paragraphs suggests that change of theme may be the basis of at

---

[4]   Grimes and Glock, "Saramaccan" (1970).
[5]   Sheffler, "Mundurukú Discourse" (ms).
[6]   Kroeker, "Thematic Linkage in Nambiquara Narrative", Appendix A of this volume. John F. Newman, "Participant Orientation in Longuda Folk Tales" (ms).

least some partitioning into paragraphs in English.[7] Christensen's model is too simple for English in that he notices only themes stated at the beginning of paragraphs; but this can be filled out by attention to Christensen's own examples of exceptions. The paragraphs he gives as topicless have a complex buildup to the topic sentence, which appears late in the paragraph. Nevertheless, his recognition of a thematic basis for partitioning of texts seems essentially correct, and may not be in conflict with Becker's observation that changes of participant orientation determine paragraphing,[8] since participant orientation itself (Chapter 18) may be a form of thematization.

Uniformity of the cast of characters (Chapter 20) may be a basis for text division. Certainly in the Odyssey the division between the episode of the Lotus Eaters and the episode of the Cyclops involves not only a change in spatial setting, "and so we sailed away from that island ...", but also a change in the characters with whom Odysseus and his crew were interacting. This is in contrast with divisions based on a new spatial setting that retains the old cast of characters, as is common in Xenophon's *Anabasis*, where the standard formula is (1:2) "From there he marched on for three days, twenty leagues to Celaenae, an inhabited city of Phrygia, great and prosperous. While there ..." Just the opposite is the case in Shakespeare's *A Midsummer Night's Dream* IV.i, where the setting remains the same but one set of characters leaves the stage, a completely different one enters, and a third set remains through most of the scene.

The point to remember about casts of characters is that a group may vary in membership and still be the same group for purposes of linguistic reference. In the example just mentioned, Odysseus lost a couple of crew members who remained among the Lotus Eaters, but he still sailed away with his crew. A candidate takes on the incumbent president, the news report has it; but in reality the candidate and his backers take on the incumbent president and

---

[7]   Christensen, "A Generative Rhetoric of the Paragraph" (1965).
[8]   Becker, "A Tagmemic Approach to Paragraph Analysis" (1965).

his backers. Divisions in the text that are based on the cast do not reflect incidental changes in the membership of the groups that participate in the action, but only in the identity of the groups as groups.

This principle of group identity may apply in different ways at higher and lower levels of segmentation. In a Cornell football broadcast, for example, the announcer may pass on the information coming in over the wire that *The Oklahoma team defeated Kansas State by a score of 35 to 10*. In giving the play by play account of the game he is witnessing, however, he will not talk about *the Cornell team* in quite the same way. Instead, he will segment his text at the point where Cornell either gains or loses control of the ball. At that point either the offensive or the defensive squad takes over, the personalities are different, the mode of play is different, and during that stretch of speech the announcer's choice of vocabulary to describe the action on the field is different, especially if he is a local announcer reporting on behalf of one of the teams. Later, however, in talking about the same game he will say *The Cornell team defeated Yale 13 to 7*, reporting that game as one of a set of games instead of as a sequence of plays, and treating the team as a unit rather than as two distinct groups.

Becker, as already mentioned, has suggested that English paragraphs are at least sometimes divided on the basis of what in Chapter 18 I describe as PARTICIPANT ORIENTATION. That is, there are stretches during which a single participant maintains a relatively high level of activity in relation to the other participants. Each stretch has a uniform orientation to the actions in the paragraph. For Nomatsiguenga, however, Wise and Lowe find that paragraphing corresponds to cycles of orientation.[9] Each cycle begins with the dominant character in a story initiating an action, followed by a response in which the secondary character initiates an action. Each time the cycle returns to the dominant character as initiator, a new paragraph is recognized. Barnard and Longacre recognize a

[9]   Wise and Lowe, "Permutation Groups in Discourse" (1972).

similar principle behind what they call lexical paragraphs.[10] In Ayoré and Jibu there are definite regularities of participant orientation, but for those languages participant orientation does not seem to contribute to partitioning of the text into paragraphs.[11]

Christensen has made the grammatical relationships of coordination and subordination the basis for his prescriptive treatment of paragraphing.[12] He looks at the clauses in a sentence and the sentences in a paragraph as a kind of tree or outline structure in which subordinate points depend on superordinate points, and in which at any level of subordination there may be two or more points that are subordinate to the same point at a higher level and coordinate with each other. Paragraph breaks in his view are appropriate whenever one returns from a lower or less inclusive level to a higher or more inclusive level. Dik adds materially to the discussion of coordination and subordination relationships, though he does not go into its relationship to paragraphing.[13]

I have made a similar point in regard to the general model of relationships among linguistic elements:[14] for many languages a tree structure or its familiar counterpart, the outline, is a very good representation of the organization of information both within sentences and in groupings of sentences and further groupings of those groupings. Meyer finds that a tree or outline representation seems to have a psycholinguistic validity in that recall of high level or more inclusive nodes is superior to recall of low level nodes except when the low level nodes give details (numbers like *1776*

---

[10] Barnard and Longacre, "Dibabawon Procedural Narrative" (1968).

[11] Briggs, "Ayoré Narrative Analysis" (ms); Bradley, "Jibu Narrative Discourse Structure" (1971).

[12] Christensen, "A Generative Rhetoric of the Sentence" (1963), "Notes Toward a New Rhetoric" (1963), "A Generative Rhetoric of the Paragraph" (1965). Christensen's use of the term *generative* is a misnomer from the point of view of linguistics. He is not characterizing the sets of paragraphs or sentences; he is telling the student how to produce certain kinds of highly valued paragraphs and sentences. Because his advice to the writer is in general good, one tends to feel lenient about his misuse of a jargon term which, after all, has tripped more than one professional linguist.

[13] Dik, *Coordination* (1968).

[14] Grimes, "Outlines and Overlays" (1972).

or proper names) that have been learned with effort in other contexts.[15] Fuller bases his system of textual exegesis on the assumption of a tree structure that involves coordination and subordination.[16]

2. LEVELS OF ORGANIZATION

Longacre makes constant use of standard levels of organization within text that are consistently present in languages of the world: morpheme, stem, word, phrase, clause, sentence, paragraph, discourse.[17] There are variations on the main pattern; for example, in many languages of Papua New Guinea there is no useful distinction between the sentence and the paragraph, in some of the Mayan languages of Middle America it is difficult and probably structurally unnecessary to tell a word from a phrase, and in some languages of Vietnam, clauses and sentences are not sharply differentiated.[18] Nevertheless, in most languages, and elsewhere in the hierarchies of even the languages in which there is some lack of distinctiveness, it is at least heuristically useful and typologically valid to expect considerable consistency from one language to another in terms of levels of organization.

My own position at the moment, as expressed in connection with outline structures,[19] is that there seem to be three general kinds of semantic units: first there are role or case relationships, which in a predicate grammar (Chapter 13) are a class of predicates that are characteristically dominated by and selected by the lexical predicates (for example, *go* selects an agent-object, the one who goes, in its use as a verb of motion). Second are lexical predicates

---

15 Meyer, *Idea units … from prose* (1971).
16 Fuller, *Inductive Method of Bible Study* (1959). Fuller's success in expressing text relationships in tree form was one of the stimuli that turned my attention to the more general problem of discourse structure.
17 Longacre, *Discourse … in Philippine Languages* (1968).
18 Watson, "Clause to Sentence Gradation in Pacôh" (1966).
19 Grimes, "Outlines and Overlays" (1972).

that correspond more or less to the meanings of words. Third come rhetorical predicates that express the relationships that unite propositions built from lexical predicates and roles to form rhetorical complexes, and that recursively unite rhetorical complexes. The minimal expression of roles and lexical predicates is in the clause, while the minimal expression of rhetorical predicates is more extensive than the clause, usually involving the sentence. Larger units are required for expressing more complex productions made within the rudimentary grammar that is implied here. Sentences, paragraphs, and the like are most conveniently thought of as packages of information that are wrapped up and labeled in a standardized form for the hearer's benefit, to help him keep track of where he is.

Whether Longacre's levels of organization have a universal basis or not, they do form a useful grid for the analysis of discourse. I will comment on them in order from least inclusive to most inclusive.

Longacre speaks of the clause as the unit whose function is to "express predications". This is not to say that no predications are expressed except in clauses, but rather that the clause is the unit that is most commonly used to express the kinds of relationships that I treat as lexical. It should also be borne in mind that some semantic configurations that could be expressed as clauses are expressed in embedded form as nouns or adverbs or relative clauses; from the semantic point of view, however, they are predications none the less.

Sentences are "propositions which may concatenate, oppose, balance, or report predications" in Longacre's hierarchy. A one-clause sentence is thus more than the simple predication of its clause component; it is the reporting or the assertion of that predication. Longacre's article on the sentence as a statement calculus and its later development by Ballard, Conrad, and Longacre exemplify Longacre's position, which in general agrees with my own observation that certain rhetorical relations (conditions, for example) cannot be expressed within the compass of a clause in surface structure, but instead require at least a sentence to say.[20] Although Longacre and I both have little to say about levels of organization between the sentence and the paragraph, I have recognized in Huichol a PERIOD consisting of a string of related sentences that seemed to play a part in the hierarchical system. Bearth reports something similar in Toura of Ivory Coast.[21]

Paragraphs in Longacre's model are "units in developing discourse". Of the principles discussed in Section 1 of this chapter for partitioning texts, I find that the unity of time or place, unity of participant orientation, and unity of subtree or suboutline structure frequently correspond to a recognizable surface configuration larger than the sentence that can conveniently be called a paragraph. Whether these units are the building blocks out of which discourse is put together directly, however, seems to me to depend on the complexity of the whole. The relationship of a paragraph to a novel is probably different from the relationship of a paragraph to an instruction sheet for a dishwasher, not only because of the difference in subject matter and style, but also because the novel is vastly more complex and requires many intermediate layers, whereas the instruction sheet may divide immediately into paragraphs. In Longacre's 1968 model these intermediate layers are assumed to be embedded discourses.

Certain groupings of paragraphs have been recognized in texts. In Ilianen Manobo, for example, Wrigglesworth finds an INCIDENT level and an EPISODE level whose surface forms are not simply strings of paragraphs, but which have their own characteristics.[22] These characteristics are expressed as constraints on the way settings may be referred to anaphorically, as formulas, and as other things: "Episode settings always involve a change of participant orientation and scene from the previous incident in the story ...

[20] Longacre, "Sentence Structure as a Statement Calculus" (1970). Ballard, Conrad, and Longacre, "The Deep and Surface Grammar of Interclausal Relations" (1971), "More on ... Interclausal Relations" (1972).
[21] Grimes, "Some Inter-Sentence Relationships in Huichol" (1966). Thomas Bearth, "Phrase et Discours en Toura" (1969).
[22] Wrigglesworth, "Ilianen Manobo Narrative Discourse" (ms).

While the opening incident of an episode takes its temporal setting from the speech of the participant thematized in the episode setting, settings for subsequent incidents are defined by their motion away from or their return to the previous setting ... Incidents nearly always conclude with evaluative paragraphs." Kayapó also has episodes in narrative.[23] They consist of a transition paragraph which links the episode to the preceding one by repeating its base paragraph, followed by one or more base paragraphs that give the action, and optionally end in an explanatory paragraph that gives non-event information. In Mambila each episode is centered around one main character to whom special rules of identification apply.[24]

The planes of an overlay (19.3) are another kind of complexity that can be intermediate between the paragraph and the discourse. In another realm, a line of argument (usually an enthymeme), may make up more than one paragraph of a nonsequential discourse, especially if some points of the argument are illustrated, say, by a narrative. As mentioned earlier (Section 1) with regard to unity of cast, an episode may consist of a series of paragraphs in which the same characters take part, so that a new episode begins when a significant change of participants takes place. The term CHAPTER is available in linguistic terminology for still larger intermediate levels of organization; there is probably no means of establishing a limit on how many intermediate levels of organization there can be between the paragraph and the discourse.

Discourse itself has to be taken as the ultimate level of organization, that level beyond which members of the culture no longer recognize the kind of closure that Pike speaks of in defining the behavioreme. Even though this notion of cultural recognizability is useful enough for me to take it as a primitive, undefined, and undefinable notion, it leaves open some questions that I cannot answer: is an unstructured conversation, as at a cocktail party, one discourse or many?[25] Is there not a form of verbal rambling

[23] Stout and Thomson, "Kayapó Narrative" (1971).
[24] Perrin, "Who's Who in Mambila" (ms).
[25] Weizenbaum, "Contextual Understanding by Computers" (1967).

that has a paragraph structure but not a discourse structure? Do marginal forms of speech such as glossolalia have a discourse structure, or only a phonological structure?[26] Can we speak of different discourse structures when, for example, a radio announcer is speaking into a microphone to his audience, stops for a commercial, talks to the engineer, goes back to talking to his audience, and perhaps even asks the engineer for coffee by turning off the microphone between sentences and calling to the engineer? Fortunately we do not have to suspend all study of discourse until questions like these are resolved, because there are enough discourses that are well behaved to give us plenty of insight into language just in describing them.

---

[26]   Samarin, "Glossolalic Private Language" (1971).

8

SEMANTIC ROLE STRUCTURE

Up to now most of what I have had to say has been heuristically rather than theoretically inclined. The different kinds of information that are found in discourse, as well as the different sizes and shapes of structures that discourses can be segmented into, now need to be discussed in contexts in which it can be seen more clearly how they contribute what they do to discourse. The reason for bringing them up together in the preceding chapters was partly to give the reader an idea of the kinds of things that can be included in discourse studies, and partly to suggest ways he himself might approach the linguistic analysis of texts.

1. CONTENT, COHESION, AND STAGING

Turning now to models of discourse phenomena that can give insight into the relationships that underlie discourse, there appear to be three distinct sets of relationships on which we need to focus.[1] The first I will call CONTENT organization. It has also been referred to as cognitive or referential structure, and more loosely has been called semantic organization or meaning structure. It embraces LEXICAL and RHETORICAL relationships; that is, both the way in which things that are perceived are said to relate to each other in the ordinary sense of dictionary meanings (Chapter 8 to 11), and the way in which these propositions about relations group together

---

[1] Halliday, "Notes on Transitivity and Theme in English, Part 2" (1967).

into larger complexes (Chapter 14). The content system of languages thus has a hierarchical side to it that is partially reflected by the kind of surface hierarchical groupings discussed in Chapter 7. It probably includes what Fillmore and Halliday call modality, though this strikes me as a separate system. It also has a side that cannot be matched to the hierarchical part without bringing into linguistic theory something that many linguists would rather keep out: reference.

A second set of relationships is fundamentally independent of the cognitive set. These are COHESION relationships, which relate what is being said at the moment to what has already been said (Chapter 19). Cohesion is cumulative and linear rather than hierarchical. It has to do with the means of introducing new information and of keeping track of old information, rather than with what the content of the new or old information actually is. It is also tied up with the speaker's estimate of the rate at which the hearer can process new information.

The third kind of relationships that operate in discourse are STAGING relationships. They are concerned with expressing the speaker's perspective on what is being said. Normally they make one part of a stretch of discourse the THEME or TOPIC and relate everything else to it. There are thematic structures that set the stage for entire discourses, thematic structures that stage only clauses, and thematic structures at intermediate levels (Chapter 21).

In the simplest instance staging, cohesion, and content support each other; the theme is selected from information that has already been introduced, and this is related to the rest cognitively as well as thematically. Frequently enough, however, at least one of the three ways of organizing information parts company with the rest; this is why they have to be distinguished.

Possibly there is a fourth kind of organization in discourse, a MODAL component that relates the discourse to the speaker (Chapter 15). If, however, the notion of performatives is capable of being fitted within the content hierarchy, then modal information might be taken as one kind of content that is introduced via the performative. As far as this book is concerned I treat modal information as part of the content system.

Now let us consider that part of the content structure that I have just labeled lexical and proceed to give it a more definite shape. The concepts discussed in this chapter and the next few are a necessary background for developing a theory of discourse, even though they do not contribute directly to discourse itself. Accordingly, we will come back to discourse as such in Chapter 14 on rhetorical content structure, and again from Chapter 16 on. Meanwhile let us build up the framework for talking about discourse.

First, it is desirable to make a distinction between those things in language over which the speaker can exercise choice and those over which no choice is available to him. The former reflect meaning; as many linguists have pointed out, meaning is possible only when the speaker could choose to say something else instead. The latter are the more mechanical components of language, the implementation process by which the results of the speaker's choices are expressed in a conventional form that permits communication with someone else. For example, a speaker of English can choose whether to talk about *cats* or about *dogs;* and in connection with that choice he can decide whether to talk about one of them or about many. If he decides to talk about *cats*, and many of them, however, he is then restricted as to where he can put the signal that lets the hearer know that he has selected the "many" option – the plural marker. It must come after the noun *cat*, not before it, and its phonetic form is constrained by the word it goes with: *-s* after *cat* and similar words, *-z* after *dog* and similar words, and so on by well known rules. The speaker has no choice over the position or the voicing; they are part of the implementation.

This distinction between choice and implementation is similar to the distinction between content and expression made by Hjelmslev and later adopted by Chafe; it also corresponds to Šaumjan's two levels of linguistic structure.[2] One way of defining the difference

---

[2] Hjelmslev, *Prolegomena* (1953); Chafe, *Meaning and the Structure of Language* (1970); Šaumjan, "The Applicational Generative Model" (1965).

between deep and surface structures is also compatible with this: that of linguists like Langendoen and Lakoff whose representations of semantic structures are capable of being independently defined, correspond systematically to surface structures, and are central to their point of view.[3] As Max Black has pointed out, this division of language into elements involving meaningful choice and the means of expressing the results of that choice is one question; whether those choices can in fact ever be made without reference to the possibilities of implementation that exist for each choice is a separate question.[4]

I adopt the position here that the choices a speaker has available within the content system can be expressed by means of PROPOSITIONAL structures (Chapter 13). Each proposition contains a PREDICATE, which expresses a semantic relation among ARGUMENTS, which may themselves be propositions.[5] Propositions, predicates, and arguments will occupy us throughout most of this chapter and the next five. The implementation that relates propositional structures to the corresponding surface forms is expressed as a set of TRANSFORMATIONS.

[3] Langendoen, *The Study of Syntax* (1969); Lakoff, *Irregularity in Syntax* (1965). The older deep-surface distinction of Hockett's *Course* (1958) and Chomsky's *Aspects* (1965) was an attempt to move linguistics in the right direction; but it went only part of the way. Chomsky's later theory (in Steinberg and Jakobovits, *Semantics*, 1971) in principle accounts for the same semantic structures and relates them to surface structures in the same way as a theory like Langendoen's; but it does so in what to me is a less insightful and revealing way by making semantics an interpretation of the syntactic structures that are associated with the language generated by his grammar.
[4] Black, *The Labyrinth of Language* (1968).
[5] The term *predicate* is used here in its logical sense: "designations for the properties and relations predicated of ... individuals" (Carnap, *Introduction to Symbolic Logic* (1958), p. 4). This should not be confused with the use of the term for the linguistic surface element called PREDICATE that involves a verb and its adjuncts (Pike, *Language* (1967), p. 250) in their relation to a SUBJECT. Complexes of propositions, in which some propositions are arguments of others, have the form of a tree generated by a recursive context free grammar whose properties are discussed in Chapter 13. Although I have a suspicion that there may be better ways than this to represent semantic relationships, tree structures are adequate for enough of what needs to be said about the organization of content in this book that I do not find them a bad or misleading representation.

Much of the content of discourse is expressible in terms of predicates whose arguments are related to them in a small number of conventional ways called ROLE or CASE relationships. The predicates whose arguments involve role specifications directly are the ones I call LEXICAL; the one that underlies English *eat* is an example. Those whose arguments are related in other ways I call RHETORICAL; the one that underlies English *because* is an example. There may be predicates that have some arguments that are limited by role specifications and some arguments that are not; if so, they constitute an intermediate class. The rest of this chapter is concerned with role relationships and the part they play in lexical structure.

2. ROLE RELATIONSHIPS

The idea that a certain few relationships operate in the semantics of a great many words is not new. C. C. Fries devoted two chapters of *The Structure of English* to structural meanings.[6] In his discussion of subjects and objects he lists five meanings which the subject of a sentence can convey: (1) performer, (2) that which is identified, (3) that which is described, (4) that which undergoes the action, and (5) that to or for which the action is performed. These meanings correspond respectively to the role categories of agent, patient of an identification, patient of a state, patient of a process, and benefactive. The role names are, however, more than just a shorthand for the kinds of subjects that Fries labeled. They correspond to similar relationships manifested in areas of surface grammar that have nothing to do with subjects and objects.

Pike recognizes, following Fries, that the notion of grammatical subject is a mixed bag.[7] In his second edition of *Language* he speaks of a "class of various different subject tagmemes".[8]

[6]   Fries, *The Structure of English* (1952), pp. 173-239.
[7]   Pike, *Language* (1954), Part 1, pp. 131, 150.
[8]   Pike, *Language* (1967), p. 196.

Pike also speaks of an analysis of discourse in which the dramatis personae are traced through a plot, and of the independence of the dramatis personae from grammatical slots such as subject and object.[9] He finds that "from the viewpoint of the tale as a whole ... the dramatis personae remain invariant". The idea is developed further in an article on matrices composed of tagmemes.[10] Longacre uses the notion of dramatis personae metaphorically along with props, scenery, local color, and plot to characterize predication clauses. His list of tagmas that are potentially suspect because of similarities in slot meaning is related to the surface manifestations of role relationships, but is not concerned with the relationships themselves.[11] Barnard and Longacre identify participant roles in relation to the discourse as a whole, similar to Pike's invariant dramatis personae.[12]

The notion of role relationships as part of the meaning of words has been most successfully exploited in tagmemics by Harland Kerr and by Forster and Barnard.[13] In dissociating role relationships from surface tagmemes, then stating explicitly the mappings that relate roles to tagmemes, Forster and Barnard paved the way for an important advance in the understanding of semantic relationships in verb systems of languages of the Philippines, as developed in papers by Hettick, Ashley, Draper, Lou Hohulin, Jeanne Miller, Rhea, and West.

As far as American linguistics is concerned, the landmark study of role relationships is Charles Fillmore's paper "The Case for Case", published in 1968. Fillmore not only summed up a lot of what had been written on the subject, but pointed the way toward an extension of role or case grammar to cover more than just verb-noun relationships. Possibly more important still, he did it in a way that caught the attention of linguists of a number of theoretical

[9] Pike, *Language* (1967), p. 246, note 14.
[10] Pike, "Discourse Structure and Tagmeme Matrices" (1964).
[11] Longacre, *Grammar Discovery Procedures* (1964), pp. 35, 63.
[12] Barnard and Longacre, "Dibabawon Procedural Narrative" (1968).
[13] Kerr, "Cotabato Manobo Voice Affixes" (1965); Forster and Barnard, "Dibabawon Active Verbs" (1968).

THE THREAD OF DISCOURSE

persuasions. Other writings of Fillmore's help round out the picture. Still other insights are given by Langendoen's applications of case grammar, and by its adoption as the frame of reference for the UCLA synopsis of work done up to that time on English transformational grammar.[14] Frantz's grammar of Blackfoot illustrates another possible formalization of role grammar, outstanding in that he makes explicit the required transformational apparatus that others tend to leave implicit.[15]

Ideas similar to Fillmore's have appeared in other works. Lyons, for example proposes a notional theory of parts of speech which, taken together with his view of grammatical functions, results in a picture of grammar that does not differ greatly from Fillmore's.[16] Halliday discusses the same kind of relationships under the label of "transitivity".[17] Chafe centers his attention on the verb rather than on verb-noun relations as such, but the effect he achieves is substantially the same.[18] Weinreich's semantics, also verb-centered, fits the same paradigm.[19] His transfer features are capable of being extended into a Fillmore grammar, as Hall's work on Subanon demonstrates.[20]

Organizing information about a language in terms of role types gives insight into an intriguingly broad range of phenomena. I take the position that role or case grammar is one of the important contributions of current grammatical theory. Even though it does not account for everything in language, yet it sheds light on enough that it should now be one of the standard areas of study in any language. Furthermore, role relationships help us understand some discourse phenomena, as we shall see in Chapter 18.

---

[14] Langendoen, *The Study of Syntax* (1969), *Essentials of English Grammar* (1970); Stockwell *et al.*, *Transformational Theories of English Syntax* (1968).
[15] Frantz, *Blackfoot* (1970).
[16] Lyons, "Towards a 'Notional' Theory of 'Parts of Speech'" (1966), *Introduction to Theoretical Linguistics* (1968).
[17] Halliday, "Notes on Transitivity and Theme in English, Part 1" (1967).
[18] Chafe, *Onondaga* (1970), *Meaning and the Structure of Language* (1970).
[19] Weinreich, "Explorations in Semantic Theory" (1966), "On the Semantic Structure of Language" (1966).
[20] Hall, "Siocon Subanon Verbs" (1969).

So far each linguist who has written on roles has come up with a different list of what the standard role relationships are. The list I give here differs slightly from every other one that I know of. What is significant, however, is not that linguists disagree on what roles there are; that is, on the exact specification of the small set of conventional relationships (quite likely a property of all languages) in terms of which a large portion of semantic structure is organized. The significant thing is that as studies of role systems continue, there seems to be a convergence in the findings of different scholars. Given the application of the idea to more and more languages, and in greater and greater depth in some languages, there seems to be an empirical shaking down of the idea of roles or cases to within the limits that normally apply to two scholars ever agreeing on anything.

Another aspect of role systems that contributes to an effect of imprecision is the likelihood that some behave differently from others. As we shall see, there is reason to believe that at the deeper levels of semantics, instrument and benefactive are themselves lexical predicates that are superordinate to the lexical base element with which they are associated. Later they are transformed in such a way that from there on they behave like the other roles. Furthermore, some role relationships may themselves be semantically more similar than others. Frantz, for example, recognizes that for certain purposes source, noninstigative cause, and instrument act indistinguishably; at that point he treats them as a more comprehensive role labelled means.[21] In the same way, the experiencer and goal roles were lumped together as dative in Fillmore's 1968 paper, but later split; yet there are times when it may be convenient to have an undifferentiated dative role that includes both.

3. ORIENTATION ROLES

This list of roles derives from the literature I have cited. I have

---

[21] Frantz, *Blackfoot* (1970), p. 161.

modified my earlier lists as a result of discussions with Gloria Risser Poedjosoedarmo, who has pointed out the need for distinguishing orientation roles from process roles and in general has provided a healthy critique of earlier role formulations. Donald Frantz has also contributed by putting his finger on the complementary properties of pairs of relations, and Bruce Hollenbach has suggested how to tighten up the agentive complex. What I give here is the kind of synthesis in which the good ideas are to be attributed to them and the bad ones to me.

Words like *flow* and *sit* have to do primarily with motion and position. The first is DYNAMIC, having to do with change of position. The second is STATIC. They communicate information about physical alignment. The roles that go with them are ORIENTATION roles.

Object (O) identifies the thing that is moving in the dynamic case, or the thing that is in a particular position in the static case. *Water (O) flows downhill; a statue (O) sits on a pedestal.* The object is the thing whose orientation to its physical environment is given by the predicate.

Source (S) applies to motions but not positions. It identifies the location of the object at the beginning of the motion, the initial boundary of the event. *The letter (O) fell from her hand (S)* indicates that as the event began, the letter was in the position defined by *her hand.* Motion implies that when the event ended the object was somewhere else.

Goal (G) also applies to motions but not positions. It identifies the location of the object at the end of the motion, the terminal boundary of the event. *The letter (O) fell to the floor (G)* indicates that as the event ended, the letter was in the position defined by *the floor.*[22]

---

[22]   The term *goal*, used as a role label, should not be confused with the use of the term by Bloomfield (*Language*, 1933) and others to mean 'grammatical object', often in the explicit sense of object as patient. I take it that this usage reflected their dissatisfaction with traditional labels of surface grammar at that time before much progress had been made in separating out surface categories from the underlying semantic relationships they express. In the same way, *object* as a role does not necessarily match the grammatical category of object.

Some languages have goal expressions that differ according whether the goal is defined by something inanimate, as in French *allons à l'opéra* 'let's go to the opera', or by something animate, as in *allons chez George* 'let's go to George's'.

In English goal does not seem to be the counterpart of what have been traditionally called purpose clauses. The purpose relationship has to be classified as rhetorical (Chapter 6) because it can coexist with goal, as in

Ride a cock horse to Banbury Cross,
To see a fine lady upon a white horse.

Banbury Cross is the goal, and *to see* ... stands in a still different relationship to *ride*.

Omie has a role relationship called TELIC that is distinct from goal yet still expressed within the compass of a single clause, which is not the case with the English purpose clause.[23] (English sentences like *he called to his wife for coffee* may make it necessary to consider a distinct telic role as well unless *coffee* can be subsumed under referent.)

Range (R) is the term I have chosen, following Halliday, for the relationship that others have labeled locative, locus, place, or site, since those terms are easily confused with the notion of setting (Chapter 4).[24] In an expression of motion, range indicates the path or area traversed, as in *the ball* (O) *rolled down the gutter* (R). With position, range indicates static location, as in *his house* (O) *is situated on top of a hill* (R) or *lever A* (O) *extends past pin B* (R).

Range is the only role associated with a class of predicates that can be called AMBIENT or meteorological. *Ithaca* (R) *is cold* has a close paraphrase *it is cold in Ithaca* (R) which sets it apart from *ice* (patient, explained in the next section) *is cold*, which has no analogous paraphrase. The *it* is a dummy subject that does not reflect any role element.

There is a question about whether a temporal role might not be

23 John Austing, "Semantic Relationships in Omie" (ms).
24 Halliday, "Notes on Transitivity and Theme, Part 1" (1967).

needed for a relation that is similar to range but is time oriented. The strongest evidence for it comes in ambient predicates. Although forms like *last week* (R) *was rainy* and *it was rainy last week* (R) fit the range pattern, this is not so easy to maintain for others: *Brisbane* (R) *is sizzling in January* (T?), *January* (T?) *is sizzling in Brisbane* (R), and *it is sizzling in January* (T?) *in Brisbane* (R) are difficult to account for and might force the recognition of a temporal role.

My current way out is to suggest that the last example is a thematically reduced counterpart of *when it is January* (R), *it is sizzling in Brisbane* (R) in which the temporal clause *when it is January* attaches to the simpler predication *it is hot in Brisbane*. One piece of evidence to support this is the awkwardness of a similar counterpart that begins **where it is Brisbane, ...* together with the observation that setting predicates can in general be expressed both in separate clauses and in a form parallel to that used for range elements. This is the case in *she knitted the socks on the porch*, in which *on the porch* is not a component of the meaning of *knit*, but has a counterpart *while she was on the porch, she knitted the socks*. A true range element could not be put into a separate clause in this way; something like **when it is on top of a hill, his house is situated* does not work.

Vehicle (V) is the final orientation role. It refers to something that conveys the object and moves along with it, as in *the letter* (O) *came by plane* (V) or *the tide* (V) *floated the oil slick* (O) *into the harbor* (G). Keith Dawson, in a personal communication, points out that it is often difficult to distinguish between vehicle and range, especially if the vehicle is a mass noun like *land, sea, air*.

These orientation roles are defined in spatial terms. They also have a nonspatial or metaphorical area of meaning in which the linguistic form is appropriate for movement but semantically nothing moves: *this idea* (O) *came to me* (G) *from Austin Hale* (S), *the tune* (O) *kept running through his brain* (R). The reason for keeping these as orientation roles rather than trying to analyze them in some other way is linguistic, not philosophical. It is simply that the forms of expression that are used in these cases are never distinct from the forms of expression that clearly spatial forms can have: *a breeze* (O) *came to him* (G) *from the sea* (R), *the ball* (O) *kept rolling around the wheel* (R).

4. PROCESS ROLES

A second set of roles, which I refer to as PROCESS roles, is independent of orientations to motion or position. Instead they have to do on the dynamic side with changes of state, and on the static side with stable states.

Patient (P) is the central role in the process system just as object is in the orientation system. It is the relation between a thing that gets changed and the process that changes it, or in the static sense, between a thing that is in some state and the state it is in. Quite a list of names has been used for this role: patient, objective, neutral, affected, theme, and undergoer are the most frequently used ones.

The exact way the patient relates to a process or state depends on what that process or state is. This gives the impression that there are many different patient-like relations, when in fact it is more profitable to assume a single relation that is tempered by the process or state it goes with.

Even though the meaning of the patient depends upon the predicate with which it is associated, there are areas of meaning that are characteristic of it. First comes that of the thing that undergoes a process, whether gradual as in *the snowflake* (P) *melted* or abrupt as in *the foundation* (P) *cracked*. As we shall see later, there may be a responsible agent on the other end of the process who brings about the change; from this end, however, it is still a process. In *the chef* (agent) *melted the butter* (P) compared with *the butter* (P) *melted*, we want to be able to say that the same thing is happening to the butter in both instances.

Processes end, leaving the things that undergo them in some terminal state. This state is the bridge between patient as undergoer of a process and patient as that which is in a particular state. In English, though by no means in all languages, the patient of a state takes a special grammatical form involving *be* as in *the snow-flake* (P) *is white, the foundation* (P) *is cracked.* Here there is also a morphological affinity between the expression of some processes like *crack* and the expression of the state that results when the process has ended, as in *cracked.*

Psychological processes such as perception and feeling employ the patient relation to identify who it is that perceives or feels: *I hear, I am dizzy, I am furious.* Formerly I followed Fillmore in assigning this relation to a special role called experiencer; but Hollenbach in a personal communication points out that the real reason this was done was because the patient role was already taken for the stimulus of the perception. If the stimulus is assigned to another role, the referent, this leaves patient available for the one who undergoes a perception or whose psychological state is described.

The most characteristic mark that distinguishes patient from range is that while a patient typically is changed in form by a process, range is not affected in any parallel way. Range is, how-ever, essential to the meaning of the predicate to which it belongs; it cannot be separated off in a dependent clause that establishes a setting.

For example, Halliday points out that *the street* in *they crossed the street* stands in a different relation to the action than it does in *they paved the street.* In the first the street provides orientation for motion, while in the second something happens to the street.[25] This is shown also by the readiness with which *pave* accepts the passive: *the street was paved by them. Cross* is awkward in the passive, unless it is taken in another sense that requires a patient, namely 'paint a cross on something', in which case *the street was crossed by them* is acceptable.

Even though it is difficult at times to know whether one is dealing with patient or range, there is evidence that they must be kept separate in some situations. In a number of languages of the Philippines the distinction is essential for one class of verbs in which

[25]   Halliday, "Notes on Transitivity and Theme, Part 1" (1967).

range and patient (or object in the orientation sense) are mutually identifying. Ashley finds a category of verbs in Tausug called FIELD OF ACTION verbs in which the range designates either the field where the action takes place or the field of which the patient (or object) is a member or component. The patient is not mentioned explicitly, but is some element that is chosen from the field identified by the range. The resultant meaning is partitive: *drink I water* (R) 'I will drink some of the water'. The patient counterpart is also possible, but has a different meaning in which the patient is treated as a whole, not as part of a range: *drink I water* (P) 'I will drink the water up' implies total rather than partial action.[26]

Material (M) and result (Rs) identify the state of something before and after it undergoes a process. There seems to be a general constraint on these two roles that requires one or the other of them to combine with patient, so that although they can be recognized as distinct from each other, they are not as readily isolated as the other roles. *She* (A) *makes dresses* (PRs) *from flour sacks* (M) represents but a slightly different view of the matter from *she* (A) *makes flour sacks* (PM) *into dresses* (Rs). Chafe uses "complement" for the result relation. Others use "factitive" from Latin *facere* 'make'.[27]

Referent (Rf) distinguishes the limitation of a process to a certain field or object from the actual application of a process to a patient. *We* (agent) *talked about politics* (Rf) tells what our discussion was limited to; politics itself suffered no change as the result of the process. This role seems to provide a haven for certain expressions of extent as well: *this book* (P) *costs three dollars* (Rf).

[26] Ashley, "A Case Classification of Tausug Verbs" (ms). Unlike English, there is an overt difference in the surface forms of the two Tausug sentences given as examples. Range in a field of action verb maps to a surface grammatical category of Tausug known as REFERENT that is signalled under certain conditions by a REFERENT FOCUS inflection in the verb coupled with a phrase proclitic in the corresponding noun phrase. Patient and object, on the other hand, both map to the grammatical object category, signalled by a verbal inflection of OBJECT FOCUS that distinguishes it from surface referent.

[27] Chafe, *Meaning and the Structure of Language* (1970), p. 156.

5. THE AGENTIVE COMPLEX

Agent (A) identifies who is responsible for an action. *My wife* (A) *made the cake* (P) asserts both that the cake took shape and that my wife did something to bring it about. Agent occurs both with process roles, as in the last example, and with orientation roles, as in *the quarterback* (A) *threw the ball* (O).

Agents are often taken to be basically animate. To push this animateness, however, has messy consequences as far as the rules that relate role structure to grammatical form are concerned. Hollenbach points out that defining the agent as animate requires an extra rule for making an inanimate tool or instrument map to the subject position when there is no animate agent present. From *Fred* (A) *fixed the engine* (P) *with this screwdriver* (instrument) it is tempting to jump to the conclusion that the subject of *this screwdriver fixed the engine* is also in the instrument role, arguing partly from the fact that *Fred* is animate and *screwdriver* is not, and partly from the fact that the two sentences are paraphrases.

Although I do not propose to adopt his terminology, I think Robert F. Simmons's use of Causal Actant One and Causal Actant Two for distinguishing these relationships clarifies what is going on.[28] Both the screwdriver and Fred are involved in the process of fixing the engine. Fred, not the screwdriver, is cast as the one responsible for the action when they are mentioned together. Both are in a single chain of action, but are ranked within that chain. If only the screwdriver is mentioned, however, it is the only causal actant present, and so stands as the responsible element in the chain of action. In other words, if only one causal element is present, it is the agent regardless of whether it is animate or inanimate, and regardless of whether there is a paraphrase that refers to the same entity as instrument. If there are two causal elements, the one cast as the more responsible is the agent, and the other is the instrument. Putting more than two causal elements in a chain, as we shall see, overloads a single proposition and has

---

[28] Simmons, personal communication.

to be conceptualized in a different way in order to account for the surface constructions that are used to express such a situation.

For a number of languages a role like "causer" or "causative agent" has been proposed as part of the role system. English does not provide a strong motivation for looking at causatives in this way, since any expression that involves explicit causation has to make use of complement verbs such as *cause, have,* or *make,* and any that does not involve explicit causation can be treated like a regular agentive. In several languages of the Philippines, however, a distinction has been made between causer and agent in order to cover examples that correspond to English *Sally* (causer) *had John* (A) *set the table,* where John set the table but Sally instigated it. If we take Frantz's principle of proposition consolidation into account, however, this distinction becomes superfluous.[29] Causatives are analyzed semantically into a predicate on the order of *cause* that takes two arguments: an agent of its own, which corresponds to *Sally* in the example, and a result argument which is itself a lexical proposition, corresponding to *John set the table* in the example. This embedded proposition in turn has its own agent, *John.* Under certain conditions (discussed in Chapter 24.3) a transformation known as PROPOSITION CONSOLIDATION applies, giving as its result a single pseudo-proposition in which *Sally* now appears as the sole agent as far as later transformations are concerned; for example, *Sally* is the subject of the output sentence. Moreover, in the subsequent application of transformations, the word *John* is no longer treated grammatically as though it came from an agent at all, but more as though it had come from a semantic goal. Proposition consolidation (11.2) results in the pseudo-proposition that contains the causative having some characteristics that also underly sentences like *Sally* (A) *handed John* (G) *the biscuits* (O) along with characteristics of *John* (A) *set the table.*

An equally strong reason for not making the agent of a causative into a separate role is that it leads to infinite regress. In *Mother made Sally have John set the table,* Mother instigates the action

29 Frantz, *Blackfoot* (1970).

and John is the agent who performs it; but a third role would have to be set up for Sally. Since there is no principle that allows us to limit the depth of embedding of causatives, neither is there a limit on the number of causer-like roles that would have to be recognized as distinct. Even if there were several, the semantic relationship of each of them to the causative would be identical.[30] It is therefore preferable to recognize that the apparent twosidedness of the role structure of *John* in the example (the "double function" Pike[31] attributes to such elements) can be accounted for by assuming proposition consolidation. The semantic distinctiveness of agents that are embedded within causative expressions is blurred as a consequence of getting them arranged into linear form for transmission in speech.

Instrument (I) or tool has already been mentioned in relation to the agent. Whereas the agent role does not necessarily imply animateness, however, as in Hollenbach's example *the locomotive* (A) *cleared the track* (P or R) *with a snowplow* (I), the instrument role does imply inanimateness. If a person, for example, or part of a person's body is used in the instrument role, it is his body as an object that is referred to, not the person acting independently. *Superman broke the window with the gangster* means that he heaved the gangster's body through the window. The gangster, it is understood, had nothing to say about it.

In some languages the instrument role implies that the tool used is equivalent to an object in motion, and that its goal is the patient, as in *he* (A) *parted the rope* (P G) *with an axe* (O I).[32] English,

---

[30]   English has a variety of lexical predicates with causative meanings: *cause, have, make,* and even *bring about.* In languages like Huichol where explicit causative verb stems are less frequent than morphological markers of the causative relation, it is correspondingly less tempting to sidestep the question of multiple layers of causative embedding by focusing on the things that distinguish, say, *cause* from *make* and *make* from *have.* The point at issue is not the obvious fact that in English these do not mean the same thing. What is important here is rather the extent to which they behave identically.

[31]   Pike, *Language* (1967), p. 574.

[32]   Hettick, "Verb Stem Classes in Northern Kankanay" (ms.).

however, permits instruments that involve no motion: *he* (A) *convinced the jury* (P) *with a syllogism* (I).

The instrument role may actually arise through proposition consolidation in the same way that agents of causatives may appear as distinct-looking roles. If instruments do result from consolidation, that goes a long way toward explaining how they are secondary to the associated agents, because each proposition that is consolidated requires an agent of its own which must be coreferential with the agent of the base predicate.

Figure 8.1 illustrates this concept of the status of the instrument role. It involves a predicate *use* which has an agent who uses a patient to bring about a result, which is the BASE proposition that we normally think of as having the main lexical content. This predicate can consolidate with *use* to give the effect of a new role element in the structure of the base predicate.

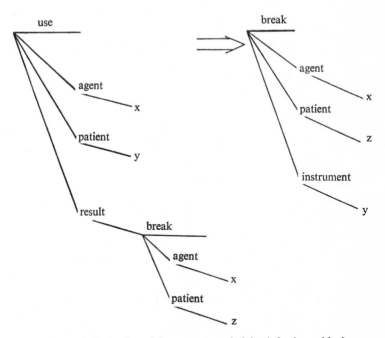

Figure 8.1 Derivation of the structure underlying 'x broke z with y'.

There are, however, cases in which consolidation does not take place, with the result that *use* remains as a full lexical predicate whose complement contains the base proposition. Constructions like these are what force us to think in terms of structures like the left hand side of Figure 8.1 in the first place. Otherwise, as seems to be the case with the patient role, the question of consolidation would never come up. Unconsolidated structures leave us, unfortunately, with the job of accounting for why the consolidation transformation fails to apply in some cases, so that instead of getting *x broke z with y* we get the unconsolidated *x used y to break z*.

Although at one time it was considered adequate to label transformations like proposition consolidation as optional, there now seems to be more to it than that. In our current concept, trans-

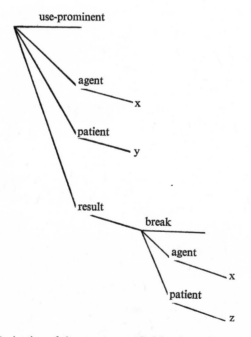

Figure 8.2 Derivation of the structure underlying 'x used y to break z', with consolidation blocked.

formations are part of the machinery of expression and hence cannot contribute anything to meaning. Yet there is a difference in meaning between the consolidated and the unconsolidated forms. It is a difference either in the prominence the speaker places on the instrument y or in the deliberateness with which the agent x uses y. I have diagrammed this possibility in Figure 8.2 by adding a special predicate *prominent* to *use*. If this is a valid way to characterize what is different about the meanings of the two sentences,[33] then the presence of the element *prominent* can be taken to block the consolidation transformation.

Looked at in another way, an element like *prominent* as used here appears to be equivalent to choosing a marked member of a set of similar predicates, say, *use actively* as opposed to a colorless *use*. The unmarked *use* allows consolidation to the instrument role form, while the marked counterpart blocks consolidation and yields the surface verb *use*.

Force (Fc) or noninstigative cause is similar to both source and instrument but must be kept distinct from both because its surface expressions are never quite the same as either of the other two.[34] It asserts a causal relation devoid of responsibility. It is incompatible with both agent and instrument. In relation to surface structure, moreover, force assumes a form that cannot be paralleled by anything in the agentive complex. For example, *kill* is generally the agentive counterpart of *die: the girl* (P) *died, the gangster* (A) *killed the girl* (P). The noninstigative *malaria* (Fc) *killed the girl* (P), however, has a counterpart in *the girl* (P) *died of* (or *from*) *malaria* (Fc) which requires a different preposition than would be permitted

---

[33] *Prominent* might attach instead to the predicate *patient* that is associated with y to represent the role relation as part of the structure. In either case, its effect is to inhibit consolidation. Note that it is a predicate of no arguments (13.1). I suspect that at the deepest level it comes from the staging or thematic system. Another possibility is to regard *use* as the kind of predicate which, like the neutral rhetorical predicates of Chapter 14, can have either a paratactic or a hypotactic form, depending on how a particular relationship is staged. "Instrument" would then be the name for the hypotactic form of the same predicate which in its paratactic form is lexicalized as *use*.

[34] Frantz, *Blackfoot* (1970).

either with an instrument *(with)* or an agent *(by)*. *?The girl* (P) *died of the gangster* is intelligible, but inappropriate for the claim that the gangster was agent. It implies rather that she found his presence mortally insufferable, and finds its closest parallel in something like *I'm* (P) *sick of his presence* (Fc) or *his presence* (Fc) *sickens me* (P).

Agent, instrument, and force share enough similarities that they can sometimes be spoken of as members of a single agentive complex. In the absence of special reasons for thematizing something else, for example, they take priority over all other roles in mapping to the grammatical position of subject. In athematic position, when some other role is subject, they are characteristically differentiated by prepositions: *by* for agent, *with* for tool, and *of*, *from*, *on*, or *in*, depending upon the action, for force.

A benefactive (B) or applicative role appears to stand outside both the orientation and the process role systems just as the main agentive complex stands outside of both. The term "benefactive" is a little misleading in spite of its widespread acceptance, since the relation includes what might be called malefactive: someone or something on whom an action has a secondary effect, good or ill. Benefactive could be considered a supernumerary role in that it can be attached to almost anything: *we chased the cats out of the attic for her*, *the milk turned sour on me*, *two plus two refuses to equal four for me*, ad infinitum.

A number of languages of West Africa regularly express the benefactive by a form of the verb meaning 'give' and an object, even when it has a malefactive sense.[35] We find the same thing in Saramaccan, a creole language of Surinam, which has sentences like *hɛ́n fufuu-man ko fufuu* DA-ƐƐN *suni fu-ɛn* (then steal-man come steal GIVE-HIM thing for-him) 'then a thief came and stole his things from him'.[36]

Like the instrument role, it seems best to consider the benefactive as a separate predicate that becomes consolidated with the base

---

[35] Pike, *Tagmemics ... in African Languages* (1966).
[36] Grimes and Glock, "Saramaccan" (1970).

predicate to which it is attached. If so, I would take it to have three arguments: an agent, which must be coreferential with the agent of the base predicate as in the case of the instrument, then a referent that indicates who the action affects, and finally a patient, which is the proposition that contains the base predicate itself.

Benefactive appears to violate a general constraint that permits at most one argument of any role type in a proposition. In *I was in the pool and he drained the water out on me* (B) *for his friend* (B), suggested by Nancy Lightfoot, there are two benefactives. If benefactive is not a separate role at the deepest level, however, the generally useful one-per-proposition constraint on roles remains intact, and we explain the double benefactive as the result of unrestricted consolidation.

6. ORIENTATION-PROCESS COUNTERPARTS

The roles set up for orientation have counterparts on the process side, and vice versa. Both kinds could be considered complementary variants of a single set of roles. Donald Frantz has already pointed out the close relationship between source and goal on the one hand and material and result on the other, and has suggested collapsing them into two dynamic and therefore time oriented roles called FORMER (F) and LATTER (L), representing the beginning and ending points of either a motion or a process.[37] Object and patient both identify what is affected, the one in terms of motion or position and the other in terms of change of state in a process. It requires no great exercise of the imagination to unite range and referent on the same basis. Agent and instrument, as we have noted, are free to go with either orientation or process predicates as causal factors, with a slight asymmetry in that both agent and instrument are incompatible with force. Neither, however, seems to be incompatible with vehicle. This leaves vehicle as the only orientation role without a process counterpart.

[37] Landerman and Frantz, *Notes on Grammatical Theory* (1972), p. 66.

A second factor is pertinent to the discussion: regardless of whether orientation or process roles are involved, the maximum number of role relations that seems to enter into the semantics of any lexical item in English or in any of the other languages for which the idea has been tried out is eight if we push the limit: for example, *we* (AS) *carried the supplies* (O) *all the way up* (G) *the cliff* (R) *for them* (B) *on our backs* (V) *with a rope* (I), which pulls out all the stops in the system.

Both this limitation on number and the complementarity of pairs of roles suggest a combined role scheme like that of Figure 8.3. There the orientation roles, the process roles, and the four that need be considered neither orientation nor process, are lined up and given a unified set of role labels. The exact meaning of those roles that combine is then dependent on a characteristic of the predicate with which they are used: orientation, either as motion or as position, or process, either as pure process or as state. Since it is likely that for purposes of distinguishing settings from events in discourse, motion and position need to be specified for lexical predicates anyway, and process and state have to be distinguished in relation to identification, we have a more compact system.

At the same time, it may be useful for some things to retain the orientation and process role labels as distinct. For example, Poedjosoedarmo in a personal communication points out that in conveyance verbs such as 'throw' in Javanese, and in their Philippine counterparts, there is an object that moves away from the agent, who is also source. An instrument is optional, or in some of the languages, grammatically incompatible. On the other hand, change

Orientation	→	Combined	←	Process
		A agent	Fc force	
		I instrument		
V vehicle	→	V vehicle		
O object	→	P patient	←	P patient
S source	→	F former	←	M material
G goal	→	L latter	←	Rs result
R range	→	R range	←	Rf referent
		B benefactive		

Figure 8.3 Interrelationships among roles.

of state verbs like 'break' involve a patient whose state is changed without its moving. There is a tool, which is handled grammatically as though it, rather than the patient, were an object that moves away from the agent as source toward a goal, which is the patient. Verbs with meanings like 'throw' are AS OP G (I) on the one hand, and verbs like 'break' are AS PG IO on the other. From here on, however, unless there is a particular reason for splitting them, I propose to use the combined terminology of the middle column of Figure 8.3.

As is evident from some of the examples already given, the same referent may appear in more than one role at the same time. Thus the agent of *send* is simultaneously the former state where the thing moved starts out, and the agent of *borrow* is simultaneously the latter state where it ends up. There are pairs of words in English (and in some other languages as well) that differ in meaning principally in the way the roles are combined: *sell* AF P L and *buy* AL P F, *lend* AF P L and *borrow* AL P F, *put* AF P L and *get* AL P F. The lexical counterparts of these words in other languages, however, may not be as specialized, but may take the form of a word like *transact* A P in which the direction of the transaction has to be specified separately.

Verbs of motion typically combine agent and patient. That is, the patient of *go* or *run* or *walk* is the same as the agent if there is an agent. Different lexical items are used when the object is distinct from the agent: *transport* separates the two.

Range and patient appear to combine in a form like *Ezra Cornell* (A) *lived in this house* (PR) or *this house* (PR) *was lived in by Ezra Cornell* (A). The lack of a parallel passive for *Ezra Cornell* (A) *lived in this state* (R) suggests that the latter involves range only, while *house* is patient as well, as though something had happened to the house but not the state as a result of Ezra's residence there.

Mamanwa of the Philippines has two kinds of predicates that combine agent and former orientation.[38] In one, the patient starts

---

[38] Jeanne Miller, "Semantic Structure of Mamanwa Verbs" (1973).

out where the agent is, but separates from the agent in the course of the action, as in *ambaligzà hao ka makaen kan Mariya* 'I (AF) will sell the food (P) to Mary (L)'. The other kind not only has the patient begin the action where the agent is; the action by its nature involves the agent moving along with the patient, as in *iolì nao ining baskit doro kan Robirto* 'I (AF) will return this basket (P) there to Robert (L)'. The range of possible clause forms that express these predicates of accompaniment is distinct from the forms for agent-former predicates that assert separation.

As already mentioned, a number of languages of the Philippines have a PARTITIVE form like 'he brought rice from the field' that implies that some rice remains behind in the field. The partitive contrasts with a total action like 'he harvested the rice', which implies that he brought all the rice from the field. This partitive effect seems to arise from a principle of mutual definition between range and patient.[39]

If the field of action is denoted by the range role, the patient is taken implicitly to be one or more of the things that normally belong in the field of action. In a sentence meaning 'I'll peel some of the mangos', for example, the grammatical form of 'mangos' is such that it has to be understood as range; this might be 'where the mangos are is where I'll do the peeling'. No patient can be expressed overtly if this meaning is to be conveyed. Nevertheless, mangos are what the action happens to; they get peeled. This could be taken as an obligatory application of the principle mentioned in Chapter 11 that if a role element is culturally conventional or is predictable from the context, it need not be expressed.

These role combinations are part of the regular meaning of certain words like *go* and *borrow*. Normally, however, each role element is expressed apart from the rest. Nevertheless, it sometimes comes about in a particular situation that two role elements denote the same thing even though in the normal meaning of the predicate involved they are not expected to be the same. The REFLEXIVE mechanism is used to express a referential identity that arises from

---

[39]   Ashley, "A Case Classification of Tausug Verbs" (ms).

the situation being talked about rather than from the meaning of the words used. For example, *cut* takes an agent and a patient that are normally distinct. For a particular instance of *cut*, however, it may turn out that the agent and the patient are asserted by the reflexive to have the same referent, as in *he cut himself*.

The compass for the expression of role relationships in surface structure is usually the clause. A predicate whose meaning is partly defined in terms of role relationships often corresponds to the verb of a clause, a predicate adjective, or a predicate nominal, while the role elements that go with it correspond to the subject, object, and prepositional phrases of various kinds. Still more restricted expressions of role relationships are possible in noun phrases: *the queen of England* (R), *his* (P) *idea*, *a ski* (I) *race*. Frequently the nominal form involves suppression of certain roles; the noun *race* implies that there are people racing against each other using skis, but neither the agent nor the range is expressed along with it.

Clauses may themselves, of course, be embedded within other clauses and compressed in various forms. Lexical propositions (that is, propositions whose predicates are lexical predicates, defined largely in terms of role relationships) may therefore be expressed not only as independent clauses but as dependent clauses like *when we get home*, or as embedded clauses like *who cut down the tree* in *the workman who cut down the tree*. Langendoen discusses the appropriateness of bringing adjectives like *sick* in *a sick elephant* or nouns like *man* in *the man*, which may correspond to a more explicit identificational form like *the one who is a man*, into the propositional scheme.[40]

Even though role relationships typically appear within the clause, the same relationships may at times be expanded into grammatical forms considerably larger than the clause itself. John Austing describes how the expression of some role relationships in Omie

---

[40] Langendoen, *The Study of Syntax* (1969), *Essentials of English Grammar* (1970).

takes one form within the clause and another form between stretches of speech that involve more than single clauses.[41]

A study of the lexical propositions of any language shows up sets of predicates that are similar in meaning but that differ from each other in specifiable ways that find parallels in other sets of predicates. The principle by which parallel sets of predicates are grouped together is that of ROLE SETS (Fillmore's case frames), which will be discussed in more detail in Chapter 10.2. All predicates that take, say, an agent, a patient, a latter state, and an instrument have the same role set. It is likely that any predicate in this group will have a second role set consisting of patient and latter state alone, and a third role set consisting of patient, latter state, and force: as an example of the first, take *the host* (A) *broke the ice* (P) *into small pieces* (L) *with a machine* (I); the second, *the ice* (P) *broke into slivers* (L); the third, *the ice* (P) *broke into floes* (L) *from the thaw* (Fc). These three role sets are systematically related; the differences among them are reflected in many other predicates as well.[42]

---

[41]   John Austing, "Semantic Relationships in Omie" (ms).
[42]   Ray S. Jackendoff's *Semantic Interpretation in Generative Grammar* (Cambridge: MIT Press, 1972) came to my attention after this book went to press. He makes some important observations about roles. His use of "theme" for patient is consistent, and therefore should not cause any difficulty with my use of the same term in staging.

9

SEMANTIC DERIVATION

To continue on with the low level content relationships out of which the more extensive semantic complexes of discourse are built, we turn to some of the relationships among role sets. These relationships can be expressed by the notion of SEMANTIC DERIVATION, in which a BASE predicate that carries what we think of informally as the main meaning is combined with one or more of a small number of what Frantz calls ABSTRACT predicates. These predicates are abstract in the sense that they are normally expressed only in combination with base predicates, whereas the base predicates can be expressed independently of any abstract predicates. It is convenient to treat most predicates that are expressed by affixes as abstract predicates; but in addition some abstract predicates have no phonological form of their own. What is an abstract predicate in one language might not be one in another, though there seems to be great consistency in the abstract status of at least a few. Abstract predicates include the developmental that relates *red* and *redden*, the agentive that relates *the water boiled* to *we boiled the water*, and others that are taken up later.

Before discussing the kinds of abstract predicates that can take part in a semantic derivation, it is useful to categorize base predicates according to some common semantic characteristics. Some predicates denote states, like *cold* and *sit*. Others denote processes, like *melt* and *rain*. Still others denote motions like *walk*, or motionless actions like *cough*. Others combine actions and processes, like *bend* and *throw*. Finally, some predicates denote experiences, like *hear*. Whether every predicate fits into one of these categories remains to be seen; but these are common enough that they keep turning up in semantic discussions.[1] They relate regularly to lexical roles, but not in a one-to-one way: states and processes both take patients, actions take an agent, action-processes take an agent for the action component and a patient for the process component, and experiences take a patient with or without a range. Some states, which correspond to the ones Chafe labels AMBIENT, take range but not patient. Some of the meteorological predicates mentioned in the last chapter are ambient states like *hot* and *cold*. There are also ambient processes with range but no patient: *rain* and *snow* in the sense that are expressed as verbs tell what is happening in a region, but do not assert that there is something it is happening to.

The first abstract predicate to be combined with base predicates is the DEVELOPMENTAL predicate.[2] The developmental denotes a process that is defined by the state that results. *Redden*, for example, denotes a process of color change that has as its terminal point the state *red*.

The inverse of the developmental derivation is the RESULTATIVE. It denotes a state that is defined by the process that brings it about. Most expressions of the resultative in English take the form of a past participle: *frozen* denotes a state that is the end point of the process *freeze*, and something that is *molten* or *melted* (depending, evidently, on how expensive it is) is the result of a process called *melt*. Resultatives from developmentals are also possible, like *reddened*, but there appear to be no developmentals derived from resultatives. In several languages of Nigeria there appears to be a preponderance of process lexical items over state words, the exact reverse of the situation in English. Resultatives are correspondingly common (including words meaning 'big' derived from 'grow', for example), and developmentals almost nonexistent.

---

[1] Chafe, *Meaning and the Structure of Language* (1970).
[2] Most linguists who write about semantic derivation have used the term *inchoative* for developmental. Since that term has a long prior history in classical grammar, used in an aspectual sense that denotes an action that is getting under way or being undertaken, I prefer to leave it as an equivalent to *inceptive* or *ingressive*, and use *developmental* instead for change of state.

The AGENTIVE abstract predicate adds an action component and the corresponding agent role to a process. In English there is a process predicate *break* as in *the rope* (P) *broke*. It has an agentive counterpart, in this case phonologically identical, that gives an action-process as in *the miner* (A) *broke the rope* (P). The process to which the action is added may itself be the result of a semantic derivation like the developmental, as in *the chef* (A) *reddened the frosting* (P). The agentive abstract predicate adds the possibility of an instrument as well as an agent, along with force in the normal way, so that we can best consider that the agentive derivation adds the whole agentive role complex: *The chef* (A) *reddened the frosting* (P) *with pomegranate juice* (I), and also *the crocodile's blood* (Fc) *reddened the water* (P).

Before going ahead with the discussion of other abstract predicates it might be wise to pause and develop a means of representing base and abstract predicates. The full scheme of representation will be discussed in Chapter 13. Here, as in the discussion of proposition consolidation given in connection with the instrument role in the last chapter, a proposition is represented as a tree. For typographic convenience it is turned on its side, with the root toward the left and the leaves toward the right. Predicates, whether base or abstract, are underlined and written immediately above the nodes that they dominate. Predicate and arguments together represent the entire proposition of which each is a part. The arguments that go with a predicate are represented by nodes beneath it, connected to the predicate itself. Role relationships are represented as one argument predicates. Some arguments could be broken down further into propositions, but are not because their further analysis is not pertinent to the example in which they appear. These unanalyzed propositions are simply cited in their output (phonological) form. Figure 9.1 shows the relationships of abstract and base predicates and roles in the state *red*, and process *redden*, and the action-process *redden*.

The CAUSATIVE abstract predicate has already been discussed in relation to the agent role. It takes its own agent, independently of the agent of the base predicate that it dominates. Its latter state

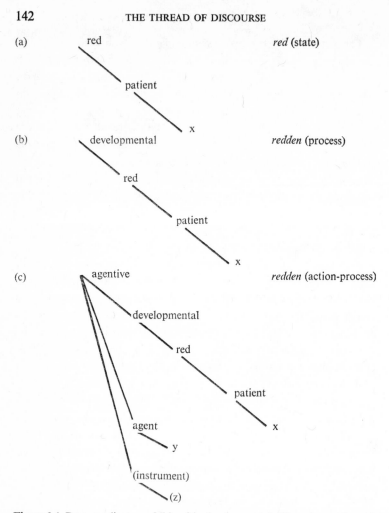

Figure 9.1 Base predicate *red* (a) with developmental (b) and agentive (c) semantic derivations.

argument is the proposition that contains the base predicate. When the transformation of proposition consolidation is applied, the causative agent is made the agent of the resultant proposition and the agent of the base predicate is shifted to another role; that is, for subsequent transformations that apply to the consolidated proposition, the agent of the base predicate is treated as though it were in the patient, benefactive, or latter role (depending on the role structure of the base predicate and probably on the language) when the role-related arguments are matched to surface grammatical categories. As far as I know causative abstract predicates never dominate state predicates directly, but only through the developmental derivation. They combine readily with process and action-process predicates, and may also combine with action and experience predicates. This is illustrated in Huichol, which has the following forms:

zúure 'red', state.
zʌʌ 'run out, terminate', process.
míe 'go', action.
qee or *qéi* 'carry in the hand', action-process.
zéiya 'see', experience.[3]

The abstract predicates are manifested in surface forms by affixes or by specialized verb phrases:

-ya or *-ríya* 'agentive'.
-tʌa 'causative', a suffix which is similar in its phonological form to one stem of 'go'.
state-*tʌ p-áa + -tʌa* (state-ing did-this-way-go) 'get to be in such and such a state; developmental' (this could be considered a specialized idiom).

The following forms illustrate possible combinations of base pred-

---

3 See Grimes, *Huichol Syntax* (1964) for a fairly complete description of Huichol surface forms. The sounds of Huichol are stops *p t c (ts) k q (kʷ)* ʔ, fricative *z* (retroflex), nasals *m n*, flap *r*, semivowels *w y h*, vowels *a e i u ʌ* (high back unrounded). Double vowels are rhythmically long. Each syllable (CV, CVV) is high (') or low (no accent) in tone. Foot boundaries are indicated by + or by word space. Huichol is a Uto-Aztecan language spoken in the states of Jalisco and Nayarit, Mexico.

icates and abstract predicates. X, Y, and Z are used instead of nouns to keep the examples short. Modal, aspectual, object, and directional affixes are used as needed, and morphophonemic changes are made without further explanation. Hyphens separate morphemes:

X p_Λ-zúure 'X is red', state.

Y p-íi+-zuuríi-ya X 'Y turned X red', agentive.

X zúu+ré-t$_\Lambda$ p-aa+-t$_\Lambda$a 'X turned red', developmental.

Y X zuu+ré-me p-áa+-yéi-t$_\Lambda$a 'Y caused X to turn red', causative (-me indicates lack of surface subject agreement between components of the developmental phrase, whereas -t$_\Lambda$ shows surface subject agreement. yéi is the stem form of 'go' in its developmental use that is appropriate in the causative).

?Z p-íi+-zuuríi+-yá-t$_\Lambda$a Y X 'Z caused Y to turn X red', causative of agentive; is plausible but grammatically over-loaded in most contexts.

X p-úu+-ti-z$_{\Lambda\Lambda}$ 'X ran out; there is no more X', process.

?Y p-íi+-z$_{\Lambda\Lambda}$-ríiya X 'Y terminated X', agentive (sounds forced).

Y p-íi+-z$_{\Lambda\Lambda}$-t$_\Lambda$a X 'Y caused X to run out', causative of process; for example, 'Y ate up all his corn supply (X)'.

X p_Λ-míe 'X is going', action.

?X Puu-míe-t$_\Lambda$ p-aa+-t$_\Lambda$a 'X got under way', causative of action; sounds unnecessarily periphrastic, but does carry the inchoative idea of beginning an action.

Y p-íi+-yeiká-cí+-t$_\Lambda$a X 'Y caused X to go' (yeiká with the connective -cí is the stem form of 'go' that is appropriate with the nondevelopmental causative).

Y p-é-i+-qei X 'Y carried X away in his hand', action-process.

Z p-é-i+-qéi-t$_\Lambda$a Y X 'Z caused Y to carry X away in his hand; Z gave X to Y', causative.

Y p-íi+-zéiya X 'Y sees X', experience.

Z p-íi+-zéi-cí-t$_\Lambda$a Y X 'Z caused Y to see X; Z showed X to Y', causative of experience.

Abstract predicates always leave a trace somewhere in the surface form, otherwise there would be no justification for recognizing them. In Huichol the trace is usually an affix. In English the trace that signals an underlying semantic configuration may be purely syntactic. Compare:

X is red (state).

X reddened (developmental, marked by -en, resulting in a process).

Y reddened X (agentive or causative, indicated syntactically).

Y made X redden (causative of abstract developmental).

Y made X turn red (causative of explicit, unconsolidated developmental).

Y made X red (causative, developmental implied but not expressed).

As mentioned earlier, the use of full words such as auxiliaries rather than affixes or zero to express abstract predicates in English probably reflects a higher degree of attention the speaker wishes to call to the abstract predicate itself.

There has been some discussion as to whether a causative abstract predicate is needed for English, or whether a simple agentive is sufficient to account for what goes on.[4] Discussion centers around the semantics of verbs like *kill*, which is semantically close to the phrase *cause to die* but not identical with it. This difference could be expressed by making *kill* simply the agentive counterpart of *die*, and leaving *cause to die* as an explicit causative that is never consolidated; in other words, the causative is not an abstract predicate in English.

Terena, an Arawakan language of southern Brazil,[5] has a system of morphological marking that shows that it is necessary to recognize both agentives and causatives in semantic derivation. For example, there is a stative stem *xuna* 'strong' that takes only a

---

4   For example, by McCawley.

5   Butler, "Verb Derivation in Terena" (ms).

patient as in *xúnati* 'he is strong'. This stem has an agentive counterpart with a prefix *ko-/ka-* 'agentive' and thematic suffixes *-k* and *-o*, together with a pronominal object suffix *-a* that represents the patient in the presence of the agent: *koxunákoati* 'he is strengthening it'. From the agentive form, however, a causative form can also be built: *ikoxúnakoati* 'he is causing it to be strong'. The difference in meaning is minimal; but in Terena it is regular throughout two classes of verbs.

The explicit indication of both an agentive and a causative derivation in Terena does not, of course, constitute a proof that all languages have both abstract predicates. It may be that English uses only the agentive, and that what corresponds to the Terena causative is parceled out in English semantics among the lexical predicates that are symbolized as *cause*, *make*, and *have*. These predicates cannot be consolidated, and are required to take sentence complement constructions.[6] On the other hand, since we are on the borders of what appear to be universal semantic relations that can be expected in all languages, perhaps our study of English to date has not been sufficiently profound to show how agentives and causatives are related in English semantics, whereas that distinction happens to be indicated obviously and consistently in Terena and is therefore easily noticed.

NONAGENTIVE probably needs to be given the status of abstract predicate as well. This semantic element takes away the agent that would normally be present in the proposition that it dominates, whether that proposition contains an action predicate, an action-process, or a causative complex.

There is a significant difference between a predicate which normally takes an agent but has had that agent suppressed by semantic derivation on the one hand, and a predicate which contains an agent semantically, yet the agent is not represented in the surface form because it is recoverable from the context on the other. In *they entered the room and found the box* there is no question

---

[6]   Rosenbaum, *The Grammar of English Predicate Complement Constructions* (1967).

as to who the agent corresponding to *found* is; by the regular deletion pattern of English it has to be *they* for both verbs of the conjunction. If, however, there is no agent, then English uses a passive-like construction: *many races were run in this arena, suppose the box is never found, finally the cargo got shipped out by air.* Even though the ordinary lexical content of the verbs involved suggests that it was people who ran the races, didn't find the box, or shipped the cargo, the reason no agents are expressed is not that they are recoverable from the context, as was the case in *they entered the room and found the box.* The agents are missing because they are irrelevant to the semantics of those particular sentences; to try to supply them from somewhere, even in the indefinite form of *by someone, by various people,* is beside the point of what is being said. The nonagentive abstract predicate expresses the speaker's decision that the agent should be eliminated from the semantic picture even though the base predicate normally takes an agent.

Nonagentives become clearer when we turn to languages where this kind of thing is indicated more explicitly. Most of the indigenous languages of the Americas have an inflectional pattern for verbs that is often called the passive voice. In very few languages, however, does the parallel with Indo-European passives hold; the Western hemisphere nonagentives (sometimes called pseudo-passives as well as passives) permit no expression of the agent. Corresponding to an expression like "John (A) cut the meat (P) with a knife (I)" there is a way of saying "the meat (P) got cut" or even "the meat (P) got cut with a knife (I)"; but it is quite rare to find a language on the west side of the Atlantic that permits "the meat (P) was cut by John (A)" or "the meat (P) was cut with a knife (I) by John (A)" within the bounds of a single clause. The nonagentive is more like the resultative inverse of the developmental derivation, in that it defines a state by telling the process, say cutting, that brought about the state, in contrast with the way the developmental defines a process by telling the state, say redness, that is the end result of the process.

The Huichol forms given a few pages back illustrate nonagentive derivation. In Huichol the nonagentive (indicated by *-ri* or *-ya*) requires the presence of at least a patient. There is no nonagentive counterpart to pure actions, as in the case of the English *many races* (L) *were run here*. I repeat the agentive forms given earlier to show how their nonagentive counterparts match. The noun surrogates X and Y are shifted around syntactically to eliminate the effects of a low level object deletion rule that might otherwise prove confusing.

> *X p-úu+-zúurii+-yá-*RI 'X got turned red'.
> (*Y p-íi+-zuuríi-ya* X 'Y turned X red', agentive.)
> *X zuu+ré-tʌ p-áa+-yéi+-tʌa-*RI 'X was caused to turn red', nonagentive causative of developmental.
> (*Y X zuu+ré-me p-aa+-yéi-tʌa* 'Y caused X to turn red', causative of developmental.)
> *?Y p-íi+-zuuríi+-yá-tʌa-*RI X 'Y got caused to turn X red', nonagentive of causative of agentive, an unlikely form.
> (*?Z p-íi+-zuurí+-yá-tʌa* Y X 'Z caused Y to turn X red', equally unlikely.)
> *?X p-úu+-zʌʌ-rii+-yá-*RI 'X got terminated', nonagentive of agentive of developmental.
> (*?Y p-íi+-zʌʌ-ríi-ya* X 'Y terminated X', agentive of developmental, sounds forced.)
> *X p-úu+-zʌʌ-tʌa-*RI, or more likely *X p-úu+-zʌʌ-cí-tʌa-*RI 'X was made to run out', nonagentive of causative of process.
> (*Y p-íi+-zʌʌ-tʌa* X 'Y caused X to run out', causative of process.)
> *?X p-úu+-yeiká-cí+-tʌa-*RI 'X was caused to go', nonagentive of causative of action.
> (*Y p-íi+-yeiká-cí-tʌa* X 'Y caused X to go', causative of action.)
> *X p-ée+-qée-*YA 'X got carried off', nonagentive of action-process.
> (*Y p-é-i+-qei* X 'Y carried X away in his hand', action-process.)
> *Y p-úu+-qéi+-tʌa-*RI X 'Y was caused to carry X away in

his hand, Y was given X', nonagentive of causative of action-process.

(*Z p-é-i+-qéi-tʌa Y X* 'Z caused Y to carry X away in his hand; Z gave X to Y', causative of action-process.)

*X p-úu-zéi+yá-*RI 'X got seen', nonagentive of experience.

(*Y p-íi+-zéiya X* 'Y saw X', experience.)

*Y p-úu-zéi-cí+-tʌa-*RI *X* 'Y was shown X', nonagentive of causative of experience.

(*Z p-íi+-zéi-cí-tʌa Y X* 'Z caused Y to see X; Z showed X to Y', causative of experience.)

The abstract predicates already discussed seem fairly well established.[7] Further thought needs to be given, however, to the status of what is readily recognized as a NOMINAL predicate. The nominal has the effect of treating a proposition as a named entity instead of as a relation.[8] The question that needs to be answered about the nominal has to do with the circumstances under which it is appropriate to nominalize. In terms of general discourse structure there is a discernible tendency for identificational information to be nominalized; but this is by no means the end of the matter. English, and the Indo-European languages in general, seem to favor the frequent use of nominalized propositions in a way that is shared by few other language families in the world. Where we would say *the explosion occurred at noon*, for example, the corresponding verb-oriented expression in many other languages would be on the order of "something exploded at noon".

One factor in the use of nominalizations seems to be the relative prominence of different propositional elements. Content elements that are more central to the staging of what is being said are less likely to be nominalized, while other content elements that are being given less attention are candidates for it. The use of nominali-

[7] Apresyan et al., "Semantics and Lexicography" (1969), list forty-seven "lexical functions", most of which might be described as abstract predicates. Some are associative relationships and some are lexical counterparts of thematic distinctions (Chapter 21).
[8] Winograd, *Procedures* (1971).

zations in discourse therefore seems to be related to thematization, discussed in Chapter 21.

Another way to approach nominalization is to notice that it ordinarily carries with it the notion of embodiment of a state. Every proposition is indexed as a whole, and can be referred to as a whole by means of words like *it* or *that*, and can be quantified. This referential permanence, by which we can keep referring back to the same state of affairs as easily as to the same object, may be a factor in the nominalization of propositions. Those propositions whose permanence as a referential entity the speaker wants to call attention to may be the ones he nominalizes; but considerable study is needed before we really understand how each of us "gives to airy nothing a local habitation and a name".

Referential permanence is part of the lexical structure of many predicates that are customarily expressed as nouns like *house* and *moment*. On the other hand, there may be a DENOMINAL abstract predicate which, in the same way as the nonagentive removes an agent, takes the element of referential continuity away from a predicate that normally requires it: *all the riders were booted and spurred* is a denominally based expression related to the nouns *boot* and *spur*.

Nominalization does not preclude the presence of other roles with a predicate. Even in the nominalized form we have *a run down the slalom course with my new skis, the generals' 1944 bomb attempt on Hitler's life*, and the like. On the other hand, role information associated with a predicate that is nominalized is so often redundant that it can be omitted as old information. The frequency with which additional roles are actually expressed with nominalizations appears on the average lower than the frequency with which additional role information is given with verbal or prepositional counterparts of the same predicates.

The relationship between nominalization and roles is not always the same. English *trainer* is a nominal form based on the agent when it refers to the person who tapes the ankles of football players, but based on the vehicle (or range) when it refers to an aircraft in which a flight instructor imparts instruction to a student pilot. *Strainer,* on the other hand, usually refers to the instrument with which a cook takes water out of food; but it can also have to do with the agent, either alone as in *this wrestler is a grunter and a groaner and a strainer,* or with the agent and other roles as in *the press officer is a real credibility strainer.* Neither example of the agentive semantics of this noun is very common; but agent is the most likely meaning with *trainer.*

Some sets of predicates are related by their role similarities. There are, for example, sets of predicates that have the same role relationships but differ in the way those relationships are staged. [9] As far as content is concerned, *I like your new coat* involves a patient who is reacting to a range as stimulus; so does *your new coat pleases me.* It is the point of departure that is different. The same holds for *Jane is Hal's wife* and *Hal is Jane's husband;* the same relationship is presented to the hearer from two different angles.

These pairs of CONVERSE predicates should be compared with other predicates for which role relationships are constant and there are distinct possibilities of staging, but for which the presence of a single lexical representation suggests that there may be no further difference in the meanings associated with each thematization. *Rent* expresses one of these predicates: *Karen rented the apartment from Mrs. Anderson* and *Mrs. Anderson rented the apartment to Karen* describe the same situation staged in two different ways. *The back yard is swarming with mosquitoes, mosquitoes are swarming in the back yard,* and *there is a swarm of mosquitoes in the back yard* are thematically distinct but have the same roles associated with the predicate.

---

[9] Other differences in meaning go along with the differences in thematic properties. *Like* does not mean exactly the same thing as *please,* nor are *husband* and *wife* completely synonymous. The point is that those differences in meaning are not related to the role system, but rather go along with the side of the role relationships that the speaker wishes to stage for the hearer. See Chapter 21.

10

OTHER RELATIONSHIPS AMONG PREDICATES

1. ASSOCIATIVE RELATIONSHIPS

Part of the meaning of a lexical item is found in its being related to other propositions in ways that were modeled in the last two chapters in the form of specialized predicates known as roles. To know the role structure of a lexical item does not imply knowing its meaning, however; it implies only that we know some of the essential elements of its meaning. Different lexical predicates like *fold* and *snap* have identical role structures, or a single lexical predicate like *hit* may take a variety of role structures.

Another part of the meaning of a lexical item involves its being related to other lexical predicates in other ways than through role relationships. A general term for these other relationships is ASSOCIATIVE, though as we shall see they can be further divided, so that the overall term for them may drop out of use as soon as the picture gets a little clearer.

INCLUSION relationships are an important property of lexical items. A *felt tip* is one kind of *pen*, which in turn is one kind of *writing instrument*, which is an *implement* or *tool*, which is an *artifact*, which is a *thing*. There are pens that are not felt tips, writing instruments that are not pens, implements that are not writing instruments, artifacts that are not implements, and things that are not artifacts. Harold C. Conklin was one of the first to show how inclusion hierarchies differ from language to language.[1]

---

[1] Conklin, "Hanunoo Color Categories" (1955).

Dixon cites a type of ethnolinguistic evidence for inclusion from a language situation that brings these hierarchies to light in a forceful way.[2] Quillian finds that each unit in his model of semantic relations must recognize another unit as its SUPERSET; in other words, a unit that represents the next most inclusive level of the inclusion hierarchy.[3] Both he and McCalla and Sampson, who follow up his work, find that the ability to trace superset chains is essential in resolving ambiguities and interpreting texts.[4]

Another kind of semantic relationship among lexical items is the COMPONENTIAL relationship. Components express analogical relationships among sets of meanings: *saw* is to *knife* as *drill* is to *awl*, or *grandfather* is to *father* as *son* is to *grandson*, and so forth. Componential analysis developed from the work of Floyd G. Lounsbury and Ward H. Goodenough, with a useful summary by Wallace and Atkins.[5]

Dixon, in the article referred to, points out that this kind of analysis is closely related to the use of semantic FEATURES by many linguists, and works well for a part of the vocabulary that he labels NUCLEAR; but it is not particularly useful for the nonnuclear vocabulary, which can be better defined by using nuclear words. The differences between two nonnuclear words that are defined in terms of the same nuclear word cannot be analogized to other pairs of words, so that the notion of semantic components breaks down there. Glock and I have also pointed out how even obvious semantic components like the progenitor relationship that is part of the analogy *grandfather : father : : son : grandson* cited above apply only within a limited range rather than throughout the vocabulary.[6] One would, for example, inquire only playfully about the progenitor component when investigating the meanings of a set of words like

[2]   Dixon, "A Method of Semantic Description" (1971).
[3]   Quillian, "Semantic Memory" (1968), "The Teachable Language Comprehender" (1969).
[4]   McCalla and Sampson, "A Model to Understand Simple English" (1972).
[5]   Lounsbury, "Pawnee Kinship" (1956); Goodenough, "Componential Analysis" (1956); Wallace and Atkins, "The Meaning of Kinship Terms" (1960).
[6]   Grimes and Glock, "Saramaccan" (1970).

house, shed, barn, skyscraper, church, store. Nevertheless, for limited parts of the set of lexical elements, there are relationships that enter into the differences between many sets of pairs, so that semantic features or componential structure is a factor to be recognized wherever it is pertinent, but not to be forced where it is not.

Some inclusion hierarchies are formed by washing out or neutralizing a distinction that is expressed by a semantic feature. In the press recently, for example, I notice that some professional societies have had their sessions conducted by *chairpersons,* since it was felt to violate the spirit of the women's liberation movement to have one session run by a *chairman* and the next by a *chairwoman* as in the olden days. The latest news tells of a meeting held under the gavel of a *chairone,* awesome indeed. The meaning of *person* is related to the meanings of *man* and *woman,* but without the male-female feature that also distinguishes *boy* from *girl* as kinds of *child, ram* from *ewe* as kinds of *sheep,* and so on through a sizable chunk of vocabulary.[7]

We are aware of CONNOTATIONS in meaning, but as yet we know little about integrating them into linguistic theory. Connotations have to do with the emotional and evaluative overtones of words. We are uncomfortable with them probably because in most of linguistics we feel happy if only we make a little sense in talking about concrete, denotative meaning. Nevertheless, connotations are always with us. Even Aristotle commented that "pirates nowadays call themselves 'purveyors'".[8]

Osgood, Suci, and Tannebaum have developed a measurement technique known as the SEMANTIC DIFFERENTIAL that makes it possible to compare connotations.[9] Their technique locates concepts in a space dominated by three dimensions: evaluation

---

[7] Another English expression for the next level up the hierarchy of inclusion from *man/woman* is *man:* to point out that *man's days on the planet may be limited by pollution or by nuclear war* does not imply that the earth will eventually be populated by women. The use of one word to express units at more than one level of an inclusion hierarchy is not uncommon.

[8] Aristotle, *Rhetoric* 3:2.

[9] Osgood, Suci, and Tannenbaum, *The Measurement of Meaning* (1957).

(exemplified by ratings on scales like good-bad, positive-negative, or pleasant-unpleasant), potency (hard-soft, heavy-light, strong-weak), and activity (active-passive, fast-slow, excitable-calm). Words with similar connotations cluster in the same region of the semantic space. While the semantic differential does not explain connotation, it does provide a way of talking about similarities in connotation.

Linguistically it is attractive to think of connotations as one kind of associative tie between lexical elements. There are fairly standard evaluative connotations attached to many words, for example, while others are neutral or take on their evaluations from the context. In one political speech, for example, I find the following:[10] Twelve terms stand for things that generally have a good connotation: *firm handling, concise, clear, vigor, heritage, spiritual, courageous, standing up for, rights, great, majority,* and possibly *architects.* Fifteen stand for things that generally have a bad connotation: *impressionable, victim, ptomaine, disparage, irretrievable, appeasement, capitulation, sellout, treason, folly, crisis, buckled under, extortionist, nondemocratic,* and *mob.* Eight terms are normally more neutral than these in their use in English in general; but in this discourse they take on the emotional coloring of Good Things: *our system, enforced, tough, children, deal, modest, traditional,* and *silent.* Thirty other terms, in a proportion that is consonant with the tone of the speech, are basically neutral but in this context are given negative connotations: *revolution, radical, spawning, sanctuary, susceptible, or* (used to state an equivalence between a neutral term and a loaded term), *left, dispensed, theatrical, problem, confronted, turbulent, patently, squads, moral, idealistic, thing, junior, secreted, smiling, benign, challenge, next, waving, nonnegotiable, demands, pitching, brown shirts, white sheets, lounges.*

The text discussed in the last paragraph illustrates another point about connotative meanings: to a greater extent than any other aspect of meaning, they are idiosyncratic. Anyone who reads the same text may query my reactions to the way particular words are

[10]   Quoted in *Time*, 1970 May 11.

used, or even to whether their good and bad connotations are conventional or by context. I am not surprised when someone disagrees with my personal readings (although I can report general agreement with the students I tried the speech out on); but I will be surprised if anyone fails to find some division of terms into good by convention, good by context, bad by context, and bad by convention.

The reason why connotations differ probably goes back to the emotional coloring of the circumstances under which each of us learns a word. How we feel about a situation is not as easy to calibrate against other people's feelings as our perception of the visible components of the situation is to calibrate against other people's perceptions of it. As a result, emotional and evaluative associations tend to be less standardized than are other kinds of associations that enter into our semantic reactions.

The idiosyncratic nature of connotations is only part of a more general problem: how in the world does anybody ever understand anybody else? Even in the supposedly straightforward area of so-called denotative meaning, where definitions can be given and tests made, speakers of the same language do not always mean the same things by the same words. This, like emotive reactions, probably goes back to the observation that everybody learns everything under different circumstances, so that there is no way of guaranteeing compatibility between the semantic systems of any two people. The amazing thing, which I do not pretend to be able to account for since as a linguist I take it as given, is that the area of compatibility is great enough that any effects of incompatibility can eventually be overcome by talking enough.

To illustrate how idiosyncratic elements are present in all kinds of meaning, one can pose the following questions to married couples of his acquaintance: (1) Is zero an even number? (2) Who are your second cousins? (3) Is turquoise a kind of blue or a kind of green? Many couples disagree on all three.

Not all kinds of associative ties are capable yet of being analyzed and classified even as well as connotations. The loosest type of associative tie is the COLLOCATION. A collocation could be thought of as a relatively high probability that if one concept is present in a discourse, another one will be as well. For me, mention of *spring* (the season) generally elicits some talk about *grass* and *warmth* and *buds*, and talking about *carburetors* calls for *tuneup* on account of my experience with carburetors I have known.

The associative relationships I have mentioned may be of two kinds: BOUNDED and UNBOUNDED. If Dixon is right, the extent to which semantic features or components in a componential system apply to the study of meanings is strictly limited. For any area of vocabulary there are a few components that operate to distinguish nuclear words. Even taken over all areas of the vocabulary, the number of these components is bounded. In the same way, if role relationships are taken to be the same in kind as other associative relationships (as Quillian's model implies), the number of role relationships is not unbounded. It is limited to something like the list given in Chapter 8. Inclusion hierarchies may be bounded in the sense that the superset chain (like *Chippendale : chair : seat : furniture : artifact : thing*) of any lexical item may have a finite maximum length. Going in the other direction from more inclusive to less inclusive, however, there is a sense in which the inclusion hierarchy may not be bounded. It seems as though for many superordinate or more inclusive elements in the hierarchy, we can always come up with one more subordinate or less inclusive element than they include; if this is so, that dimension of the inclusion relation may not be bounded.

As far as connotations and collocations go, however, there is no limit on the number of associations that a word can have. This is one reason why a model of semantic structure cannot escape taking in everything we know about everything. Furthermore, what we know and feel about everything changes constantly, even during a discourse, and that change in itself is an important element in accounting for the surface form of discourse as we shall see in Chapter 19. But as I said in Chapter 1, the way to confront the encyclopedia problem is not to duck around it and talk only about those aspects of language for which we do not need to know everything about everything, but to develop a conceptual scheme that contains generalizations powerful enough to permit us to manage a semantic system that embraces everything.

2. AREAS OF MEANING

Lexical predicates have different meanings, yet some are to a certain extent similar in meaning. In order to talk about how predicates differ or how they are similar it is useful to begin with those differences and similarities that can be attributed directly to the role relationships and associative relationships we have just discussed.

Many predicates take identical sets of role relationships. Fillmore, for example, characterizes English *break, bend, fold, shatter,* and *crack* as all having an agent, an instrument, and a patient (using the terminology of this book rather than his).[11] *Hit, slap, strike, bump,* and *stroke,* on the other hand, can take an agent, an instrument, and a latter state. The first set all denote some change of state in the patient, the second, contact with a surface indicated by the latter state.

Many predicates are capable of taking more than one set of role relationships in their arguments. *Break,* besides taking agent, instrument, and patient (which I shall abbreviate as A I P) as in *I broke the window with a brick,* also takes A P as in *I broke the window* or *the brick broke the window,* and P by itself as in *the window broke.* We can modify Fillmore's symbolization of these three sets of roles that go with change of state verbs using the common convention of parentheses to indicate optionality: *break* (A (I)) P. Surface contact verbs also take multiple role sets, but not the same sets as the change of state verbs. We can say *I hit the nail with a hammer,* A L I, or *I hit the nail,* A L, or *the hammer hit the nail,* A L. There is however, no form with L alone; **the nail hit* (the prefixed asterisk indicates a nonexistent form in the sense discussed) is not parallel to *the window broke,* but reflects still a

---

[11] Fillmore, "The Grammar of Hitting and Breaking" (1970).

different role, probably patient alone as an orientation role, parallel to *the airplane landed.* Patient can have a latter state added to it, as in *the sack* (P) *hit the ground* (L). We can use braces and a vertical line to show the disjunction in the role structure of *hit:* {A (I) L | P (L)} shows that at least one of the pair of role sets must be present.

It is tempting to try to classify predicates by the role sets that they take. It soon becomes evident, however, that clear cut groupings of predicates like the change of state group and the surface contact group are relatively rare. The reason for this is not hard to find. If we assume at most eight standard roles, as we did in the first part of the chapter, then the number of possible role sets is 2^8 or 256. (Each role set also has the possibility of appearing with a static or a dynamic predicate, and independently of that, with an orientation or a process predicate, though not many occur with all four combinations.) Even supposing that only half of the 256 combinations actually are used in a language, those 128 or so are numerous enough to suggest that classification alone is not an end in itself. Furthermore, since many predicates have more than one role set that they can take, each different combination of role sets yields a different class of predicates. *Seem,* for example, takes P like *break;* but it lacks the other role sets that *break* has. The proper study of role systems, then, is not to classify them, although classification is not impossible (and can, in fact, be done by computer).

What, then is the point of recognizing role systems, if they yield a classification that is too finely divided to tell us much? To answer this we must recognize first that a categorization of predicates in terms of role sets is not an air tight thing. We change the role set associated with a predicate when it suits us if we think we can get away with the innovation without losing the hearer. "But me no buts" is an extreme example in which a rhetorical predicate whose arguments are usually two or more complex propositions is given an agent, a patient, and a latter state for the nonce. Less radical are things like *climb me up the ladder* or *soup the leftovers,* both of which are easily recognized as nonstandard, or in the narrow sense ungrammatical, yet each of which would certainly elicit the correct reaction from most speakers of English if given as a command. There is, I think, everything to be gained by trying to build our theory of language in such a way that it not only characterizes the normal, expected combinations of elements that are the bread and butter of everyday speech, but also recognizes that speakers have liberty to innovate within bounds, and that when they do, the way in which they are understood is also systematic.

There is, then, a certain invariance in meaning inherent in each role relationship, whether it is being used in conventional association with a predicate or whether the speaker has decided to put things together in a nonstandard way. Furthermore, there seem to be characteristic patterns of role relationships that stick together. For example, for change of state verbs the A (I) complex of role sets seems to be interchangeable with (Fc), or optional force: ({A (I) | Fc}) P. Parallel to *I broke the window with a brick*, A I P, we have *the cold broke the window*, Fc P, and *the window broke from the cold*, P Fc, with the observation that *the cold* is not agent, since it is not performing any action or in any sense acting deliberately, nor is there any conceivable instrument we can think of that it might use. Neither is it instrument, since there is no normal sense in which its use could be attributed to some agent. (In suitable contexts such as fairy tales *cold* could be used by somebody to break something: *the sorcerer broke the castle walls open with cold*. This, however, is the full scale agent-instrument pattern, not force.)

Some role relationships take precedence over others in regard to their mapping to surface grammar. In English, for example, unless there are special conditions of staging and informational coherence, the agent of a proposition matches the surface subject; if there is no agent, the patient matches the subject.[12] Linguistics has a long history of classifying surface grammatical patterns.[13] It therefore comes as a mild surprise to some to find that the classification of the semantic categories that stand behind surface

---

[12] Halliday, "Transitivity and Theme", Part 1 and 2 (1967).
[13] Postal, *Constituent Structure* (1964).

patterns is many times more complex, so much so that it ceases to be useful in its own right.

Role sets, however, are not assigned helter-skelter to predicates. As a matter of fact, many of the multiple role sets associated with predicates are interrelated in just the ways that in Chapter 9 are attributed to semantic derivational processes. We can take *break*, for example, as having an underlying process predicate that takes only the patient, as in *the window broke*. The agentive derivation of this actually adds not just the agent, but the whole {A (I) | Fc} complex.

It is customary in lexicography to speak of various AREAS OF MEANING of a word. In dictionary making each of these areas is represented by a subentry.[14] One of the ways in which areas of meaning are distinguished is by role sets. *Break* as something that can happen to a stick, corresponding to P, belongs to a different subentry than *break* as something that a person can do to a rigid object, possibly aided by a tool, corresponding to A P and A I P.

There are other ways of distinguishing subentries, of course; different kinds of contexts entail different areas of meaning of a word. *Key* as an implement for unlocking a door is not the same area of meaning as *key* for following a map or *key* for keeping a wheel from turning on a shaft. Even where contextual differences are involved, however, there may be associated differences of role sets. In sports like basketball, *break* is used to describe a quick maneuver involving change of direction, and in that context takes an agent and patient combined like a typical motion verb, but no instrument.

---

[14]   Robinson, *Manual for Bilingual Dictionaries* (1968).

11

THE ARGUMENTS OF PROPOSITIONS

Role relationships hold between a predicate and its arguments. We have looked at predicates, at least to the extent that they are involved with their arguments, and we have looked at the role relationships themselves. Now we will look at the arguments.

1. CONSTRAINTS INVOLVING ROLES

The number of arguments that a predicate can take ranges typically from one, as in *the snow* (P) *is white*, to six or eight, as in *the bellhop* (A) *brought me* (L) *a note* (P) *through the crowd* (R) *from the lady* (F) *on a tray* (V). The six load down the available surface structures enough that one begins to wonder whether the vehicle really is a vehicle or part of a strange sounding source, *the lady on a tray*. Furthermore, when a predicate is capable of taking more than one role set, the sets often differ in the number of arguments involved. The familiar change of state complex ($\{A (I) \mid Fc\}$) P (L) permits one, two, three, or four arguments: P *the jar broke*, P L *the jar broke to pieces*, A P (L) *she broke the jar (to pieces)* or *the hammer broke the jar (to pieces)*, Fc P (L) *the noise broke the jar (to pieces)*, and A I P (L) *she broke the jar (to pieces) with a hammer*.

There are two senses in which it can be said that an argument is optional. For an accurate characterization of the role system of any predicate it is necessary to be able to distinguish both. An argument may be optional in the sense that it may or may not be part of the meaning of a particular use of the predicate. A, I, and Fc in the example given in the last paragraph are SEMANTICALLY OPTIONAL in this sense; when they are there, they are part of the meaning, and when they are not, there is no need to assume that they are "understood" or in some sense to be taken into account. In the first example above, *the jar broke to pieces*, there is no implication that an agent is lurking in the background with a hammer in his hand, or possibly even that there is a force to be found. The jar broke, and that is that.

The other sense in which an argument can be said to be optional I will call COHESIVE OPTIONALITY or deletability, in the sense developed in Chapter 19. Here an argument is part of the semantics, but is presumed to be known to the hearer either because it is part of the situation of speaking, because it is the culturally expected argument for that situation, or because it has been mentioned recently enough that it does not need to be mentioned again. Yet it is part of the meaning; the fact that it is not expressed falls under the general principle of recoverable deletion.[1] *All gone?* uttered with one hand on the coffee pot involves a patient, the coffee, but it is not expressed because it is pointed to nonlinguistically in the situation of speaking. *He's eating* has an explicit agent, but a patient whose deletion implies that it is a culturally expected patient for that action, and there is no attention being called to it. *He's eating fried eels* would probably not be subject to deletion, at least at our house, because the patient is unusual enough that it does not come under the cultural criterion for recoverability. In the same way, result elements with change of state predicates are usually not expressed unless there is something special about them, on the grounds that the expected results of most actions are widely known. We rarely bother with the latter state in something prosaic like *the jar broke to pieces* unless we do it to make the whole action prominent; we say *the jar broke*, assuming that everyone knows that pieces were what it broke into. On the other hand, if it were the case that *the jar broke into half-inch crescents*, something a little out of the ordinary for jars breaking, we would express the latter

---

[1] Chomsky, *Aspects* (1965), pp. 144-6.

state. Finally, in *I went to the store and bought potato chips*, we would say that *bought* has an agent, but that since this agent is the same as that of *went* and the two are grammatically conjoined within a sentence, the agent of the second verb does not have to be expressed. In other cases there may be a reduced form of expression such as pronominalization, in which only minimal information is given about an argument because the rest coheres from the preceding context.

The interrelationship of arguments within role sets has already been mentioned. One kind of condition is disjunction symbolized by braces and a vertical bar: $\{A (I) L \mid P(L)\}$ in the role specification of surface contact verbs requires that one or the other of the argument sets be present: A L *the batter hit the ball* or *the bat hit the ball*, or A I L *the batter hit the ball with the bat*, or else P alone or P L: *the ball hit, the ball hit the tree*. Disjunction within parentheses, like $(\{A (I) \mid Fc\}) P (L)$, is used for change of state verbs. (Using a vertical line to separate the terms of a disjunction is equivalent to writing one term above another and using large braces to enclose them.) This means that either one member of the disjunction will be used or the other, but not both. Many-termed disjunctions are also possible in which at most one member of the disjunction can be used.

In the notation I am using here, simple parentheses ( ) always indicate semantic optionality. If the role inside the parentheses is chosen, it is part of the meaning; if it is not chosen, then we are in a different area of meaning that does not involve that role. Braces with vertical separators indicate a different kind of optionality, in which one and only one of the arguments must be chosen.

One of the less fruitful consequences of earlier generative transformational grammars was the ironfisted way in which they claimed that you couldn't say this and daren't say that. The starred form, which I have used sparingly for things that are obviously impossible, at least in the sense I have specified for them, became a kind of invitation to instant controversy: your grammar says you can't say this, but I said it last Thursday, therefore your grammar is wrong. Once the fun and games side of counterexamples dried up, we began to wonder if the prevalence of counterexamples for nearly any starred form in the literature might not mean that a theory of grammar that rejected starred forms so roundly might not be too rigid. It was about this time, the late sixties, that people began going around muttering things like "All Chomsky grammars are square".

I think that our theory of language has now come to a point where we no longer have to tie ourselves in knots on the subject of grammaticality. We have moved to a viewpoint at which, instead of saying, "Because certain lexical elements are specified in such and such a way, it follows that Example X is ungrammatical", we have loosened up to the point where we can say, "Any semantic configuration of a certain type has the following possible forms of surface expression, and other configurations have other forms. We would have expected, judging from the way we normally use the words in Example X, that it belongs to semantic configuration A; but since it did not appear in the form that is normal for A, we must suppose that the speaker constructed it in semantic configuration B, as he was at liberty to do, and its surface form was therefore appropriate for B." In other words, when we talk about things like the role relationships and role sets of a particular lexical predicate, all we are saying is that most of the time the meaning of the predicate involves those role sets. If a speaker wishes to, however, he can use any role sets that he thinks will get him understood. For example, the predicate that underlies English *seem* takes a patient, the one who perceives things in a particular way, and a range which is itself a sentence-sized proposition. If we construct a thoroughly barbaric, non-English sentence like *why did you seem to me that he would be here by now?*, which has an agent where no agent should be, a good grammar does more than slap us on the wrist; it shows that the sentence is unusual, pinpoints the way in which it is unusual, and says in effect, "All right, I know we don't normally treat *seem* as agentive; but if you are determined to do so, then I will admit that you have given it the surface form it ought to have, just as though you had used its conventional counterpart *represent* or the explicit causative *make seem*. Next time, however, you may be better understood if you say *why did you represent to me that he would be here by now?* or *why did you make it seem to me that he would be here by now?"*

Roles that are added to the conventional role set for a predicate without further adjustment can be called SUPERNUMERARY roles. The benefactive is the most common supernumerary role. It can be added to almost anything: *the grass is green for me, shut the door for me, the rain in Spain stays mainly in the plain for them.* Even double benefactives seem to be possible: *he put the document on the table for him on me* is barely within bounds. A latter state can be added to predicates that normally do not have it: *they walked all out* ("with the result that all their energy was expended"). The notion of supernumerary roles is a special ad hoc case of semantic derivation.

2. PSEUDO-PREDICATES AND CONSOLIDATION

In Chapter 9, where I referred to developmental, resultative, agentive, causative, nonagentive, nominal, and instrumental patterns of semantic derivation, I discussed the difference between causative and agentive in considerable detail in order to clarify the agent role itself. As a result I then attempted to justify eliminating causer as a role separate from agent. The thought behind both discussions was that there are a small number of semantic relations that can be considered to be predicates themselves, but that eventually coalesce with the base predicates that they dominate. The causative, for example, has its own agent and its own latter state, which is a proposition in its own right. The base predicate, the one in the proposition that is result of the causative, may also have its own agent. When the causative and the base proposition are coalesced, however, as expressed in a transformation of PROPOSITION CONSOLIDATION like the one proposed by Frantz, the agent of the original base predicate is reassigned to another category like goal or benefactive.[2] In all further treatment of the coalesced form it behaves as though it represented the semantic role into which it has been moved, so that no problems arise from having two agents in the same proposition. I believe that proposition consolidation is the mechanism behind Pike's notion of double function, in which he notes that *him* in *I told him to go* is simultaneously an object of *told* and the logical subject of *go*.[3]

Huichol illustrates the effects of consolidation and the resulting role reassignment more readily than English, since in Huichol there are explicit affixes that distinguish between the causative derivation (*-tʌa*) and the agentive derivation (*-ra*) in which an agent is added to a predicate directly. The Huichol stem *qee* 'carry', for example, normally takes an agent for the person who does the carrying, a patient for the thing carried, and a latter state, which can denote either the destination to which the patient is carried or the direction in which it is carried. In *cʌʌkʌ p-é-i-qei paapáa* (dog assertion-away-3singularobject-carried tortilla) 'the dog carried away a tortilla', *cʌʌkʌ* 'dog' is the agent, *paapáa* 'tortilla, maize cake' is the patient, and the latter state is expressed by *e-* 'away'. *Cʌʌkʌ* 'dog' is in cross reference with the third person singular subject of the verb. *Paapáa* 'tortilla' is in cross reference with the third person singular object prefix *i-*. This role set, which is one of several related ones that are appropriate to *qee* 'carry', can be boiled down to a compact representation on the order of *qee* A P L.

Role sets are really abbreviated designations for requirements that each argument of a predicate be a proposition whose predicate is a particular role. The arguments of the role predicates themselves are either referential indices, which we will take up in Chapter 12, or other propositions whose internal structure does not concern

---

[2] Frantz, *Blackfoot* (1970). David Cranmer suggests investigating whether roles that are readjusted when they are consolidated are always moved into a role that is not otherwise taken up by the base predicate. If this is not the case, the conflict of roles would result in what could appropriately be called CON-SOLIDATION AMBIGUITY.

[3] Pike, *Language* (1967).

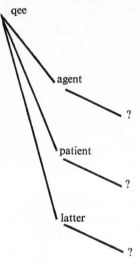

Figure 11.1

us further right now. In other words, the designation *qee* A P L says that propositions of which *qee* is the predicate normally take three arguments; one is a proposition with *agent* as its predicate, another is a proposition with *patient* as its predicate, and the third is a proposition with *latter state* as its predicate, without saying anything further about the arguments of those propositions. It is like a skeleton form where the question marks indicate the places where other propositions may be added.

It is useful to be able to distinguish between the skeleton form of a predicate and the use of that predicate in a particular semantic production in which the blanks associated with it are filled in. If *qee* A P L stands for the empty form of the predicate itself, *qee* A P L (a, b, c) is an appropriate way of designating an instance of *qee* in which some proposition *a* is assigned as the argument of the agent predicate that *qee* dominates, *b* is assigned as the argument of the patient, and *c* as the argument of the latter state. The arguments are matched in the order in which they are listed, and since it is characteristic of role systems that no predicate has more than one argument of a given type (remembering that an argument that designates a group is a single argument even though it may consist of two or more parts itself; *John and I went to town*, for example, contains a single agent-patient, *John and I*), there is no problem of duplication.[4] The example given earlier would be represented as *qee* A P L (*cᴧᴧkᴧ, paapáa, e-*). Because we are not at this point interested in the further propositional structure of the three arguments of *qee*, we simply list the forms used, as usual.[5]

Putting the causative together with a predicate like *qee* involves a double level of composition. The dominating proposition has the form *causative* A L R. Its result is the proposition *qee* A P L with its own arguments. The composite production has the form *causative* A L R (*Puukáa* 'woman', *qee* A P L (*cᴧᴧkᴧ* 'dog', *paapáa* 'tortilla', *e-* 'away'), *u-* 'there'. The second argument of *causative* matches the complete proposition cited earlier with *qee* as its predicate. A tree representation of the causative formation would be

---

[4] The notation for matching specific values like *a*, *b*, and *c* with variables like A, P, and L is a simplified form of the LAMBDA NOTATION proposed thirty years ago by Alonzo Church and modified for the representation of recursive functions by John McCarthy, "Recursive Functions" (1960).

[5] Langendoen, *The Study of Syntax* (1969).

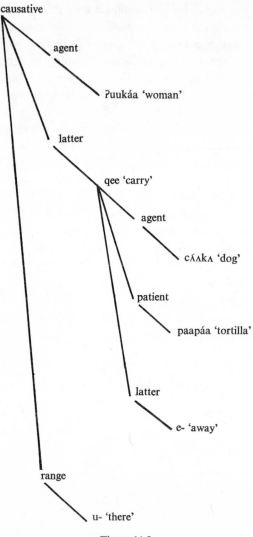

Figure 11.2

Under most circumstances these two propositions, the one with *causative* as its predicate and the one with *qee* as its predicate, are consolidated into a single proposition. The resulting proposition does not represent the semantic relationships of all the arguments directly; yet it is the basis for the surface or output form of the expression that means 'the woman gave the dog a tortilla'. In the derived proposition the predicate is the semantically complex *qéi-tʌa* 'cause to carry, give'. The new agent is the agent of the original *causative*. The patient is the patient of the original base predicate *qee*. The original *causative* (in Huichol, though not in the corresponding English) takes a range element that tells where the causative agent performed her action – an internal locative. This element is carried through into the derived proposition; but its surface form *u-* 'there' is incompatible with the surface form of the latter state of the base proposition, *e-* 'away'. As a result the latter state of the base is suppressed.[6]

The agent of the original base predicate is no longer treated as an agent after consolidation. In Huichol it behaves in relation to the syntax, but not to the morphological agreement patterns, exactly as though it were a benefactive instead. For example, in the presence of a patient, as in this example, it is expressed as the grammatical direct object, while the patient itself is expressed as a syntactic complement that lacks the cross reference that the direct object has to a verbal affix. The consolidated proposition is now *qéi-tʌa* A P R B (*Puukáa* 'woman', *paapáa* 'tortilla', *u-* 'there', *cʌʌkʌ* 'dog'). It is spoken as *Puukáa p-íi+-qéi-tʌa paapáa cʌʌkʌ* (woman assertion-3singularobject-carry-cause tortilla dog) 'the

---

[6] See Grimes, *Huichol Syntax* (1964). *E-* can cooccur with *u-* within some words. If the sequence *e-u-* were used here, however, both would be taken as the range of *causative* only. The compound locative *e-u-* conveys the idea of unspecified location, on the order of 'she gives the dog tortillas wherever she happens to be' in contrast with *u-* by itself, which implies that she was at a specific spot known to the hearer and gave the dog a specific tortilla there. *E-u-* also contrasts with *e-* by itself, which implies that she was out of sight of the speaker and hearer when she gave the dog the tortilla. In other words, the range associated with *causative* preempts the entire available surface apparatus of locative prefixes, so that the latter state of *qee* is suppressed. If that latter state were sufficiently important in the staging of the utterance, it would be expressed by repeating the base proposition without the *causative*: 'the woman gave the dog a tortilla; he carried it away'.

woman gave the dog a tortilla'.[7] The tree representation of the proposition (perhaps pseudo-proposition would be a better term) that results from consolidation of *causative* and *qee* is

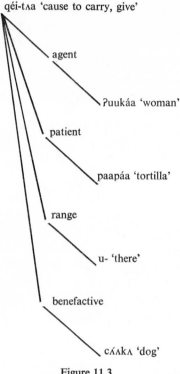

Figure 11.3

[7] This word order represents normal or unmarked thematization (Chapter 21), with agent as subject coming first. The *u-* that represents the causative range is suppressed in this form due to a positional incompatibility with *i-* 'third singular object'. The *u-* can be recovered either by moving the benefactive to just before the verb, which eliminates the third person singular object cross reference, or by using a different person or number of benefactive, which removes the positional incompatibility of the prefixes. In the first case the sentence is *Puukáa cΛΛkΛ p-uu+-qéi-tΛa paapáa* 'the woman gave the dog a tortilla', and in the second it is *Puukaa pΛ-néci+-Pu-qéi-tΛa paapáa* 'the woman gave me a tortilla'.

The roles listed as benefactive and instrument appear to be derivable from abstract predicates by consolidation in the same way as the causative is derived. A likely representation for the predicate that consolidates to give the benefactive role is something like *benefactive* A P R, where the agent must be coreferential with the agent of the base proposition if it has an agent, the patient is the base proposition itself, and the range is the element that after consolidation occupies the benefactive role. Instrument appears to have similar form but with different conditions: *instrument* A P L. The agent must be coreferential with the agent of the base proposition, and in this case the base proposition must have an agent. The patient of *instrument*, however, is the implement used to carry out the action of the base proposition, and the latter state is the base proposition itself. We could paraphrase *benefactive* A P R and *instrument* A P L loosely as 'A does P in such a way as to affect R by it' and 'A uses P in order to accomplish L'.

The general elusiveness of the range role — the problem of inner versus outer locatives — suggests that setting elements are capable of being consolidated to give a resultant range-like element that is not normally part of the semantics of the base predicate involved. *Sleep* appears to have a semantically optional range role connected with it that denotes the surface on which one sleeps: *I slept in a comfortable bed and my dog slept on the floor*. In the case of *I slept in New Orleans*, however, the relationship of *New Orleans* to the rest is not quite like that of *bed* to the rest: notice the difference in acceptability between *a comfortable bed was what I slept in* and **New Orleans was what I slept in*. This suggests that even though the grammatical expression of New Orleans is like that of the normal range element associated with *sleep* in the thematically unmarked form of the proposition, the cleft form (Chapter 21) prohibits *New Orleans* from being treated grammatically like a range element. Perhaps *in New Orleans* is really a setting element meaning 'when I was in New Orleans', which can be consolidated with the base proposition in the absence of marked thematization. Once consolidated, it is treated in the transformational shaping process like a range element. If this is so, a good deal of the problem of distinguishing range (inner locative) from setting (outer locative) can be pinpointed.

Some predicates, the ones I have labeled lexical, have meanings that are explainable at least partly in terms of a few semantic roles. A more precise way to say this is in terms of constraints on arguments: a certain lexical predicate customarily takes, say, three arguments, and one of these is expected to be dominated by agent, another by patient, and still another by latter state.

Still greater precision is desirable in some contexts. In the paragraphs immediately preceding these I suggested that at the deepest level of semantics instrument is not a semantic role of the same kind as agent. In the light of that discussion, a more exact formulation would be to say that a certain lexical predicate customarily takes, say, two arguments, agent and patient; in addition it is customarily dominated by an instrumental abstract predicate. Except where some kind of prominence condition blocks ordinary consolidation, this statement implies results equivalent to those of the less formal statement. Since either is translatable into the other, and the occasions on which it is necessary to separate them will not concern us until Chapter 21, I will use whichever form of statement fits the context best.

Role constraints are not the only ones that can be placed on arguments. There are also coreferentiality constraints. For example, the causative predicate, as already mentioned, takes an agent and a latter state. The latter state itself has as its argument a proposition that contains a lexical predicate, which I referred to earlier as the base predicate. If the base predicate has an agent, that agent may or may not refer to the same thing as the agent of the causative itself. For the instrumental and benefactive abstract predicates, however, the agent of the base predicate that they dominate must be the same as their own agent.

Still further constraints are placed on the arguments of some predicates. The requirement that the latter state of a causative be a proposition that contains a lexical predicate is that kind of constraint. It may be a tighter constraint than just that the latter state be lexical; it may exclude (at least in some languages) lexical predicates that are nominal or nominalized. In other words, causative derivations might be able to involve actions in a way that could be translated 'he made her cry', or action-process like 'he had her write the letter', or processes like 'he made the paint peel', or possibly even states like 'he caused it to be wide' without any implication that it got that way after being some other way first; on the other hand, causatives of nominals like 'he caused the balloon', either in the sense that he caused the balloon to come into existence or that he caused something to take the shape of a balloon, might or might not be possible. [8] The best way to formulate this kind of constraint on arguments is not yet clear. Weinreich's transfer features may be one way of expressing constraints; Hall used the notion to talk about semantic roles in Subanon verbs. [9]

3. THE COMPLEXITY OF ARGUMENTS

There seems to be no limit on how complex an argument can be. Each argument is represented in the semantic analysis by a subtree of the total tree. The main requirement that applies to the information content of an argument is this: the hearer must be able to recognize its referent. In many cases the speaker assumes, either on the grounds of what he has said already or on the grounds of what is present in the situation of speaking, that the hearer knows who or what he is talking about. In this case the argument will be minimally complex, represented by pronominal or zero identification. In other cases its reference must be established, and the speaker must expand the argument to the point where he feels sure

---

[8] The punch line of one Huichol folk tale comes when one dancer tells another dancer whose dancing the first one thinks is crude, *kenéu+tuizútʌa* 'go turn into a pig!', from *túizu* 'pig' and the causative -*tʌa*. He did; and since he was wearing a dark shirt with a white neckerchief, that accounts for the collared peccary. Stems like this one, built from a noun and a causative, may well represent a causative semantics that is not permitted in other languages. *He caused the riot* may be permitted because *riot* denotes an event, not an object.

[9] Weinreich, "Explorations in Semantic Theory" (1966), "On the Semantic Structure of Language" (1966). Hall, "Siocon Subanon Verbs" (1969).

the hearer knows enough to recognize what he is talking about.[10]

Identification is not the only requirement of speech that bears on the internal complexity of an argument. The hearer may be able to distinguish the thing referred to from everything else in the discourse; but the speaker also has the option of adding more to what the hearer knows about it. Description and characterization are well known factors of literary composition; they illustrate how the speaker, in addition to telling what happened, may want the hearer to associate further attitudes or visual images with the things he distinguishes. The level of detail that is managed here is completely under the speaker's control in the sense that it does not depend merely on the hearer's ability to distinguish one referent from another. The speaker may go to any lengths he likes to build up detail, color, and spice in what he says.

4. CONSTRAINTS NOT RELATED TO ROLES

We have already looked at some of the constraints a predicate imposes on its arguments in terms of semantic roles. There are other constraints as well. A number of predicates expect one of their arguments to refer to a group rather than to a single individual. *Collide* in English has one role set in which there is a patient that must be a group. In *the two ships collided* the action is bidirectional, not directed from a particular ship to the other. The sense is equivalent to that of *a collision took place in which two ships were involved*. *Pair* takes a group patient, with the further requirement that the group consist of neither more nor less than two individuals: *Al and Mary are quite a pair, buy me a pair of socks.*[11]

Langendoen discusses a requirement on reference that distinguishes between what the speaker thinks to be so and what other

---

[10] Weizenbaum, "Contextual Understanding by Computers" (1967).
[11] Even though the greatest variety of role patterns is found on predicates in English that ultimately take the surface form of verbs, those that tend to be given other grammatical forms have role sets as well.

people who are involved in a discourse believe.[12] He speaks of
REFERENTIAL TRANSPARENCY, in which the speaker's beliefs about
the state of the world hold not only for a particular predicate but
for its arguments as well, and REFERENTIAL OPACITY, where the
speaker does not have to square his own beliefs about the state of
the world with those expressed in the arguments: "referentially
opaque contexts basically permit the introduction of the beliefs
of different persons: the speaker, the person or persons who play
roles in the sentence under consideration, or people in general.
Referentially transparent contexts admit only those of the speaker
(and also perhaps of people in general)."

The concept of embedded performatives may provide a means
for incorporating constraints of opacity into a formal grammar.
For example, the range of *know*, the thing that is known, must be
referentially transparent; it must be so (hence the Kiparskys' use
of FACTIVE for this relation,[13] in the sense that we cannot know
anything that is not a fact). We can say *I know it is snowing* if it is
snowing, but we score zero if we are standing in the sun on a
tropical beach. The range of *know* must be consonant with the
state of the world both from the point of view of the patient who
knows something and from the point of view of the speaker who
reports his knowing. For the referentially opaque *believe*, however,
the patient and the speaker may see the world as different. *John
knew it was Monday* only if the speaker agrees with John that it
was in fact Monday; but if *John believed it was Monday* he and the
speaker might still have disagreed about the state of affairs.

For restrictions of another kind, there are implications that must
hold among the arguments of some predicates in order for them
to be considered appropriate. Fillmore distinguishes a group of
INTENSIONAL properties of predicates based on logical relations
among their arguments.[14] SYMMETRIC predicates like *collide* and

[12]   Langendoen, *Essentials of English Grammar* (1970), pp. 113-15. Schank and
his associates probe the same problem from another point of view in *Primitive
Concepts Underlying Verbs of Thought* (1972).
[13]   Kiparsky and Kiparsky, "Fact" (1971).
[14]   Fillmore, "Lexical Entries for Verbs" (1968).

touch have as part of their meaning the fact that if *a* touches *b*, it is also true that *b* touches *a*. ANTISYMMETRIC predicates include the opposite as part of their meaning: if we say that *a outgrew b*, then it cannot be true that *b outgrew a*. Many predicates are neither symmetric nor antisymmetric; that type of implication is simply irrelevant. Such predicates are called MESOSYMMETRIC, and are exemplified by *love*, in the sense that to assert that *Bob loves Susan* is no guarantee either that *Susan loves Bob* or that *Susan does not love Bob*.

Another relation of the same kind among arguments of a predicate is that of reflexivity, but not in the sense that in some circumstances of reference allows us to distinguish *Karen saw herself in the mirror* from *Karen saw her* (somebody other than Karen) *in the mirror*. Predicates that are inherently REFLEXIVE are those for which the possibility of saying them with arguments *a* and *b* implies the further possibility of saying them with arguments *a* and *a*, and might further entail the surface grammatical feature called the reflexive. This is the case with *equals*. We can say *this steak equals that roast in weight*, but we can also say (trivially but truly) *this steak equals itself in weight*. There are also ANTI-REFLEXIVE predicates for which it is not possible to use the same argument in both positions: **3 differs from itself in number* does not hold. Most predicates are MESOREFLEXIVE; that is, the question of reflexivity does not enter into their meaning. *Bob loves Susan* carries no implications at all about whether *Bob loves himself* or not.

The third intensional relation among arguments that Fillmore mentions is transitivity. Again, the term is not used in the ordinary grammatical sense that distinguishes verbs that take direct objects from those that do not. It is rather used in the logical sense that if *a* is related to *b* and *b* to *c* by a transitive relation, then *a* is related to *c* by the same relation. *Exceed* is TRANSITIVE in this sense; if *your entertainment bill exceeds my salary* and *my salary exceeds the Federal poverty limit*, then it is legitimate to assert that *your entertainment bill exceeds the Federal poverty limit*.[15] Other predi-

---

[15] Drawing the conclusion in that way clashes with another kind of restriction on putting things in the same sentence, namely that the result makes it sound as

cates are ANTITRANSITIVE. *Beget* has as part of its meaning in English
that if *Abraham begot Isaac* and *Isaac begot Jacob*, the two assertions
taken together would make it impossible to assert that **Abraham
begot Jacob*.[16] Other predicates are outside the transitivity scheme;
love again is MESOTRANSITIVE in that *Jason loves Sandra* and *Sandra
loves Xavier* taken together shed only dim light on the possibility
of asserting that *Jason loves Xavier*.

---

though there were a Federal poverty limit on entertainment bills, whereas the
limit actually has to do with salaries.

16   Apparently the verb in Classical Hebrew that is translated as 'beget' in the
Bible is logically transitive. The assumption that it is antitransitive in Hebrew,
as it is in English, seems to be behind Archbishop Ussher's celebrated chronology.

12

REFERENTIAL INDICES

In talking about predicates and their arguments we have considered some arguments to be monolithic blobs in the sense that their internal structure does not interest us at the moment. Others we have recognized as propositions whose internal form interests us. Even in the second case, after treating the part we are interested in (as for example, when we point out that one argument of *go* in the sense of motion must be a proposition whose predicate is the agent-patient role), we usually disregard the rest. To suggest, however, that the argument of one proposition is another proposition, immediately raises the question whether the chain of propositions within propositions ever comes to an end. We can easily imagine the content of a large discourse to be represented by a large tree of propositions; but it must not be an infinitely large tree.

The chain stops when the speaker assumes that the hearer can recognize what he is talking about.

Compare first the way in which a situation is verbalized when the speaker and hearer have shared many experiences, in contrast with the way complete strangers have to verbalize the same situation. Husbands and wives often communicate much in a few words. To speak to one's wife with the same depth of verbal explanation and identification that would be appropriate for a stranger would be either boring or insulting. *Have a good day?* answered by *Schultz called again* might convey the same thing that to a stranger would have to be spelled out — perhaps as follows: *Have a good day?* answered by *I left home and went to work at the apple squeezing factory. Things were going well, but in the middle of the afternoon our former mountain climbing partner Ross N. Schultz, who lives in a suburb of Akron, Ohio, called for the third time to tell us that he had left twenty yards of braided nylon rope in the trunk of our car, and that he would like us either to hurry up and find it and mail it to him or else pay him for it. Each time he calls he gets more disagreeable about it, with the result that the rest of my day was abnormally tense.*

Consider also the Boy Scout leader who walks into a camp dormitory at 11:30 at night, turns on the lights, and sees pillows all over the floor and the glass of a shattered light bulb, while every eyelid droops in simulated sleep and a hush that is on the point of exploding into twenty nervous giggles fills the room. He does not say, *Who scattered pillows all over the place and broke the light bulb and is pretending now to be asleep?* The only expression that really fits the situation is *All right, who did it?* The situation is already defined in sufficient detail to all concerned that no further verbiage is required.

Communication has many aspects that are like those parlor games in which one person, analogous to the hearer in a speech situation, tries either to identify an object or to pinpoint a situation on the basis of signals from the other players, whose role is analogous to that of the speaker. Suppose the game is one in which the players decide on a certain object which the one who is "it" has to guess. He comes into the room, and they help him discriminate that object from all others in the room by clapping their hands faster as he gets closer to it and slower as he gets farther away from it. As soon as his discrimination matches theirs, the round is over.

In the same way, as soon as the speaker feels that the hearer's perception of the situation he is talking about matches his own within the limits of acceptability that he sets, he can stop his semantic development; he has reached his objective. If we were to conceptualize speech situations in terms of the kind of cognitive map suggested by Kurt Lewin,[1] we would say that the speaker

---

[1]   Lewin, *Principles of Topological Psychology* (1936).

reaches a point where he is willing to assume that the hearer's map of the situation matches his own satisfactorily. This is true whether we are talking about objects, situations, or abstractions that involve whole systems of relationships. For example, there are linguists to whom I can signal a whole set of ideas by the single word *phrase* with a fair assurance that their set of ideas will match mine well enough for us to get on. There are other linguists in whose presence I am not so sure. In conversing with linguists from the second group I tend to bypass the shorthand label and go on to describe the part of the system of ideas I am talking about in enough detail that I can see they understand.

Even monologuists, including writers, lecturers, and not a few conversationalists who lose interest in monitoring how well the other person is following them, make certain assumptions about how much they have to tell their audience to get their point across.[2] Each (barring pathology) builds a semantic structure that he feels is appropriate to his audience, and terminates its elaboration when he thinks he is able to get through. He might be wrong.

The assumption on the part of the speaker that what he is trying to say is known adequately to the hearer for the speaker's purposes can now be embodied in linguistics through the notion of the REFERENTIAL INDEX. Chomsky proposed such an index to register coreferentiality, the condition in which two parts of a sentence refer to the same things.[3] In proposing it, however, he recognized that it did not fit linguistic theory gracefully. Other scholars have shown how it fails to fit, though as far as I know only Winograd has worked out a general model of language that has an explicit place for it. I discuss his model in Chapter 20.

Even the kind of grammar that claims to account for nothing larger than sentences cannot work right unless something akin to the referential index is embodied in it. Specifically, the difference between *John saw him* and *John saw himself* is tied up with the

---

[2] Ure, "Lexical Density and Register Differentiation" (1971), shows a consistent difference between speech situations with feedback and monologues.
[3] Chomsky, *Aspects* (1965), p. 145.

report that whoever John may be in the speaker's and hearer's systems of reference, the person who was seen in the first instance was not that John, and in the second instance it was. Grammars that include relations across sentence boundaries deal not only with coreferentiality but with explicit reference when they discuss pronouns.[4]

Since referential indices are part of the system of language, they should not be confused with indices of perception. Nothing is gained by going around pinning numbers on whatever speaker and hearer might each perceive as different in the world around them or inside their own heads. That is a problem for psychologists, not for linguists. The referential indices of linguistics have to do only with those judgments about sameness or difference of reference that have repercussions in linguistic form.

For example, whenever in English we have a surface grammatical configuration that involves a subject and an object, we have to know whether the subject and object refer to the same thing or not. If they do, the object is in the REFLEXIVE form; if they do not, it is in the nonreflexive form. Huichol has a second kind of reflexive in which for any surface grammatical configuration that involves a possessed noun and its possessor, we have to know whether the possessor is the same as the subject of the sentence. If it is, there is a reflexive possessive that must be used; if it is not, the regular possessive is used. The English sentence *John saw his house* is ambiguous regarding the identity of the owner of the house. It could be John's own house or it could be someone else's house. In Huichol, however, there can be no such ambiguity. *wáani yuu-kíi púu+-zéi* 'John saw his (own) house' is kept carefully distinct from *wáani kíi-ya púu+-zéi* 'John saw his (somebody else's) house'.

The idea of referential distinctness is not as clear cut as the more obvious examples make it seem. Lakoff has pointed out how in conjunctive sentences the replacement of one part by *do so* involves conditions of identity of reference similar to those involved in

---

[4] McKinney, "Participant Identification in Kaje Narrative" (ms).

pronominalization.[5] Yet a large class of examples typified by *Tarzan ate a banana and so did Jane* are not coreferential in the strict sense; each person ate a different banana, and for that matter each performed a different act of eating, probably at a different time and place. But what each did was an act of eating, and what each ate was a banana, so that the recognition criteria of the first part hold true in the second.

In other words, even though we cannot get along without the concept of reference as part of linguistic theory, neither are we able yet to articulate a theory of reference that characterizes the subject adequately. Whatever we come up with eventually, it will have to take into account at least the following observations:

(1) Speakers at times tell hearers explicitly that two or more of the things they are talking about are to be taken as having the same reference. Reflexives are one instance of this. Some equative sentences have a similar effect, as when the detective announces, *This man is the one who killed Colonel Fortescue.*

(2) Sameness of recognition criteria is not equivalent to sameness of reference. *My great-grandfather built his own house and so will I* are similar enough in reference to permit use of the *do so* construction, but refer to different houses, acts of building, and times.

(3) The assumption on the part of the speaker that the hearer has in mind a referential picture equivalent to his own, or at least should have such a picture in mind as a result of what he has said, is at the root of the speaker's decision to elaborate his semantic development no further. If we symbolize that semantic development by a tree of propositions, the end of each branch of the tree is either a predicate or a referential index.[6]

---

[5] Lakoff, "Pronouns and Reference" (ms).

[6] To say that the hearer knows what the speaker is talking about does not imply that all referential indices are definite. The speaker and hearer can be tacitly agreed on the indefiniteness of something as well as on the definiteness of something else. If I ask, *Are there any unicorns grazing in front of your house now?* and you answer *No*, we have agreed on the identity of you and me, your house, and the space around it, and also on the capacity of both of us to recognize a unicorn should one appear. But neither of us has committed himself to reference to a particular unicorn, or even that there are such things.

All that has been said about reference so far applies primarily to reference to individuals. As already mentioned in Chapter 3.2, reference to individuals seems to be fairly straightforward, even though we do not yet know all the rules of the game. When we make reference to groups, however, things are anything but straightforward. We have groups in which no individuals stand out, as in *the Goths sacked Rome*. There are groups defined by relation to a single individual in them, yet treated as groups, as in *the court went to Windsor for the season*. There are still other groups in which the defining individual is separate from the rest of the group in some instances and merged with the group in others: *The chairman reminded us that we had a three o'clock deadline. So we all buckled down and finished the plans.* The second sentence includes the chairman in the group; the first does not. Other groups are weakly constituted; they consist of individuals for most of the reference of the discourse, but the individuals are sometimes put together under a cover label: *The contenders fell apart and retired to their corners.* Other groups are indeterminate, like the conventional *they* of *they say this summer will be hot*, or the predefined *they* of some languages in which *they were fishing* in the absence of any other defining information means 'all the members of our tribe were fishing'.

Two patterns of reference are peculiar to groups. RECIPROCAL reference implies a group split into two parts, say A and B. Whatever action is involved, reciprocal forms tell the hearer that there are some members of A (possibly all) directing the action at members of B, and at the same time some members of B directing the same action at members of A, as in *the armies charged at each other*. RESPECTIVE reference, on the other hand, matches the members of one group to the members of another group ordinally. The sentence *Al and George took their girl friends to Disneyland and Knott's Berry Farm respectively* matches Al with his girl friend and Disneyland and matches George with his girl friend and Knott's Berry Farm.

The time indices mentioned in 3.2 and 20.5 are a specialized kind of referential indices. Different points in time may or may not be distinct within the particular topology imposed on the time line by a discourse.

13

THE GRAMMAR OF SEMANTIC PRODUCTIONS

The kind of semantic development I have talked about in the preceding chapters can be represented by a tree. The infinite family of trees that can serve to represent semantic productions can be characterized much more simply than, say, the syntactic trees of Chomsky.[1] These characterizations are satisfactory for any scale of magnitude from word to discourse.

1. FORMATION

The semantic grammar of propositions takes as its starting point an initial symbol F for "form", representing a proposition, and one rewrite rule that replaces F by one or more predicates P together with zero or more arguments A. The asterisk stands for a string of any number of elements greater than or equal to the subscript beneath it. This is the PREDICATE RULE:

$$F \rightarrow P_1^* A_0^*$$

The symbol A for the arguments is actually a dummy or intermediate symbol. It stands for either a referential index that terminates the recursion or for an indexed proposition. The ARGUMENT RULE has the form

$$A \rightarrow i(:F)$$

where the parentheses indicate that i, which stands for any ref-

---

[1] Chomsky, *Aspects* (1965), "Remarks on Nominalizations" (1970).

erential index, may constitute the entire argument, or that the argument may be further expanded. The Argument Rule is thus a conflation of two rules, A → i and A → i:F, just as the Predicate Rule is a conflation of a presumably limitless number of rules, F → P, F → P A, F → P A A, F → P P, F → P P A, ...

As a formal grammar this fits the standard definition G = (N, T, S, P); that is, the grammar G is a 4-tuple that consists of a set N of nonterminal symbols, a set T of terminal symbols that do not overlap with N (or in set terms, N ∩ T = Ø), a distinguished symbol S that is in N, and a set of productions P by which the distinguished or starting symbol S is related to all possible strings of terminal symbols.[2] In the formation of propositions the non-terminal symbols are F and A, propositions and arguments. The terminal symbols are P, which stands for any predicate, and i, which stands for any referential index. F is distinguished as the starting symbol. The productions are defined by the Predicate Rule and the Argument Rule.

The strings of predicates and referential indices that are implied by this grammar are of little direct interest. We are more interested in the phrase markers implied by the grammar; that is, in the tree that represents the structure or derivational history of a semantic production by telling what arguments are associated with what predicates. This is a two-dimensional representation of the semantic relationships that are implied by the grammar. Strictly speaking it is redundant because in every case it can be recovered from the string that the formal grammar implies; but for the most part we leave the strings aside and talk instead about the corresponding phrase markers.[3]

---

[2] See for example the first footnote of Griebach, "Context-Free Languages" (1969), which is equivalent though phrased in a slightly different way.

[3] Most linguists have an intuitive grasp of structural relations as presented in two dimensions, and object to having to extract structural information from string representations. Mathematicians who work with language and language-like systems, on the other hand, tend to think in terms of grammars and strings and to regard derivational history as logical excess baggage. Linguists who are interested in bridging this gap may find the game of *Queries 'n Theories* by Allen et al. (1970) useful.

This grammar of propositions is recursive in form; one of its symbols, *F*, appears both as the symbol to be rewritten in the Predicate Rule and as one of the symbols that may be used to rewrite another symbol in the Argument Rule. Because of this property there is no limit to the size of trees that are implied by it, even if we were to limit the number of arguments that could be associated with any predicate in the Predicate Rule.[4]

Our use of pronominalization patterns suggests that we treat entire subtrees composed of propositions as indexable entities: *They had to dive from the dock and swim under the hull before the ship's propellers were stopped. When I thought about it later I broke out in a sweat.* The *it* of the second sentence refers to the entire complex of events together with the background circumstance that the ship's propellers were still turning. The referential index that *it* represents is associated with that subtree as a whole rather than with a single component of it. The Argument Rule attaches an index to every proposition but the one that dominates the rest.

Chapter 10.2 implies that each language has a stock of predicates that are available to be fitted together according to the Predicate Rule. Together they constitute the SEMANTIC LEXICON. Several possible predicates of English have been mentioned, each with one or more sets of constraints on what kinds of propositions they can take as arguments: *cause* A L, *hit* {A (I) R | P}, where braces and vertical lines standing for disjunction and parentheses for semantic optionality constitute a condensed notation for distinct sets of arguments, *bend* ({A (I) | Fc}) P (L), and so forth. Each role set is associated with particular areas of meaning of the predicate. If the predicate is used with some role set other than the roles that are registered in the lexicon as the conventional ones, we can

---

[4]   The predicates I characterized as lexical in Chapter 8 normally take no more than seven arguments: *carry* takes AF P L R B V I in *they carried the supplies clear across the cliff for me on their backs with a rope*, with supernumerary B, and is about as complicated as things get. When we consider the rhetorical predicates of Chapter 14, however, it will become apparent that a relation like *and* has absolutely no limit on the number of arguments it can take.

predict that the nonconventional role set will be recognized and reacted to as strange. We can also predict that if it is understood at all, it will be understood in terms of the general meanings of the roles that are used.

Predicates have many other properties besides their conventional occurrence with certain roles. Many predicates can probably be decomposed into semantic components. All have associative and other ties to other predicates as was described in Chapter 10. All these other properties could, however, be considered as conditions that govern the appropriateness of selecting a particular predicate for a particular situation. The grammar of propositions that I have given puts certain limits on the ways in which predicates can be linked to each other. Any assemblage of propositions that is put together by the Predicate Rule and the Argument Rule is capable of being processed into speech; the grammar itself lays down no further restrictions on what can be put together. As far as the possibility of predicates being assembled into propositions and communicated is concerned, the grammar does not hinder us from bringing together the prosaic with the outlandish, the appropriate with the wildly inappropriate, truth with falsehood, and sense with nonsense if we wish to. Whether we construct utterances that are contrary to other canons of appropriateness is a matter of prudence, not grammar. There is so much evidence that language is used not only to inquire, to inform, or to command, but also to befuddle, mislead, or simply fill up time without saying anything, that a theory of language that had no room for these uses along with the more prosaic ones would be unrealistic.

Not only must a theory of grammar allow for violation of counsels of prudence and for failure to make sense; it must leave room for verbal play. Consider the poets who would have to go on welfare if they were required to obey the dicta laid down by grammarians. The soul of a good deal of poetry is in the bending of ordinary semantics to just this side, or in some case just the other side, of the bounds of conventional semantics. Sometimes what the poet bends stays bent; when the Hebrew poet had Job "escape by the skin of his teeth" he set up a deformation in the meaning of the word for 'skin' that has endured for millenia.[5]

The grammar of semantic productions implies phrase markers, as already mentioned. The representation of trees that is most generally familiar to linguists is the kind used by Chomsky to depict phrase markers in his syntax-centered grammar.[6] Chomsky's trees have their roots toward the top center of the page, or in the north. A NORTH-ORIENTED tree representation of the phrase marker that underlies the Huichol example of Chapter 11.2 would look like this:[7]

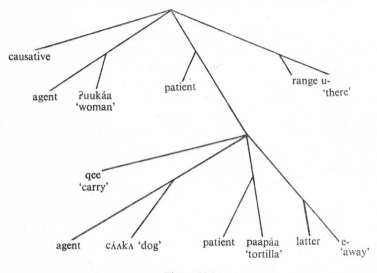

Figure 13.1

[5]   *Job* 19:20.

[6]   Chomsky, *Syntactic Structures* (1957).

[7]   In this phrase marker and the equivalent ones to follow I have not gone further into the semantic structure of the words for 'woman', 'dog', or 'tortilla', or the prefixes 'there' and 'away'. Each of these is ultimately represented by a development of its own that terminates in a referential index to indicate the speaker's judgment that the hearer has established an equivalent reference. The subtree corresponding to each of these forms develops along lines such as those suggested by Langendoen in *The Study of Syntax* (1969). Cited forms in this tree and the ones that follow indicate incomplete representation of derivations.

A whole vocabulary has grown up around north-oriented trees: *left* as a metaphor for 'preceding', *right* for 'following', *above* 'toward the root', and *below* 'away from the root'. While such a vocabulary is useful in discussing more abstract levels of representation in which temporal ordering is not in question, it adds an air of the unreal in proportion as we get closer to surface structures in which time, not graphic placement, takes an increasing importance.

The north-oriented representation is difficult to type or to set in type, therefore also expensive. Even though it is the one most linguists know, in this book I have shifted to the fully equivalent form of phrase marker representation used by Frantz, in which the root is at the top left or northwest.[8] This is reasonably simple to type. A NORTHWEST-ORIENTED tree representation of the same phrase marker is used in Chapter 11:

---

[8] Frantz, *Blackfoot* (1970).

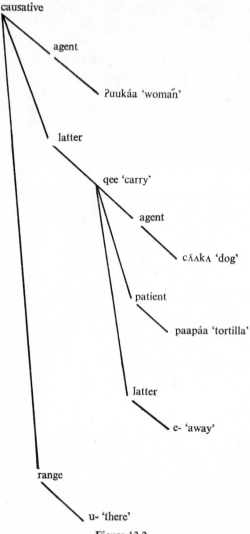

Figure 13.2

LINEAR representations of phrase markers are also possible. They are ones that can be written out on a line instead of in two dimensions, but that still give the correct grouping of elements by using parentheses. In Chapter 11, for example, I introduced a notation that distinguished the form of elements in the semantic lexicon from the values assigned to each variable in that form. This ASSIGNMENT REPRESENTATION of a phrase marker represents a proposition by its predicate, its role set, and an assignment list that tells what argument corresponds to each role in the role set. The assignment representation of the same phrase marker was also given in Chapter 11:

> causative A L R (Puukáa, qee A P L
> (cʌʌkʌ, paapáa, e-), u-)

A fully PARENTHESIZED REPRESENTATION of the same phrase marker simply moves the elements out of the assignment list of an assignment representation and groups each of them with its appropriate role symbol. A matching pair of parentheses therefore corresponds to a level in the north-oriented tree or a tabulator stop in the northwest-oriented tree:

> causative (agent Puukáa) (latter (qee (agent cʌʌkʌ) (patient paapáa) (latter e-)) (range u-)

For a representation that takes reference into account, Winograd uses proposition indexes as a basis for a nongraphic LINKED representation of propositions.[9] Like other linear representations, the linked form is equivalent to a tree, but is much easier to manage on a typewriter or in a computer. Proposition nesting is indicated by writing the index of one proposition as the argument of another. For example, if we assign referential indices from the set $a1, a2, ...,$ we can take the same causative tree in Huichol and present all the relations in it in the following form:

> (causative a1 a2 a3)
> (a1: agent a4)
> (a2: latter a6)
> (a3: range a5)
> (a4: Puukáa a5 'woman')

---

[9] Winograd, *Procedures* (1971). Simmons and Slocum (1972) use a similar representation.

(a6:   *qee* a7 a8 a9 'carry')
(a7:   agent a10)
(a8:   patient a12)
(a9:   latter a14)
(a10: *cáʌkʌ* all 'dog')
(a12: *paapáa* a13 'tortilla')
(14: *e-* a15 a16 'away from')
(a16: range a5)

In this set of propositions, the indexes *a5*, *a11*, *a13*, and *a15* refer
to objects and places that are either defined for the first time by
the statement, or that refer to entities defined earlier in the discourse, depending on context.

All four of these representations of phrase markers are completely
equivalent. There is no information about either content or organization in one that is not in each of the others. Still other representations of the same information are of course possible; one
notes the south-oriented trees used to depict evolutionary sequences
(even though specific genealogies are by tradition north-oriented).
For linguistics, however, the forms I have listed are more than
enough.

2. TRANSFORMATION

The phrase markers that are implied by the formational grammar
do not account directly for actual speech forms. None of the
illustrations given in the last section shows that what a Huichol
says is *Puukáa píi+qéitʌa paapáa cáʌkʌ* 'the woman gave the
dog a tortilla'. Why bother, then, writing a grammar in this way
if it generates things that correspond to speech so loosely?

The formational grammar of Section One is a grammar that
controls certain relationships and no others. It deals with predicates
and their arguments and relates them in a tree structure. In doing
this it aids us in noticing certain patterns or generalizations that
we recognize as part of language. We see that things like *the boy
swept the porch with a broom* shares a good deal of its meaning

with *the boy swept the porch, the broom swept the porch, the sweeping of the porch, the sweeping of the broom, the sweeping of the boy, the action of the broom,* and other expressions that differ from each other semantically, but not by much. Insofar as their meanings can be related, we want a consistent way of making that relationship clear. This we do by comparing their semantic UNDERLYING REPRESENTATIONS rather than by comparing their grammatical and phonological SURFACE REPRESENTATIONS. The surface representations, on the other hand, can be compared with each other to show a different kind of relatedness — the relatedness of *Max kissed Susan* with *the last one to leave pays the bill,* or of *leave the dishes and we'll go to the game* with *build a better mousetrap and the world will beat a path to your door,* where it is hardly any kind of semantic relatedness that is in focus.

The task of linguistics is not to prove either that surface representations are all that there is to language or that underlying representations are the whole story. The best linguistics now gives us three kinds of information about language: (1) what the surface representations of utterances are like, (2) what the underlying representations of utterances are like, and (3) how the two match each other. The matching relation, or TRANSFORMATION, is generally taken today as a mapping from the set of possible underlying representations onto the set of possible surface representations.[10]

---

[10]   The inverse mapping from surface representations to underlying representations appears to be farther from our reach at present. Sydney Lamb, for example, had hoped that his stratificational model of grammar would provide a decoding mode that used the same network of relationships as was used to express the encoding or meaning-to-sound mode, as explained in his *Outline of Stratificational Grammar* (1966). The viable fragments of grammars that I have seen written in that model, however, turn out to be unidirectional. If, as is sometimes suggested, we understand speech by producing our own analog of what we think the other person is saying, the inverse mapping would not be needed at all to account for that kind of linguistic behavior. If on the other hand we also operate in a decoding mode at times, then the inverse of a grammar is a problem that merits a good deal of study. Woods, "Transition Network Grammars" (1970), comments on the difficulties involved in arriving at the inverse of a grammar.

In order for the transformational part of language to operate it must presuppose not only the content structure that the formational grammar exemplified in Section One of this chapter provides; it must also take into account the situation in which speech is taking place, everything that has been said up to that point, and everything that the speaker assumes that the hearer already knows. This cohesion component, discussed in Chapter 19, influences the way the content is organized for presentation.[11] Thematic or staging decisions, which include the speaker's decisions about the way in which the things he says are to be brought before the speaker (Chapter 21) and the relative prominence he assigns to different parts of the content structure, are a third major kind of input to the transformational component. How the transformational component welds together the results of the speaker's content, cohesion, and staging decisions is only poorly understood, since most work in the area of transformations has concentrated on cognitive underlying structures and only tentatively reached out toward the others.

The transformational component could be thought of as the means of sorting out of the consequences of the speaker's decisions in order to express them in speech. It channels information into surface forms that are tightly constrained and therefore are appropriate vehicles of communication.

As a result of the transformational process, speech takes on a form that can be partitioned into constituents that stand in conventionally recognized arrangements relative to each other in time. The process of doing this sometimes assigns the same surface form to more than one semantic configuration. AMBIGUITY is the result; as far as we know, all natural languages have some ambiguous surface forms. The presence of ambiguity in language is by itself sufficient reason for distinguishing underlying structure from surface structure, in that underlying structure permits us to specify the nature of ambiguities in a way that we could not do by reference only to the ambiguous forms themselves.

---

[11] Cohesion is not synonymous with Chomsky's "performance" (*Aspects*, 1965). It appears to be capable of being presented formally even though it is time dependent to a certain extent.

In addition, the transformational process often results in a considerable amount of information being communicated more than once. Consider, for example, the REDUNDANCY of the subject and the verb ending in English *he drives a truck*, where *he* and the *-s* ending of *drives* both communicate that the subject is singular and third person. We do not want to assume that the choice that gives rise to *he* and the choice that gives rise to *-s* are really independent of each other. Copying transformations of the kind commonly used to express agreement permit us to recognize the multiple expressions of a single choice.

Finally, transformation results in a definite ORDERING in time of the expressions of all the surface elements. This ordering is not a necessary characteristic of the underlying semantics, but rather an accommodation to the time dependent way in which the vocal tract operates.[12]

All that I have said about the transformational process in this section is programmatic and unsupported here by examples. Nevertheless, a transformational grammar is a compelling consequence of the decision to shape linguistic theory by distinguishing fundamentally between choice and implementation. There are plenty of examples in the current linguistic literature on transformations that relate underlying structure with surface structure if we are willing to confine ourselves to single sentences. In my own work I have not yet tackled the problem of writing down the explicit relationships between deep and surface forms when more than sentences are involved; occupied with the underlying structures themselves, I have simply assumed that this can be done as an extension of sentence-based transformation theory. Frantz's work on Blackfoot includes explicit transformations that operate on an underlying structure whose form agrees with the phrase markers that I generate by the Predicate Rule and the Argument Rule of Section One. Quillian's semantic memory model and Simmons and Slocum's discourse model contain transformational components that put out information into more than one sentence when the

---

[12]   Chafe, "Language as Symbolization" (1967).

quantity of information in a semantic network is too much for the available surface structure to convey.[13] In the light of Chomsky's distinction between competence and performance, this has the consequence of making the sentence a performance notion, rather than the basic unit of linguistic competence that Chomsky assumed it to be.[14] It indicates a direction, beyond the sentence, that transformational studies could most profitably take.

3. SPECIAL MAPPINGS

The formational grammar of semantic productions given in Section One is exceedingly simple, maybe even too simple. Yet it allows the relationships that seem to be important in discourse to be expressed.

Additional complexity enters the picture in two distinct ways. The first is in the nature of the elements I have called predicates. Undoubtedly they should not be taken as simple terminal symbols as I have taken them here — ultimate elements in a theory of semantics. They probably do have some kind of internal structure of their own that is not accounted for satisfactorily by providing them with associative and other relationships to other predicates. For the present, however, I leave the composition of predicates to one side. It does not appear to affect our understanding of the structure of discourse, though it is important for our total understanding of language.

A further clarification is needed to head off possible false impressions. The formational grammar of propositions given in Section One is clear cut and definite. It purports to model the organization of meaning in language at a deep or primitive level. As a model its depth is only relative, and there may well be a structure that we do not yet see standing behind that structure.

---

[13] Quillian, "Semantic Memory" (1968). Simmons and Slocum, "Generating English Discourse from Semantic Networks" (1972).
[14] Chomsky, *Aspects* (1965).

All that the formational grammar claims is that the representation of underlying structure it provides is adequate for saying what I want to say about discourse. Even there, as should be clear from Chapter 9, phenomena like the instrument and benefactive roles can be formulated in distinct ways, each of which fits the formational grammar, but one of which possibly represents the result of the application of a consolidation transformation and hence is not as far removed from the surface form itself as the other formulation is. Deep structure, then, is relative to what we are trying to express by it.

The nature of the transformational component as I see it differs somewhat from the way Chomsky presented it. The kinds of constraints I will list are pertinent to a Chomsky grammar; if they were applied to it they could result in an artifact more appropriate to the subject matter.

The principal constraint has to do with the way in which transformations are ordered. Possibly because of the fact that grammars are written on paper, it seems to have become customary to think of the ordering of transformations (and of phrase structure rules for that matter) as fixed in a strict order. Their ordering is, however, a partial ordering rather than a strict ordering. In other words, a particular transformation does not necessarily have one and only one other transformation as its predecessor. Instead it has as its predecessors all rules, whether formational or transformational, that provide an output that is recognized by its structure index.[15] It has as its successors all rules whose structure indexes recognize the trees that it puts out. While this principle of partial rather than strict ordering has actually been implicit in all formal definitions of rule systems, it seems to have been lost sight of in practice.

The most notable point at which the ordering of transformational

---

[15] For the technical concepts of transformational grammar the reader is referred to standard works: Bach, *An Introduction to Transformational Grammars* (1964), Hale, *Transformational Syntax* (1965), Chomsky, *Aspects* (1965). A structure index is a means of recognizing a particular family of trees, and has nothing to do with the referential indices mentioned earlier.

rules has been done without reference to the connectivity relations[16] that are implicit in the rules themselves is in the distinction between a grammatical transformational component of grammar and a phonological component. I take this to be a residue of crypto-Bloomfieldian linguistics, in that there is no necessary discontinuity between grammar and phonology in a transformational grammar. Some rules recognize or introduce nonphonological features, others phonological features, others both. Possibly the sharp difference between sound and grammar has been informally carried over into formal grammar because it is useful and reflects something fundamental about language. What the detailed analysis of partial orderings in rule systems shows us, however, is the interpenetration of grammar and phonology, not the line between them.[17]

What I expect to see by the time we have looked closely at complete transformational systems that include phonology is that some phonological rules (rules that either recognize or add or change phonological information, regardless of what else there may be in the rule) presuppose nothing about the output of any of the nonphonological transformations. Some of the rules that impose meter or assonance, for example, might even recognize the output of the formational grammar directly. Naturally a great many rules that deal with phonology are ordered late; but the point is that this ordering should express a fact about language

[16]   Connectivity relations are those that are derived in the case of transformational grammar from predecessor-successor or tree producing-tree recognizing relations between pairs of rules. Their use in the analysis of affix systems, which also involve partial ordering, is discussed in Grimes, "Positional Analysis" (1967), which can be applied to rules with almost no change. See B. Kroeker, "Morphophonemics of Nambiquara" (1972).

[17]   It is sometimes pointed out that phonological rules have the form of context sensitive rewrite rules that operate on strings, while transformations operate on trees. Since, however, any string can be mapped onto a tree in which each element of the string corresponds to a daughter node and all daughter nodes go to one parent node, there is no particular justification for using context sensitive rules for phonology to the exclusion of transformations. Furthermore, Chomsky and Halle, *The Sound Pattern of English* (1968), use context sensitive rules whose context part contains a good deal of structural information in the form of labelled brackets, implying structures or trees considerably more complex than those that correspond to single strings.

rather than an arbitrary partitioning of the conceptual apparatus used to talk about language. It seems reasonable, furthermore, to treat the part of the grammar that provides explicit phonological underlying forms as though it were a set of transformations with highly specific structure indices that usually involve particular semantic predicates. Chafe has shown that rules of this kind, which we could call SYMBOLIZATION rules, have to come after the part of the grammar that adjusts idioms.[18] Most of the phonological rules in the usual sense follow the symbolization rules.

In the entire transformational system there are widely varying degrees of generality with which rules apply. The least general rules tend to be the ones that express irregularities. The most general ones express what we call regularities, but there is no clear dividing line between the two. Lakoff and others have discussed irregularity and specific irregularities in considerable detail.[19] Certain kinds of irregularities are of special interest in the framework of propositional grammar.

Transformations match underlying semantic configurations with utterances. For each kind of predicate in a semantic representation, the roles that are associated with it match surface phenomena in specific ways.

Some role elements are obligatorily represented in the corresponding surface forms. Others may be deleted under some conditions even though there is evidence that they are present in the underlying semantics. A deleted role element, however, is not the same as a role element that is not there in the first place.

Some role elements are always represented in the surface form. In Huichol, for example, any predicate that takes an agent normally has that agent represented in the surface form by something — at the very least, by a subject pronoun prefix. If in the process of consolidation with a causative (11.2) an underlying agent is shifted into a different role such as benefactive, then the representation rules for benefactive apply to it instead. (Such shifting of roles is

18   Chafe, "Idiomaticity" (1968).
19   Lakoff, *Irregularity* (1965).

done only when something else is being brought in to act as agent.) The original agent is still represented in the surface form, but not in the way most agents are represented.

As has already been pointed out, role elements may be deleted if they are redundant in terms of the previous context, or obvious from the situation of speaking, or conventional in terms of standard cultural expectations. A question about the missing role element will often elicit an answer that contains a certain amount of pique; the person who asked it should have known better. He should have been able to decipher it by rules of anaphora, or should have seen what the speaker was pointing at, or should have known what everybody knows who gets into that kind of situation.

In other cases the speaker does not know or does not wish to tell what a particular role element is. In this case a question about the missing role element elicits a definite answer. The answer may be of the "I don't know" variety, or it may give out information grudgingly that was supposed to be kept a secret. In English the passive allows the agent to be dropped in cases where filling it in might prove embarrassing as in, *A: The folder was left on the desk, apparently. B: Who left it there? A: Well, if you really must know, I did.*

Where a role is not a part of the semantics at all, rather than being deleted under the usual conditions, the reaction to a question about it is uniformly one of puzzlement, as in *A: I ran a mile and a half this morning. B: What did you ran a mile and a half this morning? A: Huh?* In this example B has taken the sense of *run* that includes a machine as patient, as in *we ran the boat across the lake*, while A began with the sense of *run* as a physical activity that combines patient with agent. The lack of communication highlights the inappropriateness of a separate patient in the only sense that A has in mind. In other words, there is nothing in A's semantics that could be construed as a patient, so that there is no deleted material to be recovered under any circumstances.

Analysis of data in terms of role systems involves keeping three things clearly separated: (1) underlying representations, (2) surface representations, and (3) the mappings between them. Practical difficulty always seems to result from trying to combine any two of the three.

An example of the necessity for keeping mappings themselves distinct from both underlying and surface forms is found in the referent assignment rules for Mamanwa of the Philippines. Jeanne Miller describes Mamanwa clauses in terms of the usual verb adjuncts of Philippine languages: subject, object, referent, and accessory.[20] In terms of the semantics of verbs, however, each adjunct type is systematically related to several different underlying roles. The roles I give here are interpreted in terms of Chapter 8; they differ systematically from Miller's earlier set.

For example, the referent is assigned as follows. There are DIRECTION predicates that take an agent together with either a latter state, a range, or a former state, depending upon the meaning of the verb. Agent matches subject; latter, range, or former match referent. The sentence *ambalik hao* DINI meaning 'I will return HERE' has the latter state as referent; *ampanik hao* KA NIZEG 'I will climb THE COCONUT TREE' has range as referent, *ampanaw* DI *hao* 'I will leave HERE' has former state as referent.

ACTION-PROCESS predicates take agent or agent-patient matched with subject, patient alone matched with object, range matched with referent, and instrument matched with accessory. No action-process predicate takes all four. *anhinang hao* KA LAGKAW 'I will watch THE CHILD' has 'child' as range in the referent slot; *ibalabag o ining kaban* DIZAN KINING PIRTAHAN 'will bar the door WITH THIS CHEST' has 'door' as range in the referent slot and 'chest' as instrument in the accessory slot. (Patient with an action-process predicate is changed or acted upon directly; range is not. 'I will build a house' and 'I will cut down a banana tree' contain patient as object, not range.)

CONVEYANCE predicates have an agent-former state matched with subject, patient matched with accessory, and latter state matched with referent: *ambaligzà hao ka makaen* KAN MARIYA 'I will sell the food TO MARY' has 'Mary', the latter state, as referent. Many

20   J. Miller, "Semantic Structure of Mamanwa Verbs" (1973).

conveyance predicates have directional counterparts with a different role set; they often include in their meaning that the agent moves along with the patient, while with other conveyance predicates such as 'sell' the patient may separate from the agent as a result of the action. *ioli nao ining baskit doro* KAN ROBIRTO 'I will return this basket TO ROBERTO' has 'Roberto' as latter in the referent slot, and implies that the agent and the patient do not separate. It differs in its role set from the directional 'I will return here'.

ACQUISITION predicates have an agent-latter state matched with subject, patient matched with object, and former state matched with referent: *paliten o ya bozag doro* KAN NOAY 'I will buy potatoes FROM NOAY' has 'Noay' as former, expressed by referent. Here the patient is not changed by the action. Instead, treating something as patient with an acquisition predicate frequently implies that it is being acquired as a whole, whereas treating the same thing as former state or range implies an area or field out of which the patient is acquired: *hinangen o* YA BANIG with *ya banig* 'mat' as object means 'I will make THE MAT', implying all of it; *hinangan o* YA BANIG with *ya banig* as referent (shown by the verbal inflection) means 'I will make PART OF THE MAT'. This whole-part relationship expressed by patient as over against former state or range is much more clear cut in other languages of the Philippines than in Mamanwa.

EXPERIENCER predicates appear to have idiosyncratic mappings to surface structure. Patient matches subject; but force matches object, referent, or accessory depending upon the particular predicate. In *masakiten si Ilina* KA BIRIBIRI 'BERIBERI is making Ilena sick', the force 'beriberi' (a deficiency disease) is object; but in *nabalikan nami* YA HILANAT 'we have FEVER again' the force 'fever' is referent.

In these ways the semantic roles of Mamanwa are combined with different predicates, and the results fall into eight definable clause patterns. The key to Mamanwa grammar is the ability to keep track of the different ways in which roles match surface categories.

In English the ways in which this matching is accomplished seem to depend more on what individual roles are present and being expressed than they do on the complete complex of roles that is there and the meaning of the predicates themselves, as is the case in Mamanwa. I have already mentioned the general rule for subject assignment. As Chafe formulates it, if there is an agent or a patient of an experiential verb, it is subject as in *I saw the President;* if not, the latter state is subject as in *I was given the best seat;* if none of those are present, the patient is subject as in *I was tired.*[21] The choice of a passive form of expression removes agent from the running for this rule, with the result that latter state or patient match the subject even in the presence of an agent as in *I was given the best seat by the manager.* Several refinements on the rule as Chafe gives it come to mind: range is ranked after patient as in *sword clanged against shield;* and in the absence of any viable candidate for subject, a dummy subject is inserted, as in *it seems to be snowing.*

I suspect that there are actually two factors involved in English subject assignment, but the details have yet to be fitted into place. The first factor is a ranking of roles in terms of priorities for subject assignment. This ranking, however, is probably a partial ordering that allows two or more roles to tie for subject position. The second factor breaks the tie; it is related to the thematic properties by which the relationship among the roles is staged for the hearer's benefit. In *this necktie* (P) *was given me* (L) *by my wife* (AF) vs. *I* (L) *was given this necktie* (P) *by my wife* (AF), neither patient nor latter state outranks the other in the general plan of subject assignment. Rather the choice is made on grounds of staging: in one case the speaker is talking about the necktie, and in the other about what happened to him.

Both Mamanwa and English illustrate an important point about deep-to-surface mappings: they are not simple. One could think of the mapping as having a job like that of the traffic officer in the parking lot at a football game. There are only so many places that can be filled; yet cars of all sizes and shapes and degrees of

21 Chafe, *Meaning and the Structure of Language* (1970), p. 244.

maneuverability come in from all directions and have to be accommodated somehow. The surface patterns of language likewise provide a limited number of places for information that comes in a wide variety. The process of accommodating each kind of information into surface constructions thus requires routings as complex as the gyrations of the man in the blue coat as he tries to get all the cars to pack in without jamming or wrinkling fenders.

As if that were not enough, individual predicates may have special properties that require them to be matched to surface structure in a particular way. Certain ones may also be prohibited from going into surface structure in the same way that most of the predicates that share their other properties are permitted to fit. The English predicate that underlies the word *seem*, for example, must undergo the process known as EXTRAPOSITION before it can appear in a surface form.[22] The semantically similar form *is likely*, on the other hand, may or may not undergo extraposition, depending probably on thematic choices. Thus we have the extraposed forms *it seems that he came* and *it is likely that he came*, but only *that he came is likely* as the non-extraposed counterpart.

---

[22] Jacobs and Rosenbaum, *English Transformational Grammar* (1968), pp. 171-78.

14

RHETORICAL STRUCTURE

In Chapters 8 through 13 we considered the area of language within which a small number of semantic roles play an important part. Role-related underlying structure, or LEXICAL structure, however, accounts for only a fraction of language content. Now we turn to the remaining propositions that are represented in underlying structure — in other words, to those propositions whose predicates do not involve specifications on roles that must be present in their arguments.

Propositions whose arguments are not related to their predicates via semantic roles are called RHETORICAL propositions. The predicates in them are called rhetorical predicates. Their main function could be thought of as that of organizing the content of discourse. They join lexical propositions together, and they join other rhetorical propositions together. In a tree that represents the underlying structure of a discourse (Chapter 13), most of the propositions near the root are likely to be rhetorical, while most of the propositions near the leaves are likely to be lexical. Nevertheless, some rhetorical propositions may be dominated by lexical propositions: *we just realized that either we will have to leave home before six or they will have to postpone the meeting*, for example, contains a lexical predicate *realize* that dominates a range element, which in turn dominates the alternative predicate symbolized by *either ... or*. In general, however, the tendency is for lexical predicates to be found in the more finely partitioned, terminal part of a derivation, and the rhetorical predicates in the upper reaches.[1] The relationship exemplified in *although we were nearly out of milk, the children didn't complain*, in which *although* relates the two lexical clauses as adversatives, is more typical of the standard arrangement in which rhetorical propositions dominate lexical ones.

Fuller's *The Inductive Method of Bible Study* was the first attempt to come to my attention in which interestingly large sections of text were grouped according to a small number of explicit organizing relations. The well established tradition of OUTLINING gives similar groupings of elements within a text; though rarely is the outliner moved to be explicit about the kinds of coordination and subordination upon which his outline is based. Fuller's analysis of a text, however, gives groupings that are equivalent to an outline, then goes on to include the semantic basis for each grouping.

Fuller's relationships between propositions correspond rather closely to the ones I list later in this chapter, though there are cases where some of his relationships can be combined on the grounds that the differences between them are attributable to differences in their arguments or to staging differences. He distinguishes two kinds, logically parallel to the grammatical notions of coordination and subordination. Logical relationships that involve "equality of class" include series, progression, and alternatives. Those that involve "equality by support" include negative-positive, general-specific, fact-interpretation, way-end, and comparison. They are in the category of restatements. There are other supporting relationships as well that involve assertions distinct from the ones they support rather than being restatements: ground, inference, cause-effect, fact-illustration, means-end, and setting-happening. Still other supporting relationships may contain contrary elements: adversative, question-answer, and situation-response.

A group headed up by John Beekman have been exchanging

---

[1] Strictly speaking, the role predicates are themselves rhetorical, since they embody no constraints on the role composition of their arguments. They can still be cut out as a separate class, however, by the fact that they are always dominated by lexical predicates, whereas rhetorical predicates in the ordinary sense are not so restricted.

papers on Bible translation that take Fuller's work together with Fillmore's case grammar as their common point of departure. These include propositional analyses of entire books of the Bible. The results of their work are to be published in a book by Beekman that should be an interesting contribution to discourse studies.

Longacre has investigated abstract relationships that have domains beyond the sentence.[2] His list of what I am calling rhetorical relationships is similar to Fuller's. He makes the interesting point that the minimal expression of most of these relationships is normally the sentence, whereas the minimal expression of the relationships that enter into lexical propositions is normally the clause. It is possible, of course, to find rhetorical relations embedded deeply within clauses as in *let's have no more of your neither-here-nor-there observations*, and to find role relationships spread out over several sentences, as in *The stone fell. It hit the ground. Zog made it happen. He used a tree trunk.* Nevertheless, his kind of observation is important in that it establishes regularities of mapping between underlying and surface structure, and thereby makes it possible to look for conditions (possibly related to staging in the first example and to rate of information transmission in the second) under which the ordinary mappings are overridden.

Rhetorical predicates are divided in two ways. The first division is along the dimension of coordination and subordination. PARATACTIC predicates dominate all their arguments in coordinate fashion. HYPOTACTIC predicates have as one of their arguments, the CENTER, a term with respect to which the proposition as a whole is subordinated to some other proposition by being added to it as an extra argument. NEUTRAL predicates have both paratactic and hypotactic forms.

Barbara Hollenbach suggests in a personal communication that there is another division of rhetorical predicates which parallels the intensional properties of lexical predicates discussed in Chapter

---

[2] Ballard, Conrad, and Longacre, "Interclausal Relations" (1971), "More on Interclausal Relations" (1971).

11, dividing them into symmetric and asymmetric (or more properly, antisymmetric) types. Symmetric predicates are such that if they assert that *a* is related to *b* in a particular way, then *b* is related to *a* in the same way without inconsistency with the meaning of the predicate; any differences in order are staging differences. Asymmetric predicates on the other hand are such that if *a* is asymmetrically related to *b*, then it is false to say that *b* is related to *a* in the same way.

1. PARATACTIC PREDICATES

There appear to be only two purely paratactic predicates; all the other candidates for the class turn out on examination to be neutral. ALTERNATIVE, however, seems to be truly paratactic. It offers a choice of this, or this, or that, in the sense that as soon as one is chosen, no further choices are possible. At the circus Johnny's mother tells him, "Johnny, you may have a hot dog, or a hamburger, or a candy apple. Or you may have some cotton candy." If she puts it that way, the rules of the game are that once Johnny has picked one thing, the rest of the game is off. In this way the alternative predicate is like the logician's exclusive OR. It is symmetric in that no matter how the arguments are listed, we can choose only one of them. Its arguments do not, however, seem to be ordered intrinsically, as are the arguments of the OR connective in the Lisp programming language.[3]

RESPONSE involves two semantic subtrees in an asymmetric relation in which the content of the second is largely taken from the first, but new material is present as well. The most obvious response arguments would be a question and its answer. The question normally contains a good deal of information about the situation that is being talked about, and a successful reply can be made only by accepting the information that is given in the question. Q: *Where were you last night?* A: *I was over at Charlie's.* begins

---

[3] McCarthy et al., *LISP 1.5 Programmer's Manual* (1962).

with the questioner stating the equivalent of *you were somewhere last night* within the framework of his question. The answerer accepts that; if he does not, then he has to disagree specifically with it — *what do you mean, where was I? I wasn't anywhere.* (The latter answer is not too good as epistemology, but fine as ethnography, since it is equivalent to *I was at home,* and goes back to the observation that the question would probably never have been asked unless the questioner had reason to believe that the answerer was not in his usual place.)

Remark and reply illustrate the response pattern without an interrogative element in the first part. The reply to a remark has to be a reply to that remark, not to some other, if the speech is normal. On the other hand, the logical relationship between the remark and the reply does not have to be spelled out directly. A: *We have a couple of crocuses in bloom.* B: *I'd better take a look at my casting rod.* is a normal remark and reply in which the connecting link, that blooming crocuses imply spring and spring implies fishing, is left unsaid. This indirect linkage is much more common in replies to remarks than it is in answers to questions, although it also takes place there. A: *Where were you last night?* B: *I haven't had a drink for a month* starts out with the explicit *you were somewhere last night; tell me where it was.* The answer, however, is not an answer so much as it is a reply to a remark like *I think you were at some bar* which is never actually uttered.

Both the plots of fairy tales and the writings of scientists are built on a response pattern. The first part gives a problem and the second its solution. The solution has to be a solution to the problem that was stated, not some other; and the problem is stated only to be solved. If the prince rescues some other maiden than the one that was originally abducted by the giant, he hasn't played the game. If the problem to be solved is one in plant breeding, the solution had better be a plant breeding solution, not a sociological one, even though some of the happiest moments of science come in fact from payoffs in the wrong area. Again, however, the content of the second part is dependent upon the content of the first part to a great extent. How to express this interlocking seems to be beyond us, especially if we try to express it as conditions on the arguments of the response predicate; but that is the shape of the relation.

I had originally regarded *sequence* as a paratactic predicate.[4] Since the development of Litteral's time index, however,[5] I find that sequence is best regarded as the neutral predicate *collection* with nonoverlapping time indexing of the arguments. Sequence is discussed further in Section Three of this chapter.

2. HYPOTACTIC PREDICATES

Hypotactic predicates are mainly asymmetric. They relate their arguments to a proposition that dominates them rather than relating their arguments among themselves. The hypotactic proposition is added as an extra argument to some other proposition, so that the hypotactic proposition as a whole is subordinate to the rest of the dominating proposition.[6]

As mentioned, one argument of a hypotactic predicate is designated as its center. This argument is the one through which the predicate is related to some other proposition as an extra argument. For example, the hypotactic predicate *specifically*, which subordinates details to a more general statement, can be taken apart from any context to have two arguments, the general element (which is the center) and the specific element, as in Figure 14.1:

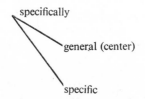

specifically

general (center)

specific

Figure 14.1 General form of a hypotactic predicate.

---

[4]   Grimes, "Outlines and Overlays" (1972).
[5]   Litteral, "Rhetorical Predicates and Time Topology" (1972).
[6]   This characterization of hypotactic predicates differs from the one I gave in

In text, however, this predicate appears to have only one argument, the specific one. The general argument is the proposition that dominates it, as in Figure 14.2:

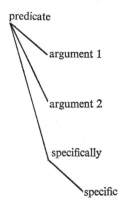

Figure 14.2 General form of a hypotactic predicate in context.

A form like *He saved the day; he made three touchdowns.* has a general-specific structure that can be represented by adding the predicate *specifically* as an additional argument to the general

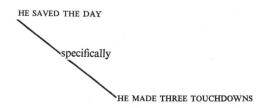

Figure 14.3 Hypotactic predicate.

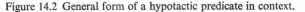

"Outlines and Overlays" (1972), in which the dominating proposition was tagged (by another rhetorical predicate) as *central* and the subordinate parts as *peripheral.* The representation of texts that this strategy gave me failed to show subordinating relationships in a way that could be capitalized on for describing mappings to surface structure. The current formulation, which was suggested by Bonnie Meyer (personal communication), is more compatible with the traditional notion of coordination and subordination.

statement *he saved the day*. Without going further into the underlying structure of either sentence, the picture is that of Figure 14.3.

In terms of a linked representation of the propositions involved,
using indices in place of propositions in full, the way in which a
hypotactic predicate fits in with others is shown more clearly:

> (a1: HE SAVED THE DAY (omitting other details))
> (a2: HE MADE THREE TOUCHDOWNS)
> (a3: specifically a1 (center) a2)

Here the link from *a3* to *a1* is preserved, rather than being lost as
it is in the tree diagram.

Although I am not completely satisfied with the basis of classification, there does seem to be some point in dividing hypotactic
predicates into SUPPLEMENTARY or SUPPORTING predicates that add
detail or explain or substantiate something, SETTING predicates
that locate things in space and time, and IDENTIFICATION predicates
that establish and maintain reference. These three kinds are similar
to the distinction made in Chapter 4 between background, setting,
and identification information in discourse in general. As a sub-
division of hypotactic predicates themselves, however, this three-
way distinction is not ideal. In the first place, it does not match
the kinds of information that were discussed in the earlier chapters
exactly in that it leaves out collateral information. In the second
place, it applies in the same loose fashion to paratactic and neutral
predicates. What I think we have is two partly independent ways
of classifying rhetorical predicates. By the form they give to a
derivational tree (possibly a staging effect) they are paratactic,
hypotactic, and neutral. By what they are used for in discourse
they divide into predicates that relate the kinds of information
communicated in discourse with each other.

So, within the framework of this inadequately loose classification,
the following seven predicates could be called supporting: ATTRIB-
UTIVE adds qualities or color to another predicate as center. It
is used most appropriately when those qualities are needed to show
consistency with actions later on. Thus Charles Dickens in *A*

Christmas Carol launches into his characterization of Scrooge with *Oh! but he was a tight-fisted hand at the grindstone, Scrooge! — a squeezing, wrenching, grasping, scraping, clutching, covetous old sinner! Hard and sharp as flint, from which no steel had ever struck out generous fire; secret, and self-contained, and solitary as an oyster.* All this adds to the characterization that is also built up by the narration of some of Scrooge's actions, and heightens the obstacle that is overcome in Scrooge's later transformation.

EQUIVALENT, rather than adding information, simply restates it, as in *we planned to leave on May 1, the day of the spring celebrations.* The subordinated information may present a different side of the thing referred to than the thing it is subordinated to. In reference, however, the two are the same. In the attributive predicate, in contrast, the reference is determined by the dominating member and imposed on the attributive; *Scrooge* is the one who has been identified, and *solitary as an oyster* is linked to *Scrooge*, but not the other way around. The equivalent relation, however, is symmetric. Either member could be used to establish the reference; which one is the dominant center and which subordinate seems to depend entirely on the staging or perspective the hearer wishes to impose on what he says. If it is the calendar date that is important, *May 1* dominates; if it is the social significance of the day, then we can say *we planned to leave on the day of the spring celebration, May 1.* Attribution does not permit this freedom of staging: **Oh! but he was Scrooge, a tight-fisted hand at the grindstone!* won't work for me.

SPECIFICALLY has already been mentioned in illustrating how hypotactic predicates fit into semantic derivations. It relates subordinate information that is semantically less inclusive to a center that is more inclusive and therefore less precise. *I heard a flock of birds flying south — geese* goes from the more inclusive *birds* to the more specific *geese.* Not only does the relation of specificity apply between single lexical items like *birds* and *geese*, however; it also applies between very large semantic subtrees: *Uncle George told me a story about a little girl and three bears. It seems that there was this little girl named Goldilocks who lived in a house on the edge of the forest. One day ...* gives the story in very general terms, then links a retelling in specific terms to it. Connectives in English like *namely* and *that is* often introduce a subordinate subtree that is related to its dominating proposition as specific to general.

Christensen points out that there are several variations on the general-specific theme.[7] One is abstract to concrete; something concrete is given as a specific instance of an abstract statement: *He was not a very ceremonious beau; he never sent her flowers or whispered silly things in her ear, and not infrequently, at the very last moment, when they had planned an evening at the theater or the opera, he would call up to say that he couldn't get away from the office.*[8] Another form is literal to metaphorical, in which the metaphorical statement stands as specific counterpart to the literal one: *she came into the room furious, all guns blazing.* A third variation is denotative-connotative, by which I gather Christensen means that the more general statement is prosaic, with little load of evaluation, while the specific one is heavy on personal evaluation: *The former tenants had painted the wall red, the most garish crimson you can imagine.*

In EXPLANATION the subordinate element is different in kind from the center that dominates it. It may be abstract, relating the dominant element to some broader context, as in *your perpetual motion machine won't work because of the law of the conservation of energy.* Abstractions used as explanations generally go back to premises that are widely accepted in the society of which speaker and hearer are a part. It may be that these premises find their natural expression almost exclusively in the explanation relationship; that is when they are needed. They may take the character of maxims: *I don't want my wife to take skydiving lessons because you can't teach an old dog new tricks.* And as in the last example, the logical connection between the explanation and the thing explained may have a number of steps left out. Explanation in the main uses

---

[7] Christensen, "A Generative Rhetoric of the Sentence" (1963).
[8] Auchincloss, "Maud", in *The Injustice Collectors* (1949).

enthymemes, not proofs. (It may turn out to be a hypotactic form of the neutral predicate *covariance*.)

The subordinate element in an explanation may on the other hand be concrete, as when a background narrative sequence is told to explain something: *your perpetual motion machine won't work because you forgot to oil it.* When an explanation consists of background events, the implication is that there is a cause-effect relationship between the background sequence and the dominating center node.

EVIDENCE has a subordinate element that goes back to a perception: *The bridge is out; I saw it fall.* Just as explanation makes uses of enthymemes rather than tight logical sequences, so the perception used for evidence may be implied rather than stated, as in *The bridge is out; I was there.* Aristotle suggests that it is more effective for evidence to come after enthymemes in making a point, since the enthymemes let the hearer know what it is the speaker is trying to establish.[9] If he presents the perceptual evidence first, Aristotle says, the hearer has to work by induction from cases to principles, and he may either induce the wrong principles or give up on the job if he does not see where he is headed.

ANALOGY ties a subordinate subtree to a dominant proposition not by logic but by likeness. Points of parallelism are exploited to support the main statement. For example, Leonard Bloomfield is said to have argued at a meeting of the Linguistic Society of America, *Trying to do linguistics without any reference to meaning would be like going into battle with one hand tied behind your back.*

MANNER is difficult to fit in anywhere. It can obviously be treated as a rhetorical supporting predicate, though if it is one it might well turn out to merge with attribution as applied to events. There is some reason, however, to think that it might be one of the roles that operates in lexical structure. It is related to the nonagentive semantic derivation (Chapter 9) in that many predicates lose their agent only in the presence of a manner element. *The farmer shells corn* does not have a straightforward nonagentive counterpart

---

[9]   Aristotle, *Rhetoric* 2:20.

corn shells or *the corn shells*, but it does have a nonagentive counterpart with manner: *the corn shells easily*. Lakoff devotes the last part of his dissertation to a discussion of the relationship of manner elements within sentences to the passive and to other things.[10] He concludes that manner elements are probably derived by a process similar to proposition consolidation (11.2) applied to a state predicate that dominates the predicate which corresponds to the main verb in surface structure. Whether this same analysis is possible for manner elements larger than the sentence I do not yet know. Consider the manner relationship of the second sentence to the first: *He got ready to shift down to go into the final turn. His hand trembled slightly on the knob, and his teeth were clenched.*

Setting predicates of LOCATION, TIME, and DIRECTION are added in as extra arguments, like any hypotactic predicate, to the proposition that dominates everything that goes on within a single setting. As has already been stated, some parts of narratives take place against a changing background; the settings of these are a special kind called a TRAJECTORY. It can be fitted into the propositional model as a particular kind of setting that has as its arguments a list of different places. Each place is matched against corresponding events by means of matching time indexes (3.1). Just as certain subtrees of content are treated as coreferential with regard to grammatical patterns like the reflexive, so arguments of the trajectory subtree are treated as coreferential in time with event subtrees when it comes to forming the surface expression of the trajectory. Each of the points named in a trajectory is likely to be treated in surface form as though it were the setting for one or more actions, even though semantically it is simply a point of coincidence between the trajectory as a whole and a particular action. Xenophon's "from there he marched on" in the *Anabasis* moves Cyrus with his ten thousand Greeks in a single sweep from Sardis to Cunaxa and battle, with incidents along the trajectory at various named points.

Much that goes under the name of identification is covered by

---

[10] Lakoff, *Irregularity* (1965).

rhetorical predicates that have already been introduced such as attributive, specific, and equivalent. There appear to be three other rhetorical predicates that are more narrowly identificational. REPRESENTATIVE singles out one element of a group and makes it stand for the group as a whole: *The average voter finds it hard to make up his mind. All through the primaries he ...* REPLACEMENT defines one thing to stand for something else. In the case of representation, the element singled out is a member of the group it represents; but in replacement there is no membership. The tie is arbitrary: *Suppose we let this coffee cup stand for the Grand Army of the Republic. The sugar bowl is Forrest's men. I move the cup so, and you see how the gap is closed.* CONSTITUENCY identifies a part in relation to some whole: *He was one of the less important members of the mob. Last Tuesday a pal of his ...*

3. NEUTRAL PREDICATES

We have seen that the hypotactic predicates relate a subordinate proposition to a proposition that dominates it, and paratactic predicates dominate the arguments that they relate regardless of what proposition dominates them. The third and most common rhetorical predicate in text is the neutral predicate, which can assume either form. In some contexts it relates a subordinate proposition to another proposition that dominates it, and in others it relates two or more propositions on an equal basis. For example, the predicate I call COLLECTION can dominate a set of coordinate elements like the items in a grocery list: *onions, cabbage, two pounds of carrots, noodles, sausage, ...* without limit. The same collection relation can hold between one item that is taken as prominent or superordinate and others that are associated with it in a subordinate way: *I went jogging with George and Henry. We did a mile and a half.* The use of *we* shows that *I ... with George and Henry* defines a referential group, but the group is defined around *I* as center.

Since each neutral predicate can have two forms, there must be

a way to distinguish the forms in a representation of the underlying structure. One possible way of doing it has already been
suggested. We have a Predicate Rule in the grammar (13.1). That
rule has to allow for more than one predicate in one proposition
anyway, in order to accommodate multiple role relationships of a
single constituent like agent-former state for *give*, agent-latter for
get, and agent-patient for *go*. I therefore propose to represent the
hypotactic use of a neutral predicate by adding a predicate (call

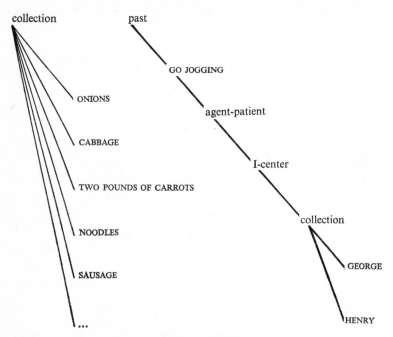

Figure 14.4 Paratactic (left) and hypotactic (right) instances of *collection*.

it *center*) to one of its arguments in its hypotactic uses, but leaving
it out in paratactic ones. This gives the two examples in the last
paragraph the underlying representations of Figure 14.4.
These are represented in the more explicit linked form as

(a1: collection a2 a3 a4 a5 a6 ...)
(a2: ONIONS)
(a3: CABBAGE)
(a4: TWO POUNDS OF CARROTS)
(a5: NOODLES)
(a6: SAUSAGE)

for the one and

(b1: past b2)
(b2: GO JOGGING b3)
(b3: agent-patient b4)
(b4: collection b5 (center) b6 b7)
(b5: I-center)
(b6: GEORGE)
(b7: HENRY)

for the other.

The hypotactic form of the collection relation has also been called *comitative* or *associative*. It has been suspected of being a semantic role, since its expression is frequently like the expression of one of them. A Liberian friend, for example, used to comment on the seeming cold bloodedness of American hostesses who one moment would be telling their friends, "We're having Gus for dinner" and the next would announce, "We're having chicken for dinner". He seemed relieved as he left the country for home that at least they had all gotten their deep structures right.

Collection when applied to events takes on a different form. Its surface expression frequently depends upon the time indexing of the events. When the events take place at different times the effect is one of temporal sequence. When they have the same time index the effect is one of simultaneous action. Because the difference in surface form (with signals like "then" and "later" for sequence and "while" and "during" for simultaneity) can be traced to differences that are expressed by the time index, it is therefore no longer necessary to retain *temporal sequence* and *simultaneity* as separate predicates.[11] Both are instances of *collection* applied to events that are indexed for time. There are even hypotactic forms of time oriented collection: *after the other team arrived we sold*

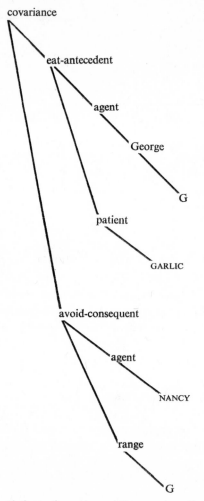

Figure 14.5 Paratactic form of *covariance:* "George eats garlic. Nancy therefore avoids him."

[11]   Grimes, "Outlines and Overlays" (1972). Litteral, "Rhetorical Predicates and Time Topology" (1972).

the last tickets subordinates the first clause, while *The highway department set up a jackhammer in my parking place. I took two Fizzy-Seltzers.* is paratactic. In simultaneous time *we descended on the place with mops and buckets, repaired the stairs, swept out the chimney, and painted the entire porch* is paratactic, and *while he was juggling a dozen eggs he kept flipping hoops with his feet* is hypotactic.

Just as temporal sequence, simultaneity, association, and collection merge into a single semantic relation whose expression depends upon several extrinsic factors, so the relations commonly referred to as *condition, result,* and *purpose* collapse into a single relation: COVARIANCE, whose surface forms are distinguished by properties of its arguments.

The covariance relation normally requires two arguments, which are distinguished as ANTECEDENT and CONSEQUENT. Although these could be defined in terms of a pure logical relation like material implication, I think it is more realistic to think of covariance in its ordinary form as having a meaning more or less parallel to the logical relation, but to take those instances of it in which the logic is actually water tight as a special case that arises in the classrooms of logicians and once in a while elsewhere. In terms of semantic structure, *antecedent* is a predicate that must dominate the proposition that forms one argument of the paratactic form of *covariance,* and *consequent* is another predicate that must dominate the other.

To illustrate, let us look at the propositional structure of a paratactic use of *covariance.* For the utterance *George eats garlic. Nancy therefore avoids him.* we might propose the analysis of Figure 14.5, *covariance* with two arguments, one of which has *antecedent* as its predicate and the other of which has *consequent.*

The hypotactic form of *covariance* has as its center the proposition that contains either *antecedent* or *consequent.* If the subordinate proposition has *antecedent* as its predicate, then the dominating proposition has *consequent* adjoined to its predicate to give a multiple predicate. If the subordinate is *consequent,* then the dominating one has *antecedent* adjoined.

A hypotactic use of the same predicate is illustrated in Figure 14.6. This arrangement corresponds to a different perspective on the relationship of the parts, and yields a sentence like *Nancy avoids George because he eats garlic*. The consequent is dominant and the antecedent subordinate.

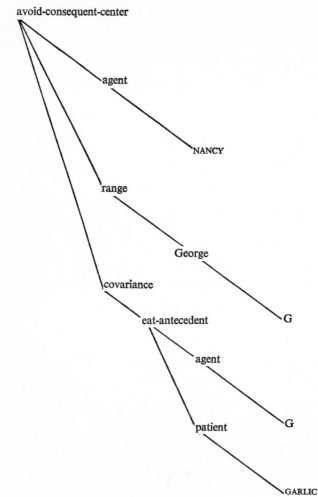

Figure 14.6 Hypotactic form of *covariance* with consequent as center: "Nancy avoids George because he eats garlic."

When the antecedent is dominant and the consequent is sub-ordinate, the hypotactic form of *covariance* appears as suggested in Figure 14.7. It would be behind something on the order of *George eats garlic, which is why Nancy avoids him.*

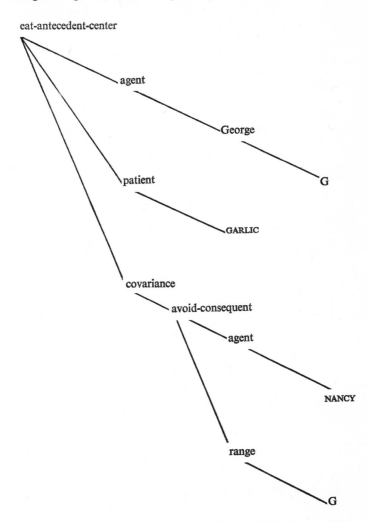

Figure 14.7 Hypotactic form of *covariance* with antecedent as center: "George eats garlic, which is why Nancy avoids him."

My reason for distinguishing one form of hypotactic predicate from another is this: relations of dominance and subordination have to do ultimately with the staging of parts of a discourse. The speaker imposes a perspective on the purely cognitive aspects of meaning. This suggests that whether a neutral predicate is taken as paratactic or as hypotactic depends upon other decisions in the area of staging. At the deeper levels of structure, the distinction between paratactic and hypotactic may very well not be important in itself, but only represent the consolidated result of the interaction between staging and content.

There are various surface expressions of the covariance relation. Which one is used depends partly upon whether covariance has the paratactic or the hypotactic form, and partly upon the makeup of its arguments. CONDITIONS are one common form for expressing covariance. They are further divided in various languages according to various criteria such as whether the antecedent is presumed to be a fact or is only hypothetical, on the one hand, and whether it is positive or negative on the other. The consequent also has different forms depending upon whether it is taken to be a real possibility or as a collateral assertion (4.4) that might have happened but did not — the well known contrary to fact or irrealis condition of classical grammar. The surface form may also depend on whether the consequent is positive or negative. I suspect that conditions represent a hypotactic form of *covariance*, with the antecedent (PROTASIS in the classical terminology for conditions) subordinate to the consequent (APODOSIS); but this may vary from language to language. REASONS appear to be closely parallel to conditions in these terms: *because ... therefore* is perhaps only a slightly more formal version of *since ... then*, which in turn accords with those varieties of *if ... then* in which time sequence is not too important.

Time sequence, on the other hand, is extremely important for purpose and result relationships. RESULT can be characterized as a condition on time indexing of the two arguments: the antecedent must precede the consequent in time. PURPOSE is similar to result except that the consequent dominates an intervening predicate *intend* whose agent must be coreferential with the agent of the base

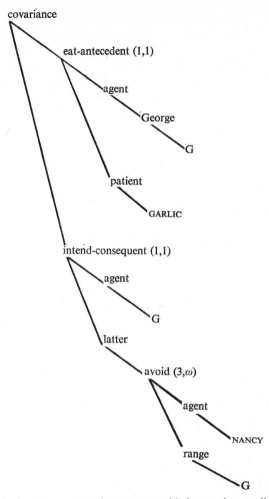

Figure 14.8 *Covariance* expressing purpose with intervening predicate *intend* in the consequent: "George eats garlic so that Nancy will avoid him."

predicate that carries the main semantic content of the antecedent. The base predicate of the consequent is the latter state of *intend*. This relationship is diagrammed in Figure 14.8, which shows the paratactic use of *covariance* with time indexing and *intend* as a means of showing purpose.

ADVERSATIVE is the predicate for collateral relationships. In its paratactic form it simply presents what happened along with what did not happen, or along with what the hearer might think happened: *it was a case of sink or swim*. More frequently the things that are not so are subordinated to the thing that is being asserted: *I'd rather have coffee than tea*.[12]

It might simplify the trees that represent semantic derivations if some of the information communicated here by means of rhetorical predicates could be added as features to some of the elements. This approach would give a representation more closely in line with some that Chomsky has suggested. The result would be that many of the connective function words in surface structure would be introduced by particle transformations, similar in kind to segmentalization transformations that add affixes to words.[13] This could be done by sacrificing the extremely simple formalism I have used for underlying structure.

The main drawback of this approach lies in the fact that semantic features are associated in a Chomsky grammar with lexical items, not with nodes that dominate major constituents. In a really high level relationship (like the one implied by St. Paul's *therefore* in *Romans* 12:1, which is generally agreed to link the first eleven chapters as antecedent with 12 through 15 as consequent) it might not be possible to decide which lexical item the rhetorical features are added to, and the transformational component would have to raise them to a much higher node anyway. It makes more sense to assert the relationship at the point where it belongs.[14]

Another reason why it seems best to stay away from a feature representation is the one Glock and I mentioned in 1970: the

---

[12]   Another possible analysis is to have all paratactic usages be assigned to the *alternative* paratactic predicate and the hypotactic ones to *adversative*, which is then no longer neutral but hypotactic. If this can be done, the two constitute a single neutral predicate *alternative*. It could be argued, however, that *adversative* is more like a negation of the *covariance* relation: "although the antecedent is true, the expected consequence did not take place; something else did".

[13]   Jacobs and Rosenbaum, *English Transformational Grammar* (1970).

[14]   Aside from this remark, I am bypassing the discussion of the place semantic features play in the lexicon itself. Since it appears possible to handle ordinary

property of redundancy, which is useful when applied to phonological feature systems, verges on being absurd if applied, as some have suggested it should be, to semantic feature systems. Redundancy fills in one feature in the presence of another; for example, in English all phonological segments that are nasal are also voiced by a regular entailment that says something that needs to be said about English. Phonological redundancy fills in a specification for every feature in every segment. To try to apply this in semantic space, however, results in a mountain of irrelevant feature specifications being heaped up over nearly everything, with no corresponding gain in insight into the system. There are local redundancies such as everything human being also animate, but they have to be stated in a way that provides reasonable local boundaries.

In short, whatever the utility of semantic features may be for talking about lexical relationships — and they are not the only way to talk about them in a generative grammar – they show little promise yet as a vehicle for expressing rhetorical relationships. Propositions, on the other hand, give a way of making useful and interesting observations in which the relevant information is located approximately where it belongs.

---

semantic features like $\pm$ human, $\pm$ count by means of the concept of associative linkages within the lexicon, I find no compelling reason for building them into the theory in a different though more traditional form. Winograd, on the other hand, builds his representation around the concept of features at every level in his *Procedures* (1971).

15

MODALITY

The simple grammar used to combine semantic elements so far has no room for modality as a separate kind of thing from propositional content. Instead it forces it to be treated in the same framework as everything else, most likely in terms of predicates that dominate lexical predicates as their arguments. This consequence of using an extremely simple model has its dangers; but in looking at the way tense, aspect, and mood relate to discourse, I find it also has some advantages.

This chapter brings together scattered observations about the relationship of modal elements to discourse in several languages. It is far from a real theory of mode, and I have not attempted to integrate it with the growing literature on English mode.

1. TENSE

The notion of time as one of the referential systems in language has been mentioned already, and will be taken up again in Chapter 20. The main thing to be observed about time as language makes use of it is that it is topological rather than metric; notions of "before", "after", and "during" are more important than the measurement of particular intervals.

Tense systems basically relate what is being talked about to the time line. If, as Litteral has suggested,[1] we can represent linguistic

---

[1] R. Litteral, "Rhetorical Predicates and Time Topology" (1972).

time by a topology on the line of real numbers, matching the zero point to right now, the time we are talking, the positive numbers to time after now, and the negative numbers to time before now, it is convenient to represent the times of events and states as open sets of points along that line.

This brings up once again the notion of the dominating performative, by which our model of linguistic structure makes explicit the extent to which systems of reference in language depend on who is speaking to whom, and where and when he is doing it. We notice that when a speaker quotes somebody else in the course of utterance, the time reference within the quoted part takes that act of speaking as its base line: *He said, "You'd really like to start right away, wouldn't you?"* transfers the time reference from the time when the actual speaker tells the hearer *he said* back to an earlier time implied by the past tense in *said*. With reference to that earlier time, the speech refers to an intention to do something later. The action referred to by *start*, if it actually happens, comes at a time later than the time referenced by the past tense of *said*, and therefore may be either earlier or later than the time of actual speaking.[2]

Displacement of time may be accomplished in other ways than by the embedding of performatives. The most usual way is to simply set a time before the time of speaking by the use of a past tense form, with or without a more explicit indication of it, or to set a time that is future to the performative time by the use of a future, potential, or incomplete tense, again with or without a more explicit indicator.

Composite displacement of time is common. Instead of restricting ourselves to times before and times after right now, we can pick a time reference point either in the past or the future from now, then refer all subsequent times to that reference point. Even in the compass of a single sentence we get composite displacements like (A) *once he received the letter*, (B) *he told his employer* (C) *that he would be quitting* (D) *as soon as he got his next paycheck* (E) *because he had finally gotten* (F) *his plans together.* Here the time reference

2 Hajičová, Panevová, and Sgall, "Recursive Properties of Tense" (1970).

is set by A at the beginning. B follows A directly in time sequence, anticipating first D and then C, with reference to E, which comes before B and after A. F is indefinite as to time. The time signals in this sentence include the past tense used throughout the passage, which seems to hold reference on the main time sequence, *once* in A, *would* in C, *as soon as* and *next* in D, and the past perfect *had gotten* in E.

Some tense systems make room for lack of reference to any particular time. Koiné Greek, for example, uses the aorist tense in independent clauses in two ways: either for an event displaced to the past time reference point as in the case of the English past, or in the GNOMIC or timeless sense suitable for general truths.

In the English example just given, the constant use of past forms throughout the passage highlights the fact that the basic reference point for all the verbs is the same past sequence. Saying so on every verb could be considered a form of discourse redundancy. For example, Bahinemo of Papua New Guinea sets the time for an entire paragraph by the use of tense on the verb of a single dependent clause at the beginning of the paragraph.[3] Godié of Ivory Coast can set the base time once for a whole text.[4] This would suggest that time reference is a property of fairly large discourse subtrees or even of entire discourses taken as wholes, and that the appearance of tense information on every finite verb in English is a language specific feature that can be represented by a copying transformation.

2. ASPECT

Two kinds of information seem to be communicated by aspect systems. The first is concerned with the shape of a particular action: taken as a whole, drawn out in time, repeated, distributed, be-

---

[3]   Longacre, *Discourse ... in New Guinea Languages* (1972), discusses Wayne Dye's analysis.
[4]   Marchese, "Time Reference in Godié" (ms).

ginning, ending, or potential. The second is concerned with the relationship between one proposition and the next: sequence, logical relation, overlap or simultaneity, or indirect effect.

Aspectual information that simply adds color or detail to the proposition with which it is associated has no implications for discourse structure. For example, communicating the difference between an action that happens all at once and an action that takes a while to accomplish may be entirely independent of how either action relates to its context. Even stating that an action happens over and over seems to be unrelated to its discourse context; a number of languages of Nigeria have iterative forms that are the same whether an action is carried out repeatedly in the same environment, like "he kept beating her", is directed toward a series of multiple objects, like "he rode all the horses in the stable", or is carried out simultaneously in various environments, like "the police rounded up the demonstrators" or, in a process, "the branches grew apart".

On the other hand, aspect systems that relate the verb they go with to other parts of the discourse are fairly common. Gleason and Cromack discuss relations of contiguity and gapping in Kâte and completion and the lack of it in Cashinawa.[5] Ronald Huisman finds an even more intricate system in Angaataha of Papua New Guinea.[6] One dimension of it he labels TIGHT vs. LOOSE, and the other he labels TEMPORAL vs. LOGICAL. Temporally tight and loose correspond fairly well to Gleason's contiguity and gapping in Kâte, loose asserting that the next action begins some time after the one with the temporally loose aspect marker ends, and tight asserting that such is not the case but that the two actions either abut or overlap. The logical counterparts are a little different; logically tight asserts that the next action is a direct consequence of the one that bears the aspect marker, and logically loose says that the earlier action has effects which persist and are factors in what takes

[5]   Gleason, "Contrastive Analysis in Discourse Structure" (1968); Cromack, *Cashinawa* (1968).
[6]   Ronald Huisman, "Angaataha Verb Morphology" (1973).

place later, but without direct causation. This idea of latent effects is not very different from the perfect tense of Koiné Greek, which also asserts relevance of the effects of an action at a later time.

A key parameter for understanding aspect systems seems to be the distinction between events and nonevents. Ruth McLeod finds that in Xavante of Brazil the aspect system works in two ways depending upon whether the verbs the aspect markers are attached to denote events or nonevents.[7] For events the aspects tell how each event is related to the next one in sequence. For nonevents the aspect system gives more like a logical structure that relates the nonevents to each other and to the events to which they correspond. The two systems are largely nonoverlapping, with few of the nonevent aspects using the same affixes as the event aspects; but the system proved difficult to analyze at first because there were some affixes that operated in both systems in different senses.

In both Mumuye and Longuda of Nigeria there is a kind of progressive aspect that is characteristic of settings.[8] One Mumuye text has near the beginning, for example, 'the horns were blowing for the ceremony' in the progressive. At this place in the text the aspect indicates that the blowing of the horns is not to be understood as one of the events in the sequence of events, but rather as a behavioral or circumstantial component of the setting. It is like what the characters in a play are doing when the curtain goes up. The same aspect used later in the text lacks this close tie with setting, and rather gives the normal shaping of a progressive action.

3. MOOD

Mood borders on being a catchall term for a variety of systems that are not mutually exclusive with each other. One suspects that we might get farther toward understanding modal phenomena if we

---

[7]   McLeod, "Paragraph, Aspect, and Participant in Xavante" (ms).
[8]   Kruesi, "Mumuye Discourse Structure" (ms); B. Newman, "The Longuda Verb" (ms).

did not put them under the terminological umbrella of modal phenomena or mood — themselves terms that some linguists distinguish and others do not. Nevertheless, quite a few things that have to do with communication options, logical status, and attitude of the speaker toward the content of the message, are customarily stirred into this pot, and until we get a really clear idea of what the differences are they are likely to remain fixed in our minds as mood.

The speaker's communication options relate to what he intends to accomplish by speaking. His intention is usually communicated by one of the standard performative forms of declarative, interrogative, and imperative.[9] His actual purpose may be classified more broadly to include intent to inform, question, command, confirm, request confirmation, contradict, or just to maintain an open communication channel, but most languages appear to grant the same three options.

The physical viewpoint from which speech is carried out appears to be related to the basic scheme of communication options in some languages. For example, in Nambiquara of Brazil, declarative statements and possibly questions require the speaker to specify one or another category of VERIFICATION.[10] This distinguishes eye-witness statements from statements based on deduction or conjecture on the one hand and from statements of what is common knowledge in the society on the other. For example, "the tree fell over" could be stated in such a way as to assert that the speaker saw it fall and is reporting what he saw, that he came across it lying on the ground and concluded that it got that way because it fell, or that he and everybody else is aware that it fell because someone else reported it first.

Oksapmin has a system for linking a happening to an account of the happening in terms of whether the source of the story is the narrator or someone else.[11] In either case, a further distinction

[9]   Ross, "On Declarative Sentences" (1970).
[10] Lowe, "Nambiquara" (1972).
[11] Marshall Lawrence, "Oksapmin Sentence Structure" (1972); Helen Lawrence, "Viewpoint and Location in Oksapmin" (1972).

is made between those actions in which the story source was the agent and those in which he was the observer. There is also a detached mode that gives the effect of an omniscient viewpoint when used in narrative.

Categories of viewpoint in English relate more directly to person assignment than to what we normally think of as mode. They are discussed in Chapter 20.

The speaker's feeling about what he is reporting enters into some modal systems. On one scale is his judgment of the certainty of what he is saying: a flat assertion, probability, possibility, and on the negative side unlikelihood and complete denial.

A number of Indo-European languages have subjunctive or optative forms that may be used to express a greater uncertainty than the corresponding indicatives. In practice the use of non-indicative forms tends to be controlled by the grammatical patterns in which a verb fits, so that in Spanish, for example, the subjunctive in *Ella quiso que yo saliera* 'she wanted me to leave', only the subjunctive fits the complement construction and there is really no option for expressing uncertainty in contrast to certainty. On the other hand, *ella no creía que yo saliera* 'she did not believe that I would leave' is noncommittal about whether I actually did leave or not, whereas the indicative counterpart *ella no creía que yo salí* is tantamount to an assertion that I did in fact leave, whether she believed it or not.

The modals of English communicate varying degrees of conjecture or uncertainty: *I might go, I could go.* On the other hand, the grammatical subsystem of which the forms that express uncertainty are a part also includes future expressions like *I will go* that are more like a part of the tense system. Rossbottom finds a tense system in Guaraní of Bolivia that similarly involves expression in something that is not a simple paradigmatic set of tense affixes,[12] so that it is likely that the modal auxiliaries of English need to be split into auxiliaries that express tense, as in some uses of *will* and *shall* on the one hand, and modals that express varying degrees of

---

[12]   Rossbottom, "Different-level Tense Markers in Guarani" (1961).

subjective certainty on the part of the speaker on the other hand.

Negatives need to be approached cautiously. Some uses of negatives, as for example in simple denials like *I did not go to Los Angeles on February 22*, are fairly straightforward expressions of the logical status of the whole sentence: "the statement that I went to Los Angeles on February 22 is false". Other negatives, however, cannot be treated in the same way. In *I didn't think she would be ready* it is not the thinking that is being denied; the negative is raised from the complement and is equivalent to *I thought she would not be ready*. In other words, the scope of what is negated always needs to be looked at thoroughly.

16

DISCOURSE SEMANTICS
AND THE SURFACE HIERARCHY

Chapter 7 sketched the kinds of units that are typically found when discourses are partitioned into their constituents: sentences, paragraphs, episodes, and the like. Each of these has a kind of semantic unity on the one hand, and embodies certain characteristic structural signals that define its nuclei and boundaries on the other. The chapters from there on talked about various kinds of underlying semantic relations in the abstract. It remains to be asked if there are any characteristic semantic configurations that seem to serve as a basis for the hierarchical phenomenon.

If the semantics of discourse is organized in anything like the way I have suggested, the cascading effect of layer upon layer of propositions with rhetorical predicates, whose arguments themselves are propositions of considerable complexity, gives no lack of richness of structure. Instead we are left wondering why the surface phenomena of discourse are organized into such regular packages, rather than being a set of signals whose intricacy matches that of the semantic tree at all its levels. Why pick just a few levels for the surface form?

The best suggestion I can offer right now is that surface form seems to offer us standard configurations for saying things at very high levels of organization, just as it offers us a limited set of forms at lower levels such as the clause and the phrase. The semantic structure that represents our choice of what we want to say is adapted until it fits one of these available forms. The addition of redundancies, the thematic highlighting of certain elements, and the subordination of others appear to be the mechanisms that are used. Some of the forms are given in the next section.

1. STANDARD CONFIGURATIONS

The OUTLINE is a model of surface form that is not only taught in schools, but also actually used by speakers of natural languages whether they learned it in school or not.[1] Its two major dimensions are coordination and subordination. Coordination, which can be expressed in terms of the paratactic predicates of Chapter 14, gives equal weight to each of its arguments. It usually involves parallel forms of expression for each argument, even when the arguments are highly complex.

Subordination, on the other hand, involves adding arguments to some predicate in a modifying capacity. The formal representation of arguments of this kind in relation to the propositions to which they are attached was discussed in Chapter 14.

Christensen's suggestion concerning the way coordinate and subordinate relationships determine paragraphing is probably not the whole story, but it does seem to account for many paragraphing phenomena. Briefly, he suggests that as long as our expression of the contents of a semantic tree goes directly from one coordinate node to another one at the same level, or from a node to another node that is subordinate to it, we encode what we have to say as a string of sentences, putting as much into each sentence as our general constraints on style permit. When we return from a deeper level of subordination to a level closer to the root of the semantic tree, however, we signal this decrease of depth by reaffirming (or changing) our orientation signals about setting and theme. In other words, we start a new paragraph.

For example, if our outline has four main points and we are on

---

[1] Christensen, "A Generative Rhetoric of the Paragraph" (1965); Becker, "A Tagmemic Approach to Paragraph Analysis" (1965). In "Outlines and Overlays" (1972) I comment on the outline as a widespread linguistic form.

the third, the transition from the third main point itself to the sub-points under it involves continuing a string of sentences. If the second subpoint has five subpoints under it, we go on through them with the same string of sentences, possibly adding special con-junctions and transitions to show the subordination, but frequently going on without special signals. When we jump from the last subpoint back to the fourth main point, however, we begin a new paragraph. This means more than just arranging the type on the page in a particular way; for most languages it involves resetting the theme of what we are talking about and reestablishing the time and place (if they are relevant) of the setting. We do the same thing when we are speaking rather than writing, using the same kinds of thematic and setting identification, and possibly making use of pause and pitch shift as phonological signals.

Change of depth in a tree of coordinate and subordinate struc-tures may not be the only basis for paragraphing. Even when a string of events in a narrative is essentially one-dimensional — this happened, then this, then this, and so on — any change in setting, the appearance of a new character whether he takes over the thematic status or not, or a shift in theme all appear capable of triggering the signals for paragraphs.

PLOT is a special kind of structure in which a complex set of semantic elements are cast into highly constrained roles. I once conjectured that plot, rather than being a part of linguistic struc-ture,[2] is more like a template which speakers place over their referential field. The plot template organizes the components of the field into an interesting relationship with each other. What is said about them, I suggested, is put together solely on the usual basis of changes of setting and theme, and does not reflect any influence of the plot form itself on the linguistic expression.

A couple of observations have come along since then, however, which have made me regard plot as a part of the higher level semantic structure of a story. The first is Labov and Waletzky's finding that speakers inject evaluative sentences like *What do you*

---

[2]   Grimes and Glock, "Saramaccan" (1970).

think he did then? or *Wasn't that something?* with great consistency just between the complication part of a story and the resolution part, even though at that point there is typically no change of scene or theme shift.[3] In other words, their placement of the evaluative sentences must be made in terms of some kind of intuition about the plot itself.

The second observation is one made by June Austing in which she finds she can account for the use of a particle *iae* in Omie only in terms of transition points between segments that are defined as elements of a plot.[4]

Besides that, it appears quite simple to construct the overall specification for a family of plots from the same rhetorical predicates that we already need for specifying other high level semantic relationships. The idea of a grammar to specify plot structure first came to my attention in a paper read by George Lakoff at a Linguistic Society of America meeting some years ago. In working over the idea, it appears that no new components are needed other than rhetorical predicates we already have in stock to give a perfectly acceptable specification of the way parts of a plot are interrelated.

The idea of plot as having this kind of structure was brought up by Propp.[5] Although not all folklorists agree with his precise specification of plot, it seems possible to take his central idea and rephrase it as a tightly constrained tree of rhetorical predicates.

The following is a representation of a large set of plots. By making some elements optional and including others in disjoint sets, in the manner of a normal context free grammar, it would be possible to extend the plot space that is defined by a considerable amount. What is given here, however, ignores the problem of optionality.

In Chapter 14 propositions are represented by an index, a predicate, and a string of arguments. In a linked representation the

3   Labov and Waletzky, "Narrative Analysis" (1967).
4   June Austing, "Omie Discourse" (ms).
5   Propp, *Morphology of the Folktale* (1958).

arguments are the indices of the propositions they represent, or else are terminal indices that represent distinguishable entities in the referential field. The representation here follows the same line, but elaborates the idea of an index in three ways: (1) Indices that stand for complete propositions are represented by mnemonically useful words written in capital letters. It needs to be emphasized that the words used as indices are chosen only for their mnemonic value to make the whole thing easier to read; they have no semantic significance in themselves. The semantic load is carried exclusively by the predicates. (2) Indices are composite. They include a time index component, expressed in Litteral's way as an ordered pair of integers that represent beginning and ending sets of points on the time line.[6] (3) Some indices represent arguments that are known to be complex but are not further developed in this list. These are replaced by a role predicate together with the referential index that it must ultimately dominate. Thus for example an argument specification *patient* (2) stands for an argument whose index is not given directly, but which consists of a proposition whose predicate is the role *patient*. The argument of *patient* itself may be of any complexity, but must ultimately result in an identification with the referential entity to which we have elsewhere given the index *2*. Here, then, is the specification for one kind of plot:

PLOT (1,37): response ante (COMPLICATION) conse (RESOLUTION)
COMPLICATION (1,15): collection DEPRIVATION VILLAINY LEAVING
DEPRIVATION (1,3): adversative ante (INTERDICTION) conse (VIOLA-
   TION)
INTERDICTION (1,1): prohibit agent (1) patient (TEST)
TEST (3,3): do agent (2) manner ...
VIOLATION = TEST
VILLAINY (5,9): collection LEARN HARM REPORT
LEARN (5,5): find-out agent (3) range (TEST)
HARM (7,7): harm agent (3) patient (2)
REPORT (9,9): inform agent (4) latter (5) range (HARM)

---

[6]   Litteral, "Rhetorical Predicates and Time Topology" (1972).

LEAVING (11,15): collection DISPATCH DECIDE SALLY

DISPATCH (11,11): inform agent (5) latter (6) range (HARM)

DECIDE (13,13): decide agent (6) patient (SALLY)

SALLY (15,15): leave agent (6) latter (RESCUE)

RESCUE (31,31): rescue agent (6) patient (2) range (3)

RESOLUTION (17,37): collection DONOR CONTEST RETURN

DONOR (17,23): collection MEET GIVE

MEET (17,17): meet patient (PAIR)

PAIR (17,23): collection 6 7

GIVE (19,23): covariance ante (ASK) conse (DONATE)

ASK (19,21): response Q A

Q (19,19): ask agent (7) latter (6) patient (8)

A (21,21): answer agent (6) latter (7) patient (8)

DONATE (23,23): give agent (7) latter (6) patient (9)

MOD (23,23): intend agent (7) patient (INTENT) range (DONATE, center)

INTENT (23,31): help force (9) range (6) latter (RESCUE)

CONTEST (24,31): collection MEET2 STRIVE RESCUE

MEET2 (25,25): meet patient (PAIR2)

PAIR2 (25,29): collection 6 3

STRIVE (27,29): collection STRUGGLE VICTORY

STRUGGLE (27,27): match-wits agent (PAIR2) range (PAIR2 (reciprocal))

VICTORY (29,29): win agent (6) range (3) instrument (9)

RETURN (33,37): collection RETRACE REWARD

RETRACE (33,33): collection BACK CONFLICT

BACK: conduct agent (6) patient (2) latter (usually 1)

CONFLICT: oppose agent (3) range (6)

REWARD (35,35): reward agent (1) latter (6) patient (MARRY)

MARRY (37,37): marry patient (PAIR3)

PAIR3 (37, omega): collection 6 (male) 2 (female)

Here the familiar plot roles are defined with reference to specific actions. The hero is the agent of VICTORY, or 6. The villain is the agent of HARM and the range of VICTORY, or 3. The victim is the patient of HARM and RESCUE or 2. The donor is the agent of DONATE and Q, or 7. The helper is the patient of DONATE and the instrument of VICTORY, or 9. The dispatcher is the agent of DISPATCH or 5. Propp's false hero does not appear in this plot.

The plot structure just given covers a wide range of fairy tales, movies, and with little modification, scientific articles. I think the structure is used to add interest to anything at all. For example, the introduction to one of Rogers's basic books on psychotherapy[7] contains a paragraph in which *our culture,* cast here as the villain, as it *has grown less homogeneous, gives much less support to the individual,* who turns out to be the victim. The consequence is that the individual is harmed; *he cannot simply rest comfortably upon the ways and traditions of his society, but finds many of the basic issues and conflicts of life centering in himself.* The resulting lack state is typical of an entire class of plots. Number 6, however, the hero, rides to the rescue, bypassing the help of the donor (who in other scientific texts may be a foundation that reviews the hero's proposal and provides him with a grant by means of which he is able to assail the walls of ignorance). Here the hero is psychotherapy. It *holds promise of resolving some of those conflicts and of giving the individual a more satisfying adjustment within himself as well as a more satisfying relationship to others and to his environment.* There is even a reward in which psychotherapy gets to be the focus of interest of both the public and of professionals.

Frankly, I would far rather have psychotherapy presented in this way, or linguistics too for that matter, than in the deadly unilinear rhetoric that much of science feels it must use. The pattern helps us identify the good guys, and whatever the outcome, we have a much more entertaining time of it than we can normally expect from the subject matter alone.

Attention to story structure brings some surprises. In Papua New Guinea there is a family of plots that run more or less like this: Boy meets girl, boy falls in love with girl, they elope. After living in the mountains for a time, they decide to seek reconciliation with their families. He kills a wild pig and roasts the meat. Early

---

[7] Rogers, *Client-centered Therapy* (1951).

the next morning he creeps into the village and leaves a piece of meat on the doorstep of each of the offended relatives, then returns to the hill above to watch. At dawn the relatives wake up, find the meat, and take it. Encouraged by this, he adjusts his decorations, stands forth on the skyline, and starts down the hill with the girl. When they reach the village, their relatives kill them. End of story.

The reason a story like this sounds a little off balance to most European readers is that we tend to make the boy the hero automatically in any boy-meets-girl story. The hero, however, is not defined that way in plot structure; instead he is the one who rectifies whatever was out of kilter. The boy, looked at from this point of view, is the one who got things out of kilter in the first place; in other words, he is the villain. Society is the hero, and the story reaches its happy ending when everything is put back into balance.

It is possible that the classical form of tragedy may consist of an adversative relation between an antecedent comedic plot in which the hero overcomes some obstacle, and a consequent retribution in which that victory puts him in conflict with superhuman forces with whom he cannot contend. Thus Oedipus saves Thebes from the Sphinx and Agamemnon returns victorious from the siege of Troy before each is cut down.

PERSUASION is another general template. Here a number of points contribute logically to a conclusion that generally involves some kind of alteration of the behavior of the hearer. More has been studied about persuasion from the rhetorical point of view than from the linguistic point of view.[8] Nevertheless, there seem to be two basic patterns, which might be called the star pattern and the chain pattern.

The STAR pattern can be thought of as having a central point, the conclusion, to which a number of other points contribute more or less independently of each other. Each stands in a relation to the main point itself. In the formal terms in which we have discussed

[8] Most studies of discourse phenomena have begun with attention to narratives, where the signals seems to be relatively clear cut and the structures somewhat regular. Speech that is intended to persuade needs much more attention from linguists than it has gotten so far.

rhetorical relations, the basic predicate in a star pattern is a co-variance relation focused on the consequent element. The antecedent is a simple collection of points, any one of which would support the consequent, and which taken together it is hoped will have a cumulative effect.

The CHAIN pattern is also based on the covariance relation. Its antecedent, however, is itself a single proposition based on co-variance with its own internal antecedent and consequent, and so on recursively through a whole chain of reasoning. The result is on the order of "A is true, and therefore B follows. B has C as its consequence, and from C we can establish D. D leads directly to E, which is the main point."

The star pattern is illustrated by a Borôro text collected by Thomas Crowell.[9] The text consists of a collection of stories about various depradations made by jaguars against one community's livestock. In one incident the jaguars chase some cattle into a river. In another they frighten two Indians who come across a pair of them in the ruins of a deserted house. In another they kill a calf belonging to the speaker. None of the stories is connected with the rest except through the common theme of being about jaguars; but after the whole series of incidents is finished, the speaker concludes with a point that is equally derivable from any one of the embedded narratives by itself: his community needs some good dogs to hunt jaguars.

The formal study of logic has gotten its greatest impulse from classical times to the present from the observation that not all that passes for persuasion is logically sound. This is made the antecedent of a covariance predicate whose consequent is that people ought to become more familiar with how logic really works so that they can avoid the traps set for the unwary. From Socrates to Quine there is an unbroken chain of practitioners who impart knowledge of how to tell reason from fallacy. And yet for all that, it seems clear enough that from the linguistic point of view, it is enough that a discourse merely sound logical in order to achieve its desired effect, whether it actually is logical or not. A few well placed

9   Crowell, "Cohesion in Borôro Discourse" (ms).

"therefores" and "consequentlys" seem to be all most users of language require to feel that they are reacting to persuasion — never mind a misplaced quantifier or an invalid middle term here or there. Logic, as seen by a linguist, appears to be a deity whose festal observers are many but whose true worshippers are few.

Still another pattern of discourse organization is the PROBE, which requires two or more participants in the action of speaking. Weizenbaum characterizes this discourse type as having the form of a tree.[10] The tree represents a conceptual structure in the mind of one of the participants. He and the other participant or participants converse back and forth until the one who put together the conceptual structure is satisfied that the other has substantially the same set of ideas, and the other person feels he has adequately grasped what the first speaker has to say. In a conceptual structure of any complexity, the participants follow it to the point where they feel they understand each other adequately, then back up to a higher node and go on to the next point leading out from that node.

This is an oversimplification of what goes on in conversation, but it is a helpful one. To make it more realistic we need to add only two factors. The first is that each participant in a conversation usually has his own conceptual structure and is interested in communicating it. The flow of information in one direction and elicitation in the other is thus multilateral; I may be learning from you at the same time you are learning from me. The result of a successful probing is that each of the participants goes away with an apparently adequate counterpart of the conceptual structure of each of the other participants.

The other factor is that the conceptual structure of each initiating participant is changed during a probing. The change may come about either because new relationships within the structure become apparent to the person who is explaining it while he is talking, or because his conceptual structure interacts with that of another participant in a way that may modify both. The content of the communication during a probe is therefore best taken as dynamic,

[10]   Weizenbaum, "Contextual Understanding from Computers" (1967).

changing from one part of the probing interaction to another. Other conceptual structures share this dynamic property to some degree, in that even the teller of a well known story may perceive new relationships and try to communicate them in the course of speaking; but in probing this modification of the participants' systems of underlying semantic relationships is taken for granted.

There is a related phenomenon. We have all heard of the politician who, when asked what he thought about a certain issue, replied, "How can I know what I think about it until I've given a speech on it?" There is a sense in which many of our own conceptual structures become well defined to us only in the process of talking about them. It seems to require the exigencies of a speech situation, particularly an informal or low pressure one, to crystallize some of the semantic relationships that are inherent in what we intend to say. The questioning and elicitation of a prober can force implications to our attention that elude us in our own attempts to express what we want to express. The feedback loop involved in bringing these things to the surface appears to be the attempt of the person we are talking with to restate what we have been saying in his own words. He puts our ideas in a perspective that differs enough from our own that it forces a weak strand of our own conceptualization to be noticed and made more precise.

2. ALTERNATIVES TO CONSTITUENCY GRAMMARS

Linguistics has a long tradition of treating the surface form of language by partitioning what is said into its constituents or linear components, then further dividing these until we reach some ultimate element. Even in transformational grammar, the basic model is one of constituency in the base component; any phenomena of surface form such as reordering or copying for agreement that make it difficult to square our observations with our constituency model are normalized by means of the transformational component. The idea of constituency, applied recursively and made flexible by transformations, is reasonably easy to use and gives results we understand.

It helps to ask from time to time, however, whether partitioning is the best of all possible bases for a grammar. There are points at which we might argue that it leaves us with more cleaning up to do than a really elegant theory might.

The outstanding area in which a pure constituency grammar seems awkward is in reference. We have mentioned several times how reference to real world time is topologically ordered; but it now remains to point out that its ordering implies the breakdown of our notion of constituency.

Take for example a folk tale with the structure given in the first section of this chapter. To abstract the referential information about time relationships and put it into the form of an index obscures the fact that the time sequence itself implies a partitioning of the text. It has a different basis from a grammatical or rhetorical

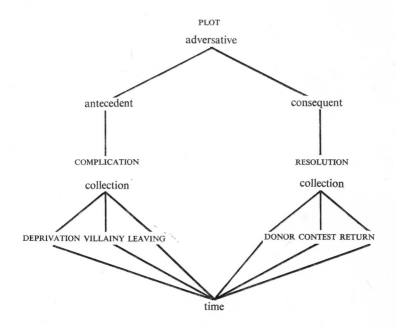

Figure 16.1 Double constituency.

partitioning; but it is a segmentation of the text and it affects the linguistic form of the text. We could think of it as another tree with the same terminal elements as the content tree, but imposing a different structure. We could diagram it as a double tree, as in Figure 16.1.

In the upper tree, which is a simplification of the plot structure, all the leaves happen to be at the same distance from the root. In a full tree this is not usually so; different subtrees are usually developed to different distances from the root. Regardless of the distance from the root of the upper tree, however, the partitioning by time applies equally to all the terminal elements that denote events in a sequence.

In the same way a rhetorical relation like *result* can be decomposed into two kinds of organization: the logically antecedent and consequent terms, and the temporal first and last terms. When applied to a single rhetorical predicate, it could be argued that what we have is a single complex predicate, parallel to other complex predicates like agent-former state. When one predicate dominates another, however, as in the chain structured argument mentioned a few pages back, it becomes evident that the temporal structure is a simple partitioning in terms of time spans, while the logical component is a nested structure like that of Figure 16.2:

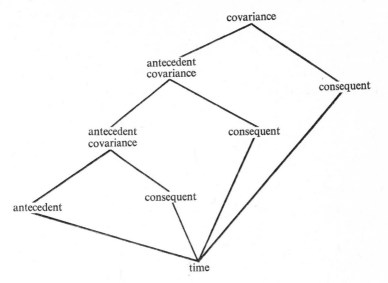

Figure 16.2 Double constituency of *result*.

A second phenomenon that makes one wonder whether a tree represents everything adequately is the phenomenon of thematization or staging (Chapter 21). We have gone into content structure in terms of lexical and rhetorical relationships; but cutting across those relationships we recognize another kind of relationship that carries information about the perspective from which the content is presented. It includes judgments of relative centrality and peripherality to a theme and the identification of that theme. It may involve considerable reorganization of the content material without losing any of the content relationships: *my wallet they returned, but it was the loss of my rabbit's foot that I couldn't bear* is a highly thematized counterpart of *they returned my wallet, but I couldn't bear the loss of my rabbit's foot,* which is in turn related to things like *I lost my rabbit's foot* and *I had a rabbit's foot* (in this context, at any rate, rather than *my rabbit had a foot*) and *I have a wallet.*

Still another principle that cuts across regular lexical and rhetorical structure is the principle of information blocking and the placement of centers in terms of a cohesive judgment about the relation of each word and construction uttered to what has gone before (Chapter 19). Even in a thematically unmarked clause like *we ordered* SAND*wiches* (using capitalization to mark the placement of the intonation nucleus) a calibration of each element in terms of relative predictability or unpredictability in relation to what has already been said amounts to a different structuring from the one implied by the grammar, whether we look at the underlying semantic structure or at the surface grammar.

The overlay structure (Chapter 19) that is found in several parts of the world poses still another problem. In an overlay a story is told over and over several times in sequence, with a few elements being carried forward from one telling to the next and some of the other elements being brought in as new information each time around. The parts that are carried forward are referentially — and frequently grammatically — identical with their counterparts in earlier tellings. For any one telling the rhetorical structure can be represented in the form of a tree, and the time structure is uniform. The moment we get two tellings one after the other, however, some of the branches of the tree that represents one telling line up with some of the branches of the tree that represents the next telling. Some of the branches do not line up; however, the time elements in one telling are referentially relatable to the time elements in another telling. At this point it seems of less interest to try to represent what is happening in the form of a tree than to try to devise some more revealing mode of abstract modeling.

The same questions are actually with us in ordinary sentence grammar. Conditions for reflexivization are represented by identical indexes of coreferentiality at different points in a representation of underlying structure. One suspects, however, that using indices (which are not, by the way, part of the definition of any formal grammar I have seen; they appear to have come to the rescue out of nowhere as far as theoretical formulations are concerned) for perceptual reference is just as much a notational trick as using indices for time is. We could equally well have a separate structure imposed on the terminal elements of a semantic representation that enumerates all the things that are referentially distinct and matches each enumerated element with one or more terminal elements. The shape of this structure, however, would be completely at variance with the semantic structure we normally think of, just as the partitioning according to time cuts across the partitioning by rhetorical structure in the examples given a few paragraphs back. Lesser referential similarities include the kind required for replacement by *do so*, in which for *I drank a Coke and so did Jean* the most likely reading is that two distinct Cokes were consumed, and it is possible that the times may be different; the similarity is between two referentially different events that permit the same specification as Coke-drinking events. These also strain the idea of using the familiar tree structures for talking about everything in language.

Several alternatives to a tree representation have been proposed for linguistic structure. One is the stratificational network representation of Sydney Lamb.[11] This lies behind the representation of texts begun by Gleason and his pupils, mentioned earlier, which is drawn upon in this book for the Thurman chart in Chapter 6. As a means of representing linguistic structure it has the advantage of being easily picturable and the drawback of appearing to be unbounded.

With regard to the problem of reference, the stratified representation does offer a possible interface to the world out there through its many-to-one realization rules that map semantics on semology. One suspects that not all stratificational linguists would be happy with realization rules that apply to the field of reference of a particular text rather than to a generalization of the possible referents of texts. Nevertheless, this is a line of possible development.

The semantic networks of Ross Quillian are definitely not trees, but associative networks.[12] Here too, however, the association is

---

[11] Lamb, *Outline of Stratificational Grammar* (1966).
[12] Quillian, "Semantic Memory" (1967), "The Teachable Language Comprehender" (1969).

between semantic element and semantic element, and it is not clear how reference is to be brought into the picture.

The semantic networks of Robert F. Simmons represent a development of discourse theory that is in many ways parallel to my own.[13] The deep structure from which Simmons works can be easily related to the lexical and rhetorical predicates that I talk about here, with the difference that he treats role predicates and rhetorical predicates as kinds of arcs in the implied tree graph rather than as nodes. Each of these arcs has transformations associated with it that modify the semantic structure in a direction that results in its eventually being changed into the equivalent surface structure. The result is a model of discourse quite in keeping with what I am talking about, with a fuller attempt at stating exactly how to get from the underlying representation to the surface form than I have made.

The notion of a back link from a subordinate part of the tree to the proposition that dominates it is due to Simmons. He finds (with certain precautions that need to be taken to prevent limitless embedding) that besides showing what other propositions a given proposition dominates, it aids in the production of connected discourse to know which propositions each subordinate part is dominated by, especially a noun centered one. The possibility of having one proposition back linked to two or more others has the effect of pulling together diverse branches of the same tree without appearing to violate the general pattern of tree structure on which the transformations operate. This is an important step toward being able to recognize several parts of the tree as being referentially equivalent.

As Simmons and Slocum point out, they have not yet incorporated a full referential component outside the semantic component to tell them whether two uses of a noun, say, refer to the same thing twice or to two different things. They feel, however, that the machinery necessary to perform this identification is avail-

[13] Simmons and Slocum, "Generating English Discourse from Semantic Networks" (1972).

able in their conceptual scheme. On the other hand, they do make considerable use of a time index that is not too different from Litteral's to help control embedding. It is possible that entering their model at a nonverbal node might help explain the staging concept.

Probably the most complete linguistic theory in that it incorporates a working model of reference is that of Winograd.[14] The key to his model of linguistic behavior is an INFERENTIAL component that stands between the grammar and a model of the referential field. This frees the referential field from being simply a list of perceptions or distinguished entities and relationships among them. Instead it allows anything that can be deduced from the information already encoded in the referential field to be treated on the same basis as direct referential statements. Winograd incorporates a fairly complete treatment of anaphoric reference into his system for figuring out pronominalization and antecedent temporal and logical relationships.

The kind of underlying structure with which Winograd works, like that of Simmons, keeps the form of a tree in the grammatical component, but links it to referential entities in a way that allows different parts of the discourse to refer, directly or by inference, to the same part of the referential field. The referential field itself changes during the discourse, through a working model of linguistic time that is built into the system. It is possible that as this approach is assimilated into linguistics (for it began in the area of artificial intelligence) it will provide the most satisfactory account of what at the moment is a difficult problem.

[14]   Winograd, *Procedures* (1971). See Chapter 20.

17

LINEAR ORGANIZATION

The preceding chapters have discussed semantic relationships of various kinds that are important for understanding how discourse goes together. One thing that they leave aside, however, is the linear organization of discourse. This will occupy the chapters that follow.

Speaking is a time dependent activity. The process of arranging elements of speech one after the other can be separated from the process of deciding what to say and putting it together in pyramided, hierarchical fashion. As Chafe pointed out in 1967, it makes a good deal of sense to regard the putting together of what we decide to say as independent or nearly independent of how the signals that go with it are arranged in the order that allows them to be transmitted one at a time through the relatively narrow band offered by our organs of speech or our typewriter. The next few chapters discuss this linearization of what we want to say.

It is in this area that we raise the question about how different kinds of information such as identifications, explanations, foreshadowings, reports, and the rest are welded together. The integration of various kinds of information is partly independent of decisions about how much information to put in each sentence of the discourse, but to a certain extent it does depend on those decisions. Near the beginning of a paragraph in a narrative, for example, several sentences may be taken up with setting the scene, explaining the background, and identifying the participants. The action of the narrative, though it is central to the paragraph, may be reported at the rate of several events per sentence, while at the same time a setting for the paragraph is drawn out to several sentences.

On the other hand, certain decisions about where to put identificational information seem to depend upon where the sentence boundaries are placed. The pronominalization systems of many languages prohibit the inclusion of too much identificational information in any one sentence, especially after the initial identification of a character.

Different kinds of discourse seem to select different kinds of information around which to organize the rest. Narratives and procedures, as Longacre has pointed out,[1] take the time oriented parts of the material as their backbone and hang identifications and explanations on as peripheral elements. Explanations and exhortations, on the other hand, put the covariance relationship in the center of things and subordinate events to it. Complex combinations of these and other relationships can make the organizing principle vary from one part of a text to another.

Where time is central, the mechanisms for handling it appear to be elaborate, though at heart they may all be based on a simple recursive principle.[2] One common means of setting time reference is by nesting verbs of saying or thinking in such a way that each furnishes the time reference point for everything in the content of the speech or thought. Another means of setting time is in the specification of sequence in narrative, where different events may occur in order at a fast or slow pace or may take place simultaneously.

McCawley and Langendoen have suggested that identificational information is essentially independent of other kinds, but that it is inserted into texts that are organized around something else at appropriate points.[3] This agrees with the general principle of informational cohesiveness that permits the speaker to quit

---

[1] Longacre, *Discourse ... in Philippine Languages* (1968).
[2] Hajičová, Panevová, and Sgall, "Recursive Properties of Tense" (1970).
[3] McCawley, "Where Do Noun Phrases Come From?" (1970); Langendoen, *The Study of Syntax* (1969).

elaborating what he has to say at the point where he has reason to believe that the hearer knows what he is talking about.

Setting is frequently worked into event sequences where one large unit ends and another begins. In some languages a re-specification of setting, even if the actual setting does not change, is an essential signal of the beginning of a paragraph. Temporal and circumstantial setting as well as spatial setting tend to make use of grammatical constructions that are not frequently used for other kinds of information, such as equatives and locatives.

Background information, as Labov and Waletzky have shown, has certain places where it characteristically appears in some languages.[4] The difference between background information and time oriented information appears to be shown by aspect systems, in which the same form may be used in different senses depending upon whether the section in which it appears is intended as events or background, or in which some aspect forms are used only in one kind of information or another.[5]

Collateral information is often identified with specialized grammatical forms: negatives, modals, questions, and the like. There is often a strong cohesion between the earlier part of a text in which some event is predicted or foreshadowed and the later part where it does or does not happen. Frequently much of the content is built into the early part, so that the later mention of the event is largely anaphoric.

All the foregoing patterns of integration of different kinds of information have been concerned with the part of language that I have referred to as content or cognitive organization. The order in which linguistic elements go into a linear sequence, however, appears to be determined only partly by content. Even more important are the cohesive and thematic phases of language, for which order variations are the primary means of communicating differences, especially in those languages that have traditionally been said to have free word order.

---

[4]   Labov and Waletzky, "Narrative Analysis" (1967).
[5]   McLeod, "Paragraph, Aspect, and Participant in Xavánte" (ms).

The cohesive side of language structure involves relating what is being said at the moment back to what has already been said. Ultimately it relates back to any shared experience of the speaker and the hearer. Information is divided up into blocks or quanta which are transmitted to the hearer at a rate the speaker thinks he can assimilate. The amount of information that is put into each block is related to the speaker's estimate of the probability that the hearer already knows what he is going to say. Furthermore, within each block the speaker (in English and at least some other languages) singles out one part of the information as least predictable of all, and adds an intonational or morphological signal to inform the hearer which part the speaker wants him to take as most informative. There are a variety of devices in language for controlling the rate of injection of unpredictable information, ranging from the telegraphic style used in English to communicate the most information in the fewest words to the overlay style used by some languages to slow down the rate of new information to a minimum.

A number of linguistic patterns are related to the general idea of referring back to what was said earlier. Linkage, or repetition of what was just said as a means of getting started on the next part, provides cohesion within paragraphs in some languages and between paragraphs in others. Other devices, such as the use of conjunctions and even the prediction ahead or "chaining" of certain grammatical categories that is practiced in the highlands of Papua New Guinea, have a similar effect of tying the parts of the discourse to each other in time. Pronominalization is the most common of these anaphoric patterns.

The deletion of constituents under the condition that they have already been identified is a similar cohesive device. Under the right circumstances, anything that has already been mentioned need not be mentioned again.

There are linguistic relationships that involve making a separation between assertions, which frequently imply relatively unpredictable information or else they would not be needed, and presuppositions (also called assumptions and happiness conditions), which must fit the shared background of the speaker and hearer in order to provide the proper context so that the assertion makes sense. To say that I bought a pound of candy implies that I had enough money to buy it, up until the time of the transaction.

A considerable portion of the linear arrangement of speech needs to be attributed to the factor of staging or thematization. The more we look at it, the more evident it becomes that everything we say is phrased from a particular perspective, just as everything that a cinematographer shows on the screen is photographed from a particular perspective. He sets his camera in a definite place and trains it principally on one character; in speech we choose one element that we are referring to as the point of departure for the relationships to all other elements. This affects word order,[6] choice of pronouns in some languages,[7] and decisions concerning subordination.

Chapters 18 through 22 depart from the hierarchical and content side of language and look into the linear factors implied by cohesive and thematic phenomena. As will be evident, these phenomena do not operate independently of either hierarchical organization or content, but interpenetrate both.

[6] Halliday, "Notes on Transitivity and Theme, Part 2" (1967); Gieser, "Kalinga Sequential Discourse" (ms).
[7] Wheatley, "Pronouns and Nominal Elements in Bacairí Discourse" (ms); John Newman, "Participant Orientation in Longuda Folk Tales" (ms).

18

PARTICIPANT ORIENTATION

The study of participant orientation systems[1] has turned out to be helpful in the analysis of some kinds of texts. It starts out from two simple ideas.

The first is that in any single event in a story there are very few participants involved,[2] usually not more than three. The other basic idea is that the relationship of participants to events in a sequence is conventionally constrained in some languages. In other words, there is a regular sequencing of the orientation of participants to events through a story. Becker suggests that the point where this orientation changes is structurally significant.[3]

The conceptual machinery needed to understand participant orientation was worked out by Ivan Lowe.[4] He first traced the principle discussed in Chapter 5 that intervenes when pronominal reference is embedded in quotations, a problem originally proposed by Kenneth L. Pike.[5] The principle turned out to be not only simple but complete in the sense that there is no depth of embedding

---

[1] This chapter is adapted from a paper that was presented to the Linguistic Society of the Philippines in July of 1971 and published in the Philippine Journal of Linguistics.

[2] This principle was suggested by Bellman's approach to dynamic programming, in which the number of factors that influence any decision in an optimal sequence of decisions is taken to be very small: Bellman and Dreyfus, *Applied Dynamic Programming* (1962).

[3] Becker, "A Tagmemic Approach to Paragraph Analysis" (1965).

[4] Lowe, "An Algebraic Theory of English Pronominal Reference" (1969).

[5] Pike and Lowe, "Pronominal Reference in English Conversation" (1969).

for which it does not apply. It is worked out using mathematical group theory.

Later Lowe worked with Mary Ruth Wise, who had studied the identification of participants in discourse.[6] On investigating where pronouns and noun phrases come in text, they began to notice a regular rotation of participant reference. This rotation, however, applied to sequences rather than to embedded constructions. They applied the group principle to discourse and found that there is an independent basis in the referential system for recognizing segments of text that would also need to be recognized on other grounds as paragraphs, whether by unity of setting, by introduction of characters, or by linkage.[7] The exact relation between participant orientation and paragraphing, however, seems to be language specific.

1. PERMUTATIONS

Before going into participant orientation as a linguistic phenomenon, a concise way of talking about it in the abstract is needed. First of all, there are only a few ways of arranging two or three items. For example, if we have any A and any B we can put them either in AB order or in BA order, and no other.

To apply the Wise-Lowe model to text, an appropriate order principle or ranking of elements has to be established to permit different orderings to be distinguished. The ranking used is based on underlying role or case (Chapter 8). It was arrived at empirically, but seems to hold up in a number of languages.[8] Agent is the

[6] Wise, *Identification of Participants* (1968).

[7] Wise and Lowe, "Permutation Groups in Discourse" (1972).

[8] Because it is not clear on theoretical grounds whether instruments and benefactives are best considered primitive roles or abstract predicates, I am not ready to integrate participant orientation into a general theory of the semantic structure of discourse. It seems that the sequencing of role sets is a topicalizing mechanism (Chapter 21). If so, it operates in the area of assigning the referential indexes that correspond to participants in such a way that they match underlying roles, and thus controls the choice of lexical items indirectly. Most topicalization with which we are familiar operates on surface order; this is considerably deeper.

highest ranked role; the others are ordered below it in a way that will be given in detail later.

To change the ordering of two items so that the one that ranked lower in case now ranks higher and vice versa is an operation of REVERSAL (r). For two items, say 1 and 2, reversal is symbolized as (12), which expresses a PERMUTATION in which the elements between parentheses are moved one position to the right, and the last element is brought around to the front. The notation is a general one that permits permutations of any number of elements to be included in a single statement. Here it has the effect of interchanging 1 and 2: (12) = 21.

Reversal is the only orientation operation in certain texts, including the text on which Wise and Lowe first worked out the idea. It starts out with one character as agent and the next as, say latter state, then reverses so that the second character is agent and the first is a lower ranked role. A second reversal brings them back into the original orientation, which signals a new paragraph.[9]

Another text based on reversal alone is reported by Virginia Bradley for Jibu of Nigeria.[10] The characters are a bridegroom and his group and the narrator and his group. The story starts with the bridegroom extending an invitation to the narrator, an agent-latter situation in which agent ranks higher than latter state. The narrator responds by going to where the bridegroom is; the narrator as agent now outranks the bridegroom as latter state. Then the bridegroom and his group do something as joint agent with reference to the guests at the wedding as a patient group; and the guests, changing to agent, react. The structure of the text revolves around the regular return to the initial configuration in which the bridegroom ranks high and the narrator ranks low; each reversal that gives this state begins a new section.

[9] Philippine languages appear to rely to a small extent on participant orientation; but more explicit means of identification via pronouns and noun phrases are common. Some languages of Papua New Guinea (S. Litteral, "Orientation in Anggor", ms), Bolivia (Briggs, "Ayoré Narrative Analysis", ms), and Nigeria (Bradley, "Jibu Narrative Discourse Structure", 1971) make more extensive use of it.

[10] Bradley, "Jibu" (1971).

Other texts juggle three participants. There are six different possibilities of rearranging three things. (The number of possibilities is equal to the factorial of the number of things permuted. Factorial $n! = n (n - 1) \ldots 1$.) To generalize operations, a reversal involving three things is defined as (12) (3), signifying that 1 and 2 permute with each other and 3 permutes with itself, or in other words stays where it is.

A second operation, SWITCH (s), instead of interchanging the first and second things, interchanges the second and third things: (1) (23). Notice that the reversal of a reversal ($r \cdot r$ or r^2) goes back to the starting arrangement, and so does the switch of a switch ($s \cdot s$ or s^2). This provides the INVERSE relation.

A third operation, IDENTITY (I), the operation of doing nothing (1) (2) (3), completes the system. These three elementary operations provide for all participant orientation orders for three participants, and are related as $I = r^2 = s^2$.

Using A, B, and C, to stand for participants and left to right order for high to low role ranking, let ABC be the base or identity state of the participants. Then r(ABC) = BAC, which can be called the reversal state, and s(ABC) = ACB can be called the switch state. The states are named from the operations it would take to get to them by starting from the ABC or identity state. Going on, BCA is the rs state: rs(ABC) = s(r(ABC)) = s(BAC) = BCA.

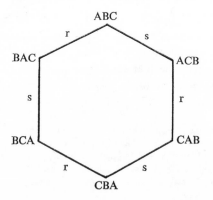

Figure 18.1 Permutations of three things.

CAB is the sr state: sr(ABC) = r(s(ABC)) = r(ACB) = CAB. CBA is the srs or the rsr state: srs(ABC) = s(sr(ABC)) = s(CAB) = CBA, but also rsr(ABC) = r(rs(ABC)) = r(BCA) = CBA. We summarize all this in Figure 18.1.

These operations, simple and compound, form a mathematical group. That is, they have the following four properties: (1) Closure. Any sequence of operations results in another operation in the same system. No sequence of operations goes out of the system. For example, rsIrrsrIrss = r, since $r^2 = s^2 = I$ and most of the string cancels out on that basis. (2) Associativity. Grouping operations by parentheses makes no difference. (rs)r = r(sr) = rsr. (3) Inverse. Every element has an inverse, and there is no sequence of operations that cannot be inverted by another sequence of operations. $r \cdot r = s \cdot s = sr \cdot rs = rs \cdot sr = rsr \cdot rsr = srs \cdot srs = I$. (4) Identity. There is an operation I which, applied to any operation in the group, gives the same operation: $I \cdot r = r$, $I \cdot s = s$, and so forth.[11]

2. SEQUENCES OF PERMUTATIONS

Orientation, as mentioned, requires a ranking of semantic roles or cases. The ranking that seems to give the clearest results is a composite of rankings that have been worked out in several languages. It is tantamount to a scale of relative involvement in actions: agent, former state, latter state, patient, instrument, force, benefactive, range, and zero to represent a participant who is wholly removed from an action. On this scale agent outranks patient and patient outranks benefactive.

A text in Ayoré of Bolivia illustrates a ranking with three

---

[11] An equivalent group could be defined starting with two other operations, say x = (123) and y = (13) (2) together with I. Defining the r and s operations in the context of role ranking, however, gives us a linguistically insightful way talking about the phenomenon that would not be as apparent if we began from other operations.

participants.[12] The first sentence is an introduction or verbal title: 'I killed a jaguar on another occasion'. It has two participants, narrator and jaguar, who are agent and patient. If A is the narrator, B the jaguar, and C a third character not yet mentioned, and agent outranks patient and patient outranks zero, the ranking is ABC: A kills B with C not mentioned.

The story goes on: 'I killed a jaguar' $I(ABC) = ABC$. 'He jumped at me' $r(ABC) = BAC$. 'I lanced him as he came' $r(BAC) = ABC$, 'but he took out my lance' $r(ABC) = BAC$,[13] 'and I followed him and found him far away' $r(BAC) = ABC$. 'I went to kill him with my lance' $I(ABC) = ABC$, but 'Bague's father found me' $sr(ABC) = CAB$, 'and killed him right under my nose' $s(CAB) = CBA$. 'He and his friends carried him back' $I(CBA)$. The end of the story has the form of a coda: 'The place where I killed him is in that direction' $srs(CBA) = ABC$.

The regular progression of events in a story is carried by single permutation operations: r and s. Whenever we get composite operations, sr, rs, rsr, or srs, there is a surprise, an interruption, or a point where things go wrong; and this happens not only in Ayoré but in several languages.

In Koiné Greek, in the first chapter of *St. John*, John tells his disciples who Jesus is, his disciples follow Jesus and talk with him, then Andrew goes off and gets his brother Simon and brings him to Jesus. Jesus says to him, "You are Simon, son of John; you shall be called Cephas" (meaning 'a stone'). The point where Jesus addresses Simon directly is an sr transition, the surprise point of the whole narrative. What happens is completely unpredictable to Peter. The story up to that point goes by the simple transitions r, s, and I. But that is the point at which Peter gets the shock of his life.

Back to the jaguar story, the same thing happens. From the point of view of the narrator, the jaguar hunt has been going

---

[12]   Briggs, "Ayoré Narrative Analysis" (ms).

[13]   The lance is considered a prop (3.2) rather than a participant because whether it is considered or overlooked makes no difference to the orientation analysis. Note Wise and Lowe's partitioning of referents, which allows their analysis to be based on the relationships of the people alone.

normally. Then just as he is standing over the jaguar ready to finish him off with his spear poised in the air, out of the jungle comes C and kills the jaguar instead. The shock even affects the linguistic structure at this point.

Going from the actual killing of the jaguar to the coda, which reminds us that it was really A's jaguar hunt, we have a concise description of what could be called a roundabout mental process. The narrator brings the story back to the state in which he started it, the equilibrium state or base line, even at the cost of twisting the arm of reason in order to get back there.

One function of an equilibrium state, as Labov and Waletzky point out in their paper on narrative structure,[14] is to relate the narration itself to the performative situation in which the narration is given. The narrator does that first of all by identifying himself in the title as both the teller and the major actor. The phrase "on another occasion" in the introduction has the effect of placing the story in some entirely different time. At the end, "the place where I killed him was in that direction" brings the story back to the place of telling, so that at both ends it is hooked into the performative. Not all stories do this, but it is a common device. The English formula *Once upon a time ...* matched with *They all lived happily ever after* has that function, among others.

3. PERMUTATION STATES

Up to now we have labeled operations. We can also label states in terms of the operations that are performed in order to get to that state from some other state. Looked at in this way, BAC is the r or reversal state if we take ABC as the starting state, and CBA is the rsr or srs state.

In a story with an identifiable starting state and ending state such as is defined by the title and the coda, we can go through and name the states, taking the starting state as the identity state, and

---

[14] Labov and Waletzky, "Narrative Analysis" (1967).

using the operations to name each of the six states of the system. ABC is the I state, BAC the r state, ACB the s state, BCA the rs state, CAB the sr state, and CBA the rsr or srs state, each calculated with reference to the identity state. During the early part of stories the states tend to stay around the I, the r, and the s state. The tension point of the story, however, almost always comes in the srs state. In the jaguar story, "C killed B right under A's nose" is the srs state, and is obviously the tension point. This turns out to be a formal means of recognizing it in a number of languages.

The notion of a tension state is distinct from state transition operations. The composite operations sr, rs, and srs give jumps in the action. But stories can build up to an srs tension state without any jumps. Also, the development from the tension state back to the equilibrium state is frequently smooth. Therefore the information we get from plotting states and the information we get from plotting sequences of operations do not necessarily coincide.

In texts with a recognizable identity state there is an interplay between the role a character has in the discourse as a whole and the role of that character in each action. DISCOURSE ROLES distinguish the participant who is characteristically the INITIATOR throughout the discourse from the one who is characteristically the REACTOR throughout the discourse, and cast all others in a tertiary role. In the jaguar story A is the one who moves things along. The jaguar is cast as the reactor, and C is neither initiator nor reactor. The identity state is then the one in which the initiator is acting as initiator, the reactor is acting as reactor, and the other is acting as other: ABC. In other configurations like BAC or CBA there is a temporary discrepancy between the relation of the participant to a single action and his overall role in the story. State analysis gives a kind of measure of that discrepancy from the identity state, and thus fits the idea of a tension state.

There are texts for which it is hard to tell what the identity state is; possibly no identity state exists for them. The only significant thing in this case is the sequence of operations that give the transitions between one state and another. There it still holds true that the smooth development of the story is built on identities, switches, and reversals, and surprise points follow composite operations.[15]

In some languages where up to now it has been hard to tell what pronouns refer to, one of the principles that may operate is this regular progression of the relation of participants to actions.[16] If it is built so deeply into people's mental makeup as to recur in widely spaced languages around the world, it could operate even when other more obvious principles of reference do not.

The usual principles for pronoun reference include: who was mentioned last? who is the story about? who is the paragraph or sentence about? Lines of distinction in a pronoun system, like person or number or gender distinctions, also serve to keep reference sorted out. But in a story with four participants, all of them "he", and in a language that is sparing of pronouns anyway, there must be some other principle operating. We observe as a matter of fact that people can keep references untangled in a situation like this. (Not everybody keeps all his pronoun references untangled all the time, even in languages that make this easy.) When they do get their reference right, what are they doing? Participant orientation is a possible model.

Four participants operating at once has not been found yet. Nevertheless, Figure 18.2 covers four. In addition to the three operations of identity, reversal, and switch, there is a TRADE operation (1) (2) (34). The hexagon in the middle of the figure corresponds to the diagram given earlier. In three dimensions Figure 18.2 would come out a fourteen-sided figure composed of eight hexagons and six quadrilaterals.

Bradley, as already mentioned, describes the expansion and shrinkage of participant groups; the participants in the orientation system do not necessarily include the same individuals at each stage. Part of her Jibu text also includes a change of scope in the orientation system. A group that throughout the main part of the

---

[15] Barnard and Longacre, "Dibabawon Procedural Discourse" (1968), find that what I would think of as an identity state cannot be identified clearly until the discourse is nearly over. It becomes clear at the point where the characters accomplish what they set out to do.

[16] Larson, "Pronominal Reference in the Ivatan Narrative" (ms).

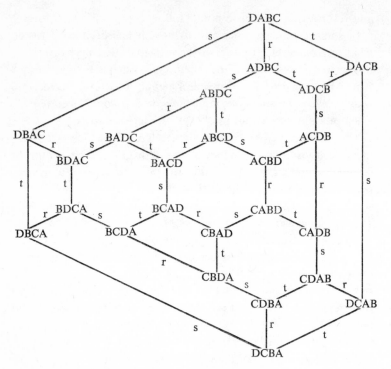

Figure 18.2 Permutations of four things.

ELEMENTARY PERMUTATIONS
r = (12)(3)(4)
s = (1)(23)(4)
t = (1)(2)(34)
I = (1)(2)(3)(4)

text is one participant, the initiator group, appears in one scene in a closeup view that splits the members of that group temporarily into initiator and reactor subgroups. After that scene the group returns to single participant status without further internal differentiation.

ROLE SUBSTITUTION takes place when a series of individuals take turns in the same relation to one of the participants. For example, in an Ilianen Manobo tale brought to my attention by Hazel Wrigglesworth, a lizard, the main character, confronts a deer, a woodpecker, a crocodile, and a shrimp in turn. While the lizard is talking with one of them as initiator to reactor, the reactor mentions the next one in the series, and is told to call him: the lizard (A) tells the reactor (B) to call the next character (C). The next character appears and the former reactor drops from the story. But rather than the next character's reply to A's call being a switch-reversal, which would give CAB, the character who was called as C rather seems to shift into the reactor role of B by substitution, while the former B drops out of sight. By role substitution, then, the operation becomes a simple reversal: from ABC to BA(C), but with B_2 taking over the identity of the former C and the former B_1 dropping out as a dummy C, no longer active.

19

COHESION

Most of linguistics has been directed toward the study of the content structure of language. I have already mentioned that there seems to be evidence for two other kinds of structure that interlock with content. The first, which I discuss in this chapter, is the system of COHESION. It has to do with the way information mentioned in speech relates to information that is already available. The other, which is introduced in Chapter 21, is what I call STAGING. It has to do with the kind of perspective from which each section of a discourse is presented to the hearer.

Cohesion, probably because it is partly time dependent, tends to be dropped into the performance category of Chomsky's competence-performance dichotomy.[1] Even within the limits for which that distinction is useful, however, I think it must be granted that part of the speaker's or hearer's knowledge of his language includes the capacity to assign and interpret correctly the features that signal cohesion, to recognize aberrations, and to disambiguate — in short, if there is a basis for talking about linguistic competence in the area of content, where most of the discussion has taken place, whatever arguments justify it there also support it in the area of cohesion.

Much of my thinking on the subject of cohesion has been influenced by Michael A. K. Halliday's articles on transitivity and theme in English.[2] I have, however, departed from his terminology

---

[1] Chomsky, *Aspects* (1965).
[2] Halliday, "Notes on Transitivity and Theme in English" Parts 1 and 2 (1967), Part 3 (1968).

for two reasons. The first is that some of the terms he uses are chosen from the gray area of nomenclature in which each linguist does that which is right in his own eyes, and few do the same as anyone else. His terms "unit" and "focus" fit here; there are enough different uses of each in the current scene that his use, no matter how carefully it is defined, is bound to be misunderstood. My own preference is for terms that are a little easier to associate with the phenomena they describe, and a little less likely to be used in a different sense by the next person who happens to be looking for a term. The second reason for not following Halliday's terminology is that other terms he uses tend to be put into morphological paradigms that are not transparent. For example, he distinguishes "mode" from "modal" and "encoding" from "decoding" in a tightly defined way; but I (and a number of other linguists I have asked about it) have to keep turning the pages back to keep track of which means what. I have tried, therefore, to select terms that stand far enough apart from each other in the associative relations I have for each that I can retain some idea of how they are distinguished as well as the fact that they are distinct.

I follow Halliday rather than Wallace Chafe in discussing cohesion because Chafe blurs the distinction between it and thematization or staging.[3] For his purposes this lack of distinction does not hurt, because his remarks on the distribution of new and old information apply mainly to unmarked thematization in Halliday's sense. He does not, for example, worry about cases like *my hat I had to leave at the cleaner's*, under the circumstances that the theme *hat* and the most predictable information *I* are different. In a fuller treatment of the phenomena, or in an expansion of his generally stimulating ideas so as to embrace discourse, I doubt that Chafe would remain satisfied for long with this initial underdifferentiation.

1. INFORMATION BLOCKS

The first observation to be made about the cohesive structure of

---

[3] Chafe, *Meaning and the Structure of Language* (1970).

language is that the speaker, in addition to having to decide on the content of what he is talking about and how it is to be organized, decides also how much of it he thinks his hearer can take in at one time. He makes this decision in the light of what he thinks the hearer already knows. The package of information that results, or INFORMATION BLOCK (Halliday's "information unit"), may or may not correspond to some easily recognized substring of the content. In English its extent is signalled by a single intonation contour, while in Oksapmin it is delimited not only by intonation but by verbal inflection as well.[4] An utterance like THIS / *is the* FIRST TIME / *we have* EVER / DONE *anything like this* (using capital letters for words that are intonationally prominent, following Gunter, and slashes to separate intonation contours) has a different information blocking from *This is the first time we have ever* DONE *anything like this*, even though they are the same in content.[5]

Several factors enter into the decision to block information in one way or another. The first is the information a speaker has already given in the discourse. Anything that the speaker feels is already clear is not as likely to be singled out by being put in a separate block as are expressions for things concerning which he is sure the hearer knows nothing. The same thing holds for expressions that refer to the immediate situation of speech. Performative elements like *I* for the speaker and *you* for the hearer, or *this* and *that* for visible entities in their surroundings, are not likely to be put in separate information blocks, especially after attention has been called to them linguistically for the first time.

Besides these first two factors, which we might label TEXTUAL and SITUATIONAL for convenience, there seems to be an overall decision on the part of the speaker about the rate of INFORMATION

[4] Marshall Lawrence, "Oksapmin Sentence Structure" (1972).
[5] The notation follows Richard Gunter, "On the Placement of Accent in Dialogue" (1966). This simple notation for intonation overlooks the variety of pitch patterns that make up intonation and a good deal of the dynamics as well. These factors, however, seem to be controlled largely by the speaker's attitude on the one hand, and by certain grammatical traits on the other. They are on the margin of the system that communicates cohesion as such, the main traits of which are all this notation represents.

INJECTION that he wishes to establish. In English the highest rate of information injection is that of telegraphic style, in which the apparatus of cohesion is squeezed to the minimum that grammar will permit. The famous *sighted sub sank same* of World War II is about as far as we can go in making every word count. In idealized journalistic style we get a high rate of information injection in the lead paragraph and a constant decrease in the rate for succeeding paragraphs. At the other end of the scale we might have the well padded term paper or the television talk show, where the frequency of introduction of new information per line or per sentence is decidedly low.

The natural tendency is for the speaker to help the hearer by making his information blocks short when his rate of information introduction is high. The wartime message cited in the last paragraph, for example, is usually punctuated with a comma in the middle, presumably to indicate blocking, though I doubt that the original dispatch contained one. On the other hand, when the speaker is acting as though his rate of new information is low, the tendency is for the information blocks to be long. As an example we might consider a linguist who is uncertain of himself presenting a paper to an audience who he suspects know nearly everything he is going to say anyway; he is likely to drone on and on with uniformly long information blocks.

There are two interesting deviations from this pattern in contemporary American English. The first is the practice of some radio and television newscasters to speak in rather large, well organized information blocks even when they are communicating new information at a high rate. When compared with the practice of those announcers (most sports announcers and some newscasters) who follow the normal rule of short blocks for a high rate, their adopted pose makes sense. If their information blocks were as short as the newness of the news implies, they might leave their listeners breathless at the end of five minutes. By lengthening their information blocks they may be suggesting the fiction, "You are well posted on the world situation. Nothing I have to say will surprise you. There are, however, a few details I can add to what you already know, and these may interest you." That listeners accept this fiction gratefully is backed up by what appears to be a positive correlation between the salary of the newscaster and the average length of his information blocks.

The other exception is in the opposite direction. As is well known, politicians tend to speak in very short information blocks: *My* FRIENDS / *I* COME *here this evening* / *to* TELL *you* / *that we are* ALL / FACED / *with a* GRAVE DECISION. / *We* MUST / ELECT / *the* BEST / *most* HIGHLY QUALIFIED / CANDIDATE / *from among our* RANKS. Here any hearer who could not predict the rest of the speech himself is simply a novice at politics. The content is highly redundant; the real rate of information injection is extremely low. The blocking, however, is characteristic of a very high rate of information injection. Perhaps the fiction is this: "You and I need to feel that what we are doing is important. Important things are characterized by a high information flow. I will talk and you will listen under the trappings of a full flow of information, and neither of us will question how new the associated content really is."

Information blocking segments an oral discourse into an integral number of blocks, with no fractional residue. We would not, for example, find a speech that consisted of 103.7 information blocks, but we might find 103 or 104. Some writers punctuate by information blocks, though my experience is that most editors punctuate by surface grammar more often than by information blocking. (Example: *Some writers, punctuate by information blocks, though my experience is, that most editors, punctuate by surface grammar, more often than by information blocking.*)

Cohesion in discourse appears to involve the further grouping of information blocks into larger units, rather like the way sentences are grouped into paragraphs in written discourse. The intonational grouping of mesosegments into macrosegments in Sierra Náhuat reflects this kind of block grouping.[6] In Oksapmin the normal inflection of verbs aids in delimiting information blocks,

---

[6]   Robinson, *Sierra Nahuat Word Structure* (1966).

working along with intonation; but there is a special final inflection that terminates a group of information blocks.[7]

In English it seems possible for one information block to be
interpolated within another in a parenthetic fashion: *Bill wrote | or*
SAID *he was going to write | the* NOTE *last week*. This utterance
consists of two information blocks, even though phonetically it
consists of three breath segments.[8] The first has no point of
intonational prominence in it, and hence is capable of being taken
as part of the third breath segment, forming a two-part information
block that is interrupted by the second breath segment. The second
segment is itself a complete information block.

Although we have already seen how information blocking is
independent of content, the two lock together at certain points.
To explain these points it helps to make use of the notion of
MARKEDNESS mentioned earlier in Chapter 8.3. There are many
things in language that come in small sets: pronouns, vowels,
affixes, certain transformations, and others. In these sets there is
often one member that seems to be used in the absence of any
special reason for choosing one of the others. All the other members
of the set have some more specific motivation attached to their use.
The members of the set that are picked up under specific conditions
are called the MARKED members, while the one that is used by
default is called the UNMARKED member.

Information blocks that correspond to single clauses are unmarked in their relationship to content organization. In English,
and in several other languages at least, we make our information
blocks the same size as our main clauses unless there is a particular
reason for not making the two match. *Bill wrote the* NOTE *last week*,
for example, is a single clause uttered as a single information block.

Embedded clauses are normally treated as part of the matrix
clause (that is, the clause within which they are embedded) as far
as information structure is concerned. They are not blocked
separately in the unmarked case. *The people who visited us wrote*

---

[7] M. Lawrence, "Oksapmin Sentence Structure" (1972).
[8] Grimes, *Phonological Analysis* (1969).

the NOTE *last week*. Clauses used as adjuncts to other clauses within sentences, however, are normally split off intonationally rather than being treated like embedded clauses: *Bill wrote the* NOTE / *as he* SAID *he would* is the normal form. Both the dependent and the independent clauses are unmarked information blocks in this case.

A MARKED information block is one that does not correspond to an independent or dependent clause. In other words, the speaker has some reason for overriding the natural affinity between clause boundaries and information block boundaries. The most common kind of marked information block covers less than a clause: BILL / *wrote the* NOTE *last week*. In most speech the average number of information blocks per clause is somewhat greater than one, but less than two.

On the other hand, more than one clause may be included in a marked information block: *Bill wrote the note last week and then he had to leave* TOWN.

The use of marked information blocks implies a judgment on the part of the speaker about the hearer's capacity to assimilate what he is saying. It is related to the fact that each information block has a CENTER that represents the least predictable part of the block; this will be discussed in the next section. If everything that is being said is predictable, the block may be allowed to grow fairly long,[9] as in the last example. On the other hand, a large quantity of new information ordinarily calls for more frequent blocking so as to provide more centers. We have already considered how newscasters and politicians manipulate this blocking principle, the one to play down the quantity of new information, and the other to give the appearance of new information even when there is none.

Marked information blocking may also be used when the speaker wishes to prevent misunderstanding of content structures that are

---

[9] Since information blocking is connected with intonation contours in English and many other languages, physiological constraints on the length of contours may force the effect of blocking even when the speaker's estimate of his message does not demand the end of a block. The limiting constraint is that the speaker has to take a breath once in a while regardless of his information structure.

otherwise ambiguous. For example, within a noun phrase there may be postnominal qualifiers that define or restrict the reference of the noun phrase as a whole. These tend to be blocked together with the head noun: *The* MAN *who is over there* / *is* WATCHING *us*, for example, tells which man the hearer is to attach *watching* to. Other postnominal qualifiers, however, assume that the hearer already knows what the phrase refers to. They add incidental information, and so are appropriately blocked by themselves: *The* MAN / *who is over* THERE / *is* WATCHING *us*. A similar pattern of difference between defining the head of a noun phrase and throwing in additional details about it for the hearer's interest is seen in *The* CHECKS *which were ready yesterday* / *are still on the* DESK versus *The* CHECKS / *which were ready* YESTERDAY / *are still on the* DESK. When the second kind of information block (the so-called NONRESTRICTIVE relative pattern) is used, the pitch of its intonation contour tends to echo that of the contour that ends on the head word.

Information blocking can also be used to clarify just how far certain adjuncts carry. In general they tend to apply to only one information block. If the adjunct is marked off in a block of its own, then it applies to the block next to it. If it is included within a larger block, then it applies within that block. For example, in *On* WEDNESDAY / *Uncle* GEORGE *arrived* / *and we had a* PICNIC the sentence initial adjunct is blocked by itself, and so applies to Uncle George's arrival. What day the picnic took place is anybody's guess; it could even have been on Thursday, because the adjunct does not apply beyond the block next to it. A similar effect can be gotten by putting the adjunct inside the same block as the clause it modifies: *On Wednesday Uncle* GEORGE *arrived* / *and we had a* PICNIC.

On the other hand, the adjunct can be applied to both clauses by putting them into a single information block. If we say *On* WEDNESDAY / *Uncle George arrived and we had a* PICNIC, or even *On Wednesday Uncle George arrived and we had a* PICNIC with everything in one block, then the picnic could only have been held on Wednesday because the adjunct is tied to both of the clauses in the block.

There are final adjuncts that work in the same way as the initial adjuncts, but in the opposite direction. *Only, neither,* and *too* imply a constituent prior to the one to which they are bound by the information blocking. *They got there late and missed the bus* TOO implies something in the situation or earlier in the discourse to which the current misfortunes are being added; so may *They got there late and missed the* BUS / TOO. The latter, Dwight Bolinger points out in a personal communication, seems to suggest less strongly that what came earlier was necessarily a misfortune. If each clause is blocked separately, however, then the first one is the earlier element that *too* looks for; there is no need to scan farther for it: *They got there* LATE / *and missed the bus* TOO, or the nearly equivalent form with *too* as a separate block, *They got there* LATE / *and missed the* BUS / TOO.

2. INFORMATION CENTERS

Each information block contains at least one CENTER. The center is that part of the block in which new information is concentrated. The rest of the block contains more predictable material. In English the center of an information block is identified by intonational prominence, just as the extent of an information block is identified by intonational boundaries. In *The* MART / *is having a* SALE *today, Mart* and *sale* are the centers of their respective information blocks, and communicate the least predictable information within each block.

Just as the quantity of information that is contained in one block is decided on by the speaker, so the placement of the center is under his control. He has to designate the "part of the message block the speaker wishes to be interpreted as informative", in Halliday's words; he can direct the hearer's evaluation of what is to be taken as new and what as given. He does not, on the other hand, exercise any choice over whether the block will have a center or not, any more than in English he exercises a choice over whether an independent verb will have a tense or not. Something in the block has to be picked out as its center, if only in relative terms. Bolinger uses the terms "relative semantic weight", "informativeness", and "unpredictability" in this sense.[10]

The decision about what is to be considered relatively new is independent of the constituent structure of the block. It is also independent of the underlying content structure which the constituency reflects. Perhaps we all played games with center placement in childhood, like repeating

> MY puppy is black.
> My PUPPY is black.
> My puppy IS black.
> My puppy is BLACK

All four have the same underlying content, but they differ as to the speaker's decision about the informativeness of the parts. All are natural in the right contexts.

New information corresponds to the information that could be given as the answer to some question. For this reason questions are useful tools in tracking down information centers. The game is to find a question to which a particular information block is the natural answer.

The search for questions is complicated by a further characteristic of given information, however: answers often leave out part or all of the presupposing statement that is behind the question. *Whose puppy is black?* for example, can elicit MY *puppy is black* as an answer under some circumstances, but the familiar principle of deletion recoverability — that anything that can be supplied from the context does not have to be repeated — leads more often to MINE as the answer.

Intonation centers that reflect the answer to a question illustrate center assignment on a CUMULATIVE or CONTEXTUAL basis. The information is new with reference to the text that has gone before and the situation. *On* FRIDAY / CAROL *came* / *and she* TOLD *me* / *she*

---

[10]   D. Bolinger, "Accent is Predictable (If You're a Mind-Reader)" (1972).

wanted to get a JOB illustrates singling out the center of each block by testing words against the previous text, with the result that *she* is never a center but *Carol* is on her first appearance, and against the situation, so that *Friday* fits at an unpredictable distance in time from the day of the speech situation.

Other intonation centers, on the other hand, are placed to FORESTALL misapprehension. They reflect a guess by the speaker that the hearer might understand something wrongly if he applies the normal rules to it. Forestalling center placement can apply to anything at all, while contextual placement is restricted almost completely to content words, for reasons we will look into later. *I saw* HIM illustrates a forestalling information center placed on an anaphoric word that would never be a center in the contextual sense. What the forestalling placement means is "be careful — the reference you would understand by ordinary backtracking is the wrong one for this use of *him;* so look for the next most likely referent instead". Forestalling stress on the modal, as in *My puppy* IS *black*, means "I think you misunderstood an earlier assertion of mine on its positive-negative dimension". It could also be used to clarify a misunderstanding about tense, contrasting with *was*.

An information block may have more than one center under certain conditions. In English the secondary center usually follows the primary one as a second point of intonational prominence within the same contour. The second intonational nucleus is not as high in pitch as the first: *They have a* CLASS *on* WEDNESDAYS. This could be taken as a compressed answer to a double question: *What do they do? and when do they do it?*, in which the second question depends on the answer to the first, so that its range of unpredictability may be less.

Secondary information centers are thus used to communicate information that is relatively unpredictable, yet is dependent in some way on the primary center. In *We'll* BE *there if we* CAN the secondary center CAN involves a contingency. In *They cost* LOTS *you* KNOW the secondary center is a confirmatory tag on the main part of the information block. In the clause final adjunct of *He wrote the* LETTER *on* FRIDAY the time designation is new, but not as importantly new as the primary center. Each of these secondary centers could, of course, be uttered as a separate block: *We'll* BE *there* | *if we* CAN and so forth. The speaker has the option of separating them; but if he chooses to combine them, he is making the second one definitely subordinate in its impact on the hearer.

Another kind of secondary information center could be thought of as halfway between being new by forestalling and being contextually new. Halliday characterizes this as given information that is 'to be noted'. It appears regularly in thematic tags (22.4) in which the tag consists of given information, as in *He fixed it* FAST *did* GEORGE.

There is a special kind of secondary information center in which the pitch is not only lower than that of the primary center, but distinctly lower than the general pitch of the rest of the block. In our oversimplified notation for those parts of intonation that reflect the information blocking system we can symbolize this by a falling arrow before the word: GEORGE *doesn't* ↘ THINK *so*. This deviation of the pitch line to the low side of normal seems to be capable of being used for adding a negative evaluation by the speaker.[11] It has a special affinity for evaluative words, though it may be used to cast a bad light on something relatively innocuous. In *He* REALLY *had a* ↘ BAD *night* only the lowered secondary center fits; the same statement with ↘ GOOD in place of ↘ BAD sounds ironical. On the other hand, *The* STEAK *was* ↘ OKAY sounds grudging rather than complimentary. In contrast, just as negative words like *terribly* and *horribly* are used more often for good things than for bad things, deviation on the low side may also give the effect of a superlative: Bolinger mentions *I was* DAZZLED *by their* ↘ LOVELINESS.

One wonders, accordingly, about the airline stewardess who announces *we* HOPE *you've* ↘ ENJOYED | *your* FLIGHT *with us* | *and we* HOPE *to* ↘ SEE *you again* | SOON | *on* GAMMA ↘ AIRLINES ... Is it because she was trained to use a singsong chant over the public address system, or does this express what she thinks of the pas-

---

11   Donald Hayes, personal communication.

sengers? Clearly this class of information structures requires further research.

Epithets that are tagged on the end of a clause frequently appear as lowered secondary centers. This is in keeping with their mildly negative meaning: *He* SAID *he'd get here the* ↘ SO-AND-SO.[12]

Oksapmin of Papua New Guinea has already been mentioned as having a cohesive structure that handles given and new information in a slightly different way. As in English, the basic information block corresponds to the clause in the unmarked case. Centers, however, come in two varieties. Some centers involve information that is new in the technical sense of being relatively unpredictable in terms of the text or situation. Others are new in that sense; but in addition the speaker considers it appropriate to call the hearer's attention to that newness. Thus in Oksapmin information centers could be thought of as unmarked or marked in terms of how their newness is presented.

The kind of center that is involved in Oksapmin has direct grammatical consequences. Unmarked centers have an inflection pattern called MEDIAL on the main verb of the clause. With medial inflection no information is given about tense and mode; this is held off until the next marked center comes along. At the marked center, where the speaker is telling the hearer that the new information he is giving him is not only new but worth singling out as new, he employs a FINAL inflection pattern. This expresses the tense and mode that apply to the entire string of medial clauses ahead of the final one as well as to the final clause itself. In effect, the final inflection is what indicates the relationship between the speaker and what he is saying, while the medial inflection puts off that question. Thomas Bearth finds a similar pattern of primary and

---

[12] This discussion skips over several factors that need to be brought into a full description of the way intonation relates to informative structure. Dwight Bolinger (personal communication) has called my attention to the part terminal distinctions between drop and upturn in pitch play in information blocking, the behavior of pitch in relation to thematic inversions and in conjoined sentences, doubly centered blocks in which the second center is higher than the first, and the relation of the whole matter to presuppositions as well as to things that are mentioned earlier.

secondary information in Toura of Ivory Coast, even though its signals are quite different from those of Oksapmin.[13]

Up to now our discussion of centers has been concerned with the number of centers per block. We have considered the fact that centers placed to forestall misunderstanding can go on anything in the block.[14] Now it remains to look into where the center comes in the block when it is contextual.

This is best explained by working up to it through a series of approximations. The first level of approximation is the observation that unmarked centers usually fall on the last word of a block. The stressed syllable of that word is the one with which the intonational nucleus coincides: *Here are some* BOOKS. The fact that unmarked centers do not always come on the last word will give rise to another round of approximation later. For now let us concentrate on the cases in which the unmarked center is last.

One consequence is the generally valid observation that given information is presented before new information. It lays the groundwork for it, so to speak.

The given-new sequence, however, has a built in point of ambiguity. The longer the block, the more possible division points there are between where the given information leaves off and the new part begins. In other words, we do not know how far the center extends; all we really know is where it ends.[15]

There are cases where everything in the information block is new; the center carries all the way back. Blocks of this type are characteristic of the beginning of discourses,[16] especially discourses

---

[13]   Thomas Bearth, "La Structure d'Information en Toura" (ms).

[14]   Forestalling centers can even fit on fragments of words: *The engineers designed this pump to* EX*pel rather than to* IM*pel.*

[15]   Chafe's rules for assigning *new* status to the elements of a sentence in *Meaning and the Structure of Language* (1970) miss this point, which really requires discourse conditions on the assignment of *new*.

[16]   C. C. Fries, in *The Structure of English* (1952), took most of his data from the initial sentences of telephone conversations. He found that they showed a greater variety of structure than later sentences. I would guess that the later sentences make heavy use of cohesive mechanisms, but beginning sentences have to rely on the full expression of content in the absence of given information.

like telephone conversations and narrations in which situational factors are at a minimum: *Two* MEN / *were walking down a* ROAD / THREE MILES / *from* BIRMINGHAM contains a series of information blocks in which all the information is new. Blocks of this kind are typically elicited by nonspecific questions like *What happened?*

Halliday suggests that in some cases information blocks that contain all or nearly all new information may be phonologically distinguished from blocks that begin with given information, provided the whole block is short enough.[17] In English phonology, intonation contours consist of one or more FEET or rhythmic units. Each unit consists of one to five syllables, and in the main is co-extensive with a word. Each foot has one stressed syllable; the rest are unstressed. Halliday notes that some syllables have the rhythm of unstressed syllables, but the stressed syllable they should go with is nowhere to be found. Its place is taken by a pause, the timing of which is equivalent to the timing of a foot nucleus in ordinary speech rhythm. A foot can thus consist either of a stressed syllable as nucleus with peripheral unstressed syllables, or it can consist of a SILENT STRESS as nucleus with peripheral unstressed syllables. Using an acute accent for rhythmic nuclei, including the accent by itself for silent stress, and writing a plus sign to indicate rhythmic foot boundaries, we could show the rhythmic substructure of an all new information block as ´*He* + *wrítes* + NÓVELS, with a complete foot as well as one with silent stress in the part before the center.

For a given-new information block, the information center begins somewhere in the middle of the block. It is the last constituent, figuring constituency far enough down the tree of surface grammar that it does not embrace the entire block. This kind of information structure is elicited by specific questions that assert while they query: *What do you have in that* SACK? asserts *you have something in that sack*, so that in the answer anything that entered into the assertion will be given information, and only the contents of the sack will be new: *I have an* ORANGE. Halliday suggests further that

[17]   Halliday, "Transitivity and Theme, Part 2" (1967).

for given-new information blocks that are short enough to permit it, the part preceding the center may not contain any full feet, but only one with silent stress: *'I have + an* ÓRANGE. In answer to a specific question like *Whát does + he* WRÍTE? the answer is likely to be phonologically marked as given-new by its rhythm: *'He writes +* NÓVELS. This is in contrast with the block of nearly all new information elicited by a general question like *'What does + he* DÓ?, which is more appropriately answered *'He + writes + * NÓVELS.

Keeping to the approximation that the unmarked center of an information block falls on the last word of the block, it follows that any other placement of the center is marked, implying a special reason for putting it elsewhere than at the end. ALL *the reports have to be in by tomorrow* illustrates a marked placement of the center. It is frequently the first constituent of the block that is marked, especially in cases where the center coincides with a marked theme. As before, placement of the center may be contextual or forestalling.

The same ambiguity appears with marked information centers as we had for unmarked centers; namely, we are often uncertain whether the center covers a larger or a smaller constituent. All we know is that the intonational prominence comes on the last word of some constituent. For example, there are two informational readings for *The six kids on the* CORNER *might have seen them.* The first reading takes the entire noun phrase constituent *the six kids on the corner* as the new part. It could, for example, imply a contrast with *the five adults down the block.* The second reading, however, takes only the prepositional qualifier *on the corner* as the new information. It could imply a contrast with *on the balcony.*

On the other hand, a center like the one in *I've eaten* BETTER *pizzas* is unambiguous because the only constituent that ends with *better* is the word itself.

Marked intonation centers can thus cover rather large constituents or single words. They can also single out parts of words: *The effect you expect should be an* IM*plosion, not an* EX*plosion.*

If we use the question-answer approach to localizing new information, we find that marked information centers are appropriate in the answers to information questions, and correspond to the WH-word:

Q. Who wrote the NOTE?
A. BILL wrote the note.
Q. What did Bill do about the NOTE?
A. Bill WROTE the note.
Q. What did Bill WRITE?
A. Bill wrote the NOTE.

The last answer is also appropriate for the less specific questions that elicit unmarked centers in their answers:

Q. What did Bill DO?
Q. What HAPPENED?

We began with the principle that unmarked information centers fall on the last grammatical constituent of an information block, but recognized that that statement is only an approximation to the real principle. The placement of information centers is skewed because there are some kinds of constituents that are incapable of being contextually new (although they can, of course, be new in the forestalling sense). When these elements come last in an information block the unmarked center comes on the first constituent ahead of them.

The most obvious class of items that cannot be informationally new are ANAPHORIC elements. These include both words that point to the earlier part of the discourse and words that point to standard features of the situation of speaking like time, the speaker and hearer, and objects that are under their immediate attention.

The elements that are anaphoric by reference to the text (Halliday uses the word "substitution" for this relation) include relative markers, demonstratives, pronouns and quasi-pronominal nouns, and other proforms. Relative markers like *whom* in *It's the man for whom you* ASKED are already defined by the head noun, therefore are always anaphoric. They come at the end of information blocks only when the blocks are very short: *It's the* MAN / *for* WHOM / *you* ASKED. Demonstratives refer back: *I just* SAID *that.* (When demonstratives are used cataphorically to refer to something that is yet to be explained, they are not anaphoric and so are quite likely to be information centers.) Anaphoric pronouns like *We already* SAW *him* are common. Inclusive nouns behave in much the same way as pronouns when they are used anaphorically: *He drives a* BEETLE / *but his wife prefers a* BIGGER *car* is anaphoric provided one knows that a *Beetle* is a kind of *car.* To make *car* in this sense the information center would constitute either a joke or a confession of ignorance. There are other proforms like *so* that point back anaphorically to parts of the text other than designations for objects: *When will he* LEAVE? *I think he's already* DONE *so.*

Other elements are anaphoric in the sense that they refer to things in the situation of speaking that do not need to be pointed out. (Halliday's term for this is "reference".) Interrogatives may operate this way: *Which* IS *it?* is situationally anaphoric when a collection of objects is in view, as when a rental car customer enters the parking lot to pick up his vehicle. Demonstratives that refer to something already under attention are anaphoric in the same sense: *He won't* LIKE *that one,* for example, fits the situation of a woman shopping for a necktie for her husband when the salesman shows her a particularly garish one. Pronouns do not have to be defined textually to be anaphoric; consider a scene in which one golfer walks up to another who is fuming at the tee and says *Did you* MISS *it?,* referring all too obviously to the ball that is still sitting there. Quasi-pronominal nouns can also be situationally anaphoric, as when one person turns to another while inspecting the pits before the Grand Prix race at Watkins Glen and says, *Looks like a rather* FAST *car.* Adverbs that take their meaning directly from the situation of speaking are anaphoric and therefore not eligible to be made into unmarked information centers: *Bill wrote the* NOTE *this morning, I wish they'd* COME *now, Let's have a little* QUIET *here.*

There is also a set of forms that are not in the running to be unmarked information centers even though they are not in any sense anaphoric. These are members of small closed classes of function words like modals, prepositions, and conjunctions. Even though the information in modals, for example, may be new, the modal is not treated as an unmarked information center: *Forgot his* WALLET *did he?* Prepositions frequently specify a location or direction more precisely than the general role relationships that form the framework for their use; but that does not qualify them as centers: *What tree did you* LEAVE *it under?* Conjunctions like *and, or,* and *but* are rarely centers, though scope indicators like *both, either,* and *neither* may be treated as new (and may be called for in lieu of making an information center out of their matching conjunction): BOTH *Peter and Julie came.*

In contrast, some words carry new information more often than not. Whenever a situational reference is being defined (as opposed to its being taken as obvious and therefore given) the DEICTIC word referring to that situation is new and is the prime candidate to be an information center: THAT's *the one I want* (pointing to it), HERE *is where we camp tonight* (said while standing on the spot). Interrogatives may be treated as centers: HOW *is it done?* highlights the fact that the presupposition of the question, *it is done,* is accepted, whereas *How is it* DONE? treats the whole block as new.

CATAPHORICALLY defined demonstratives have reference to something the hearer has not been told yet. They are new in the sense of promising that information will be given later that is to be treated as a unity: THIS *is what we demand | an* IMMEDIATE CESSATION | ...

REPETITIVE questions refer to something that has been asked or answered already. The interrogative element in them is treated as the center; but they are distinguished from ordinary intonation blocks by their continued high pitch after the center. They are questions about an earlier piece of the discourse, and imply that the one who asks should know the information but missed it. They come in both yes-no and information forms. The yes-no form goes: A. *Do you* THINK *so?* B. DO *you think so?* A. *Yes, that's what I asked.* The informational form is WHO *did it?* (I know you already said who did it, but I missed it); WHAT *time did you say it was?*

Forestalling information centers, as we have already seen, may locate new information anywhere in a block. Their meaning, however, is of a special kind. It says, "the interpretation of this element is not what I think you expect it to be". Thus a modal element may be a forestalling center in *they* WILL *go* (even if you say they will not, I assert my positive modal against your negative one). They may point to a reference that is not the ordinary reading for anaphora: THAT'S *what I said* (not the other thing that I think you are referring to). The switch in reference is seen plainly in the following example from Langendoen:[18]

JOHN / tried to shout to BILL / but he misunderSTOOD him.
(Bill misunderstood John)
HE misunderstood HIM.
(John misunderstood Bill)

Finally, elements that are anaphoric by situational reference may be made into forestalling centers in cases where more than one possible referent is present in the situation: THAT'S *the one* is appropriate to go along with pointing to single out one of several possible referents for *that.*

We can return now to the formulation of how information centers are indicated in English by intonation. Recognizing that some elements inherently go with given information, we can say first that contextually new information is contained in the constituent on whose final accentable foot the nucleus falls. This leaves us with a potential ambiguity in that, since constituents may be embedded one within another, we may not know whether we are dealing with, say, a whole sentence or a single word. We also must stipulate that normally, accentable feet exclude anaphoric items and small closed system items. If on the other hand, the information is new in the forestalling sense, the center may fall on anything.

[18]   Langendoen, *Essentials of English Grammar* (1970).

Bolinger goes one step further in characterizing the principle of placing the intonational nucleus on the last accentable syllable as a gradient principle: "the speaker will put the main accent (nucleus) as far to the right as he dares, when assertive pressure is high; and he frequently dares to put it on a syllable (almost but not always one containing a full vowel) farther to the right than the recognized lexical stress." He cites examples like *This altered the program some*WHAT.[19]

3. OVERLAYS

In working on several unrelated languages I became aware of a pattern of handling new information that does not fit Halliday's given-new paradigm too well.[20] This pattern was first called to my attention by educators and others who found that speakers of some languages insisted on writing English in school in what the educators regarded as a prolix style that involved going around and around in multiple cycles, each of which said approximately the same thing.

On looking further it became apparent that a tightly structured rhetorical pattern was involved, but one that was constructed on different lines than the patterns with which English speakers are familiar. One could say, in an approximation to Halliday's terms, that these structures (which I have labeled OVERLAYS) distinguish three kinds of information: given, new, and HIGHLIGHTED. So far all the overlay patterns I have seen have been related to event sequences.[21]

The overlay technique involves putting together two or more PLANES, each of which constitutes a narration of the same sequence

---

[19] Bolinger, "Accent is Predictable (If You're a Mind-Reader)" (1972).
[20] Grimes, "Outlines and Overlays" (1972).
[21] This is true even in Loron of Ivory Coast, where overlays are used in messages rather than in narratives. Within each plane of the overlay, events and potential events are ordered in time, according to Leenhouts, "Overlays in Loron Discourse" (ms).

of events. The first plane consists largely of new information. The second plane, and others that follow it, begin the sequence over again. Furthermore, they consist partly of new information that is being given for the first time in that plane, partly of given information such as that which is referred to anaphorically, and partly of information that is being repeated piecemeal from an earlier plane. This repeated information has a special status; it is the highlighted information that ties the whole overlay together. Informationally it is the backbone of the whole structure. One could think of the highlighted information that carries through from plane to plane as information that is being made to stand out by being placed in slightly different environments, just as a stereoscopic visual image makes the foreground objects stand out by relating them to slightly different backgrounds.

For example, in a Borôro text reported by Thomas H. Crowell we could list the actual sequence of events that are narrated as follows:[22]

A   A calf and its mother arrive in Colonia.
B   I arrive in Colonia.
C   My companions run to me.
D   The Brazilians, the Borôros, and my companions say the calf is mauled and I should go to it.
E   I say the calf will not die.
F   I go to the calf.
G   I see the calf lying beside a machine and the mother standing nearby.
H   The calf dies.

If we arranged the events along the time line, following Litteral's idea of an index, they would come out in order ABCDEFGH as listed. They are not, however, told in that order. The planes of the overlay are

[22]   Crowell, "Cohesion in Borôro Discourse" (ms).

1 B D G
2 D F G
3 C D F G H
4 A E H

We notice first that within each plane the action proceeds in time sequence, while between planes it backs up. The first three planes are tied together by D G, the last two by H — in other words, in the first part of the overlay the speaker is highlighting D G (between 1 and 2), then expanding the highlighted part to D F G (between 2 and 3), then shifting to H (between 3 and 4).

Ivan Lowe in a personal communication has pointed out that when we extrapolate from the relationships that are present in the actual telling, we find a surprising consistency. This consistency can be seen by representing the text as a lattice that shows its TOPOLOGICAL form as follows.[23] Each of the four tellings of the story is taken as a subset of the universal set ABCDEFGH that describes the total series of events. These four tellings are considered OPEN SETS in a topology. The rest of the topology is filled in according to the following three principles: (1) The universal set and its complement, the null set ∅, are in the topology. (2) For any two open sets in the topology, their union is also an open set in the topology. The union of two sets is a set that contains every element that occurs in either of the two; the union of DFG and BDG is BDFG. (3) For any two open sets in the topology, their intersection is also an open set in the topology. The intersection of two sets is a set that contains only elements that occur in both of the intersecting sets; the intersection of DFG and BDG is DG.

The open sets in the topology all fit this picture. Listed by the number of elements in them, they are represented in Figure 19.1 italicizing the original sets). In the figure unions are represented

---

[23] A finite topology is one way of representing relationships that may or may not fit into the tree structures that linguists are most familiar with. See the references to topology in Chapter 3. A lattice is a graph like Figure 19.1 in which for every pair of nodes there is some node that serves as their common upper bound and another that is their common lower bound.

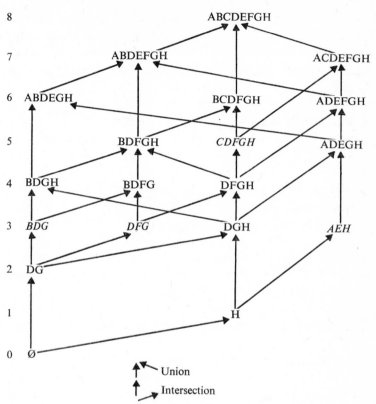

Figure 19.1 Lattice representation of open sets in the topological structure of a Borôro overlay.

by arrows whose heads meet, intersections by arrows whose tails diverge.

Given the four GENERATING SETS of the topology, there are exactly nineteen open sets in the topology.[24] On the other hand, there would be a possibility of having a topology that includes all subsets of the universal set if we had different generating sets. The

---

[24] We can observe that this topology has a BASE consisting of the four generating sets together with Ø, H, and DG. Every set in the topology can be formed by the union of sets in the base.

maximum number of sets in a topology on eight elements is $2^8 =$ 256 sets; a topology that contained all of them would be called the DISCRETE topology. How is it that less than a tenth of the sets that would be present in the discrete topology actually turn up in the topology related to this discourse?

If we read back the open sets in the topology as possible tellings of the tale or planes of an overlay, we see that each one is a valid plane. On the other hand, sets that are not in the topology (such as AB or CH, for example) do not fit the picture; they are out of joint as expressions of the story. (The relevance of a telling becomes even clearer if we look at the context of the story. In this case the narrator was documenting a request for hunting dogs to help control the depredations of jaguars, first by establishing himself as an attested eyewitness using the DG complex, and second as having suffered a personal loss using the H complex.) The topology thus expresses a kind of internal coherence that is far from a random selection of possible tellings. What the nature of this coherence is needs to be explored in detail; the topology simply gives us a means of recognizing that it is there.[25] In languages that do not make use of overlay we have no way of approximating this kind of structure.

Some languages make little or no use of the overlay mechanism. Formal English does not use it, though I have detected snatches of it in the kind of oral explanatory discourse that we characterize informally as going "round and round". I have also picked it up in conversational Mexican Spanish — always when I have no tape recorder with me. Alan Healey has suggested that portions of the Bible like *Judges* 20: 29–48 are overlays.

---

[25] There may be other valid tellings of the tale that are not in the topology but lie close to it in the sense that the generating sets that would have to be added would intersect so thoroughly with the existing topology that the total number of sets would not increase by very much. We can thus consider three distinct topological representations of a narrative: (1) The topology derived from a telling without overlay, which would consist of only the null set and the universal set; (2) the topology derived from an overlay, as presented here, which has as its limiting case (3) the topology derived from all possible overlays, which would contain all possible relevant planes and no irrelevant ones.

In English we do have patterns of summarizing and abstracting that look superficially like overlays but are not. In an initial or final summary or an abstract, the only information that can appear is information that is also in the body of the text. No new information can be introduced. In topological terms, the body of the text is identical with the universal set. In all likelihood the only other sets in the topology would be the summaries or abstracts themselves, since their unions and intersections would not yield any new sets.

The difference between an overlay and a summary is thus that in an overlay each plane introduces some new information at the same time that it highlights information that each new plane after the first has in common with earlier planes. There is no plane that acts like the body of a text with summary in being equal to the universal set. Instead the universal set of an overlaid text is built up by union of the planes.

4. INFORMATION RATE

We have already considered the rate of introduction of new information as a factor in determining the length of information blocks. A high rate tends to go with many short information blocks. It also seems to go with a generally low reliance on anaphoric means of maintaining reference. In other words, when the information rate is high, speakers tend to rename and reintroduce things rather than to employ complex means of keeping track of who did what.

On the other hand, some languages seem to favor a more leisurely rate of information introduction. Many of the languages of Papua New Guinea, for example, use techniques like linkage and overlay in a way that keeps the information rate generally low.[26] They tend at the same time to exploit the mechanisms of anaphora,

---

[26] Thurman, "Chuave Medial Verbs" (ms). See also the discussion of linkage in Chapter 20.3.

and to permit fairly long information blocks. Saramaccan of Surinam seems to have a fairly low average rate of information introduction, and it is possible that casual styles in most languages show this kind of increased redundancy when compared with more formal or business-like styles.[27]

Jean Ure points out the consistently higher lexical redundancy of English texts from situations where there is feedback from the hearers as opposed to a higher rate of information injection in situations without feedback.[28] It should prove instructive to analyze the effect of writing on languages whose normal information rate is relatively low. Although good writing does not require that the reader scan back to pick up what he is not given redundantly, the nature of the artifact freezes the preceding context so that it is there if the reader wants to go back to it.

In writing for new literates or in training writers to produce material for new literates, it might be worth considerable effort to try to match information blocks with eye spans, so that each chunk that is read (once the reader gets past the syllable-by-syllable or word-by-word barrier) is informationally complete.

[27]   Grimes and Glock, "Saramaccan" (1970).
[28]   Ure, "Lexical Density" (1971).

REFERENCE

When we talk, what do we talk about? We have to know in order to characterize linguistic forms correctly. In the first place, the speaker's judgment that the hearer does or does not yet know what it is he is talking about determines the effort he puts into elaborating his descriptions. Second, we have already seen how in forms like reflexives a judgment that different parts of a sentence refer to the same thing is taken for granted. Third, it appears to be necessary for the understanding of overlays (Chapter 19) for the hearer to be able to recognize when the speaker is talking about the same event a second time rather than a new event of the same kind. Finally, tense sequences lock into a special part of the referential system.

1. THE FIELD OF REFERENCE

We are moving toward a consistent theory of reference that can be related to grammar at the points where it is needed. Even now there are some things we can say both about what it is we refer to and about the way that reference relates to linguistic form. It must be recognized that what a linguist needs to know about reference is not necessarily what a philosopher or a psychologist want to know about it, though linguists need the help of both (and they probably need ours).

The idea of a FIELD OF REFERENCE in terms of which each of us forms his speech and understands the speech of others provides a useful model for discussion. The field of reference is not to be equated with the way our perceptions are organized, though it is likely that everything in the field of reference has at least indirect ties to perception somewhere. But it can also include things that are not direct consequences of perceptions, and even things that run counter to perception; it takes in our total mental world.

Perhaps any flight of the imagination, mathematics included, goes beyond what the imaginer has experienced. Lincoln Barnett refers to Albert Einstein's rejection of the common sense notion that objects retain the same dimensions when they are in motion that they have while at rest.[1] He points out that "common sense is actually nothing more than a deposit of prejudices laid down in the mind prior to the age of eighteen. Every new idea one encounters in later years must combat this accretion of 'self-evident' concepts." Einstein's ability to imagine the universe in a way that did not agree with perception was fundamental for our modern views of physics.

Literature creates parts of referential fields with abandon. The ancient *Book of Job* contains an account of a meeting between God and the Devil that is unlikely to be an eyewitness report. Dante's Hell is a detailed landscape, the nine circles of which are picturable even without Doré's engravings to help us visualize them; the people in them are surprisingly like people we know. There are lands of fairy tales and wonders given to us in folk and formal literature. In them not all the laws of our more immediate universe work in the same way; Fafnir the dragon and Cerberus the three-headed dog are just as out of kilter with our perceptions as is Einstein's yardstick that changes its length as it speeds up. Lewis Carroll in *Through the Looking Glass* sets out to build a universe in which things do not work quite as one thinks they should. In our own day Tolkien's Middle Earth is a monumental creation of a highly structured field of reference (complete with maps, grammars, and history) about which engineers and computer scientists

---

[1]   Barnett, *The Universe and Dr. Einstein* (1957).

converse almost as familiarly as they would talk about a trip to the lake for the weekend.

Another literary creation of a field of reference gives us a metaphor for what every speaker of language does for his hearers part of the time. In *The Magician's Nephew* C. S. Lewis transports five people from London to a totally dark place. They are aware that they are standing on something, but otherwise have no inkling of where they might be. Suddenly light begins to grow and they hear a song. As the Singer comes closer they see parts of the landscape spring into existence with the notes of his song; boulders appear with the bass notes, and the high trills create waving rows of trees in the green of spring. The song continues until a whole new world is there, and the five meet the Singer.

As a figure of the way the speaker creates a field of reference for his hearers out of nothing, Lewis's metaphor reflects the linguistic experience which in a less rich context we speak of as "painting pictures with words". We tell people of things that we have seen or thought of and they have not, and in doing so we extend their field of reference beyond their own experience. Actions and feelings are also part of that field of reference, not just the visible details of the setting. In the example given in Chapter 6 (coincidentally taken from the same author), not only do different kinds of information take their place on the Thurman chart; but as we read the passage we build up a picture of a rain-washed bit of England in which the sunset illuminates a chestnut tree beside a road, and a Pedestrian steps out to continue some journey, though we do not know yet where he came from or where he is headed. But our reaction to the words has been to organize a new corner of our own field of reference.

The independence of the field of reference from perception is also important for understanding motivation and inspiration. A leader leads by helping his followers recreate his own vision of a state of affairs that is different from the one in which they live. Martin Luther King says, "I have a dream", and thousands of American black men and women follow him in it.

The idea of a referential field appears to make generally good sense. What has not been easy until now has been to link that idea with what we know about linguistic structure. The most serious proposal that I know of to date is the one advanced by Winograd in the form of a simulation of speech behavior by computer. The rest of this section is my condensation of Winograd's model.[2]

A general idea of the model is given by the following diagram:

LANGUAGE	FIELD OF REFERENCE

GRAMMAR ↔ SEMANTICS ↔ INFERENCE ↔ DATA BASE

On the left, grammar covers our ordinary understanding of linguistic processes including phonology. On the far right, the data base includes the dynamic, constantly changing representation of what an individual knows, concrete or abstract, perceptually based or not. (I tried to call this the "memory" component of the model, but found that it became confused so easily with popular and psychological uses of the word that I had to pick a nonpsychological equivalent.) The inferential mechanism embodies his knowledge of how the world works, of how things that are to be distinguished in the data base can be expected to relate to each other. Semantics, finally, is the bridge between grammar and inference. It operates when we understand language by making use of the organizing signals that are transmitted by grammar in order to build up complex inferential structures that allow us either to find information in the data base or add to it. Operating in the reverse direction, semantics tells how to encode similarly complex inferential structures into linguistic form.

Winograd points out that the data base component is essentially unorganized, rather than being a logically tidy structure. Part of the information in it may even be inconsistent with the rest, and there

---

[2] The textual critic will be aware that this chapter was written considerably later than some of the others that mention reference less optimistically. In the interim I became acquainted with Winograd's *Procedures* (1971).

are gaps in the information. New information does not have to be integrated with what is already there, although occasionally (especially in flashes of insight and conversion experiences) rather large parts of the data base may be made less redundant by being subsumed under some new inferential principle.

In order to talk about the data base (to characterize it, that is; to enumerate the contents of any individual's data base is at present beyond our abilities) we need two kinds of conceptual elements: OBJECTS and RELATIONS. Relations include not only relations that involve two or more objects like the ones implied by *between* or *hit*, but also those that take only one object like *red* and *hot*, which are often called ATTRIBUTES. Objects here include actual entities that are perceived as distinct, like the chair that is on the other side of the table from me as I write this sentence. They also include names of relations that in turn have other elements for their own objects, and so include abstract entities. Winograd's class of objects thus coincides with the referential indices of Chapter 12, and his relations correspond to predicates. Together they form propositions.

Some relations can be taken as primitive and others as complex, built up out of more primitive ones, but I agree with Winograd that it probably does not matter whether we know which the primitive ones are, since they themselves are susceptible to redefinition in terms of other relations that are not necessarily primitive. Taking a relation as primitive, then, is more an assertion of convenience than it is a claim about how human thought is structured.[3]

[3] Robert A. Hall, Jr. in "Why a Structural Semantics is Impossible" (1972), takes the absence of any identifiable minimal unit of meaning as one reason why a structural semantics is impossible. It seems reasonable, however, to suggest that if we can identify the characteristics of any unit of meaning, minimal or not, and learn something by using those characteristics, then we can progress farther than if we insist that we have the minimum in hand before we move. Furthermore, having an inferential component between language and the data base relieves us of having to assume that the data base is structured in neat hierarchies. Schank et al., "Primitive Concepts Underlying Verbs of Thought" (1972) discuss the potentially infinite regress in some semantic areas like the instrumental relation.

The relations in the data base at this moment seem to be best taken as language specific.[4] They are probably also more concerned with topological relations than with purely metric ones, as Lewin suggests.[5]

The information that is in the data base comes from several sources. Sensory perception is probably basic. Our visual information processing, for example, allows us to take in at a glance things that if communicated verbally would take a very long time; the experience of blind people like Helen Keller would suggest that without sight the rate of information intake is drastically cut. I would hazard a guess that until a perceived object has been associated with some relation, however, it has not been noticed in a way that can be talked about; this has the effect of keeping down the amount stored.

There are, however, propositions in the data base that are not just inferences from perceptions. Suppose that someone says to us, "Suppose that ...", and takes us off on a flight of fancy with words. We can follow him through the bizarre and the topsy-turvy as long as he keeps general touch with our basic understanding of the way the world works.

There seems to be a tradeoff between things that are stored as propositions and things that can be reconstructed inferentially from other propositions. One thinks of an airplane pilot who is quite accustomed to calculating cruising range against the rate of fuel consumption for various types of aircraft at different power settings, but who on a particular flight commits the range figures to memory lest he need them in an emergency when he does not

---

[4] Šaumjan gives the hypothesis in "Outline of the Applicational Generative Model" (1965) and *Structural Linguistics* (1971) that the genotype language is universal. This hypothesis is not necessarily contradicted by the assumption that data base relations are language specific. Even in the light of the remarks made in the preceding footnote, there could easily be a universal set of semantic units from which the working units of the world's languages are derived. Our present understanding of meaning is far enough removed from the genotype language that Šaumjan begins with that we are neither in a position to confirm his conjecture nor to invalidate it.

[5] Lewin, *Principles of Topological Psychology* (1936).

have the time to reconstruct them. Here too is probably where the balance comes in education between filling people's heads with facts and teaching them to find relationships.

The inferential component goes beyond the data base's collection of objects and relations that are put together in unconnected propositions. It incorporates two other related concepts: VARIABLES, and STRATEGIES for knowing under what circumstances relations apply and when they do not.

Variables can take as values anything in the class of objects in the data base. In other words, they are referential variables, not feature valued variables like the ones used in transformational grammar and phonology. When joined with relations, they define potential classes of entities that might fit those relations.

The strategies of the inferential component are ways of deciding when variables fit things in the data base and when they do not. They can be thought of as recognition criteria for classes of objects and relations. Recognition, however, is not limited here to perceptual recognition. Most native speakers of English would have no difficulty determining whether something is a unicorn or not even if they have never seen one, and most can recognize abstractions like "an irrelevant point in an argument" just as well.

The inferential component thus forms the basis for generalizing. If I know that Bobo the pet dogfaced baboon has an intense desire to untie my shoelaces, I am likely to incorporate this into what I know of the world and generalize it to all baboons and anybody else's shoelaces. Enough has been written about the bad effects on society of overgeneralizing that it is enough here to point out that it has a linguistic side, perhaps due to the adoption of simplistic inferential strategies.

There is a special set of strategies in the inferential component that attach themselves to variables in ways that control how inferences may match the data base. These are the QUANTIFI-CATIONAL strategies, which impose limits on variables in a small number of standard ways. Linguistic quantification may restrict a variable to a single unique object, to a set of objects that is small in number, to a set of a specific number, to no objects at all, to some member of an ordered set, to all objects that satisfy the strategy, or even to generic classes of objects that include ones not in the data base. Quantificational relationships are signalled by special parts of the grammar, and obey special inferential rules.

Winograd's notation for the data base, inferential, and semantic components of language brings out the kinds of things we have been discussing. I will introduce it briefly here, aware that we are short of systematic attempts to bridge the gap between reference and language as explicitly as this one. The notation, therefore, is expectedly out of the ordinary for linguistics. The examples given are adapted from Winograd's.

Each proposition in the data base consists of a relation predicate that has at least one other object or relation associated with it. Object labels in the data base are not linguistic names of objects, but arbitrary sequences of symbols that stand for their referential indices. Object labels are prefixed with a colon to distinguish them from everything else: :OBJ72, :ME, :JONES (a particular individual). Names of relations are prefixed with a double quotation mark: "ON, "RED, "SUPPORT. The logical processes that are involved in inferential strategies are all prefixed with TH (for THEOREM). Finally, variables used in strategies are prefixed with $? and a few similar signs ($_, ?) that depend upon how they are used.[6]

A simple declarative sentence directs that information be added to the hearer's data base. This direct link to the data base is symbolized by the theorem THASSERT, which to simplify matters can be taken to stand both for declarative information and information derived from perception. Thus (THASSERT ("HUMAN :JONES)) tells the inferential mechanism to put the proposition ("HUMAN :JONES) into the data base, referring to a particular object labelled :JONES. THASSERT would be the appropriate response of the inferential mechanism whether somebody tells us that Jones, whom we both

---

[6]   The notation is based on Carl Hewett's PLANNER system, which is a goal oriented theorem prover for logical manipulation. It is implemented in Sussman and Winograd's Micro-Planner version for simulating linguistic behavior by computer. Both are expressed in the LISP language of McCarthy et al., *LISP 1.5 Programmer's Manual* (1962) for representing complex data structures.

know already, is human, or whether we see Jones and reach that conclusion from our own observation.

The basic tool of the inferential mechanism is the CONSEQUENT theorem. Rather than starting from some set of premises and working toward a conclusion as is the practice in ordinary logic, a consequent theorem tells us that if such and such is what we are trying to prove, here is the best way to go about it. In other words, it starts with the desired conclusion and states what else needs to be known (that is, available in the data base) for that conclusion to be valid. Consequent theorems are identified in the notation by THCONSE. They usually contain one or more instances of THGOAL followed by a propositional form that has to be proved in order for the stated consequence to hold.

For example, part of what we know about people can be expressed in the following consequent theorem involving a variable X. Let us name this bit of what we know THEOREM1 so that we can refer to it again, and identify its formal definition as such with DEF-THEOREM. Then the Micro-Planner representation for this bit of our knowledge has the form

```
(DEFTHEOREM THEOREM1
   (THCONSE (X)
      ("FALLIBLE $?X)
      (THGOAL ("HUMAN $?X))))
```

Even though this shorthand seems a little ponderous for such a simple thing, it acquires a considerable advantage over all its verbal paraphrases the moment relationships become complex. For now, however, a verbal paraphrase is in order. Since THCONSE after the name of the theorem tells us that THEOREM1 is a consequent theorem, it means that we are showing how to prove ("FALLIBLE $?X) for some X, a variable. The way we can prove it is to prove X is human; if we can do that, then we also know that X is fallible.

An English expression like *is Jones fallible?* or *Oscar, who is fallible* (as long as *Oscar* refers to the same referential entity that is labeled in our data bank as the specific object whose index label is :JONES), when analyzed grammatically and semantically, activates the inferential mechanism of THEOREM1 by trying to prove (THGOAL ("FALLIBLE :JONES)) from the data base. The simplest form of proof would be to find the goal proposition ("FALLIBLE :JONES) itself in the data base; but in this case all we have there is ("HUMAN :JONES). THEOREM1, however, says that that is enough for a link to the data base by inference. :JONES, then, is the value which the variable X of THEOREM1 takes on, and so we can say that between the inferential component and the data base, the proposition ("FALLIBLE :JONES) fits our view of the world. The answer to the question form of it would be *Yes*, and the response to the relative clause form would be our assent that this is the way things are, that we have the right person in mind.

THGOAL may have a second argument besides the proposition that is to be proved. The second argument is a list of names of other theorems that might help in proving it. This list is headed THUSE, and stipulates that the most effective way to prove the proposition in the first argument is by trying the theorems listed there in the order they are given. In the absence of other advice, the general inferential strategy is to try all theorems whose consequent matches the form of the goal proposition.

Other kinds of theorems are also available to express quantification. THGOAL, as we have seen, asks about a specific instance and thus matches the idea of unique quantification naturally. If there is a possibility that more than one object might fit a relation, however, as is implied by the use of determiners like *some*, then a continuing search of the data base is necessary even after one instance is found. This search is performed under a strategy called THPROG, which is the logician's existential quantifier in inferential form. A question like *Is anyone fallible?*, for example, is expressed to the inferential component in the form

(THPROG (Y)
   (THGOAL ("FALLIBLE $?Y)
     (THUSE THEOREM1))).

It operates as follows. THPROG sets up a potential variable Y, without knowing ahead of time whether anything in the data base fits Y or not. The body of the expression then goes through all likely propositions in the data base using the same THEOREM1 that we defined earlier. That theorem tells how we are to know if a particular object is fallible or not. Nothing is listed in the data base as fallible, but since Jones is listed as human, THEOREM1 says that that suffices. The answer to the question *Is anyone fallible?* can be as simple as *Yes* or as helpful as *Yes; one person; Jones.* If nothing ever sets Y, then the answer is *No;* if several propositions set Y, all are available.

THFIND is like THPROG but is concerned with specific quantities like *all, three, at least five,* or *more than I have.* THAMONG looks for a match between a variable and any one of a list of things. THAND, THOR, THNOT, and THCOND (for if-then relations) add the power of Boolean logic to put together complex semantic relationships. THERASE removes information that is no longer needed from the data base. In addition to consequent theorems, there may be ANTECEDENT theorems labeled by THANTE that direct the inferential mechanism to conclude that if a certain proposition is in the data base, then some other proposition that follows from the first should be there too.

Seen from this point of view, the task of the semantic component in understanding language is to get clues from the linguistic form that will permit it to put together an inferential complex that can find information in the data base and can add information to it. Grammatical constructions are thus the framework for bringing together semantic information in a way that can be matched to the field of reference.

Paradoxically, we have a better account of the semantic-inferential link to the field of reference for understanding language than we do for producing language, where Simmons and Slocum's model goes from semantic structure to surface form well enough, but is not yet explicitly tied to reference via the inferential component in the way Winograd's model is in the other direction.[7] The

---

[7] Simmons and Slocum, "Generating English Discourse from Semantic Networks" (1972).

rest of this discussion is therefore from the point of view of understanding language rather than producing it.

Those parts of the field of reference that are quantified in a particular discourse are generally expressed in noun phrases of one kind or another. The words in a noun phrase contribute to an OBJECT SEMANTIC STRUCTURE in a way that is determined partly by the meanings of the words themselves and partly by their arrangement.

Semantically the key word in a noun phrase of English is the head noun, which tells what kind of object the object semantic structure is dealing with. The words ahead of the noun add further information about properties of the object. Modifying nouns and adjectives are therefore examined in reverse order from that in which they were uttered in order to progressively restrict the class of objects in the data base to which the whole noun phrase might apply. Next the initial parts of the noun phrase enter the picture, the quantifier and determiner structures. These give the entire object semantic structure its logical status. Finally, the postnominal modifiers contribute further restrictions, some of which must be interpreted in the light of the quantifiers and determiners, as in the case of ordinals.

On analyzing an input text, Winograd's grammar forms object semantic structures for each noun phrase it encounters, using semantic definitions of words taken from the dictionary. These semantic definitions are either condensed instructions about how to go about finding things in the data base that match the word, or else are special instructions for words like function words.

English nouns and adjectives have a special defining form called NMEANS. It is followed by a list of one or more pairs of lists, one pair for each area of meaning of the word. Each pair consists of a SEMANTIC MARKER list and a condensed Micro-Planner statement that is reconstituted in full when the object semantic structure is put together. The markers act as filters to screen out broadly conflicting areas of meaning; for example, the festive meaning of *ball* does not need to be weighted as heavily as the manipulable object meaning in a context that deals with the handling of physical objects as in *pick up the ball*. The semantic definition of *pyramid* in Winograd's data base example is

(NMEANS)
  (("PYRAMID)
  ("IS — "PYRAMID)))),

where the special relation "IS identifies the basic property by which an object known to the data base is characterized, and the relation "PYRAMID is a primitive one associated with any object that is a pyramid. (There may be a consequent theorem that decides when some object is or is not a pyramid.)

When the indefinite noun phrase *a pyramid* is encountered in the input, it results in the creation of an object semantic structure that has nine elements: (1) a label, which may be omitted, (2) a list of the variables that are needed in the definition implied by the object semantic structure, (3) the priority of the first expression in the definition, which is usually derived from the semantic definition of the head noun in the noun phrase, but may in principle be replaced by an expression derived from some other part of the noun phrase if this would simplify the process of matching with the data base, (4) the actual sequence of Micro-Planner (TH) instructions that sets up the inferential link to the data base, (5) a marker list, beginning with a priority for each marker set, assigned whenever a possible ambiguity is detected to represent the basis of plausibility of that interpretation within its context, and following with the markers that are given for the head noun in its dictionary entry, each filled in with the hierarchy of more inclusive markers that are taken from a generalized marker tree that is also part of the semantic component of the grammar, (6) a system list of choice points in the marker tree from which a choice has already been made, to help in locating marker clashes, (7) the particular variable from the variable list in 2 that stands for the object being defined, (8) the determiner categories of number, definiteness, and interrogation, in that order, and (9) the ordinal specification.

The object semantic structure for *a pyramid*, with parentheses enclosing things that belong together, is

((((X2) 200
   (THGOAL ("IS $?X2 "PYRAMID)))
   (O "PYRAMID "MANIP "PHYSOB "THING)
   ("MANIP "PHYSOB "THING))
X2
(NS INDEF NIL)
NIL)

In this object semantic structure (1) the label is not used (2) X2
is the only variable needed, (3) the first expression has a priority
of 200, (4) the dictionary entry for the noun yields a single THGOAL
expression, (5) the marker "PYRAMID has the rest of its hierarchy
added: a pyramid is a kind of manipulable object, which is a kind
of physical object, which is a kind of thing, with priority O because
no decisions about ambiguity have had to be made, (6) in the marker
hierarchy three choices have been made to get down to "PYRAMID
level, (7) the only variable in the list, X2, is the one that stands for
the object being defined, (8) the determiner *a* is singular, indefinite,
and not interrogative, and (9) no ordinal is involved.

A more involved noun phrase also yields a single object semantic
structure, but has a more elaborate Micro-Planner section for
linkup with the data base. If the example above were incorporated
into *a red block which supports a pyramid* the object semantic
structure would be

((((X1 X2) 200
   (THGOAL ("IS $?X1 "BLOCK))
   (THGOAL ("COLOR $?X1 "RED))
   (THGOAL ("IS $?X2 "PYRAMID))
   (THGOAL ("SUPPORT $?X1 $?X2)))
   (O "BLOCK "MANIP "PHYSOB "THING)
   ("MANIP "PHYSOB "THING))
X1
(NS INDEF NIL)
NIL)

where the object semantic structure for *a pyramid* is added in with the total structure in accord with its grammatical position.

There is a second kind of semantic structure in Winograd's scheme, a RELATION SEMANTIC STRUCTURE. It is less complex than the object semantic structure because it involves neither quantification nor variables. It may, however, include a TIME SEMANTIC STRUCTURE, the third kind of semantic structure in the model.

Clauses give information on relationships with the possibility of reference to time, place, and manner. Prepositional phrases, on the other hand, though they give information on relationships, divest those relationships of time, place, or manner reference. Some adjective phrases emphasize relationships, while others are treated like adjectives that contribute to object definitions.

Instead of variables, relation semantic structures incorporate the labels of particular object semantic structures as their terms. When the relation semantic structure is handed over to the inferential mechanism, the variables that stand for the objects being talked about (Element 7 of each object semantic structure) are substituted for the names of the structures they represent and the matching procedure is carried out.

Relation semantic structures are derived from dictionary definitions that use the special defining form CMEANS. It is followed by one semantic marker list for each of the role elements involved in the definition, ranked in order of candidacy for subject status. (In Winograd's dictionary the role labels themselves are not given, but only their relative rank.) Then comes the reduced Micro-Planner statement that is reconstituted in the relation semantic structure. For a word like *support*, which appeared in the last example, the definition shorthand is

(CMEANS
   ((((("PHYSOB))
   (("PHYSOB))
   ("SUPPORT "1 "2)
   NIL))),

where "1 and "2 are the rankings of the roles, in this case patient

and range respectively, and the final NIL is in the place available
for a list of markers for the relation itself, including features like
"CHANGE and "MOTION, neither of which applies here.

The relation semantic structure that is derived when a word like
a verb or a preposition is encountered in text has four parts: (1) a
label, which in the case of a modifying relation is the same as the
label of the object semantic structure which the relation modifies,
(2) the proposition that embodies the relation which the inferential
mechanism must try to match against the data base, with the names
of the appropriate object semantic structures inserted in place of
its terms, (3) the negative or positive status of the relation, either
NEG or NIL, and (4) the marker list for each role in order, including
a priority number for resolving ambiguities as in the object
semantic structure. Thus if the relative clause *which supports a
pyramid* is being attached to an object semantic structure labeled
NG1 and the element *a pyramid* has been given the object semantic
structure NG2, the relation semantic structure for the relative
clause is

((NG1
("SUPPORT NG1 NG2)
NIL)
(O))

The label (1) identifies the relation semantic structure as a modifier
of NG1, (2) sets up the proposition form ("SUPPORT NG1 NG2) in a
way that the inferential system can modify for matching, (3) NIL says
that the relation is asserted positively, and (4) omits any marker
lists other than the ones that are part of the object semantic structures themselves. The way in which this relation semantic structure
is incorporated into a larger object semantic structure has already
been shown.

Time semantic structures may be added to the proposition that
is the second component of a relation semantic structure by making
it the final element of that proposition. If they refer to the time of
speaking, they are omitted. The time semantic structure has four

components: (1) the tense, a list of one or more tenses taken from the verb phrase structure, (2) a progressivity indicator T (for true, that is, progressive) or NIL (for false or nonprogressive), (3) a limit at or after which the action takes place, and (4) a limit at or before which the action takes place. There is a special class of objects in the data base that are always associated with time, namely indices of the kind suggested by Litteral, together with the performative index :NOW. Time limits are set by adverbs, by temporal noun phrases, by prepositional phrases, and by dependent clauses whose time may in turn be specified by other means. Dependent clauses with *after* set only the first limit and those with *before* or *until* set only the second. The time of a construction that is not a clause is usually carried forward from the time semantic structure of the closest clause that dominates it, and in the absence of an explicit setting of time, the time semantic structure of an earlier clause may be carried over to a later one.

Here are some time semantic structures appropriate for the clauses that go with them:

((PRESENT) T :NOW :NOW) *A supports B*
((PAST) T NIL :T23) *A supported B before :T23*
((PAST) NIL NIL :T23) *A hit B before :T23,*

where *support* and *hit* differ in progressivity. If we have another event, say :E657, whose own time semantic structure is ((PAST) NIL :T3 :T7), then the following inversion of times for the starting and ending limits helps characterize the progressive in English:

((PAST) NIL :T3 :T7) *you hit it during :E657*
((PAST) T :T7 :T3) *you were hitting it during :E657;*

in other words, the action was in progress later than :T7 and before :T3.

A formal apparatus like Winograd's, sketched here only briefly enough to give an idea of the way the parts are put together, does offer a possible way of integrating reference into linguistics via an inferential component. It relieves us of the inconsistency of having to talk about reference solely within a system that has no place for reference.

2. COHESIVE STRUCTURE AND REFERENCE

A surprisingly large proportion of linguistic reference is redundant. As we saw in Chapter 19, new information is generally presented in the context of old information. This makes it possible for the hearer to keep his bearings; too much new information without any old information to tie it to would be impossible to process.

When things are referred to for the second time, however, they are not necessarily identified by simply repeating the words that were used the first time. It is more usual to use a more condensed linguistic form. Furthermore, noninitial reference does not have to go into the same level of detail as initial reference. Instead, it is possible to refer to only the dominating propositions of that part of the field of reference, and take in every thing that they dominate by implication.

The linguistic identification of referential entities that have already been mentioned is called ANAPHORIC or backward-looking identification. The most common form of it is pronominalization, already discussed in Chapter 3.2. Pronominalization gives a minimal identification for objects that have already been identified by noun phrases. It may also be used to refer to relations, as in *that's what the boss told me too*, in which *that* may refer to a referential entity of considerable complexity.

The anaphoric LINKAGE pattern (Chapter 6.2) described by Thurman is another use of anaphoric reference.[8] Here a clause is repeated or paraphrased in dependent form as a means of leading into an independent clause that contains new information: *He broiled the steaks. When he had broiled the steaks, he called the guests. After he called them, they came* ... gives the flavor of linkage systems, which seem to be used in many parts of the world.

---

[8] Thurman, "Chuave Medial Verbs" (ms).

There seem to be two distinct uses of linkage. The first is to separate large units of text one from another. In Saramaccan of Surinam, for example,[9] linkage is one of the signals of paragraph boundaries, but there are no linkages within paragraphs. The other use is the opposite: consecutive sentences within a stretch of text are linked to each other, but the linkage stops at paragraph boundaries. In Sanio-Hiowe of Papua New Guinea the lack of linkage is one of the signals that can indicate a paragraph break if other signals of the paragraph complex are also present; linkage breaks within paragraphs are occasionally possible as well.[10]

The most extravagant use of linkage seems to be that of the Kayapó of Brazil, as described by Stout and Thomson.[11] There, besides a sentence-to-sentence linkage pattern, it is customary in a narrative to repeat an entire action paragraph almost word for word before beginning a new action paragraph.

There are many other anaphoric signals that indicate that reference is being made to a part of the referential field that has already been established for the hearer. English has a pattern of *do so* substitution that reactivates a relation in the data base but requires a distinct assignment of the variables associated with that relation. In *Albania produced a surplus and so did Gambia*, the repeated reference is to the relation *produced a surplus*, but a different surplus is meant than in the first use. There are anaphoric words for nearly every grammatical part of speech: *then* and *there* for time and place, *thus* for manner, and anaphoric prepositional objects like *with it*, *in spite of that*, and *until then* practically without limit.

Less frequently than he uses anaphoric reference, the speaker promises to identify something that he has mentioned with only enough identification to induce his hearer to assign a referential object to it. This CATAPHORIC or forward-looking reference has a certain attention-getting value, as though human nature abhorred

9   Grimes and Glock, "Saramaccan" (1970).
10   Ronald Lewis, "Sanio-Hiowe Paragraph Structure" (1972).
11   Stout and Thomson, "Kayapó Narrative" (1971).

a referential vacuum. In *Here's what we have to do first*, the cataphoric *here* looks ahead to what the speaker is about to say. Presumably in the next sentences he will fill in the details associated with *do*, which can also be taken as cataphoric in that it has no specific content at the point in the text at which it is used.

Pronominalization is cataphoric at times. In *Until he was* TEN / *Prince William had* NO IDEA / *that poor people even* EXISTED, the pronoun *he* is a promise to define a referential entity later. Walter Archer in a personal communication has questioned whether cataphoric pronominalization actually refers to new information as often as is assumed; he points out that not only does *he* in examples like the one given have the position and intonational features of given information (Chapter 19), but *Prince William*, the noun phrase that defines it, has the same characteristics, suggesting that the construction as a whole might be appropriate only for texts where the thing referred to cataphorically is already presumed known to the hearer. Paul Chapin summarizes several of the points that bear upon cataphoric pronominalization in English and Samoan,[12] including the COMMAND relation between a noun phrase and all other noun phrases within its clause and within all clauses that are subordinate to that one. A noun phrase may precede a coreferential pronoun within the same sentence, as in the case in anaphora, or it may command it, permitting cataphoric reference, but it may not be in both relations to it at once.

Thurman in the paper already cited discusses a specialized form of cataphoric reference known as CHAINING which is found only in the highlands of New Guinea. Certain verbs are not inflected explicitly for the person and number of the subject, as are others, but have a MEDIAL inflection that says that their subject is referentially the same as or different from the verb of the next clause. Sentences consist of chains of verbs of this kind, ending in a FINAL verb that does have subject person and number inflection and possibly a nominal identification of the subject. Over a dozen clauses at a time are not uncommon in this pattern, each predicting

---

[12]   Chapin, "Samoan Pronominalization" (1970).

either compatibility or incompatibility with the subject of the verb of the next clause, but never giving any indication as to what that subject might refer to until the end of the chain.

3. VIEWPOINT

It seems to be a special property of sentient participants that the amount of information the speaker is allowed to impute to each of them is limited according to rather strict rules. Just as we use linguistic identification to attach the names of different physical characteristics to people that we talk about, so that we build up a picture of a person named *Billy* who is five years old, blond headed, and cute, we use similar means to establish that he likes cotton candy, saw a parade go by last Saturday, and just had a fight with his sister. In other words, we use speech and inference to build up an image of a data base that we impute to him, in which his experiences are accessible to us, and his attitudes and feelings at each stage of our talking about him are open to inspection. The rules for proper management of the speaker's picture of what is inside the heads of the persons, real or fictitious, about whom he is talking, are collectively known as VIEWPOINT.

Frequently the speaker adopts an OMNISCIENT viewpoint towards the participants of his discourse. Under this viewpoint he considers himself to have complete access to all that they perceive or feel. In situations where each is said to be acting in partial ignorance of what the others know, the speaker knows more about each participant than any of the other participants does, and may describe their thoughts and motives accordingly.

On the other hand, the speaker may choose to limit himself in any of several ways. He may adopt the FIRST PERSON PARTICIPANT viewpoint, in which he himself is or imagines himself to be one of the actors. If he does, he has access to his own mental processes, but the rules of that viewpoint cut him off from the free access to the data bases of the other participants that a speaker with the omniscient viewpoint has. Instead of telling what some other participant thinks or remembers, the speaker with a first person participant viewpoint can only tell what the other does and says.

The THIRD PERSON SUBJECTIVE viewpoint is similar except that the speaker himself is not cast as one of the active participants in the discourse. Instead he talks about others as participants. In this viewpoint, however, there is one participant to whose mental data base he still has access, so that he can report to us what that one person thinks. As far as the other participants are concerned, however, he can only say what the person whose eyes he is using can see and hear. His reporting must therefore be consistent with that viewpoint; we consider him to be mismanaging his reference system if he jumps inside the mind of any other character, so to speak, or tells us anything about that character that his key character is not in a position to observe or deduce.

The most completely external viewpoint is the THIRD PERSON OBJECTIVE one. Here the speaker orients what he says around one character, but denies himself access to what that character thinks and feels. He can report what he or any other character says and does, but the hearer must work out the internal component by himself.

Viewpoint on a larger scale is similar. to REFERENTIAL TRANS-PARENCY on a scale of complement constructions. Some verbs of saying and knowing allow their complements to contain anything whatever; others impose restrictions on them that have to do with the state of affairs represented by agreement between the data base of the speaker and the imputed data base belonging to the subject of the verbs.[13] For example, *believe* allows any complement, whether it is so or not: *Muriel believes that yesterday was New Year's* could be true on any day of the year. *Believe* is thus said to be referentially OPAQUE in that the veracity of its complement makes no difference. *Know*, on the other hand, is referentially transparent in that its complement has to reflect a state of affairs on which both speaker and hearer can agree. *Muriel knows that yesterday was New Year's* is acceptable only on January 2, because that is the only day on

---

[13] Langendoen, *Essentials of English Grammar* (1970).

which the speaker and his hearers can have the complement fit their data bases compatibly. The content of the complement of a referentially transparent verb is thus limited to what the subject is able to know in the circumstances for which the verb is used. Verbs of saying and knowing are responsible for other constraints on their complements, as mentioned in Chapter 5. Pike and Lowe have expressed the patterns by which a series of embeddings of verbs of saying refer to the participants being talked about, using the same group theoretic treatment as was employed in Chapter 18 for participant orientation.[14] Briefly there are two patterns of pronominal use under embedding.[15] The DIRECT pattern of pronominal use takes its person assignments from the role structure of a verb of saying that immediately dominates the quotation within which the pronouns in question are used. The agent of the verb of saying is represented by the first person in the quotation, and its latter state element is represented by the second person. Any other participant is third person: *The chief* (A) *said to his followers* (B), "*I* (A) *will give the signal. Then you* (B) *cross the river and surprise them* (C)".

The INDIRECT pattern of pronominal use takes its person assignments in the same way, but not with reference to an immediately dominating verb of saying. The verb of saying that is involved is higher up in a chain of embeddings. The implicit performative that dominates the whole discourse may be the verb of saying whose role structure is indexed: *Gladys told her that I* (the speaker) *had suggested that she* (ambiguous: Gladys, her, or someone else other than the speaker or the hearer) *see a doctor.*

A number of languages of West Africa appear to combine direct and indirect approaches to reference. In Abidji of the Ivory Coast any reference to the speaker of a quotation inside the quotation is made by indirect reference, and any reference to the person spoken

---

[14] Pike and Lowe, "Pronominal Reference" (1969); Lowe, "An Algebraic Theory of English Pronominal Reference" (1969).
[15] Perrin, "Direct and Indirect Speech in Mambila" (ms), gives a comprehensive discussion of various embedding possibilities in a language that uses extraordinarily complex patterns.

to is made by direct reference.[16] Since both policies result in other participants being given the third person category, it is impossible to tell which kind of reference is being used for them. Mambila of Nigeria not only has the direct-indirect distinction; it has three distinct kinds of direct reference, each of which is used in a definable set of contexts.[17]

[16]   Donald Webster, personal communication.
[17]   Perrin, cited in Footnote 15.

21

STAGING

Every clause, sentence, paragraph, episode, and discourse is organized around a particular element that is taken as its point of departure. It is as though the speaker presents what he wants to say from a particular perspective. I find it convenient to think in terms of how various units are STAGED for the hearer's benefit. This staging is at least partially independent of both content structure and cohesive structure. It operates at many levels of text organization simultaneously.

In choosing a term like "staging" I am trying to break out of a terminological bind. We have the words "topic", "focus", "theme", and "emphasis" appearing freely in the linguistic literature, but with such broad ranges of overlap and confusion that they are nearly useless. I hope not to add to the confusion, but rather to help map a way through what we are trying to describe. My choice of terms like "information block" and "center" in Chapter 19 fits in with this attempt, since the words we are concerned with here have also been used for the phenomena of cohesion, and we need to stop mixing them up.

In the area of staging I have found it useful to continue the general strategy of distinguishing semantic choices from the phenomena involved in communicating those choices. For example, in discussing content structure I have distinguished predicates, which express content in an abstract way, from the nouns and verbs that are used to express that content. In cohesive structure I have distinguished information blocks and centers from the intonational boundaries and nuclei which in English are used to communicate the extent of the blocks and something about the placement of the centers.

In discussing staging I wish to maintain a parallel distinction between the semantic choice of a THEME or point of departure on the one hand, and the designation of a constituent in the grammar as the TOPIC by means of appropriate signalling devices. In *my dog has fleas*, for example, there is a choice to treat the subject as theme. This is implemented by putting it first, which makes it the topic. If the thematic choice fell on *fleas* instead, the same topicalizing mechanism would be invoked, giving *fleas my dog has*.

It is evident that thematic choice is independent of content structure; both examples in the preceding paragraph have the same predicates and arguments. Thematic choice is also independent of the cohesive structure. Although a marked topic (in English declaratives, a topic that is not the subject) is frequently informationally new as well, as in FLEAS *my dog has*, it can also be given information, as in

A: I wonder where I can get some fleas for my biology experiment?
B: Huh! Fleas my DOG has.

1. THEME AND MODALITY

English uses word order in several ways. This makes it sometimes difficult to untangle all the factors that are involved in a particular ordering. Because the staging of a clause and its mode are two of the main factors, we will begin by attempting to separate out mode from topicalization in clauses.[1]

As in cohesion, so also in staging it makes sense to talk about unmarked and marked patterns of staging. In English the unmarked theme in clauses[2] depends on the mode.

[1] Halliday, "Transitivity and Theme, Part 2" (1967).
[2] I speak of clauses here rather than sentences because, for complex sentences at least, there is a separate set of thematic options. *I'll go if they invite me* and *if they invite me I'll go* are thematically different sentences, but each clause in them is thematically unmarked.

The content structure that corresponds to a clause contains at least one lexical predicate and its role related arguments. The consolidation transformation (Chapter 13) gives each clause a single dominating predicate, which may be semantically complex, and retains most of the role related arguments, though it may delete some and reassign others. There is then a mapping rule that assigns one of the arguments to the subject category and others to other surface functions. This rule is part of the staging system; it interacts with the selection of mode to give unmarked word order, and has other semantic inputs that give distinctions of voice.

Mode in English is expressed by the way the subject, selected on this basis, is related to the modal elements, more or less independently of the rest of the clause. In the declarative mode the subject precedes the modal element, which may be carried by the main verb as in *Max ate the apple* or by an auxiliary as in *Max has eaten the apple*. The subject is the unmarked topic. In independent clauses a subject must be present; so strong is this requirement that English uses dummy subjects where none is supplied by the mapping from the role system: *It's raining*, or *there is a possibility that we will leave a week early*. In terms of the modal system, the declarative is without doubt the unmarked mode.

In the polar or yes-no interrogative mode the modal element is itself the unmarked topic, and the subject follows it. In contemporary English the topicalization of the modal requires the use of an auxiliary, as in *Did Max eat the apple?* (In earlier English the main verb itself could have been moved forward as a carrier for the modal: *Ate Max the apple?*) The rest of the clause following the modal gives the area of uncertainty that the modal questions, and implies a disjunction. If the disjunction is not spelled out, it is taken to be between a positive and a negative value: *Either Max ate the apple or Max did not eat the apple; tell me which*. A disjunction that is not made on yes-no lines must be spelled out: *Either Max ate the apple or Max ate the orange; tell me which*, with its less redundant form *Did Max eat the apple, or the orange?*

The nonpolar interrogative has as its topic a WH or question element. The rest of the clause states the presuppositions or background assumptions that will be considered acceptable in an answer. *Who ate an apple?*, for example, sets the requirement for answering as agreement that somebody ate an apple. The presuppositions even extend into the word that contains the WH element, since *who* implies that a person ate the apple, while *what* would imply that the eater was not a person.

Nonpolar interrogatives like *who, what, when, where, why*, and *how* focus the answer on clause and sentence constituents. *Which, how much*, and *how many*, and occasionally *what*, on the other hand, point to the determiner element of some noun phrase within a clause: *Which student did the best work this semester?* Nonpolar interrogatives of either kind can be raised out of embedded clauses: *Who did you say I ought to send the letter to?* begins with a *who* that actually belongs with the final *to*. Prepositional phrases with nonpolar interrogatives may also function as topic in relation to the modal: *To which senator did you say I ought to send the letter?*

The main verb itself is unmarked topic in the imperative mode, and the subject is deleted as predictable from the mode: *Eat an apple today*.

Dependent clauses have their introducer word as unmarked theme, as in *if you keep doing that I'll scream*. Following the introducer, however, a few thematic options (though no mode-related ones) are still possible, enabling sentences like *I'll talk to him because me he respects*, with fronted *me*.

Whenever anything is put first in the clause other than the element that normally signals the mode, it constitutes a marked topic in English. This kind of thematic marking is most common in the declarative mode; in other modes, the unmarked topic is less frequently preceded by anything: *This picture I want for the living room* (declarative), *Max did he eat an apple?* (polar interrogative), *The carpenters what did they finish today?* (nonpolar interrogative), *You guys clear out* (imperative), *Me if I get there I'll phone you* (dependent). Note that where the subject is the marked topic, a pronoun is left behind in its regular position. In English this REPRISE pattern prevents loss of the modal information that depends on the order of subject and finite verb form; but the same phenomenon occurs obligatorily in some languages of West Africa in which the order of subject and verb is fixed.

Clearly the marking of thematization is related to a semantic factor of PROMINENCE. It is as though stage directions were given to the spotlight handler in a theater to single out a particular individual or an action, or as though one actor were placed close to the audience and another off to the side. In fact, staging metaphors appear to be highly appropriate for the marked varieties of a whole range of linguistic phenomena that have a long history of being hard to handle.

One such area is the semantic relations that I have spoken of in connection with proposition consolidation (11.2). For example, both the similarity in meaning and the difference in form between *we used pliers to bend the wire* and *we bent the wire with pliers* can be expressed by saying that in the first example the staging involves a prominence factor attached to the abstract instrumental predicate. This prominence of staging blocks the consolidation transformation that normally yields an instrument role as in the second example.[3]

Another area where staging seems to be at work is in the decision about what to embed and what to make grammatically independent. The propositions (1: *man* (P x)), (2: *enter* (A 1) (R 3)), and (3: *store* (P y)) combine in more than one way: *The man entered the store, the store was where the man entered, enter the store the man did.*[4] In relation to other propositions we might also have *the man who entered the store, the store's entry by the man, entering,* and a

---

[3] If prominence explains failure to consolidate, this moves the area of difficulty over to characterizing the difference between *we used pliers to bend the wire*, *with pliers we bent the wire*, and *pliers we bent the wire with*. In the first of these prominence attaches to the predicate underlying *use*, and in the last to *pliers*; but in the second either it goes with the entire proposition (*use* (A *we*) (P *pliers*) L), or there is a better explanation yet to be found that will also preserve the semantic similarity shared by all these sentences.

[4] There are also propositions related to the speech situation and cohesion that influence the form of these examples: (4: *know* (P :HEARER) (R x)), (5: *know* (P :HEARER) (R y)), (6: *inform* (A:I) (L :HEARER) (R 2)), (7: *precede* (P 2) (R :NOW)), and possibly others.

number of other forms. Given a collection of propositions that are interconnected by shared references, the speaker's decision about what is, so to speak, front and center on the stage, what is present in a secondary way, and what is unimportant enough that it need not even be mentioned, is a thematic decision. Looked at in this light, we see that staging concerns much more than grammatical topicalization.

Quite a few languages use sentence initial adjunct clauses as part of their staging. Thurman discusses the general process of LINKAGE, also mentioned in the last chapter, in which a clause that describes an event is repeated to provide the point of departure for the next event.[5] The repetition may be verbatim, or it may take a reduced or dependent form. Like ASYNDETON or absence of a conjunction in Greek, the lack of a linking clause may signal a thematic shift. A typical example of linkage is cited by Ronald Lewis from Sanio-Hiowe of Papua New Guinea: *Krismasi ta saro uriye.* KRISMASI TA SARO URIYE, *teitiye sosu a'i masta nomo eimawiye pranteisin.* NOMO EIMAWIYE, *nomo ta apo inawe.* 'We were here for one Christmas. WE WERE HERE FOR ONE CHRISTMAS; then the boss sent us to the plantation. HE SENT US; we went to it.'[6] Stout and Thomson cite entire paragraphs repeated as linkages in Kayapó of Brazil.[7]

In one sense a linkage is the topic of the sentence it introduces; yet the main clause of the sentence may have its own internal topic. This may make linkages be parallel to dependent clause introducers in English, where the relator is the unmarked topic but secondary thematic options are also available within the clause. On the other hand, the sentence topic expressed by linkage and the internal clause topic may be independent.

Nonanaphoric connectives like *and* and *but* appear to be athematic even though they are initial. They are followed by the full range of thematic possibilities for clauses. This independence

5   Thurman, "Chuave Medial Verbs" (ms).
6   R. Lewis, "Sanio-Hiowe Paragraph Structure" (1972).
7   Stout and Thomson, "Kayapó Narrative" (1971).

establishes them as outside the system. Some discourse level connectives like *first*, ... *second*, ... may go with chunks of speech much larger than clauses, but they also appear to be athematic for the same reason.

In between athematic elements like these and fully thematic things like object topicalization, there seems to be a range of semi-thematic introducers that restrict some of the possibilities of what can be topicalized after them but leave others open. We have already considered subordinating conjunctions like *although* and *because* in this sense. Linkage clauses appear to impose mild restrictions in some languages. Modally oriented introducers like *perhaps* have a similar effect.

2. THEME AND COHESIVE STRUCTURE

The best way to show the independence of theme from cohesion is by displaying a series of paradigms adapted from Halliday's article already mentioned. Each paradigm gives one mode: declarative in Figure 21.1, polar interrogative in Figure 21.2, and nonpolar interrogative with a WH-word as subject in Figure 21.3.

Unmarked center		John saw the PLAY.
Marked center:	S	JOHN saw the play.
Marked center:	V	John SAW the play.
Marked center:	O	ambiguous with unmarked center.

		Verb as marked theme
Unmarked center		Saw the play did JOHN.
Marked center:	V	SAW the play did John.
Marked center:	O	Saw the PLAY did John.
Marked center:	S	ambiguous with unmarked center.

		Object as marked theme
Unmarked center		The play John SAW.
Marked center:	S	The play JOHN saw.
Marked center:	O	The PLAY John saw.
Marked center:	V	ambiguous with unmarked center.

Figure 21.1 Theme and cohesion, declarative mode.
Subject as unmarked theme

Unmarked center		Did John see the PLAY?
Marked center:	S	Did JOHN see the play?
Marked center:	V	Did John SEE the play?
Marked center:	M	DID John see the play?
Marked center:	O	ambiguous with unmarked center.

Subject as marked theme

Unmarked center		John did he see the PLAY?
Marked center:	S	JOHN did he see the play?
Marked center:	V	John did he SEE the play?
Marked center:	M	John DID he see the play?
Marked center:	Pr	John did HE see the play?
		(note that this center is a residue of topicalization.)
Marked center:	O	ambiguous with unmarked center.

Verb as marked theme

Unmarked center		Saw the play did JOHN?
Marked center:	V	SAW the play did John?
Marked center:	O	Saw the PLAY did John?
Marked center:	S	ambiguous with unmarked center.

Object as marked theme

Unmarked center		The play did John SEE?
Marked center:	S	The play did JOHN see?
Marked center:	O	The PLAY did John see?
Marked center:	M	The play DID John see?
Marked center:	V	ambiguous with unmarked center.

Figure 21.2 Theme and cohesion, polar interrogative mode.
Modal as unmarked theme

The first block in each paradigm gives the unmarked theme for that mode and within that thematization gives various options for placement of the information center. Besides the unmarked information center that corresponds to that thematization, the subject, verb, object, modal, or pronoun may be marked information centers. All the examples consist of single clauses that are unmarked with respect to information blocking; that is, one clause, one block.

Before he reacts to the examples in Figures 21.1, 21.2, and 21.3 as bad English, as many do the first time they encounter them, the reader should observe his own thematizing behavior for a day or so. Our grammatical tradition is heavily biased toward regarding

Unmarked center		Who saw the PLAY?
Marked center:	S	WHO saw the play?
Marked center:	V	Who SAW the play?
Marked center:	M	Who DID see the play?
Marked center:	O	ambiguous with unmarked center.

Verb as marked theme

Unmarked center		Saw the play did WHO?
Marked center:	V	SAW the play did who?
Marked center:	O	Saw the PLAY did who?
Marked center:	S	ambiguous with unmarked center.

Object as marked theme

Unmarked center		The play who SAW?
Marked center:	O	The PLAY who saw?
Marked center:	S	The play WHO saw?
Marked center:	V	ambiguous with unmarked center.

Figure 21.3 Theme and cohesion, nonpolar interrogative mode, WH- as subject. Subject as unmarked theme

unmarked thematization as well behaved and proper, and marked thematization as aberrant. Not so; it is part of the language, used constantly, related systematically to the rest. In fact, many of the phenomena written off in grammars as free word order are in contrast with each other thematically.

Marked topics are likely to be blocked separately, rather than be included in the same information block with the rest of their clause as they are in the three figures. The subject and the object are most likely to be blocked separately; other adjuncts moved to the front are less likely to be separate information blocks. For these adjuncts, as has already been mentioned (19.1), blocking is a means of making their scope explicit.

When the marked topic is a separate information block, the block that follows it may begin with a foot that contains a silent stress: *Tén* + DÓLLARS / ' *he* + *tríed* + *to* CHÁRGE *me*.

3. VOICE

Voice has to do with a further relationship between staging and content. We have already mentioned the mapping rules that relate content structure to surface grammar by assigning one role as subject and other roles as other clause functions. We have also seen that in English (and in some other languages as well) the subject element is tied up with the expression of mode — for imperative, no subject; for polar interrogative, modal before subject; and for declarative, subject before modal.

Unmarked mapping relates the agent role when it is present, and otherwise some other role, to the subject, and the subject in turn to the topic via the modal system, in the ACTIVE voice. In the active sentence *George brought these pickles, George* is in the agent relationship to *bring* in the content structure, is at the same time the subject in relation to the mode and the surface form, and is the unmarked topic.

The marked mapping pattern dissociates the agent from the subject position and thus from unmarked theme and mode. At the same time it leaves the theme unmarked. In this PASSIVE mapping the agent is treated in one of two ways that are not easy to handle in the active voice. In the first instance the agent can be treated as new information by making it the center of an information block, but an unmarked center: *These pickles were brought by* GEORGE. In the second instance the agent is left out, either because it is vague as in *the city was bombed* or because it is irrelevant as in *I was just told that my uncle died.*

Other nominal elements can be made the unmarked topic in the passive voice; thematic status is not restricted to whatever role maps to the grammatical object: *These strawberries were given me* and *I was given these strawberries* are equivalent in content but different in staging. Robert Port finds that in Swahili nearly any role can map to the subject, depending upon staging; one would conjecture that this is less constrained than in English because the modal information is not tied to the subject position.[8]

The nonagentive derivation discussed in Chapter 9 is distinct from the passive in English. While the passive retains its agentive

---

[8]   Port, "Focus and Participant Rules in Swahili" (ms).

meaning even when the agent is omitted, the nonagentive leaves out the agent explicitly, giving us pairs like *the houses were sold (by someone)* versus *the houses sold*, or *the door was opened* versus *the door opened.* Where the mapping patterns do not include a voice distinction, as in Huichol, the nonagentive may appear to be the closest translation equivalent to an English or Spanish passive; but there is no way an agent can be brought into the same clause.

Many languages of the Philippines have an inflectional pattern called FOCUS for topicalizing within a clause. The clause typically consists of a verb followed by a subject, an object, a referent, an associative, and in some languages a fifth adjunct that does not participate in the focus system. Every independent verb is inflected for focus on one of the first four adjuncts: in most of the languages the inflection is *ma-* or the infix *-um-* for subject, *-en* or *-on* depending on the language for object, *-an* for referent, and *i-* or *pag-* for associative. The focused element in the clause is either taken from a special set of topic pronouns or, if it is a noun phrase other than a pronoun, is introduced by a special proclitic which shows that it is the topic of the clause. In relation to the clause, order has nothing to do with signalling what the topic is. In relation to the sentence and paragraph, however, putting an element (not necessarily the one that is clause topic) ahead of the verb topicalizes that element over a more extensive stretch. The focus system is different from a true voice system, although it has been dubbed that more than once; but there is only one set of mapping rules involved in subject selection. If an agent, for example, is present, it can never be anything but the subject. Some of the Philippine languages use a nonagentive form that, unlike the typical nonagentive of the Americas, leaves open the question whether the agent is absent because it is redundant or because there is no agent in the semantic picture at all.

4. STAGING AT VARIOUS LEVELS

We have considered whether embedding and subordination in

surface grammar might not express the results of thematic choices. The whole dimension of structural coordination and subordination in discourse — of how we decide what goes where — seems to be related to the concept of staging at least as much as to the organiza- tion of content. One could even suggest that hypotactic rhetorical predicates (14.2) are a part of content structure onto which staging decisions are mapped.[9]

Within the clause we have seen that thematic choices have two kinds of effects: subordination of some elements, and ordering of others. Voice distinctions in some languages and focus in others also appear to be controlled by the speaker's choice about how he wants to present what he has to say.

Sentences represent a different range of thematic options. LINKAGE systems like those of Sanio-Hiowe and Kayapó maintain a thematic continuity by having a new sentence start from the repetition of the one that preceded it. CHAINING systems, found mainly in the highlands of Papua New Guinea, point ahead rather than back to maintain thematic continuity by predicting whether or not the subject of the next verb will be the same as the subject of the current one.

Kalinga of the Philippines allows the sentence to have a topic, shown by putting the topic ahead of the verb, that may be different from the topic of its principal clause as shown by focus inflection.[10] Borôro of Brazil begins many sentences with a linkage-like element that gives the point of departure for the sentence; but unlike a typical linkage it may single out not only the main clause of the

---

[9] It is quite possible that both cohesion and staging, though ultimately not dependent on content structure, are projected on it. For example, the decision to talk about a particular referent could be expressed by attaching a predicate *topic* to the index of that referent. This then implies that the ordinary trans- formations of language operate on a representation of the result of linking content, cohesion, and staging together into a single structure, while an earlier set of transformations whose form has not yet even been sketched operates on the separate representations to link them. Sgall and Hajičová, "A 'Functional' Generative Description" (1970), link theme with the performative by assuming that it can take the form, "I hereby inform you CONCERNING JOHN that ...", where the complement then has to say something about John.

[10] Richard Gieser, "Kalinga Sequential Discourse" (ms).

preceding sentence, but also any other clause or noun element or location.[11]

Paragraphs also have topics, and these may be independent of the topics of their component sentences. The paper by Menno Kroeker on Nambiquara of Brazil that forms the appendix to this book illustrates the kind of linguistic bookkeeping that allows hearers to keep track of several levels of staging at once. Longuda makes heavy use of a distinction between the global theme of an entire text and the theme of a particular paragraph.[12]

Mundurukú, also of Brazil but unrelated to Nambiquara, uses change of theme to divide a text into paragraphs. A particle announcing that the theme is to be changed introduces the first sentence of a new paragraph. The object or goal of the next main verb is the new topic.[13] In Ivatan of the northern Philippines, Hooker reports that the theme of a paragraph is usually the subject of the first independent clause of the paragraph, though two paragraphs may have the same theme and be broken by a discontinuity in the time or space setting.[14]

Ilianen Manobo of the southern Philippines has a highly elaborated narrative form in which there is thematization by EPISODES as well as by paragraphs and smaller units.[15] In episodes the topics are participants in the plot. They are introduced by set formulas: *Hane* DIYA' *te pe' ma te kenakan ne mevantug.* 'Note: THERE we are now with the young man who was famous.' 'There' introduces a character formally for the first time, even when he has been mentioned before in passing. 'Here', on the other hand, brings back as topic a character who has already been the topic of an earlier episode: *Engkey pe' be imbe iya te riya' te pe'* KAYI *te raha.* 'What but indeed there we are HERE with the young woman.'

Bacairí of Brazil has a pronominal system that distinguishes thematic third person referents from athematic ones with reference

---

11 Crowell, "Cohesion in Borôro Discourse" (ms.).
12 John Newman, "Participant Orientation in Longuda Folk Tales" (ms.).
13 Sheffler, "Mundurukú Discourse" (ms.).
14 Hooker, "Cohesion in Ivatan" (ms.).
15 Wrigglesworth, "Ilianen Manobo Narrative Discourse" (ms.).

to the clause.[16] Both kinds are further divided into focal and non-focal varieties. David Cranmer in a personal communication suggests that the focal category may represent a higher level theme, on the order of a paragraph theme.

Entire discourses frequently have identifiable topics. Kroeker's study of Nambiquara illustrates this. Behind it lies Aristotle's observation that "necessarily, you state your case, and you prove it".[17] The title of written discourse is a form of topicalization.

---

[16]   Wheatley, "Pronouns and Nominal Elements in Bacairí Discourse" (ms).
[17]   Aristotle, *Rhetoric* 3:13.

22

TOPICALIZATION

The last chapter introduced the area of language that has to do with staging or thematic prominence. This chapter goes into further detail on some of the processes used by various languages to identify the topic, which is that part of the surface form that represents the speaker's thematic choice.

1. DEVICES

A range of devices for distinguishing the topic has already been mentioned in Chapter 21. Initial position in the clause is distinctive in English. In many of the languages of the Philippines initial position is distinctive, but with reference to the sentence and paragraph rather than to the clause itself. In Bacairí of Brazil position is distinctive for expanded noun phrases that act as topic, but not for pronouns.[1]

Morphological marking of thematic distinctions has been reported for several languages. Bacairí pronouns, for example, distinguish two distinct kinds of thematization, clause-related and possibly paragraph-related. Longuda of Nigeria uses different pronouns for the theme character of a paragraph and the athematic characters;[2] but occasionally the fact that a character is thematic for the discourse as a whole overrides the status of the paragraph

---

[1] Wheatley, "Pronouns and Nominal Elements in Bacairí Discourse" (ms).
[2] John Newman, "Participant Orientation in Longuda Folk Tales" (ms).

thematic character for determining prominal usage. When this happens the perspective of the discourse is shifted from closer attention to the paragraph action back to the global picture.

The inflectional cross reference between the verb in most languages of the Philippines and the nominal elements that accompany it has already been mentioned. A variation on this is the PREFOCUS of verbs in the Bilaan of Sarangani Province, Mindanao, where each verb takes one of the four focus categories as inherent.[3] It is then inflected only for the three other focus categories; absence of a focus inflection does not denote lack of focus (such as is found in embedded clauses in many of the other languages), but rather the particular focus category that is inherent for that verb.

Most of the simple topicalization found so far is a matter of either position in the clause or of inflectional marking of topic. More complex structures for delimiting the topic, however, are apparently quite widespread.

2. THEMATIC PARTITIONING

English and a number of other languages mark topicalization in a special way by PARTITIONING the content of a sentence into two parts that are joined by an equative construction, the so-called 'pseudo-cleft' construction. The two parts are related to each other in the same way that a question and its answer are related, and in fact are generally expressed by grammatical patterns similar to those used for questions on the one hand and for relative clauses on the other. Rather than adopt a separate terminology for these sentences, I will simply speak of the question part and the answer part: in *What he thinks is that money will cure all ills* the question part comes first. It is the nominalized counterpart of *What does he think?*, and the answer to it, on the other side of the verb *be*, is *that money will cure all ills*. In *Another chance is what he wants*, the answer part comes first, *another chance*, followed

---

[3]   Rhea, "Prefocus in Sarangani Bilaan" (ms).

by the question part, the nominalized counterpart of *what does he want?*

As Halliday points out,[4] the answer part of a partitioned construction may be nearly anything. It may be a major clause constituent such as the subject in *He is the one who brought the pickles*, answering *Who brought the pickles?*, or the object as in *What this country needs is a good five cent cigar*. It may be the verb itself as in *What I would like you to do with that pet snake is give it away*.

The answer part may also be an adjunct that is not a major clause constituent: *How he did it was with mirrors*, *The park is where the action is*. It does not even have to be a direct constituent of the clause, but may be a constituent of a constituent, as in *He's the one whose arm was injured*.

When the answer part is itself an embedded clause, the thematically partitioned construction can turn ambiguous. *What I want is what John wants* has two patterns behind it. If the question part comes first, *What do you want?*, the answer is *I want what John wants*. If the answer comes first, the question is *What does John want?* and the answer is *John wants what I want*.[5]

More than one constituent may be included in the answer. As was the case before when the verb was in the answer, the question part must contain an auxiliary verb. Furthermore, it appears that if there are two or more constituents in the answer, one of them has to be the verb. Halliday gives an extensive set of examples containing more than one constituent in the answer part: *What John did last week was paint the shed*, *What happened was that John painted the shed last week*, *What John did to the shed was to paint it last week*, and so on, always keeping within the basic Q-*be*-A or A-*be*-Q pattern.

The question part of a pseudo-cleft sentence is always a nominalized clause. It may have a head noun introduced to give it the nominalized form, as in *The one who saw the play was John* from an underlying question *Who saw the play?*[6] On the other hand, the question word itself may act as the head of the nominalized construction, as in *What I told him was that he should resign.*

The nominalized question is always definite rather than indefinite. When a head noun is added to the question to give it nominalized form the determiner *the* is required: *The thing Susie wanted most was a drink of water, The car I was driving then was a Plymouth.* These head nouns are always generic, at least in relation to nouns in the answer part: *person, kind, thing, time, place, fact, reason, way,* and *one* are the normal dummy head nouns, while slightly more specialized ones like *car* in the second example in the paragraph are still generic in relation to answers like *a Plymouth. Thing* in this context covers an especially wide range. It may refer to an object as in *the thing he saw was a floating box,* an abstraction as in *the thing that bothers me most is the effect of hyperconductivity,* or a mass noun as in *the thing we have to watch out for on this stretch is fog.*

Without a head noun, *what* is the usual introducer of a question nominalization. Its definiteness may be specified by a demonstrative in the answer, or simply by the fact that it is in the question part of a thematically partitioned construction. In *What we ought to do is this* the demonstrative *this,* though cataphoric, provides the definiteness that *what* in itself lacks. In *What we ought to do is pack the courtroom* the total construction is sufficient to account for the definiteness. The same is true in a wishy-washy but not impossible construction like *What we ought to do is something,* where the definiteness of the total construction cannot be attributed to the nature of the answer part.

In a thematically partitioned construction either the question

---

[6] Anna Granville Hatcher's monograph *Theme and Underlying Question* regards numerous features of Spanish syntax, not just partitioning, as related to the type of question that elicits a sentence. The characteristic of partitioning that is under discussion here is the fact that the question is given along with its answer. Hatcher's approach looks as though it could be applied profitably to discourse, but so far I do not know that it has been.

part or the answer part may be thematized by being put first: in *The play was what John saw* the answer comes first, and in *What John saw was the play* the question comes first. Furthermore, either the question part or the entire equative may be negated: *What John did not see was the play* puts the negative in the question, while *What John saw was not the play* negates the equative.

Thematically partitioned constructions differ systematically from the corresponding simple clauses. One might say, following Halliday, that a simple construction involves a process and the participants in the process, whereas a partitioned construction defines one of the participants, the one in the answer part, by the fact that he participates in the process.

Halliday also points out that the identification given by thematic partitioning is exclusive. He cites the British brewery advertisement *What we want is Watney's*, which implies 'and nothing else', as over against the more broadminded *We want Watney's* 'but anything else will do'. Furthermore, the construction gives a clear ending for the topic of the clause. Whereas in a simply topicalized clause like *he put on his coat* it is easy enough to say that *he* is the thematic starting point but not as easy to say that the next word, *put*, is not part of the topic, with a pseudo-cleft sentence like *what he put on was his coat* the topic includes everything up to the form of *be* that forms the equative framework. This topicalizing property is what is behind my term for the phenomenon in its relation to discourse studies: thematic partitioning.

A large class of CLEFT sentences can be related to thematically partitioned sentences in Q-*be*-A form. Here the question part in relative clause form is moved to the end of the construction, after the answer part, and a dummy *it* or *there* is left in its place in initial position to preserve the modal information: *It was me who said it* has an extraposed question part *Who said it?* and an answer part, *me*, that is actually the topic. It is topic in a different sense, however, than the topic of the pure cleft construction. Whereas the pseudo-cleft topic is exclusive in terms of the definition given it, the topic of the extraposed form is exclusive as theme. In *I was the one who said it*, the implication is that I and nobody else was

involved in saying it, while in *It was me who said it* the implication
is that I and nobody else am being talked about as theme.[7]

Extraposition relates to more than topicalization alone, and
applies to other things than the question part of a cleft sentence.
It is, for example, obligatory for some verbs such as *seem*, where a
subject complement clause is extraposed: *it seems that he left us
to pay the bill*. Here no form of *be* is involved.

3. TAGGING AND REPRISE

Noun phrases with an auxiliary placed at the end of a clause are a
special type of marked topic: *he's sick, is John*. This final position
is unmarked for adverbial elements like time and place elements,
but it is marked for subjects and objects. (Frontshifting is marked
for the adverbial adjuncts.) These final TAG constructions constitute
the backbone of the pseudo-Irish dialect writing of some authors:
He kissed the Blarney Stone in his early youth, did Paddy.

A noun phrase put at the beginning of a clause, but echoed at
the normal place in the clause by a pronoun, constitutes a REPRISE:
John, he's always late for the subject, or *The commissioner, I could
shoot him* for the object. Like the answer part of a thematically
partitioned sentence, the fronted element in a reprise does not have
to be a clause constituent, but may be embedded within one:
The commissioner, I could wring his neck. The reprise pattern is
more common in French than in English: *Moi, je suis fatigué*. It
is also reported for Welsh,[8] and is the unmarked pattern for use
of a noun as subject in many languages of West Africa.

4. COMPOUND TOPICALIZATION

The various ways of indicating the topic of a clause or sentence

---

[7]   Those dialects of English that use *It was I who said it* have the same pattern
of extraposition; the difference is in the assignment of case forms of pronouns.
[8]   Macqueen, "Reprise Construction in Welsh" (1957).

TABLE 22.1
Compound topicalization patterns.

	Front	Infl	Pron	Agree	Part	Extrap	Tag	Rep
Fronting	+	+	−	?	−	+	+	+
Inflection		+	?	?	+	?	−	−
Pronouns			+	?	?	?	?	?
Agreement				−	?	?	?	?
Partitioning					−	−	+	+
Extraposition						−	+	+
Tagging							−	+
Reprise								−

can be combined, but not all combinations seem to be possible. If we make a table of the different mechanisms available in languages for topicalizing, we will see that some combinations are easily documentable (+), others appear to be impossible (−), and we simply lack empirical evidence on about others (?) due to never having asked this kind of question about most languages.

The impossible combinations (−) are only impossible with reference to our present range of experience with languages. We do not know enough yet about why languages topicalize anything at all to be able to explain why certain combinations should or should not occur.

Going through Table 22.1 row by row we find the following types of compound topicalization to match the plus signs. Double fronting occurs in English: SHOES AT THAT TIME *we could buy for three* dollars a pair. Fronting with inflection is reported by Gieser for Kalinga, with the focus inflection affecting the clause and the fronting affecting the paragraph.[9] Fronting and extraposition give THE OTHER DAY IT *was the green dress that you wanted.* Fronting and tagging combine in LAST TUESDAY *he was feeling better,* WAS GEORGE. Fronting and reprise give JOHN, LATELY *he's been acting strange.*

The inflection patterns of the languages of the Philippines enter into other combinations besides with fronting. Northern Kankanay

9   Gieser, "Kalinga Sequential Discourse" (ms).

has some double focus inflections; it is not clear how they fit the thematization patterns of texts.[10] Several grammars of Philippine languages have an equative construction that looks suspiciously like a thematically partitioned sentence pattern and whose parts are independent of the inflection for focus of the verb involved.

Bacairí has the fullest set of topic-related pronouns found so far.[11] Furthermore, they distinguish two thematic levels simultaneously, and so are capable of communicating compound thematic information.

The patterns of agreement between the use of certain pronouns at certain points in the text and the thematic status of the referents of those pronouns is characteristic of Longuda; but I do not know that it enters into any patterns of compound topicalization.[12]

Thematic partitioning and tagging go together in English *What he wants to do* IS *get married*, DOES BILL. Partitioning also goes with reprise: ME, *what* I'D *like* IS *a cup of coffee*. It is possible to suggest that the reason thematic partitioning does not go with fronting is because the partitioned construction itself has to be arranged in one of two thematic orders, question first or answer first, so that the fronting pattern itself is, so to speak, used up by the mechanics of partitioning.

Tagging and reprise, finally, can go together: BILL, *he hates him*, DOES JOHN.

This brief survey of linguistic devices that are used for topicalization leave open a question on which considerable research still needs to be done: what is the precise role of each in discourse? In some languages topicalization is a signal of a new theme in the broadest sense of changing the subject. In others topicalization is used in more specific ways such as to introduce new characters. But even though the general idea of theme as having to do with the principle by which a speaker presents what he says not only with a certain content but from a certain perspective, we are still a long way from getting to the bottom of that principle.

[10] Hettick, "Verb Stem Classes in Northern Kankanay" (ms).
[11] Wheatley, "Pronouns and Nominal Elements in Bacairí Discourse" (ms).
[12] John Newman, "Participant Orientation in Longuda Folk Tales" (ms).

23

VARIABILITY

So-called freely varying phenomena — word order, for example — often turn out to communicate distinctions like staging that linguists had not been too aware of until recently but that follow patterns as definite as those of the content related part of linguistic structure. Nevertheless, there do seem to be some things in languages that are communicated by variations that are perceivable by their mass effect and can be analyzed using the tools of statistics.

The variable frequency rules discussed by William Labov and Ralph Fasold seem to be an instance of this.[1] A variable frequency rule in a grammar has a form like the following: a particular underlying configuration is expressed in one way a certain percentage of the time, in a second way another percentage of the time, and a third way the rest of the time. The minimum number of alternatives is two, but there may be more depending on the rule. In the case of so-called optional rules in grammar, it simplifies assigning probabilities to speak in terms of a choice between two rules, the rule in question and an identity rule that leaves everything unchanged, rather than in terms of the presence or absence of one rule, or of its use or nonuse.

Suppose we begin with sets of rules that have two alternatives. If we assign to one the probability p, a number between 0 and 1, then the other rule has the probability $1 - p$. The probability p

---

[1] Labov, "Contraction, Deletion, and Inherent Variability of the English Copula" (1969); Fasold, "Two Models of Sociolinguistically Significant Linguistic Variation" (1970).

expresses the proportion of instances in which the first rule is applied in the production of some class of texts, while in the rest of the instances the other rule is applied instead.

Now suppose in a different text the same speaker gives the first rule a different probability, say q, and the second the probability $1 - q$. Assuming that the two probabilities, p and q, are significantly different from each other, it is likely that the choice of the PROBABILITY VECTOR $(p, 1 - p)$ in the one case communicates a different meaning from the choice of the probability vector $(q, 1 - q)$ in the other. In other words, differences in probability vectors are capable of expressing semantic choices.

An example of how this works can be given by relating it to Simmons and Slocum's grammar for producing texts from underlying semantic representations.[2] They describe how semantic structures whose expressions could be embedded in terms of the surface grammatical structure are first recognized by the grammar, then subjected to decision by a random process that is the computational equivalent of flipping a coin. If the coin falls heads, the expression is embedded; if tails, it is made syntactically independent. In the terms I have just given, Simmons and Slocum's grammar contains a pair of rules whose probability vector is (.5, .5). One rule results in embedding, the other does not.

The probability vector (.5, .5) is taken for granted in Simmons and Slocum's current implementation. Let us change the grammar, however, in such a way that the probability vector is under the control of the speaker. In other words, the speaker can make a semantic choice whose expression is not a particular word or construction, but a probability vector for the pair of embedding rules. If, for example, the speaker has the choice between sounding pedantic or casual (to oversimplify things grossly enough to make them plain), perhaps a choice to communicate pedantry would be expressed as a probability vector of (.8, .2) over the two rules, and a choice to sound casual as a vector of (.3, .7) over the same two

[2] Simmons and Slocum, "Generating English Discourse from Semantic Networks" (1972).

rules. Semantic predicates whose expression is of this form can be called PARAMETRIC predicates, since they control the mass behavior of another part of the grammar.[3]

In terms of producing texts, a probability vector of (.8, .2) says that on about eight out of ten occasions when the possibility of embedding comes up, the speaker will embed if he is trying to sound pedantic. The vector gives us no indication about which eight instances will be embedded, but simply sets the overall effect at a certain ratio. In the same way, if he is trying to sound casual, the corresponding parameter on the same rule of the grammar stipulates that he will embed on the average only two times out of ten opportunities, again without giving any idea which two times out of any given ten, since the choice is a random process.

In terms of understanding texts, the concept of parametric predicates suggests that hearers are sensitive to mass effects of choices that come up repeatedly in texts. The range of semantic choices that can be communicated parametrically is nowhere near as great as the range of choices that can be communicated by the well tuned oppositions of the phonological system; nevertheless, it does appear to play a part in language.

One can even suggest that the hearer's task is to decide which of several possible probability vectors is being used by the speaker. If so, his task can be simulated by a Bayesian statistical decision process.[4] In such a process, each time he encounters a point in the semantic structure where embedding could have taken place, the observation whether it did or not constitutes one piece of evidence. Each piece of evidence tends to bolster one of the possible hypotheses and not to support another. The more consistent instances are found, the less uncertainty is attached to one interpretation of the overall effect over against all the other possible ones. The more text, the less risky is the choice of one particular probability vector.

The idea of choosing one probability vector over another extends, of course, to longer vectors that represent more than two

[3] This phenomenon is discussed in Grimes and Glock, "Saramaccan" (1970).
[4] Chernoff and Moses, *Elementary, Decision Theory.*

alternative rules at some point in the grammar. Furthermore, it seems likely that different decisions which involve the same set of parametric predicates can be made at different points in a text, with the implication that one probability vector holds for a particular subtree of the whole. Authors who use very short sentences for one kind of subject matter and long ones for other kinds exemplify some such principle.

Parametric predicates appear to be a good field for the expression of GRADIENT relationships in semantics. Instead of having a binary choice between pedantic and casual expression, for example, it is just as likely that pedantic and casual are points on a continuum. In this case the choice the speaker makes can fall anywhere along that continuum, and the probabilities that he uses reflect where on the continuum he has placed himself. In the case of embedding in the Simmons-Slocum model, for example, a speaker who uses a probability vector of (.5, .5) is not speaking ungrammatically in the sense that he has not committed himself to (.8, .2) or (.3, .7). Instead he has placed himself somewhere near the middle of a scale that runs from pedantic to casual.

The concept of variability can be followed out in text by taking note of all points in the grammar where there are sets of alternative rules, including optional rules as a special case. The differences in probability vectors associated with each of these sets of rules in different kinds of text then become data to be accounted for semantically in much the same way that differences in words and phrases have to be accounted for semantically.

24

POSTSEMANTIC SHAPING

Up to now, in discussing how underlying forms relate to their surface representations, we have tended to speak about direct implications for surface form. The full picture, however, requires us to recognize that the surface form is influenced not only by the choices the speaker makes, but by intermediate semantic patterns that are entailed by those choices. This entailment is automatic. Components that are entailed on some occasions and chosen independently on others have similar effects on surface form regardless of how they come into the picture.

Wallace Chafe refers to entailments of this kind as POSTSEMANTIC.[1] They are not directly involved in the expression of what the speaker wants to say, yet the elements that are involved are semantic predicates and their arguments, not surface forms. Only after these processes have taken place, argues Chafe (based on the semantic properties of idioms and the ways in which they are expressed), is the underlying form amenable to LINEARIZATION, in which the actual surface forms are matched to the underlying forms.

1. REDUNDANCY TRANSFORMATIONS

Inclusion hierarchies incorporate information into the semantic structure by redundancy. Bierwisch and Fillmore, among others, have commented on such things as the way a query about linear

---

[1] Chafe, *Meaning and the Structure of Language* (1970).

measure is phrased according to properties of the thing being measured.[2] If an object has an essentially limitless dimension, like a road or a river, a query about the distance across it at right angles to that dimension refers to a *wide-narrow* measure by using the unmarked term *wide: How wide is this road, how wide is the river at Centerville?* While the question simply names the dimension about which information is wanted, the answer is in terms of the member of the opposition that is appropriate: *It's wide enough for two lanes, it's pretty narrow right there.* If a specific measure is given, however, it again is attached only to the more inclusive term that names the dimension rather than to the scale along the dimension: *It's twenty feet wide* but not **it's twenty feet narrow.* The choice of the dimension is open to the speaker, but in the general question and the kind of answer that involves a specific measure, the terms that are appropriate are the redundant ones.[3]

Winograd's incorporation of semantic marker hierarchies in his model of a semantic system reflects inclusion redundancy in language.[4] In understanding speech, redundancy helps disambiguate the possible readings of a text. Where a word has multiple meaning possibilities (the meanings of *ball*, for example, were mentioned in Chapter 20), incompatibilities between marker hierarchies for words in constructions are used to eliminate superfluous readings. The incompatibility does not have to be stated in terms of the specific marker that is associated with the word in the dictionary, but may call on the redundancies built into the system by looking for more inclusive markers. Thus the likely reading for *The ball was attended by many wealthy people* is the one that takes *ball* to be an event instead of a physical object; but the dictionary entry for the physical object meaning of *ball* is actually that of a manipulable

---

[2] Bierwisch, "Some Semantic Universals of German Adjectivals" (1967); Fillmore, "Lexical Entries for Verbs" (1968).

[3] A question that uses the marked term, like *how narrow is it?*, implies that the speaker has already made up his mind about where on the *wide-narrow* scale it fits and wants a specific measure as his answer. The answer, however, is still *twenty feet wide*, regardless of the other assumptions in the question.

[4] Winograd, *Procedures* (1971).

object, which is only one kind of physical object, because the more precise marker is needed in other contexts. The marker that is needed in this context, however, is found farther up the inclusion hierarchy to which the marker for manipulable objects belongs.

The inferential processes used in Winograd's model to specify how access is to be made to the data base also involve a redundancy. Instead of a specific match, an entire family of possible matches is defined.

Redundancies are often involved in the expression of anaphoric linkages. The linkage pattern used in many languages, which has been mentioned already several times, involves a repetition in dependent form of a preceding sentence, something like *John cut the grass. After John cut the grass, he put the mower away. After he put the mower away, he got himself a drink.* On the other hand, there are two other kinds of redundant linkages that are common in a number of languages. The first makes use of inclusion hierarchies by repeating with a less specific word than the one used the first time: *John cut the grass. After he did that, he put the mower away. After he took care of it, he got himself a drink.* The second kind makes use of inferential sequences in which a process that is represented as having started is referred back to in terms of the assumption that it finished: *John cut the grass. After he finished, he put the mower away. When it was inside, he got himself a drink.* These inferential sequences, which Longacre refers to as expectancy chains, embody fairly extensive assumptions about the culture of the speakers.[5]

2. SEMANTIC NEUTRALIZATION

Related to the inclusiveness is the differing fineness of the semantic grid in terms of which the same distinctions of meaning are encoded in different situations. Distinctions that are available in some environments are simply not there in others. Chafe shows how the

[5] Longacre, *Discourse ... in Philippine Languages* (1968).

Onondaga verb permits a rather rich system of distinctions in its overall pattern.[6] Certain combinations of distinctions, however, eliminate differences in the expression of the meaning categories involved, so that in the surface form it is impossible to tell which of several possible categories is intended by some forms. (This is not to say that semantic categories are created by the linguist in great profusion and then neutralized down to an irreducible few in violation of Occam's principle. Rather, every distinction in the system corresponds to a surface distinction somewhere, though not necessarily in all its possible combinations.)

Many languages of West Africa show a different tense-aspect system in the negative than they do in the positive.[7] In some the positive categories are related to those of the negative, but the full set of distinctions is neutralized in the negative to give a different system. In others the negative aspects seem to be independent of the positive ones.

The suppression of some of the role-related arguments of lexical predicates can be thought of as a type of semantic neutralization, since the resulting form appears to have a different role set from the one it normally takes.

The typical case of argument suppression takes place when one of the arguments is culturally conventional, so predictable that it is not worth commenting on. A suppressed patient in English gives us a form that looks like it should belong to a pure action verb like *be careful;* but the patient is still in the picture semantically. We suppress the patient in *he is eating*, where the patient is taken to be whatever it is that people normally eat under the circumstances, and *he is drinking*, where the patient is a liquid that (perhaps a commentary on the habits of our linguistic forebears) contains alcohol. If there is anything out of the ordinary or specific to be said about the patient it cannot be suppressed: *he is eating caviar* or *he is drinking Coke*. Other roles can also be suppressed by a similar principle: the result in *they broke the window* assumes

---

[6]   Chafe, *A Semantically Based Grammar of Onondaga* (1970).
[7]   Flik, "Dan Tense-aspect and Discourse" (ms); Dawson, "Remarks on Negation in Tépo Krou" (ms).

that it broke into small, irregular pieces; but in *they broke the window into two halves* or *into shimmering hexagons* it cannot be suppressed.

Some languages regularly delete to show anaphora rather than replacing a role element by a pronoun as English does most of the time. Many languages of Papua New Guinea appear to operate almost without nominal adjuncts to their verbs: "he left, crossed, climbed, threw a spear, escaped" gives the effect of the normal mode of story telling. In this case it is not culturally predictable elements that are involved, but textually predictable elements. Considered one verb or one clause at a time, texts of this kind would appear to be highly ambiguous; taken as a whole, however, they are not. It is probably best not to speak of semantic neutralization in such a case, since the full meaning is recoverable from the discourse context.

Semantic neutralization that is brought about automatically as a postsemantic process, as in Chafe's Onondaga, also needs to be distinguished from deliberate bypassing or washing out of semantic distinctions by the speaker. In discussing semantic derivation in Chapter 9 we saw how a nonagentive derivation in many languages makes an action word behave like a process word by suppressing information about whether an agent is involved or not. In most languages of the Americas the nonagentive form is related in its expression to the developmental or change-of-state form of a predicate. The Huichol nonagentive *puu + qéiya* 'it got carried off', for example, with the nonagentive *-ya* suffix, is completely noncommittal about whether anybody is responsible or not, while its agentive counterpart *péi + qei* 'he carried it off' implies that the agent is identifiable in the discourse.

3. PROPOSITION CONSOLIDATION

This process, discussed in detail by Frantz,[8] has already been

---

[8] Frantz, *Blackfoot* (1970).

mentioned in Chapter 11 in relation to its effects on the apparent role structure of semantic predicates. It operates on particular predicates like the ones that express causative and instrumental relations, and on the propositions that act as their arguments. The effect of consolidation is to take the dominating predicate of the pair and attach it to the other one as though it were another role-related argument of it.

As we have seen, the kind of underlying representation that needs to be assumed for discourse involves many, many layers of branching. Proposition consolidation acts to reduce this branching depth by combining two propositions, one of which directly dominates the other, into a single consolidated proposition. It does this, however, at the cost of obscuring the role relationships of the dominated predicate, because it then appears to have the role set of some group of predicates other than the one it really belongs to.

Proposition consolidation appears to be closely related to concepts of staging. Applied to an instrumental predicate, as discussed in Chapter 11, it yields what appears to be an instrument role like that of *knife* in *he buttered the toast* WITH A KNIFE. If *knife* is made prominent in some way, however, this may give us an account of the blocking of consolidation such as needs to be assumed for HE USED A KNIFE *to butter the toast*.

It is possible that there is something similar to this behind the patterns that present the same information either as an independent proposition, a proposition embedded in some other, or as a reduced proposition that yields a minimum of information. We can illustrate this by drawing a parallel between a full sentence, a relative clause, and a noun, all used for the same individual: *he acted in the play*, *the one who acted in the play*, and *the actor*. Though we can in one sense choose to say more or less about any item in our data base, observations like the ones made about identification spans in Chapter 6 show that the places where we say more and the places where we say less are constrained by where we are in a discourse. We can give information greater prominence or less prominence according to how it fits our overall perspective, and according to how familiar we think the hearer is with it already.

4. PERFORMATIVE SATURATION

In Chapter 5 we discussed the influence on linguistic form of the speaker's knowledge about who he is, who the hearer is (or at least his mental image of who the hearer is), and the time and place at which he is speaking. This influences the speaker's choice of person categories in pronouns and deictic categories in demonstratives, adverbs, prepositions, and verbs of place and motion. It pervades his use of tense.

Rather than assume that this kind of information, which I have lumped together as performative information, is chosen afresh for every proposition in whose expression it is involved, it makes more sense to think of a small number of performative choices that are then spread throughout the semantic structure by post-semantic processes. If we think of the semantic structure of a discourse as a rooted tree, the propositions that embody perform-ative information are at or near the root of the tree, and are per-colated down to nodes farther away from the root by copying transformations. Some process such as this can be used to explain how a language like Bahinemo of Papua New Guinea can have tense information represented mainly at one point in each para-graph,[9] and a language like Godié of Ivory Coast can have it as infrequently as once per discourse,[10] while other languages like English indicate tense on nearly every verb; yet as far as content is concerned the time relations that the tense represents in all three languages are not essentially different.

It is also necessary to recognize that verbs of saying and related verbs (often lumped together as a LOCUTIONARY category on the basis of the very property I am about to mention) may entail

[9]   Longacre, *Discourse ... in New Guinea Languages* (1972).
[10]   Marchese, "Time Reference in Godié" (ms).

different person and tense assignments within the subtrees that form their patients. If I, the speaker, tell you, the hearer, that A said to B, "I'll see you at eight," within the quotation that acts as the patient of *A said to B* the assignment of person categories is sharply distinct from that of the rest of the sentence. Within the quotation both I and you are identified as *he*, and it is A who takes on the first person, B the second. With reference to the subtree it dominates, a locutionary verb, when used in the way known as DIRECT discourse, has the same effect on person assignments, deictic categories, and tense as the implicit performative that dominates the entire discourse has. The work of Lowe, Pike, and Perrin on patterns of direct and indirect person assignment with locutionary verbs has already been discussed in detail in Chapter 5.

One could think, then, in terms of fairly simple transformations that copy the person assignments determined by a locutionary verb in direct discourse from that verb, with appropriate shifts, to its patient, and on down by a process of saturation to all nodes that are dominated by the patient. The process begins with the implied performative that dominates the entire discourse. It is blocked, however, by any embedded locutionary verbs that are also used in direct discourse. They shift the person assignments that come from above in the tree to a new set, following Lowe's law. These assignments are the ones they pass on to their own patients.

5. LEVEL FORMATION

As was mentioned in the discussion of proposition consolidation, the complexity of surface structure in language, whether we look only at sentences or at entire discourses, is not the same as the complexity of the underlying structures that have to be assumed in order to account for what those constructions communicate. Proposition consolidation is one process that reduces the depth of embedding. There are also others.

A number of linguists, especially the tagmemicists on the one hand[11] and those who follow M. A. K. Halliday on the other,[12] have commented on the relatively small number of surface constructions that have to be assumed for language. They observe that grammatical patterns frequently sort themselves out into discrete levels, usually word, phrase, clause, sentence, paragraph, episode, and discourse. Much of the apparent complexity of language is a consequence of the ability of a unit of one level to be embedded as a constituent within a unit that is normally at a lower level, so that for example a relative clause may be part of a noun phrase or a narrative discourse may be the object of a single verb within a clause. Longacre refers to this phenomenon as backlooping and Halliday as rankshifting.

The concept of a hierarchical level has not been as strongly followed out in generative grammar, except for the development of the embedding concept. There considerably more effort has been expended on characterizing underlying form than on the possibilities of surface form; but even there a surface hierarchy does appear at the interface between grammar and phonology. It comes at the point where cyclic rules are invoked that behave according to the surface partitioning of sentences.[13]

The grouping of information into surface units at various levels seems to relate to several factors. One could be thought of as the capacity of a surface construction to hold a quantity of information. In Saramaccan, for example, Glock and I noticed that verb phrases seemed to allow room for one or at most two nominal elements like objects or complements.[14] Other information that might be present in the same semantic complex had to spill over into another verb phrase in a string of verb phrases, or even into another clause. Even in languages that permit considerable complexity in sentence structure, there seems to be a limit (perhaps a probabilistic one as was suggested for parametrically controlled embedding in Chapter

---

[11] Pike, *Language* (1967); Longacre, *Grammar Discovery Procedures* (1964).

[12] For example Winograd in his *Procedures* (1971).

[13] Chomsky and Halle, *The Sound Pattern of English* (1968).

[14] Grimes and Glock, "Saramaccan" (1970). Philip Hewer traces further consequences of surface constraints in "Clause Clusters in Kasem" (ms).

23) as to how much one sentence can hold. Metaphorically one thinks in terms of ladling out one's semantic soup in small spoonfuls.

The grammatical structures that are available for expressing a particular semantic complex may also be restricted by cohesion and staging. With cohesion, the amount that needs to be said in order to communicate a particular part of the semantic structure depends upon what reference has already been made to that information. Whatever has been talked about need only be identified in the least explicit way that is available. If it has been mentioned recently, a pronoun or a generic noun or even no mention at all suffices; if it has been some time and other things have come to the fore since then, a more specific identification is called for.

Also within the general calibration of how familiar information is to the hearer, there lies the ordering of what is to be said relative to intonation. As was discussed in Chapter 19, less predictable information tends to be shifted toward the end of an information block unless it is to be specially marked as new, in which case English moves the intonation to it and away from the end. Languages of the Papua New Guinea highlands pick a different verb inflection pattern, and languages that make use of overlay repeat such information in another plane.

Staging or imposition of a thematic perspective also plays a part in grouping things together. It is especially important in ordering the elements within a grammatical grouping. The principle seems to be universal that topics are mentioned early within their constructions. This holds to a certain extent even in languages that also have inflectional patterns or special pronouns that permit them in some cases to identify topics without recourse to the order of elements.

The delimitation of larger units seems to be a special case of topicalization. Quite a few languages, for example, have a paragraph-like unit that begins with some indication of a change in time, place, or characters. At least one of these, and often more than one, are mentioned explicitly at the beginning of the paragraph. They hold throughout the paragraph without further mention. The early mention of time, place, or characters thus gives the paragraph its starting point. Something similar happens on a larger scale in Longuda episodes, in which one of the characters is referred to in a way that shows that he is the thematic character for that episode.[15] Around him the action revolves even when other characters are doing things. From then on in the episode his thematic status affects the use of all pronouns.

Although most discussions of staging seem to concentrate on the topic, that is, on one element that is made thematically prominent, the other end of the same scale needs to be investigated in order to understand how underlying semantic structures relate to surface forms. The opposite of prominence is the near oblivion that is imposed on embedded information — it may be needed to help establish the reference of a nominal construction, for example, but nothing more. It is cast into a grammatical mold that informs the hearer that this information refers not to what is taking place at the center of his mental stage, but to the borders of his attention.

This concludes our review of observations about discourse and the ways in which it seems to fit together with the rest of what we know about language. Discourse studies have been made in more than sixty languages at the time I write this, and more are on the way. Nothing approaching a grammar of discourse has been developed yet, however. One investigator concentrates on linkage, another on units in a hierarchy, another on pronouns; yet a composite picture is beginning to emerge.

What we do not know is more important at this stage than what we have found. The biggest gap in our understanding is in the area of staging. We know how to recognize topicalization patterns; but we have not figured out yet why any language really needs them. The terms I have used for staging are at best metaphors, not terms defined within a system that explains anything.

A second area that needs considerable attention is finding out how far principles apply. We recognize various types of cohesion

---

[15] John Newman, "Participant Orientation in Longuda Folk Tales" (ms).

spans, for example, that have to do with participants and places and events and times. They are not particularly hard to find in paragraphs. The idea of a span, however, needs to be pushed up to large units like epics and down to small units like noun and verb phrases and affix strings. Are rules of pronominalization, for example, a specialized instance of the effect of cohesion spans on linguistic structure? Or in the realm of topicalization, is it enough to recognize topics of clauses, sentences, and paragraphs, or are there parallel phenomena that pervade parts of linguistic structure where we do not ordinarily look for such things? Is the difference between *give the sandwich to me* and *give me the sandwich* a purely thematic difference, or are there other factors? At least we have taken a few steps already on the way to understanding discourse.

Appendix

THEMATIC LINKAGE IN NAMBIQUARA NARRATIVE

MENNO H. KROEKER

(This paper explores some of the evidence that staging applies at several levels. – *JEG*)

INTRODUCTION

The linkage system employed between sentences, paragraphs, and themes is one of the more complex elements in the analysis of Nambiquara[1] narrative. It involves several sets of connectors depending on the element to be linked, i.e. whether one is referring to sentences, paragraphs, or larger discourse units.

TYPES OF LINKAGE

Sentence linkages are most numerous. Some linkages indicate

[1] Nambiquara was classified by McQuown and Greenberg as in the Ge-Pano-Carib Phylum of languages (Sol Tax, "Aboriginal Languages of Latin America", 1960). There are approximately 200 speakers of Nambiquara in northwestern Mato Grosso, Brazil. The number of dialect groups remains uncertain at present. The data for this paper were gathered on field trips to Nambiquara villages between the years 1961 and 1970 in accordance with a contract with the Museu Nacional do Rio de Janeiro and with the cooperation of the Fundação Nacional do Índio. The present paper was written under the auspices of the Summer Institute of Linguistics at a field workshop held in 1970 at Cuiabá, Mato Grosso, Brazil, under the direction of Joseph E. Grimes.

A concordance of 21,960 morphemes taken from Nambiquara texts was used in the analysis done for this paper. The concordance was prepared at the University of Oklahoma Computer Laboratory under the Project for Computer Support for Linguistic Field Research, partially supported by National Science Foundation Grant GS-1605.

relative ordering of events in relation to time as follows. [2] SIMULTA-
NEOUS: $x\tilde{a}u^3xain^1t\varrho^3kxai^3lhu^2$ $a^2l\tilde{u}^1a^2$ $a^3li^3na^2h\tilde{e}^3ra^2$ (sleep-they-
while tapir left-past) 'While they were sleeping the tapir left'.
FOLLOWING: $x\tilde{i}^3yai^3nain^1nu^2la^2$ $ai^3ain^1na^2h\tilde{e}^3ra^2$ (eat-they-after
hunt-they-past) 'After they had eaten they went hunting'. PUNC-
TILIAR: $xw\tilde{a}^3ain^1t\tilde{a}u^3$ $ya^2na^1la^2$ $\tilde{i}^2ain^1na^2h\tilde{e}^3ra^2$ (arrive-they-when
jaguar see-they-past) 'Upon arriving they saw the jaguar'.

Other linkages indicate logical relationships. CAUSE AND EFFECT:
$x\tilde{u}h^3w\varrho^3ai^1nha^2kxai^3$ $k\tilde{a}^3txa^2$ $x\tilde{i}^3yai^3nain^1tu^1wa^2$ (plant-they-
because later eat-they-future) 'Because they planted, later they will
eat'. CONTRARY TO FACT CONDITIONAL: $x\tilde{i}^3xi^2ke^3la^3te^2kxai^3$
$x\tilde{i}^3yai^3nh\tilde{i}^3na^1wa^2$ $xy\tilde{a}n^1ta^1$ $x\tilde{i}^3xi^2xna^3wa^2$ (come-if eat-would-I
but come-not) 'If he would come I would eat; but he hasn't come'.

Still another type of linkage adds aspects of modal logic in a
similar manner to those listed above. SUPPOSITION: $x\tilde{i}^3xi^2na^3na^1$
$h\tilde{a}x^2xw\tilde{a}^3txa^3nu^2$ $xwa^3na^1tu^1wa^2$ (come-supposition later go-I-
future) 'If he comes (as supposed), later I will go'. INTENTION:
$wa^3ko^3na^1kx\tilde{a}i^2n\tilde{a}n^2tu^3$ yen^3kxa^2 $so^1kxi^3na^1tu^1wa^2$ (work-I-
intention things earn-I-future) 'If I work (as intended), I will earn
things'.

In all of these examples the linkage is attached to the verb in
place of the tense element that occurs in the verb of all independent
clauses. Independent verbs always occur in the final clause of a
sentence, and dependent verbs in the non-final clauses. Only the

---

[2] The phonemes of Nambiquara are p, t, k, d (implosive alveolar stop), x
(glottal stop), j (alveopalatal affricate), n (with six allophones: [m] after nasalized
vowel glide $\tilde{a}u$, [bm] after oral vowel glide au, [gŋ] preceding a velar stop and
following an oral vowel, [ŋ] preceding a velar stop and following a nasalized
vowel, [dn] on all other occasions following oral vowels, and [n] on all other
occasions following nasalized vowels), N (voiceless nasal), r (only in the final
syllable of the independent verb), l ([ř] after front vowels, [l] after all other
vowels), s, h, w, y. Vowels occur in oral and nasalized series (written with tilde
$\tilde{v}$): i, e, a, o, u, and two vowel glides ai and au. Both series of vowels also occur
laryngealized, indicated by a hook γ under the vowel letter. There are three
tones in Nambiquara indicated by raised numbers [1] [2] [3] at the end of every
syllable. [1] is a downglide, [2] is an upglide, and [3] is a low level tone. See Barbara
Kroeker, "Morphophonemics of Nambiquara" (1972) and Lowe, "Sememic
Matrices ... from Nambiquara" (1972) for further details of linguistic form.

verb to which the linkage is attached and the following independent verb are involved in the relationship implied by the linkage. The persons of the verb are suffixed to the independent verb after the stem and before the tense element, or before the linkage element in the case of the dependent verb, to indicate the subject. A pro-verb may be substituted for the dependent verb.

A sentence linkage may also be an inflected free form (i.e. un-attached to verbs) between two independent clauses. The reference in such cases is not limited to the immediately preceding clause. It could refer to several closely related clauses. $xĩ^3yai^3nain^1na^2hẽ^3ra^2$ $ain^1nu^2la^2$ $ai^3ain^1na^2hẽ^3ra^2$ (eat-they-past they-after hunt-they-past) 'They ate. Afterward they went hunting'.

Paragraph linkage, on the other hand, indicates a change of focus either from one actor to another or from one type of activity to another (for example, a change from an action by an actor to an act of speech by the same actor). $a^2lũ^1ai^2li^2$ $an^3nu^2la^2$ $xwã^3sxã^3$ $e^3sĩn^1na^2hẽ^3ra^2$ $xna^2ha^1te^1$ $xã^3yo^3li^3kix^3tu^1wi^1$ (tapir-that kill-after arriving told-us-past then eat-we-future-quote) 'After killing the tapir he arrived and told us. Then, "Let's go there and eat it"', (we said)'.

On a higher level still is found linkage for theme, which is the major concern of this paper.

THEMATIC LINKAGE

Each narrative has at least one theme. The entire narrative can be considered to have an underlying structure which is representable by a tree. The narrative has a GLOBAL theme, and subtrees within it can have LOCAL themes of their own. Each subtree can be further broken down into subtrees which are actually paragraphs.

$-jut^3$ is the base form of the main thematic link. It occurs with up to three orders of prefixes and up to four orders of suffixes. The central meaning of $-jut^3$ is theme reference. Delimiting factors are supplied by the affixes.

PREFIXES

From the stem $-jut^3$ outward the following prefixes occur.

Person

There are two series of person markers corresponding to subject and object. These are identical in form to the obligatory verb person suffixes. They provide identification with a previously mentioned event. If, for example, the previous event was focusing on a first person theme, $-jut^3$ would always occur with the first person marker when referring to that theme.

Normally the subject series occurs. If, however, an object pronoun is used to refer to the theme in the verb immediately preceding an occurrence of $-jut^3$, the person marker prefixed to $-jut^3$ will reflect it: $h\tilde{a}i^1xn^3ti^3x\tilde{a}^1$ $ya^2lun^1txi^3$ $hxan^3ki^2\text{SA}^3na^2h\tilde{e}^3ra^2$ $j\tilde{a}^1xne^3\text{SA}^2ju^3kxai^3lhu^2$ ... (all dying disappeared-from-ME-object-past again-thus-ME-object-theme ...) 'Every one, dying, disappeared from me. Again thus with me, my situation ...'

Subject person markers are first singular na^1-, second singular $n\tilde{\imath}n^1$-, third singular zero. Plurals are prefixed to the corresponding singular forms. The first plural is $s\tilde{\imath}n^1$-, second plural lxi^3-, third person plural ain^1-; there is also a second dual yah^3-. Object person markers are first singular sa^3-, second singular xna^2-, third person zero. The plurals immediately follow the corresponding singular object forms. The first plural is $s\tilde{\imath}n^1$-, second plural lxi^3-, third person plural ain^1-, as with the subject markers; but there is no second person dual.

In an autobiographical text by one of my informants we have the following examples, which are cited in reverse sequence from the order in which they occur in the text. Each of these sentences refers to the local theme, which is enunciated at the beginning of Sentence 3 and repeated in the same sentence. They are the only ones in that part of the text in which a first person $-jut^3$ is found. Therefore we conclude that each occurrence of $-jut^3$ refers back to the local theme of 'my early past'.

Sentence 14. $j\tilde{a}^1xne^3na^1ju^3kai^3la^1$ $txa^2si^3ton^1yau^3xna^1hi^1nu^1$-$tai^2kxai^3la^1$ $kox^3nha^2tet^2tx\tilde{a}^3wa^2$ (Again-I-theme my-past-child-dwelt-when-remote-past know-not-I) 'Again this my theme, about the time when I was a child I don't know first hand'.

Sentence 11. $j\tilde{a}^1xne^3na^1jut^3su^2$ $\tilde{a}in^2txi^3sa^2hxai^2h\tilde{e}^1ra^2$ (Again-I-theme sad-me-past-tense) 'Again this my theme, I was sad'.

Sentence 9. $j\tilde{a}^1xne^3na^1ju^3kai^3la^1$ $kat^3ja^3la^2$ $xw\tilde{a}^2\tilde{a}n^3tsi^3xwe^3$ $yah^3lxi^1nhi^1ni^2$ xne^2 $\tilde{a}^2nu^2la^3$ $x\tilde{\imath}^3ton^3sx\tilde{a}^3$ $ya^3lu^2x\tilde{a}n^3tsi^3xwe^3$-$san^3t\tilde{a}^1$ $xne^3hxai^2na^1h\tilde{e}^1ra^2$ (Again-I-theme whiteman arrive-begin-you pl. thus people sickened died-began-deduction thus-it-always-was) 'Again this my theme, when you white men began to come, thus the people began to sicken and die'.

Sentence 3. $txa^2si^3kx\tilde{a}^3xna^3u^1thi^3n\tilde{a}n^2tu^3$ $k\tilde{a}x^3nh\tilde{\imath}^1nu^1tai^3n\tilde{a}n^2$-$tu^3$ $txa^2si^3don^1xyau^3na^1t\tilde{a}u^3u^1tai^2n\tilde{a}n^2tu^3$ $x\tilde{\imath}h^1te^2sa^1wa^2$ (My-past-time-remote long-ago-remote my-past-childhood-long-ago was-I-know) 'My early past, long ago, my childhood days were thus, I know'.

In the same section of text we have $-jut^3$ occurring with third person in one instance. The theme in this case is a third person referent, the story itself. And the only reference made to it is in Sentence 12. As shown in the example, reference goes back to where the third person theme is introduced at the beginning of the text:

Sentence 12. $j\tilde{a}^1xne^3jut^3su^2$ $x\tilde{\imath}^3ye^3a^1tu^1wa^2$ (Again-theme speak-I-future) 'Again this theme, I will speak'.

Sentences 1 and 2. $x\tilde{\imath}^3ye^3a^1tu^1wa^2$. $ain^3ki^2sa^2h\tilde{e}^1ra^2$. (Speak-I-future. Listen-me-imperative.) 'I will speak. Listen to me'.

Pro-verbs

The pro-verb xne^3- 'thus' provides additional reference to the previously mentioned theme. It always occurs immediately preceding the person marker: $ja^1xne^3na^1jut^3su^2$ (Again-thus-I-theme) 'Again thus my theme'. Pro-verb in this paper is used in much the same way that the verb *do* is used in English, as in *I like ice cream*, *don't you?* It differs from other verbs in that it cannot have the prefixes found on verbs.

Occurrences of other verb stems with -jut^3 are very infrequent. Since -jut^3 refers to a theme, it is rarely possible to insert a verb stem in this position. An example where this does occur is xne^3-$sa^2jut^3su^2$ $a^3ye^3a^1jut^3su^2$ ... (Thus-me-theme see-I-theme ...) 'The event being thus, I seeing the event ...' In this case the narrator is giving the proof of his story by emphasizing that he had seen it.

Repetition

The repetition indicator $j\tilde{a}^1$- occurs in the third position before -jut^3. It refers back to an event that is part of a theme already mentioned. This reminds the hearer that the event is in progress. $j\tilde{a}^1$- informs the hearer that the event it goes with is the same as one already given, not a different event of the same kind. $x\tilde{i}^3yai^3$-$na^1h\tilde{e}^3ra^2$ $j\tilde{a}^1xne^3jut^3su^2$ $x\tilde{i}^3yai^3na^1h\tilde{e}^3ra^2$ (Eat-I-past again-theme eat-I-past) 'I ate, again referring to that previous occasion, I ate'. $x\tilde{i}^3yai^3na^1h\tilde{e}^3ra^2$ $xne^3jut^3su^2$ $x\tilde{i}^3yai^3na^1h\tilde{e}^3ra^2$ (Eat-I-past thus-theme eat-I-past) 'I ate. Thus referring to that previous occasion, I ate'. In the first example $j\tilde{a}^3$- indicates that it is the same action in both verbs. In the second example, however, eating occurred on two occasions. The first instance where $j\tilde{a}^1$- does not occur in the text mentioned comes in Sentence 23; the speaker up to there is discussing a single situation using many linked sentences to do it. In 23, however, we find only $na^1jut^3kxai^3la^1$ (I-theme-nominal). Following this form the narrator tells a specific incident relating to the continuing theme of the narrator's past. By omitting $j\tilde{a}^1$- he makes a fresh start and gives new information though the new incident is by no means unrelated to the situation already described.

Prefixes thus inform the listener as to the person of the theme and as to how the action is progressing.

SUFFIXES

From the stem outward the following suffixes occur.

$-n\tilde{u}^3$ follows $-jut^3$ directly. It signifies an addition to present information similar to the English *also*. $j\tilde{a}^1xna^1jut^3t\tilde{u}^3kxai^3la^1$ (again-thus-I-theme-also-nominal) 'also I on the same theme'.

$-ai^2$ is in the second position following $-jut^3$. It refers to remote past time, setting the theme into the past and emphasizing the earliest aspects of the theme. $jut^1tai^2kxai^3lhu^2$ (theme-past-nominal) 'about that time earlier in time'.

$-kxai^3lhu^2$ and $-su^2$ are endings of the third position after $-jut^3$. They are normally found on nouns as stem formatives as in sxi^2su^2 'house' and $in^3txa^2kxai^3lhu^2$ 'man'. They imply that a subtree in the development of the theme may be terminated with the next sentence, which is normally a summarizer.

$-la^1$ is also in the third position after $-jut^3$, and therefore mutually exclusive with $-kxai^3lhu^2$ and $-su^2$. It indicates that there is more to come on the same theme.

$-ta^3la^3$ is a negative when it occurs on nouns. Its use here, however, is limited to occurrences correlative with an immediately following connective form $na^2ha^2kxai^3$ which together have the literal meaning 'not, therefore then'. Idiomatically it signifies the completion of one theme and presupposes a new theme immediately following. It does not cooccur with other suffixes.

GLOBAL VS. LOCAL THEMES

One can think of narrative themes as being global or local in scope. A global theme is the overall theme for the entire narrative. Local themes are those which are in force for only a part of the narrative before giving way to a new local theme or returning to the global theme. The global theme constitutes the hierarchical framework of the narrative in its entirety, and subtrees within it join to make up the substructure of the narrative.

Frequently the global theme of the narrative is given in one of the first two sentences. A subsection of the narrative tree, however, may also be introduced immediately afterwards with its own local theme. It is usually accompanied by a temporal setting and a possible locational setting. These settings occur as free temporal phrases or free locative phrases elsewhere in the theme sentence.

The theme of this subtree remains in force as long as a single temporal or logical sequence is being followed. When, however, a break occurs, the narrator must inform his listener as to which theme he will be talking about and as to which theme he has been talking about in the immediate context.

Continuation of the same sequence is signalled by means of $-la^1$ as previously described. When $-la^1$ is not used the preceding local theme is taken as summarized by the event just narrated. A frequent occurrence of this is found when the narrator gives his own reactions to events as a logical sequel to them in the development of the theme. $xne^3jut^3su^2$ $\tilde{a}in^2txi^3sa^2hxai^2h\tilde{e}^1ra^2$ (Thus-theme-referent sad-me-past) 'The situation being like that, I was sad'.

A theme may continue on with several occurrences of $-la^1$. There is no apparent limit on the number of times $-la^1$ may occur; but something new is added to the story after every occurrence. A sequence thus expands the theme by giving more details in the second telling. In such a case, ja^1xne^2- signals that it is a retelling of the same sequence. However, reference back to the narrative theme by means of $-jut^3$ can be made only at the end of the telling of an event. Thematic links pointing to a different theme, either global or local, are signaled by the person markers (unambiguously marked only if one is third person and the other first person), and in the repetition of the verb that was used to introduce the theme in its first occurrence.

The theme of a new subtree is introduced only after the old subtree has been closed off by $jut^1ta^3la^3$ 'event referent, negative'. When this has been signaled a new local theme will be developed in the same manner as the first one was.

Once all local themes have been discussed, $-jut^3$ is not required to refer back to previous themes in a final summary. A specific time reference of identical form to the one used for the introduction of a theme is all that is required.

BIBLIOGRAPHY

Works that have resulted from the Cross-Language Study of Discourse Structures project are indicated with an asterisk * after the reference. Those cited here as manuscripts are in the process of publication; those that are further tagged with *POD* are to appear in a report tentatively entitled *Papers on Discourse*.

Allen, Janice D.
1972 "Relationships between Sentence and Discourse in Halia", *Pacific Linguistics* series A, 31.*
Allen, Jerry
ms. "Tense/aspect and Conjunctions in Halia Narratives", to appear in *Oceanic Linguistics.**
Allen, Layman E., Peter Kugel, and Joan Ross
1970 *Queries 'n Theories: The Science and Language Game* (New Haven: Wff 'N Proof Publications).
Aristotle
1954 *Rhetoric*, ed. by Friedrich Solmsen (New York: Modern Library).
Arndt, William F., and F. Wilbur Gingrich, trans.
1957 *A Greek-English Lexicon of the New Testament and Other Christian Literature*, by Walter Bauer, 4th revised and augmented edition (Chicago: University of Chicago Press).
Arnold, Bradford Henry
1962 *Intuitive Concepts in Elementary Topology* (Englewood Cliffs: Prentice-Hall).
Ashley, Seymour
ms. "A Case Classification of Tausug Verbs", to appear in *Anthropological Linguistics.**
Auchincloss, Louis
1949 *The Injustice Collectors* (New York: New American Library).
Austin, J. L.
1962 *How to Do Things With Words*, ed. by J. O. Urmson (New York: Oxford University Press).
Austin, Virginia Morey
1966 *Attention, Emphasis and Focus in Ata Manobo* (= *Hartford Publications*

in Linguistics 20) (Hartford: Hartford Seminary Foundation).

Austing, John
ms.   "Semantic Relationships in Omie", to appear in *Language Data*.*

Austing, June
ms.   "Omie Discourse".*

Bach, Emmon
1964   *An Introduction to Transformational Grammars* (New York: Holt, Rinehart and Winston).
1968   "Nouns and Noun Phrases", in *Universals in Linguistic Theory*, ed. by Emmon Bach and Robert T. Harms (New York: Holt, Rinehart and Winston), 91-124.

Ballard, D. Lee, Robert J. Conrad, and Robert E. Longacre
1971   "The Deep and Surface Grammar of Interclausal Relations", *Foundations of Language* 7(1), 70-118.
1971   "More on the Deep and Surface Grammar of Interclausal Relations", *Language Data*, Asian-Pacific series, 1.

Barnard, Myra L., and Robert E. Longacre
1968   "Lexicon Versus Grammar in Dibabawon Procedural Narrative Discourse", in Longacre (1968), 194-222.

Barnett, Lincoln
1957   *The Universe and Dr. Einstein*, revised (New York: New American Library).

Barr, James
1961   *The Semantics of Biblical Language* (Oxford: Clarendon Press).

Bearth, Ilse
ms.   "Discourse Patterns in Toura Folk Tales", *POD*.*

Bearth, Thomas
1969   "Phrase et Discours en Toura", *Cahiers Ferdinand de Saussure* 25, 29-45.
ms.   "La Structure d'Information en Toura".*

Becker, A. L.
1965   "A Tagmemic Approach to Paragraph Analysis", *College Composition and Communication* 16(5), 237-42. Reprinted in *NCTE* 1966, 33-38.

Beekman, John
1970   "Propositions and Their Relations Within a Discourse", *Notes on Translation* 37, 6-23.

Bellman, Richard
1956   "The Theory of Dynamic Programming", *Modern Mathematics for the Engineer*, ed. by Edwin F. Beckenbach (New York: McGraw Hill), 243-78.
1957   *Dynamic Programming* (Princeton: Princeton University Press).

Bellman, Richard, and Stuart E. Dreyfus
1962   *Applied Dynamic Programming* (Princeton: Princeton University Press).

Benveniste, Émile
1966   *Problèmes de Linguistique Générale* (Paris).

Bierwisch, Manfred
1967   "Some Semantic Universals of German Adjectivals", *Foundations of Language* 3, 1-36.

Bishop, Ruth, Ella Marie Button, Aileen Reid, and Robert E. Longacre
1968   *Totonac: From Clause to Discourse* (= *Summer Institute of Linguistics Publications in Linguistics* 17) (Norman: Summer Institute of Linguistics and University of Oklahoma).

Black, Max
1968   *The Labyrinth of Language* (London: Pall Mall).

Bloomfield, Leonard
1933   *Language* (New York: Henry Holt).

Bock, Philip K.
1962   "The Social Structure of a Canadian Indian Reserve", Harvard University Ph.D. dissertation.

Böckh, Augustus
1968   *On Interpretation and Criticism*, ed. and translated by John Paul Pritchard (Norman: University of Oklahoma Press), from *Encyclopädie und Methodologie der philologischen Wissenschaften* (Berlin: B. G. Teubner, 1886, 2nd ed.).

Bolinger, Dwight L.
1968   *Aspects of Language* (New York: Harcourt, Brace, and World).
1972   "Accent is Predictable (If You're a Mind-reader)", *Language* 48(3), 633-44.

Borgman, Donald M.
ms.   "Deep and Surface Case in Sanuma", to appear in *Linguistics*.*

Bradley, Virginia
1971   "Jibu Narrative Discourse Structure", *Anthropological Linguistics* 13(1), 1-15.*

Bridgeman, Loraine Irene
1966   *Oral Paragraphs in Kaiwá (Guaraní)*, Indiana University Ph.D. dissertation.

Briggs, Janet
ms.   "Ayoré Narrative Analysis".

Burton, E. D.
1920   *A Critical and Exegetical Commentary on the Epistle to the Galatians* (International Critical Commentary Series) (New York: Charles Scribner's Sons).

Butler, Nancy E.
ms.   "Verb Derivation in Terêna", to appear in *Language Data*.*

Callow, Kathleen
1970   "More on Propositions and Their Relations Within a Discourse", *Notes on Translation* 37, 23-27.

Carnap, Rudolf
1958   *Introduction to Symbolic Logic and its Applications* (New York: Dover Publications).

Carroll, Lewis [Charles L. Dodgson]
1872   *Through the Looking Glass*.

Chafe, Wallace L.
1967   "Language as Symbolization", *Language* 43, 57-91.
1968   "Idiomaticity as an Anomaly in the Chomskyan Paradigm", *Foundations of Language* 4, 109-27.

1970   *Meaning and the Structure of Language* (Chicago: The University of Chicago Press).

1970   *A Semantically Based Sketch of Onondaga* (= *Indiana University Publications in Anthropology and Linguistics*, memoir 25).

Chapin, Paul G.
1970   "Samoan Pronominalization", *Language* 46(2), 366-78.

Chase, J. Richard
1961   "The Classical Conception of Epideictic", Cornell University Ph.D. dissertation.

Chernoff, H., and L. E. Moses
1959   *Elementary Decision Theory* (New York: John Wiley).

Chomsky, Noam
1957   *Syntactic Structures* (= *Janua Linguarum*, series minor 4) (The Hague: Mouton).
1965   *Aspects of the Theory of Syntax* (Cambridge: The MIT Press).
1970   "Remarks on Nominalizations", in Jacobs and Rosenbaum (1970). Reprinted in Noam Chomsky, *Studies on Semantics in Generative Grammar* (= *Janua Linguarum*, series minor 107) (The Hague: Mouton, 1972).

Chomsky, Noam, and Morris Halle
1968   *The Sound Pattern of English* (New York: Holt, Rinehart and Winston).

Christensen, Francis
1963   "A Generative Rhetoric of the Sentence", *College Composition and Communication* 14(3), 155-61. Reprinted in *NCTE* 1966, 1-7.
1963   "Notes Toward a New Rhetoric", *College English* 25(1), 7-11, 12-18. Reprinted in *NCTE* 1966, 8-19.
1965   "A Generative Rhetoric of the Paragraph", *College Composition and Communication* 16(3), 144-56. Reprinted in *NCTE* 1966, 30-32.

Conklin, Harold C.
1955   "Hanunoo Color Categories", *Southwestern Journal of Anthropology* 11, 339-44.

Conrad, Joseph
1900   *Lord Jim* (= *Everyman's Library*, 925, 1935) (London: J. M. Dent).

Conybeare, William John, and J. S. Howson
1860   *The Life and Epistles of St. Paul*, 7th ed. (New York: Charles Scribner).

Cromack, Robert E.
1968   *Language Systems and Discourse Structure in Cashinawa* (= *Hartford Studies in Linguistics* 23) (Hartford: Hartford Seminary Foundation).

Crowell, Thomas H.
ms.   "Cohesion in Borôro Discourse", to appear in *Linguistics*.*

Davis, Donald R.
1973   "Wantoat Paragraph Structure", *Linguistics* 110.*

Dawson, Keith
ms.   "Remarks on Negation in Tépo Krou", to appear in *Language Data*.*

Dickens, Charles
A Christmas Carol.

Dik, Simon C.
  1968 *Coordination: Its Implications for the Theory of General Linguistics*
        (Amsterdam: North Holland).
Dixon, R.
  1971 "A Method of Semantic Description", in Steinberg and Jakobovits
        (1971), 436-71.
Draper, Marjorie
  ms.   "Underlying Case Structure in Northern Kankanay".*
DuBois, Carl
  1973 "Connectives in Sarangani Manobo Discourse", *Linguistics* 110.*
Dundes, Alan
  1962 "From Etic to Emic Units in the Structural Study of Folktales",
        Journal of American Folklore 75, 95-105.
  1963 "Structural Typology in North American Indian Folktales", *South-
        western Journal of Anthropology* 19, 121-30.
  1964 *The Morphology of North American Indian Folktales* (Helsinki).
Edersheim, Alfred
  1883 *The Life and Times of Jesus the Messiah* (New York: Anson D. F.
        Randolph).
Elkins, Richard E.
  1968 *English-Manobo Dictionary* (= *Oceanic Linguistics*, special publication
        3).
Elson, Benjamin F., and Velma Pickett
  1969 *Morphology and Syntax* (Santa Ana, California: Summer Institute of
        Linguistics).
Ennulat, Jürgen
  ms.   "Participant Categories in Fali Stories", *POD.*
Fasold, Ralph W.
  1970 "Two Models of Socially Significant Linguistic Variation", *Language*
        46(3), 551-63.
Fillmore, Charles J.
  1966 "Deictic Categories in the Semantics of 'Come'", *Foundations of
        Language* 2(3), 219-27.
  1968 "The Case for Case", in Bach and Harms (1968), 1-88.
  1968 "Lexical Entries for Verbs", *Foundations of Language* 4(4), 373-93.
  1969 "Types of Lexical Information", in Kiefer (1969), 109-37.
  1970 "The Grammar of Hitting and Breaking", in Jacobs and Rosenbaum
        (1970).
Fillmore, Charles J., and D. Terence Langendoen, eds.
  1971 *Studies in Linguistic Semantics* (New York: Holt, Rinehart and
        Winston).
Flik, Eva
  ms.   "Dan Tense-aspect and Discourse", *POD.*
Forster, Janette
  1964 "Dual Structure of Dibabawon Verbal Clauses", *Oceanic Linguistics*
        3, 26-48.
Forster, Janette, and M. L. Barnard
  1968 "A Classification of Dibabawon Active Verbs", *Lingua* 20, 265-78.

Frantz, Donald G.
1970 *Toward a Generative Grammar of Blackfoot*, University of Alberta Ph.D. dissertation, reissued in Summer Institute of Linguistics Publications in Linguistics.
Fries, Charles Carpenter
1952 *The Structure of English* (New York: Harcourt, Brace).
Fuller, Daniel P.
1959 *The Inductive Method of Bible Study*, 3rd ed. (Pasadena: Fuller Theological Seminary, mimeo).
Gieser, Richard
ms. "Kalinga Sequential Discourse".*
Gleason, H. A., Jr.
1968 "Contrastive Analysis in Discourse Structure", *Georgetown University Monograph Series on Languages and Linguistics* 21, 39-64.
Goodenough, Ward H.
1956 "Componential Analysis and the Study of Meaning", *Language* 32, 195-216.
Gratrix, Carol
ms. "Godié Narrative", *POD*.*
Grebe, Karl
ms. "Verb Clusters of Lamnsok Described by the Transition Network Grammar Model", *POD*.*
Griebach, Sheila A.
1969 "An Infinite Hierarchy of Context-free Languages", *Journal of the Association for Computing Machinery* 16(1), 91-106.
Grimes, Joseph E.
1963 "Measuring Naturalness", *The Bible Translator* 14, 49-62.
1963 Review of *The Semantics of Biblical Language* by James Barr, *American Anthropologist* 65, 1189-90.
1964 *Huichol Syntax* (= *Janua Linguarum*, series practica 11) (The Hague: Mouton).
1966 "Some Inter-sentence Relationships in Huichol", *Summa Antropológica en Homenaje a Roberto J. Weitlaner* (México, D. F.: Instituto Nacional de Antropología e Historia), 465-70.
1967 "Positional Analysis", *Language* 43, 437-44.
1968 "The Thread of Discourse", *ERIC* microfiche no. ED-019669.
1969 *Phonological Analysis* (Santa Ana: Summer Institute of Linguistics).
1971 "Kinds of Information in Discourse", *Kiving* 4(2), 64-74.*
1972 "Outlines and Overlays", *Language* 48(3), 513-24.*
1972 "Participant Orientation", *Philippine Journal of Linguistics*.*
Grimes, Joseph E., ed.
forthcoming *Papers on Discourse (POD)*.
Grimes, Joseph E., and Naomi Glock
1970 "A Saramaccan Narrative Pattern", *Language* 46(2), 408-25.
Gulstad, Daniel E.
1973 "A Generative Discourse Model", *Linguistics* 99, 5-70.

Gunter, Richard
1966 "On the Placement of Accent in Dialogue: A Feature of Context Grammar", *Journal of Linguistics* 2, 159-79.
Haas, W.
1957 "Zero in Linguistic Description", *Studies in Linguistic Analysis* by J. R. Firth et al. (Oxford: Basil Blackwell), 33-53.
Hajičová, Eva, J. Panevová, and Peter Sgall
1970 "Recursive Properties of Tense in Czech and English", *Prague Bulletin of Mathematical Linguistics* 13, 9-39.
Hale, Austin
1965 *Worksheets for a First Course in Transformational Syntax* (= Supplement to the 1965 Work Papers of the Summer Institute of Linguistics) (Grand Forks, North Dakota: University of North Dakota).
Hall, Jr., Robert A.
1972 "Why a Structural Semantics is Impossible", *Language Sciences* 21, 1-6.
Hall, William C.
1969 "A Classification of Siocon Subanon Verbs", *Anthropological Linguistics* 11(7), 209-15.
Halliday, M. A. K.
1967 *Intonation and Grammar in British English* (The Hague: Mouton).
1967 "Notes on Transitivity and Theme in English, Parts 1 and 2", *Journal of Linguistics* 3, 37-81, 199-244.
1968 "Notes on Transitivity and Theme in English, Part 3", *Journal of Linguistics* 4, 179-215.
Harris, Zellig S.
1952 "Discourse Analysis", *Language* 28, 1-30.
1952 "Discourse Analysis: A Sample Text", *Language* 28, 474-94.
1957 "Co-occurrence and Transformation in Linguistic Structure", *Language* 33(3), 283-340.
1963 *Discourse Analysis Reprints* (The Hague: Mouton).
Harrison, Michael A.
1965 *Introduction to Switching and Automata Theory* (New York: McGraw-Hill).
Hatcher, Anna Granville
1956 *Theme and Underlying Question: Two Studies of Spanish Word Order* (= *Word* monograph 3) (New York: Linguistic Circle of New York).
Herdan, Gustav
1956 "Chaucer's Authorship of the 'Equatorie of the Planetis'", *Language* 32, 254-59.
Hettick, Donna
ms. "Verb Stem Classes in Northern Kankanay".*
Hewer, Judy
ms. "Kasem Questions", *POD.**
Hewer, Philip L.
ms. "A Semantic Approach to Clause Clusters in Kasem", *POD.**

Hewitt, Carl
  1971 "Description and Theoretical Analysis (Using Schemata) of PLAN-NER: A Language for Proving Theorems and Manipulating Models in a Robot", MIT Ph.D. dissertation.
Hjelmslev, Louis
  1953 *Prolegomena to a Theory of Language*, tr. by Francis Whitfield (= *Indiana University Publications in Anthropology and Linguistics*, memoir 7).
Hockett, Charles F.
  1958 *A Course in Modern Linguistics* (New York: Macmillan).
Hofer, Verena
  ms. "Types et Sequences de Propositions en Wobé", *POD.**
Hohulin, Lou
  ms. "Complex Predicates in Keley-i Kallahan".*
Hohulin, Richard
  ms. "Cohesive Organization in Keley-i Kallahan".*
Hollenbach, Bruce
  1969 "A Method for Displaying Semantic Structure", *Notes on Translation* 31, 22-34.
Hooker, Betty
  ms. "Cohesion in Ivatan".*
Howard, Olive
  ms. "The Paragraph in Gagou (Gban) Narrative", *POD.**
Huisman, Roberta D.
  1973 "Angaataha Narrative Discourse", *Linguistics* 110.*
Huisman, Ronald D.
  1973 "Angaataha Verb Morphology", *Linguistics* 110.*
Hunt, Geoffrey
  ms. "Paragraphing, Identification, and Discourse Types in Hanga", *POD.**
Jacobs, Roderick, and Peter Rosenbaum
  1968 *English Transformational Grammar* (Waltham, Mass.: Blaisdell).
Jacobs, Roderick, and Peter Rosenbaum, eds.
  1970 *Readings in English Transformational Grammar* (Waltham, Mass.: Blaisdell).
Jakobson, Roman
  1957 *Shifters, Verbal Categories, and the Russian Verb* (Cambridge: Harvard University).
Jordan, Dean
  ms. "Tense-aspect in Nafaara", *POD.**
Katz, Jerrold J., and Jerry Fodor
  1963 "The Structure of a Semantic Theory", *Language* 39, 170-210.
Kelkar, Ashok R.
  1970 "Some Notes on Language and Literature", *Indian Linguistics* 31(3), 69-79.
Kemeny, John G.
  1969 "Facing Up to Large Systems", *Scientific Research* (January 6).

Kerr, Harland
1965 "The Case-marking and Classifying Function of Cotabato Manobo Voice Affixes", *Oceanic Linguistics* 4, 15-47.
Kiefer, Ferenc, ed.
1969 *Studies in Syntax and Semantics* (= *Foundations of Language* supplementary series, vol. 10) (Dordrecht: D. Reidel Publishing Company).
Kiparsky, Paul, and Carol Kiparsky
1971 "Fact", in Steinberg and Jakobovits, 345-69.
Kroeker, Barbara J.
1972 "Morphophonemics of Nambiquara", *Anthropological Linguistics* 14(1), 19-22.*
Kroeker, Menno H.
1974 "Thematic Linkage in Nambiquara Narrative", Appendix of this book.*
Krüsi, Peter
ms. "Mumuye Discourse Structure", *POD*.*
Labov, William
1969 "Contraction, Deletion, and Inherent Variability of the English Copula", *Language* 45, 715-62.
Labov, William, and Joshua Waletzky
1967 "Narrative Analysis: Oral Versions of Personal Experience", *Essays on the Verbal and Visual Arts*, ed. by June Helm (Seattle: University of Washington Press).
Lakoff, George
1965 "On the Nature of Syntactic Irregularity" (= Report NSF-16) (Cambridge: Harvard Computational Laboratory), reissued as *Irregularity in Syntax* (New York: Holt, Rinehart & Winston, 1970).
1970 "Counterparts, or the problem of Reference in Transformational Grammar", (= Report NSF-16) (Cambridge: Harvard Computational Laboratory).
ms. "Pronouns and Reference".
ms. "Structural Complexity in Fairy Tales".
Lamb, Sydney M.
1966 *Outline of Stratificational Grammar* (Washington, D.C.: Georgetown University Press).
Landerman, Peter, and Donald Frantz
1972 *Notes on Grammatical Theory* (Lima, Perú: Summer Institute of Linguistics and Ministry of Education).
Langacker, Ronald
1969 "On Pronominalization and the Chain of Command", in *Modern Studies in English*, ed. by D. Reibel and S. Schane (Englewood Cliffs: Prentice-Hall), 160-86.
Langendoen, D. Terence
1969 *The Study of Syntax* (New York: Holt, Rinehart and Winston).
1970 *Essentials of English Grammar* (New York: Holt, Rinehart and Winston).
Larson, Virginia
ms. "Pronominal Reference in the Ivatan Narrative".*

Lawrence, Helen
1972 "Viewpoint and Location in Oksapmin", *Anthropological Linguistics.**
Lawrence, Marshall
1972 "Oksapmin Sentence Structure", *Pacific Linguistics* series A, 31.*
Leenhouts, Inge
ms. "Overlay in Loron Discourse", *POD.**
Lewin, Kurt
1936 *Principles of Topological Psychology*, trans. by Fritz Heider and Grace M. Heider (New York: McGraw-Hill).
Lewis, Clive Staples
1938 *Out of the Silent Planet* (London: The Bodley Head).
1955 *The Magician's Nephew* (London: The Bodley Head).
Lewis, Ronald K.
1972 "Sanio-Hiowe Paragraph Structure", *Pacific Linguistics* series A, 31.*
Lightfoot, J. B.
1892 *Commentary on St. Paul's Epistle to the Galatians* (London: Macmillan).
Link, Christa
ms. "Units in Wobé Discourse", *POD.**
Lipschutz, Seymour
1965 *Outline of Theory and Problems of General Topology* (New York: Schaum Publishing Co.).
Litteral, Robert
1969 *A Programmed Course in New Guinea Pidgin* (Marrickville, N.S.W.: Jacaranda Press Pty. Ltd.).
1972 "Rhetorical Predicates and Time Topology in Anggor", *Foundations of Language* 8(3), 391-410.*
Litteral, Shirley
1972 "Orientation to Space and Participants in Anggor", *Pacific Linguistics* series A, 31.*
Longacre, Robert E.
1964 *Grammar Discovery Procedures* (The Hague: Mouton).
1968 *Discourse, Paragraph, and Sentence Structure in Selected Philippine Languages*, vol. 1 (Santa Ana: Summer Institute of Linguistics).
1970 "Sentence Structure as a Statement Calculus", *Language* 46(4), 783-815.
1972 *Hierarchy and Universality of Discourse Constituents in New Guinea Languages*, 2 vols. (Washington, D.C.: Georgetown University Press).
Loos, Eugene
1963 "Capanahua Narration Structure", *Texas Studies in Literature and Language* 4, supplement 697-742.
Loriot, James, and Barbara Hollenbach
1970 "Shipibo Paragraph Structure", *Foundations of Language* 6(1), 43-66.
Lounsbury, Floyd G.
1956 "A Semantic Analysis of the Pawnee Kinship Usage", *Language* 32, 158-94.

Lowe, Ivan
1969 "An Algebraic Theory of English Pronominal Reference", *Semiotica* 1(2), 397–421.
1969 "On the Relation of Formal Sememic Matrices with Illustrations from Nambiquara", *Foundations of Language* 8(3), 360-90.
Lyons, John
1966 "Towards a 'Notional' Theory of the 'Parts of Speech'", *Journal of Linguistics* 2, 209-36.
1968 *Introduction to Theoretical Linguistics* (Cambridge: Cambridge University Press).
Macqueen, J.
1957 "A Note on Reprise Construction in Welsh", *Archivum Linguisticum* 9(1), 62-66.
Mansen, Richard
ms. "Guajiro Narrative Discourse".*
Marchese, Lynell
ms. "Time Reference in Godié", *POD.*
Marriott, Alice
1945 *The Ten Grandmothers* (Norman: University of Oklahoma Press).
Martinet, André
1965 *La Linguistique Synchronique* (Paris).
McCalla, Gordon I., and Jeffrey R. Sampson
1972 "MUSE: A Model to Understand Simple English", *Communications of the Association for Computing Machinery* 15(1), 29-40.
McCarthy, John
1960 "Recursive Functions of Symbolic Expressions and their Computation by Machine", *Communications of the Association for Computing Machinery* 3, 184-95.
McCarthy, John, Paul W. Abrahams, Daniel J. Edwards, Timothy P. Hart, and Michael I. Levin
1962 *LISP 1.5 Programmer's Manual* (Cambridge: The MIT Press).
McCarthy, Joy
1965 "Clause Chaining in Kanite", *Anthropological Linguistics* 7(5), 59-70.
McCawley, James D.
1970 "Where Do Noun Phrases Come From?", in Jacobs and Rosenbaum (1970). Rewritten and published under the same title in Steinberg and Jakobovits (1971), 217-31.
McGuire, Martin R. P.
1964 *Introduction to Medieval Latin Studies* (Washington, D.C.: Catholic University of America Press).
McKinney, Norris P.
ms. "Participant Identification in Kaje Narrative", *POD.*
McLeod, Ruth
ms. "Paragraph, Aspect, and Participant in Xavánte", to appear in *Linguistics.*
Mendelson, Bert
1963 *Introduction to Topology* (London: Blackie and Son. Also Boston: Allyn and Bacon, 1968).

Meredith, Robert C., and John D. Fitzgerald
1963 *The Professional Storywriter and his Art* (New York: Crowell).
Meyer, Bonnie J. F.
1971 "Idea Units Recalled from Prose in Relation to Their Position in the Logical Structure, Importance, Stability, and Order in the Passage", Cornell University M.Sc. thesis.
Miller, Helen
1973 "Thematization in Mamanwa", *Linguistics* 110.*
Miller, Jeanne
1973 "Semantic Structure of Mamanwa Verbs", *Linguistics* 110.*
Moravcsik, Edith A.
1971 "Some Cross-Linguistic Generalizations About Yes-No Questions and Their Answers", *Stanford Language Universals Project Working Papers* 7, 45-193.
National Council of Teachers of English (NCTE)
1966 *The Sentence and the Paragraph: Articles on Rhetorical Analysis from College Composition and Communication and College English* (Champaign, Ill.: NCTE).
Newman, Bonnie
ms. "The Longuda Verb", *POD.*
Newman, John
ms. "Participant Orientation in Longuda Folk Tales", *POD.*
Nida, Eugene A.
1964 *Toward a Science of Translation* (Leiden: E. J. Brill).
Osgood, Charles E., George J. Suci, and P. H. Tannenbaum
1957 *The Measurement of Meaning* (Urbana: University of Illinois Press).
Perrin, Mona
ms. "Direct and Indirect Speech in Mambila".*
ms. "Who's Who in Mambila Folk Stories", *POD.*
Pike, Kenneth L.
1954 *Language in Relation to a Unified Theory of the Structure of Human Behavior*, Part 1 (Glendale, Calif.: Summer Institute of Linguistics). Second edition 1967 (The Hague: Mouton).
1964 "Discourse Structures and Tagmemic Matrices", *Oceanic Linguistics* 3, 5-25.
1966 "A Guide to Publications Related to Tagmemic Theory", in Sebeok (1966), 365-94.
1966 *Tagmemic and Matrix Linguistics Applied to Selected African Languages* (= Final Report, Contract no. OE-5-14-065) (U.S. Department of Health, Education, and Welfare, Office of Education, Bureau of Research).
Pike, Kenneth L., and Ivan Lowe
1969 "Pronominal Reference in English Conversation and Discourse — A Group Theoretical Treatment", *Folia Linguistica* 3, 68-106.
Popovich, Harold
1967 "Large Grammatical Units and the Space-time Setting in Maxakalí", *Atas do Simpósio Sobre a Biôta Amazónica* 2, 195-99.

Port, Robert
   ms.   "Focus and Participant Roles in Swahili".

Postal, Paul M.
   1964   *Constituent Structure: A Study of Contemporary Models of Syntactic Description* (= *Indiana University Research Center in Anthropology, Folklore, and Linguistics*, publication 30).
   1964   "Underlying and Superficial Linguistic Structures", *Harvard Educational Review* 34, 246-66.
   n.d.   "Problems in Linguistic Representation of Reference",

Powlison, Paul S.
   1969   "Yagua Mythology and its Epic Tendencies", Indiana University Ph.D. dissertation.

Price, Norman
   ms.   "Nchimburu Narrative", *POD.**

Propp, Vladimir
   1958   *Morphology of the Folktale* (= *Indiana University Research Center in Anthropology, Folklore, and Linguistics*, publication 10). Reissued (The Hague: Mouton).

Quillian, M. Ross
   1968   "Semantic Memory", in *Semantic Information Processing*, ed. by Marvin Minsky (Cambridge: The MIT Press), 227-70.
   1969   "The Teachable Language Comprehender: A Simulation Program and Theory of Language", *Communications of the Association for Computing Machinery* 12(8), 459-76.

Rhea, Mary
   ms.   "Remarks on Prefocus in Sarangani Bilaan", to appear in *Philippine Journal of Linguistics.**

Rich, Rolland
   ms.   "Tense and Discourse Particles in Arabela".*

Robinson, Dow F.
   1966   *Sierra Náhuat Word Structure* (= *Hartford Studies in Linguistics* 18) (Hartford: Hartford Seminary Foundation).
   1968   *Manual for Bilingual Dictionaries* (Santa Ana: Summer Institute of Linguistics).

Rodgers, Paul C., Jr.
   1966   "Contribution to Symposium on the Paragraph", *College Composition and Communication* 17(2), 72-80. Reprinted in *NCTE* 1966, 61-69.

Rogers, Carl R.
   1951   *Client-centered Therapy: Its Practice, Implications, and Theory* (Boston: Houghton Mifflin).

Rosenbaum, Peter S.
   1967   *The Grammar of English Predicate Complement Constructions* (Cambridge: The MIT Press).

Ross, John R.
   1970   "On Declarative Sentences", in Jacobs and Rosenbaum (1970), 222-72.

Rossbottom, Harry
1961 "Different-level Tense Markers in Guaraní", *International Journal of American Linguistics* 27, 345-52.

Rowan, Orland
1972 "Some Features of Paressí Discourse Structure", *Anthropological Linguistics* 14(4), 131-46.*

Salton, Gerard
1968 *Automatic Information Organization and Retrieval* (New York: McGraw-Hill).
1971 *The SMART Retrieval System: Experiments in Automatic Document Processing* (Englewood Cliffs: Prentice-Hall).

Samarin, William J.
1971 "Evolution in Glossolalic Private Language", *Anthropological Linguistics* 13(2), 55-67.

Sanders, Gerald A.
1970 "On the Natural Domain of Grammar", *Linguistics* 63, 51-123.

Šaumjan, S. K.
1965 "Outline of the Applicational Generative Model for the Description of Language", *Foundations of Language* 1(3), 189-222.
1971 *Principles of Structural Linguistics* (= *Janua Linguarum*, series maior 45) (The Hague: Mouton).

Sawyer, Louise
ms. "Aspect in Amganad Ifugao", to appear in *Anthropological Linguistics*.*

Schaefer, Nancy
ms. "Gurenne Clause Structure", *POD*.*

Schank, Roger C., N. Goldman, and C. J. Rieger
1972 *Primitive Concepts Underlying Verbs of Thought* (= National Technical Information Service microfiche AD-744 634) (Stanford: Department of Computer Science).

Searle, John
1969 *Speech Acts* (London: Cambridge University Press).

Sebeok, Thomas A., ed.
1966 *Current Trends in Linguistics* 3, *Theoretical Foundations* (The Hague: Mouton).

Sgall, Petr, and Eva Hajičová
1970 "A 'Functional' Generative Description (Background and Framework)", *Prague Bulletin of Mathematical Linguistics* 14, 3-38.

Sheffler, E. Margaret
ms. "Mundurukú Discourse".

Simmons, Robert F., and J. Slocum
1972 "Generating English Discourse from Semantic Networks", *Communications of the Association for Computing Machinery* 15(10), 891-905.

Steinberg, Danny D., and Leon A. Jakobovits
1971 *Semantics: An Interdisciplinary Reader in Philosophy, Linguistics and Psychology* (Cambridge: Cambridge University Press).

Stennes, Leslie
 1969 *Participant Identification in Adamawa Fulani* (= *Hartford Studies in Linguistics* 24) (Hartford: Hartford Seminary Foundation).
Stockwell, Robert P., Paul Schachter, and Barbara Hall Partee
 1968 *Integration of Transformational Theories of English Syntax* (= U.S. Air Force Contract no. 19(628)-6007, Command Systems Division, Electronic Systems Division, Air Force Systems Command).
Stout, Mickey, and Ruth Thomson
 1971 "Kayapó Narrative", *International Journal of American Linguistics* 37(4), 250-56.*
Strange, David
 1973 "Indicative and Subjunctive in Upper Asaro", *Linguistics* 110.*
Sussman, Gerald, and Terry Winograd
 1970 *Micro-Planner Reference Manual* (= AI Memo 203, Project MAC) (Cambridge: MIT).
Taber, Charles R.
 1966 *The Structure of Sango Narrative* (= *Hartford Studies in Linguistics* 17) (Hartford: Hartford Seminary Foundation).
Tax, Sol
 1960 "Aboriginal Languages of Latin America", *Current Anthropology* 1(5-6), 431-36.
Taylor, John
 1970 "A Propositional Analysis of the Book of Jude", *Notes on Translation*.
Thomas, David
 1955 "Three Analyses of the Ilocano Pronoun System", *Word* 11, 204-08.
Thompson, Sandra Annear
 1971 "The Deep Structure of Relative Clauses", in Fillmore and Langendoen (1971), 79-94.
Thurman, Robert C.
 ms. "Chuave Medial Verbs".*
Ure, Jean
 1971 "Lexical Density and Register Differentiation", in *Applications of Linguistics: Selected Papers of the Second International Congress of Applied Linguistics, Cambridge 1969*, ed. by G. E. Perren and J. L. M. Trim (Cambridge: Cambridge University Press), 443-52.
Wallace, Anthony F. C., and John Atkins
 1960 "The Meaning of Kinship Terms", *American Anthropologist* 62(1), 58-80.
Wallis, Ethel E.
 1971 "Contrastive Plot Structures of the Four Gospels", *Notes on Translation* 40.
Watson, Richard
 1966 "Clause to Sentence Gradations in Pacoh", *Lingua* 16(2), 166-89.
Weinreich, Uriel
 1966 "Explorations in Semantic Theory", in Sebeok (1966), 395-477. Reprinted with a preface by William Labov (= *Janua Linguarum*, Series minor 89) (The Hague: Mouton, 1972).
 1966 "On the Semantic Structure of Language", in *Universals of Language*,

ed. by Joseph H. Greenberg (Cambridge: The MIT Press), 142-216.

Weizenbaum, Joseph
1967   "Contextual Understanding by Computers", *Communications of the Association for Computing Machinery* 10(8), 474-80. Reprinted in Young, Becker, and Pike (1970), 330-44.

West, Anne
1973   "The Semantics of Focus in Amganad Ifugao", *Linguistics* 110.*

Wheatley, James
ms.   "Pronouns and Nominal Elements in Bacairí Discourse", to appear in *Linguistics.**

Wiering, Elisabeth
ms.   "The Indicative Verb in Dowaayááyo", to appear in *Linguistics.**

Willis, Raymond S., Jr., and Frederick B. Agard
1941   *Spanish from Thought to Word* (Princeton: Princeton University Press).

Winograd, Terry
1971   *Procedures as a Representation for Data in a Computer Program for Understanding Natural Language* (= Artificial Intelligence Laboratory Report AI TR-17) (Cambridge: MIT).

Wise, Mary Ruth
1968   "Identification of Participants in Discourse", University of Michigan Ph.D. dissertation, reissued in SIL Publications in Linguistics.

Wise, Mary Ruth, and Ivan Lowe
1972   "Permutation Groups in Discourse", *Georgetown University School of Languages and Linguistics Working Papers* 4, 12-34.

Woods, William A.
1970   "Transition Network Grammars for Natural Language Analysis", *Communications of the Association for Computing Machinery* 13(10), 591-606.

Wrigglesworth, Hazel
ms.   "Ilianen Manobo Narrative Discourse".*

Young, Richard E., Alton L. Becker, and Kenneth L. Pike
1970   *Rhetoric: Discovery and Change* (New York: Harcourt, Brace and World).

INDEX